Tempest over Teapot Dome

THE OKLAHOMA WESTERN BIOGRAPHIES
RICHARD ETULAIN, GENERAL EDITOR

Albert B. Fall as secretary of the interior in the Harding cabinet, 1921–1923. (Courtesy of Emadair Chase Jones)

Tempest over Teapot Dome

The Story of Albert B. Fall

David H. Stratton

UNIVERSITY OF OKLAHOMA PRESS : NORMAN

Also by David H. Stratton

The First Century of Baptists in New Mexico, 1849–1950 (Albuquerque, 1954)
(ed.) *The Memoirs of Albert B. Fall* (El Paso, 1966)
(coed.) *The Changing Pacific Northwest: Interpreting Its Past* (Pullman, WA, 1988)
(ed.) *Spokane and the Inland Empire: An Interior Pacific Northwest Anthology* (Pullman, WA, 1991)
(ed.) *Washington Comes of Age: The State in the National Experience* (Pullman, WA, 1993)

This book is published with the generous assistance of Edith Gaylord Harper.

Library of Congress Cataloging-in-Publication Data

Stratton, David H. (David Hodges), 1927–
Tempest over Teapot Dome : the story of Albert B. Fall / David H. Stratton.
p. cm. — (The Oklahoma western biographies ; v. 16)
Includes bibliographical references and index.
ISBN 0-8061-3078-4 (alk. paper)
1. Fall, Albert B. (Albert Bacon), 1861–1944. 2. Cabinet officers—United States—Biography. 3. Teapot Dome Scandal, 1921–1924. I. Title. II. Series.
E748.F22S77 1998
364.1′323—dc21
[B]
97-51347
CIP

Tempest over Teapot Dome: The Story of Albert B. Fall is Volume 16 in *The Oklahoma Western Biographies.*

The paper in this book meets the guidelines for permanence and durability of the Committee on Production Guidelines for Book Longevity of the Council on Library Resources, Inc. ∞

1 2 3 4 5 6 7 8 9 10

For Wanda

Contents

Illustrations

Series Editor's Preface

STORIES of heroes and heroines have intrigued many generations of listeners and readers. Americans, like people everywhere, have been captivated by the lives of military, political, and religious figures and of intrepid explorers, pioneers, and rebels.

The Oklahoma Western Biographies endeavor to build on this fascination with biography and to link it with two other abiding interests of Americans: the frontier and the American West. Although volumes in the series carry no notes, they are prepared by leading scholars, are soundly researched, and include a list of sources used. Each volume is a lively synthesis based on thorough examination of pertinent primary and secondary sources.

Above all, the Oklahoma Western Biographies aim at two goals: to provide readable life stories of significant westerners and to show how their lives illuminate a notable topic, an influential movement, or a series of important events in the history and culture of the American West.

David Stratton's lively, smoothly written biography of Albert B. Fall more than achieves the major goals of volumes in this series. The appealing product of years of research and reflection, Stratton's book on Fall is the first full-length, thoroughly researched, and well-rounded biography of this notable western figure.

From the opening scene to the closing pages, David Stratton proves himself a polished, able writer. He knows how to tell an interesting, even engrossing story. Early on, he provides dramatic vignettes of Fall as a young person, as a family man, as a political novice, and as an opinionated and individualistic leader.

As Stratton demonstrates, Fall's participation in New Mexico political conflicts and his deals with friends and competitors help explain his later controversial actions in the Senate and in President Warren G. Harding's cabinet. Fall's biographer exhibits his narrative talents as he moves through these foreshadowing events, carefully pushing his story toward illuminating, dramatic moments. All readers will be impressed with the author's obvious literary talents in this biography.

In addition, Stratton provides particularly revealing links of continuity among the western, national, and even international experiences of Fall's career. For example, the opinions Fall advanced as a westerner adumbrate his later decisions vis-à-vis the federal government's role in developing natural resources and in pressuring Mexico and Colombia to recognize and protect American investments in those countries. Overall, Stratton advances the most convincing explanation thus far of why Fall became involved in the unfortunate events surrounding the Teapot Dome controversy. Painting a more complex and balanced picture than earlier historians, Stratton also points out how politicians, Democrats and Republicans alike, quickly and easily made Fall the scapegoat for the political and economic corruption of the 1920s.

Stratton's sparkling biography is an especially notable contribution to the Oklahoma Western Biographies. He not only furnishes an appealing study of a westerner whose life illustrates important regional and national events, he also provides the definitive life story of a complex western character. After reading David Stratton's biography of Albert B. Fall, no one will view the Teapot Dome scandal and Fall's participation in it in the same way. This revealing, judicious, clearly written, and engrossing biography is a rewarding addition to the most important books about major political figures of the American West.

RICHARD W. ETULAIN

Author's Preface

MORE than thirty-five years ago at the Huntington Library, the prolific historian Allan Nevins strongly advised me to begin any biographical study of Albert B. Fall and the Teapot Dome affair with a ringing prefatory statement that Fall was a crook and a scoundrel, and that the purpose of my work was to show how he got that way, not to whitewash him. Otherwise, he said, the reviewers would tear my book to pieces. Nevins probably hoped to spare me, a young scholar, from the abusive criticism he had received for his anti-robber-baron revisionist views on American industrialists, particularly his study of John D. Rockefeller. As I had already decided then, however, I want to present Albert Fall as a complex person, not a stereotype; as a human individual, without cloven hooves and horns, perhaps possessing some admirable qualities. Also, as much as possible, I intend to portray Fall on his home ground in the Southwest, rather than as a typical Harding-era politician. Without these ingredients, I still think, there is no compelling story in the Teapot Dome saga. But deciding the general approach was the easy part; how to interpret a historical figure often considered an archtraitor, on the order of Benedict Arnold, was a more difficult problem.

During the extended litigation resulting from his naval oil–leasing arrangements with Harry F. Sinclair and Edward L. Doheny, Fall protested the defense lawyers' steadfast refusal to put him on the stand so that he could tell his own story. At one point he even threatened to argue his own case in the courtroom, no matter how unorthodox it might seem—a threat he never pursued. Not surprisingly, I have tried to take the viewpoint of a historian in this biography, not that of a sympathetic defense counsel or of Fall himself, had he testified in court. Under the legal system lawyers have to focus on a limited body of evidence dealing with questions about their client's guilt or innocence. That is why the attorneys would not call Fall as a witness; they feared that within the narrow confines of the law his testimony would be impeached, or discredited, or he might lose his well-known temper, say more than was prudent legally, and do the case more harm than good. If Fall had actually testified, or taken control of his own defense, he undoubtedly would have expanded and placed a different emphasis on the main points of evidence. But he, too, was an experienced trial lawyer, and probably he would not have ventured far outside the time-honored bounds of courtroom practice. A historian, on the other hand, enjoys far more freedom in gathering and using a wide array of information than a defense attorney does. Although deeply concerned with guilt or innocence, the historian can go beyond such specific issues, examine the background events, consider the broad historical context, and, most important, engage in well-reasoned speculation. In short, unlike a defense counsel, I have attempted here to follow the historian's tribal code by letting the accused tell his version through the sources, while judging it in scholarly terms.

Drawing on the historian's expansive freedom, I have included many events and forces in Fall's life that may seem to have little relevance to his guilt or innocence for oil sins. Historically, his name and reputation are inextricably bound to the Teapot Dome scandal, which explains the main title of this comprehensive biographical account. He was a hard fighter and was always surrounded by conflict and controversy. One of his longtime comrades, the western writer Eugene Manlove Rhodes, said that in New Mexico Fall had no mere acquaintances, but that everyone there was "his steadfast friend" or "bitter enemy," and they all admired him. Before President Warren G. Harding, a close friend, appointed him secretary of the interior in 1921, he had been seasoned in public office, first in tumultuous territorial New Mexico and then for nine stormy years in the United States Senate. His firsthand knowledge of revolution-torn Mexico made him a frequent critic of President Woodrow Wilson and an adviser of former President Theodore Roosevelt. As a western developer and corporation lawyer, he had been using the natural resources for nearly forty years. His belief in the unrestricted and immediate disposition of the public lands was as typically western as his black, broad-brimmed Stetson hat. Fall's Senate record clearly revealed that he had no sympathy for the conservation movement. In fact, the conservationists regarded him with contempt, and he held the same opinion of them.

Unsurprisingly, then, Interior Secretary Fall negotiated separate agreements with oil magnates Sinclair and Doheny for drilling on the Teapot Dome Naval Petroleum Reserve in Wyoming and a similar reserve in California, both set aside for the navy's emergency fuel supply. The surprise came when a Senate investigating committee revealed that Fall had received $404,000 from the two oilmen. Nearly a decade of congressional inquiries, incriminating headlines, and courtroom accusations besmirched Fall's name and finally sent him to prison in 1931, the first American cabinet officer to suffer such a fate.

There is little danger that an author will give Fall's historical reputation "protective custody" as some biographers of unblemished national icons have been accused of doing. Several of Fall's prominent associates later tried to conceal their previous admiration for him by saying that everyone always knew he was a scoundrel even before Teapot Dome. At his death in 1944 the press portrayed him as the villain of "the most sordid scandal" of American national politics. Such a rock-bottom historical reputation actually provides unaccustomed latitude for a biographer by obviating the inclination to safeguard the subject's integrity in every detail and overlook faults, or, even worse, to turn weaknesses into virtues. Instead a writer can freely explore an exciting life such as Fall's chiefly for its dramatic qualities, drawing harsh conclusions without the customary restraint required in consideration of a sacrosanct hero. In the process, more pathos, enduring lessons, and valuable insights may be revealed than in the usual biography. And one thing is certain, if Albert Fall were not such a colorful, intriguing historical character, I could not have sustained the interest to dog his trail for more than forty years.

The degree of Fall's guilt in Teapot Dome is a major emphasis at the end of this account. Because of his anticonservation views, and for this reason alone, Fall no doubt would have turned over the naval reserves to representatives of private enterprise. In fact, the money he took from Sinclair and Doheny, which led to his imprisonment, played little or no role in determining his actions. Fall's greatest offense actually involved his strident attempts to undo Progressive Era reforms, particularly conservation of natural resources and the bridling of corporate power. In the broader historical framework, however, recent federal decisions to sell naval petroleum reserves to the highest private bidders tend to make Fall's oil policy seem surreally visionary.

Besides my wife, Wanda, and our three children, Michael, Nancy, and Scott, who have heard far too much about Teapot Dome, I owe debts of gratitude to so many friends, relatives, colleagues, students, and secretaries that a list of them would probably be longer than this book. At the risk of offending this multitude, I must limit my acknowledgments to these: the late Robert G. Athearn, for whom my original project was the first doctoral dissertation he directed at the University of Colorado; Fall's daughter, the late Alexina Fall Chase, who graciously opened countless doors to crucial source materials; Michael P. Malone, for his early research assistance and his interest since then; Peter Blodgett and the manuscript staff at the Huntington Library, for their many courtesies over the years; Richard W. Etulain, series editor, who gave me wise guidance and suggestions; and John N. Drayton, director, Randolph Lewis, acquisitions editor, Sarah Iselin, who edited my manuscript, and all of the other helpful people at the University of Oklahoma Press. In addition, Baylor University, Washington State University, the American Philosophical Society, and the Huntington Library have aided this project through research grants or fellowships.

DAVID H. STRATTON

Pullman, Washington

Tempest over Teapot Dome

CHAPTER 1

The Origins of a Friendship

THE Sunday newspapers of May 22, 1927, headlined the dramatic news that on the previous night Charles A. Lindbergh, in his sleek, silver Ryan monoplane, *The Spirit of St. Louis*, had successfully completed his lonely nonstop flight across the Atlantic. Others attempting the same feat had failed or died. On his arrival at Le Bourget Aerodrome near Paris, the "Lone Eagle" received an enthusiastic welcome from a cheering mob of one hundred thousand people, but it could hardly match the "frenzied acclaim" and jubilant hero worship awaiting him when he returned to the United States. His fellow citizens, it seemed, had seized upon Lindbergh's flight as a symbolic act of national catharsis and spiritual regeneration. Americans of the 1920s had been sorely disillusioned by a number of traumatic experiences: the greedy peacemaking following World War I, the hypocrisy of prohibition, highly ballyhooed gangster racketeering and crimes of violence, a jarring revolution in manners and morals, and shocking graft and corruption in politics. As historian John William Ward has observed, "The grubbiness of the twenties had a good deal to do with the shining quality of Lindbergh's success." By putting ethics "above any desire for wealth," according to a leading periodical, the Lone Eagle had shown Americans that they were "*not* rotten at the core, but morally sound and sweet and good!"

Although Lindbergh, a Minnesotan, more nearly represented the new age of technology, the image makers of the day often chose to stress that he came "out of the West" and thus embodied the pioneer qualities of America's frontier past. The late

Theodore Roosevelt's eldest son and namesake proclaimed that Lindbergh was the "lineal descendant" of Daniel Boone, Davy Crockett, and other frontier heroes who had "made America." Ironically the major instance of "grubbiness" in politics contributing to the widespread public disillusionment in the twenties also had western origins. The Teapot Dome scandal, which involved Secretary of the Interior Albert B. Fall, a New Mexican, and his leasing deals for Wyoming and California naval oil fields, became a major preoccupation of Americans during that decade.

Teapot Dome caused journalist Lincoln Steffens, who had gained fame for exposing chicanery in government, to despair of his muckraking role, at least in successfully uncovering big-business graft. In the New York gubernatorial contest of 1924 Mrs. Franklin D. Roosevelt and her daughter toured the state in an automobile with a rebuilt body resembling a giant steam-spewing teapot and labeled "TEAPOT DOME," making speeches for the victorious Democratic opponent of her Republican cousin, Theodore Roosevelt, Jr. Young lawyer and future federal judge John J. Sirica, who graduated from Georgetown University Law School in 1926 and experienced some lean years around Washington in the late twenties, spent much of this slack time observing and admiring the courtroom tactics of the brilliant attorneys hired by the Teapot Dome defendants. "Perhaps the greatest trial lawyers of this century," he later called them. Sirica never dreamed that he would one day preside over the courtroom proceedings of the equally notorious Watergate scandal of the 1970s. And, as a lad of eleven, future President Richard M. Nixon became so outraged from listening to his father talk about the Teapot Dome scandal that he decided then and there on a career as a public servant. "When I get big," he told his mother one day in 1924, "I'll be a lawyer who can't be bribed." According to Nixon's mother, "That was the first step [toward political greatness]." Ironically a half century later the media would make repeated comparisons between Teapot Dome and the Watergate affair that brought down Nixon's presidency.

In time the Teapot Dome scandal came to epitomize all the evil in what is usually regarded as the worst of all presidential administrations, that of Warren G. Harding. It also became the darkest stain of corruption on a political party in the twentieth century, until Watergate in the 1970s. In American political folklore Teapot Dome stands as a symbol of wrongdoing in government, and the man most responsible for it, Interior Secretary Fall, is considered an archtraitor, only slightly less despicable than Benedict Arnold.

This monumental scandal resulted from Secretary Fall's separate leasing agreements with two petroleum magnates, Harry F. Sinclair and Edward L. Doheny, for the drilling of Teapot Dome Naval Oil Reserve in Wyoming and Elk Hills Naval Oil Reserve in California, both set aside for the navy's exclusive use only in case of emergency. First in 1924, and later in 1928, a Senate investigating committee, directed by Senator Thomas J. Walsh of Montana, revealed that Fall had received personally at least $404,000 from Doheny and Sinclair. With the aid of the extended, sensational court action following the 1924 inquiry, the "oil scandal" stayed continually in the headlines for almost a decade. In 1929 Fall was found guilty of accepting a bribe from Doheny. Old and ill, the former interior secretary, leaving his home in an ambulance, went to prison in 1931, becoming the first American cabinet member convicted and imprisoned for a felony committed in office.

Even though most Americans of the twenties probably failed to realize it, Teapot Dome was a complicated web of events. In a sense the oil scandal more accurately reflected the frontier experience than did the flight of *The Spirit of St. Louis*, and Fall, the New Mexican, more nearly represented western traits than did Lindbergh. For the informed observer the scandal was packed with western drama. A large part of the western patrimony was at stake because Teapot Dome involved an important battle in the conservation movement, which was largely a master plan for the future development of the West. In addition, the scandal concerned national defense in the form of the navy's emergency fuel supply, the arrogant exercise of presidential power, the unsavory influence of big business in politics, and bribery, corruption, and deceit at the highest level of government. But only the basic sin of human greed—the love of money as the root of all evil in the wrongdoing of Secretary Fall—captured the public imagination. The deeper issues remained fuzzy and obscure.

Walter Lippmann, writing in the twenties, contended that the enforcement of criminal laws depends on "how earnestly citizens object to certain kinds of crime." In symposium proceedings published in 1922 under the title *Civilization in the United States*, thirty intellectuals agreed among themselves that hypocrisy was one of the three major characteristics of American life. To most Americans, the panelists maintained, the unforgivable sin was being caught red-handed, not the immorality or dishonesty of the act itself. Although perhaps it is an oversimplification to say so, this indictment of American life helps explain why Fall's conspicuous sin made him the scapegoat of Teapot Dome. In short, he had scorned conservation policy by stealthily leasing the navy's emergency oil supply, but it was more damning in the public mind that the interior secretary had been caught with his hand in the till. He had, as the Democrats charged in the 1924 election, broken the Eleventh Commandment, "Thou shalt not get found out."

The origins of the Teapot Dome scandal, or at least the name of it, go back to an unpretentious rock formation in eastern Wyoming. There, in the rich oil fields about thirty-five miles north of Casper, stands an insignificant little butte jutting up above the rough, brown prairie country. Even today, antelope, jack rabbits, and rattlesnakes far outnumber the people living in the area. The butte's soft sandstone, which is crumbling and eroding away more each year, has been splotched with the mud nests of swallows. It vaguely resembled a jagged teapot until the long finger of the rock spout was knocked off by a tornado in 1962. From other angles it might be a kneeling camel or a British imperial lion.

Although Teapot Rock itself had no importance historically, the naval oil field where the curious butte is located, and to which it gave a name, assumed a prominent place in newspaper headlines during the 1920s. Like the mines, forests, and abundant lands of the West, this petroleum deposit exemplified the potential wealth of the region. Under the field's surface is a geological structure, known as a dome, in which the layers of rock rise to a common apex, forming a spacious reservoir underneath. From these two earthen formations Teapot Dome, or Naval Oil Reserve No. 3 (so designated by President Wilson in 1915), got its name. Two other petroleum reserves in California, Elk Hills (Reserve No. 1) and Buena Vista Hills (Reserve No. 2), had already been withdrawn from the public domain by President Taft in 1912 as parts of an emergency underground resource to be used by the navy only when regular oil supplies became inadequate. None of the three reserves had been opened for the exigencies of World War I. Because questions about Secretary Fall's handling of the Wyoming reserve gained widespread publicity first, Teapot Dome gave a popular name to the scandal involving his leasing of all three of them.

The central figure in this controversy, Albert Bacon Fall, made his home in another western state where he had spent most of his adult life deeply involved in the development of natural wealth like that offered by the sage-covered prairie surrounding Teapot Rock. While New Mexico was still a territory, Fall had gone there as a young man to get a new start. He had mastered the rough-and-tumble politics of that unhewn southwestern territory at a time when partisan rivalries often led to shooting in the streets, bloody range wars, and the mysterious disappearance of opponents. Early in his law practice in southern New Mexico and nearby El Paso, Texas, he won acquittals for defendants in several celebrated rustling and murder trials, but more and more he began to represent development and industrial interests including irrigation enterprises, mining companies, timber concerns, and railroads. He devoted much time to his own mining investments, which were always his real love—not oil. Small-scale ventures across the border in northern Mexico led to his involvement in some of the multimillion-dollar operations of William C. Greene, the "Copper King of

Cananea," from which he gained a substantial, but short-lived, income and the ownership of several potentially valuable Mexican mining properties. From his profits Fall acquired a historic ranch near Three Rivers, New Mexico. Then his hopes for great wealth in mining were dashed by the revolutionary upheavals in Mexico, which, beginning in 1910, threatened American business concerns south of the border.

In 1912 the brand-new state of New Mexico elected Fall as one of its first two United States senators. When he entered President Harding's cabinet in 1921, the politically inconsequential state could justly take pride in his accomplishment, for no other New Mexican had ever risen to such heights. Although most people had not heard of the Teapot Dome oil field at that time, Fall had become a relatively well-known national figure as the most outspoken Senate advocate for the protection of American lives and property rights in revolution-torn Mexico, frequently demanding military intervention by the United States. In Senate debates he was bombastic, often cynical, and a combative Republican partisan. A bitter critic of President Wilson's Mexican policy, Fall also opposed the Treaty of Versailles; usually he was classed among the irreconcilables. He liked to tell stories about his experiences on the southwestern frontier and in Mexico, and one colleague who loved these yarns was Senator Warren G. Harding of Ohio. Fall and Harding became poker-playing cronies while they served together on the Senate Foreign Relations Committee. To the surprise of many professional politicians, "dark horse" candidate Harding emerged as the Republican nominee and was elected president in 1920. He at first toyed with the idea of naming Fall secretary of state, but, after more serious reflection, appointed his friend instead as secretary of the interior.

Fall is not renowned for outstanding achievements in the Senate or in the Harding cabinet. It was the Teapot Dome scandal that put his name on the front page of every daily newspaper in the country during the twenties, and since then in the index of most American history textbooks. But his story is hardly the one of unadulterated human greed that so impressed his contemporaries. In fact, the money he took from the two millionaire oilmen, Doheny and Sinclair, played only an incidental role in determining his actions, although there would have been no public outcry if he had not taken it. From long practical experience in the West and Mexico, Fall had acquired the conviction that private business enterprise possessed vested rights in the use of natural resources. This strong empathy with economic individualism, especially in the exploitation of nature's bounties, had gained him the reputation of a "corporation man" back in the Southwest. More than anything else, Fall's economic philosophy explained his decisions in not only the naval oil–leasing episode but in his entire political career as well.

By the time Fall had become interior secretary, he had been utilizing the natural resources in the Southwest and Mexico for almost forty years as a prospector, hard-rock miner, mining investor, land speculator, farmer, rancher, and corporate attorney. He placed an emphasis on "use" and "development" for "the satisfaction of human needs." He believed that the land, timber, and minerals of the western states should be used for the immediate benefit of that region, as had been done in the older states. His unsuccessful efforts in the Senate to donate the remaining public domain to the states were as typical of his western background as his black Stetson hat and his love of fine horses. Once, while Fall was secretary of the interior, a National Parks official challenged him on his wide-open attitude toward the natural resources, asking what sort of heritage this would leave to his grandchildren. Fall replied easily: "I'm surprised at you. You've had a good education. You know something about history. Every generation from Adam and Eve down has lived better than the generation before. I don't know how [succeeding generations will] do it—maybe they'll use the energy of the sun or the sea waves—but [they] will live better than we do. I stand for opening up every resource."

Such flagrant utilitarianism was already incomprehensible to many Americans at that time, and it became increasingly so as the twentieth century unfolded. But Fall was a remnant of an extravagant age, the nineteenth century, when the natural resources had seemed unlimited and open for unrestricted exploitation. His Senate record had made it crystal clear that he was no conservationist. It should have come as no surprise that Fall, shortly after taking office as interior secretary, gained control of the naval petroleum reserves and then negotiated drilling agreements with Doheny and Sinclair. The astonishing part was that he had taken money from the two oil magnates at about the same time the leases were made. Fall went to prison for accepting a bribe, but it must be said in his behalf that with his belief in the unrestrained and immediate disposition of the natural resources, regardless of other considerations, he undoubtedly would have turned over the reserves to representatives of private enterprise anyway.

Back in the days of a young, undeveloped America, Fall might have had wealth and honor all the days of his life. Many American politicians and captains of industry had lived in respectability with deeds fully as devious as his. But the times had changed; it was the twentieth century, not the nineteenth. The decline of laissez-faire and social Darwinism during the Progressive Era of the early 1900s, the accentuation of idealism in World War I, and especially the continuation of the uniquely twentieth-century struggle for conservation of natural resources had brought about a new political order in which people like Fall were anachronisms. With his supreme self-confidence, and no small measure of arrogance, Albert Fall tried to turn the clock back and failed. In an ironic way the natural resources of the West and Mexico both made and broke him. His life was an untimely western tragedy. Perhaps one might say it was an "American success story," but with an unhappy ending.

Fall had not always lived in the Southwest, where natural wealth was so readily accessible. Born at Frankfort, Kentucky, in the first year of the Civil War (November 26, 1861), he grew up in the Reconstruction South at a time when money was so scarce that even the price of a small piece of land seemed out of reach. In fact, his most cherished ambition early in life became the acquisition of enough means to buy a Kentucky farm. During the turmoil of the war years and for extended periods thereafter, he lived with his paternal grandparents in Nashville, Tennessee, and at the family's Poplar Hill farm near Frankfort, only occasionally staying with his parents. His mother, Edmonia Taylor Fall, came from a prominent Kentucky family; one branch distilled Old Taylor whiskey at Frankfort. His itinerant schoolteacher father, Williamson Ware Robertson Fall, who served with Confederate cavalry General Nathan B. Forrest and was later incarcerated in a military prison at Nashville, appears to have been irresolute, and he often was dependent upon his son in later years. A brother and a sister also frequently relied heavily on their older brother for financial support.

His grandfather, Philip Slater Fall, became the single most powerful influence in young Albert's life. The elder Fall, who preached the gospel for seventy-one years, originally as a Baptist and then as a Campbellite minister, has been called the father of the Christian Church (Disciples of Christ) in the South. A follower and close friend of Alexander Campbell, he was a leader in establishing the Disciples of Christ in Kentucky and Tennessee, principally while in pastorates at Louisville, Frankfort, and Nashville. Scholarly, polished in manners, and eloquent (although purportedly "somewhat heavy" in the pulpit), he also distinguished himself as an educator. Because of his work conducting academies for young ladies, he reputedly "educated a large portion of the most accomplished women in Kentucky" and pioneered the movement in Nashville to "dignify female education." In 1856 he turned down an invitation to become the president of Transylvania University, the oldest institution of higher education west of the Appalachians.

Albert Fall, as befitting a self-made man, later claimed to be self-educated, which was true only in the sense that he lacked formal advanced training. He always owed a great debt to his scholarly grandfather, who early instilled in him a passion for books and learning, and from whom he acquired the habit of reading omnivorously. In later years Fall often spent the entire night reading in bed, sometimes finishing three or four books. His library at the Three Rivers ranch was renowned in that part of the Southwest for the number and variety of its volumes, especially on Mexico but also the classics and English literature.

Philip Slater Fall stood as firm in matters of principle as in tenets of the faith. His Civil War sympathies undoubtedly lay with the Confederacy since young Albert's father served under General Forrest and another son, Albert Boult Fall, was killed as a member of the Confederate forces defending Fort Donelson. When Federal troops occupied Nashville during the war, he reportedly refused the demands of the military governor, future President Andrew Johnson, to take the oath of loyalty to the Union. The resolute minister, who had emigrated from England to this country as a youth in 1817, supposedly declared, "If the oath I have taken, in order to become a voter, is not sufficient, I prefer to remain a British subject." Family tradition says that he then went home and defiantly raised a British Union Jack over his residence. Neither he nor his church building was disturbed for the rest of the war, even though many other prominent Nashville ministers were either imprisoned or sent out of the city and many meetinghouses were confiscated for use as Federal barracks and hospitals.

Young Albert, while living in his grandfather's home under the influence of this quiet man of learning and strong convictions, attended church regularly as a matter of course. In such Campbellite surroundings after the Civil War the boy was exposed to fervent evangelical preaching and heartfelt hymn singing, as well as heated disputes over the proper role of ministers and the use of instrumental music in worship services. The Protestant ethic, with its apologia for materialistic success, constituted an implied part of this ideology. It was only natural that young Albert should become aware of the importance of oratorical skill, especially since he apparently felt an early calling toward the ministry.

In time Fall drifted away from these moorings; he was not known in the Southwest as a churchman. Of the eleven original members in the Harding cabinet, only Fall was listed as "unaffiliated" with regard to religious membership. Near the end of his life, as he lay desperately ill in an El Paso hospital, he became a member of the Catholic Church. Perhaps his self-righteous, authoritarian style in partisan debates in later years had a source in his boyhood religious experiences, although few references to Scripture marked those political discourses. Likewise, at the time of his election to the United States Senate in 1912, the *Albuquerque Morning Journal* attributed his extreme partisanship to Reconstruction conditions in the South, or the "strenuousness of the times," which might well have left their influence on one "reared among the grim scenes of a civil strife."

Certainly the post–Civil War South offered only limited horizons for an ambitious young man. On December 31, 1876, Philip Slater Fall, then seventy-eight years old, retired from his Nashville pastorate and soon afterwards moved back to the Poplar Hill farm near Frankfort, although he continued to preach occasionally until his death at ninety-two in 1890. A leading Louisville newspaper stated in a eulogy of the revered old Campbellite patriarch that his life had been "guiltless and pure, and to everybody like an open book." Albert was fifteen when his grandparents left Nashville. He remained there for several months, working in a cotton mill, and then joined his schoolteacher parents for a while at Springfield, Tennessee, where he pursued his studies and obtained a part-time job as a "bottle washer and general roustabout" in a drugstore that made "Rangum Root" liniment. After attending various schools conducted by his father in Tennessee and Kentucky, in which he also assisted with the younger children, he became a teacher himself. He probably first taught on his own for a five-month term in the tough "Bald Knob" district near Frankfort. Later, when helping his father, he proudly wrote his grandfather from Morganfield, Kentucky, in March 1881 about having charge of his own class, and that the pupils "appear to be very agreeable, affectionate children, and seem to have become attached to me already." He was also using the law library of a family friend, he told his grandfather, and when the school term ended would continue those studies "as before." For at least one extended period during those years he lived at

Poplar Hill with his grandparents and an aunt and helped run the farm. It was a life of meager returns.

By 1880, when he was about eighteen, Fall had started reading law books on his own, although he sought advice about the profession from Judge William Lindsay of Frankfort, later a United States senator from Kentucky. The next year, as previously mentioned, the law library of a Morganfield attorney was available to him. Fall wanted to obtain an apprenticeship in the office of some prominent lawyer, such as Judge Lindsay, but he apparently could never arrange it. Intermittently he continued to "read law" until he finally became a practicing attorney in New Mexico in 1889.

Meanwhile, because Fall was plagued by debt and poor health, the most attractive option was a new start in the West. Borrowing $100 from the Morganfield lawyer whose books he had used, he and two companions left Kentucky in late 1881 for Clarksville near the Red River in northeastern Texas. He had worked briefly as a farmhand in that area about a year earlier while on a "prospecting trip" (perhaps taken mainly as a cure for some sickness), which had also included Eureka Springs, Arkansas, and Indian Territory (now eastern Oklahoma). For a time Fall retained the ambition of amassing enough wealth to buy a farm in the Blue Grass country, but he would never again live for long in his native state.

Like countless other "lungers," Fall was first drawn to the West by its salubrious climate. From his youth Fall's health was always precarious, beginning apparently with tuberculosis. Such respiratory ailments as severe colds, influenza or grippe, chronic bronchial inflammations, and pneumonia frequently plagued him unmercifully. At age sixty-nine, just before going to prison as a result of the Teapot Dome prosecution, he was diagnosed as suffering from hardening of the arteries and a heart ailment, severe arthritis, and chronic but inactive tuberculosis. In fact, according to one of his daughters, there was hardly "a good pair of lungs in the Fall family." His wife's respiratory problems were one of the reasons he later moved his family to sunny New Mexico.

Work as a bookkeeper in Clarksville temporarily impaired the young man's eyesight and affected his fragile health, and so he became a cowboy, hoping that an outdoor life and hard exercise would prove therapeutic. As a Kentuckian and Tennessean, he had early acquired the ability to ride a horse well. While working for Texas cattle outfits, first as a drover of a Kansas-bound herd and then as a cowhand on a plains ranch near San Angelo, Fall got his first real taste of the wild West. A local feud, the "Buffalo Gap War," was in progress when he arrived in San Angelo, where he saw three men lying dead on the sidewalk. Besides the regular tasks of a cowboy, Fall also tried the most celebrated calling of any cow camp, chuck wagon "bossing," or cooking.

Fall's uncertain health apparently improved enough for him to return to a more sedentary life at Clarksville. Again, in a desultory manner, he read law. He also dabbled in real estate and the insurance business, ran a grocery store, and, on May 7, 1883, married nineteen-year-old Emma Garland Morgan, whose late father, railroad developer Simpson H. Morgan, had died while serving as a representative from Texas to the Confederate Congress. Emma at first rejected Fall's suit, and she left town to visit relatives; but Fall, never one to give up easily, followed her to Readyville, Tennessee, where they were married. It was a good marriage, although not without the occasional tiffs to be expected between two high-strung persons. They had four children: John ("Jack") Morgan, Alexina, Caroline Ann, and Jouett Adair. Tall, slender, with a finely sculptured face, and full of impetuous energy, Emma Fall virtually worshiped her husband and defended him to the end. Perhaps because of his love for "Miss Emma," or "Old Lady," as he affectionately called his wife in family circles, or perhaps because of his intense devotion to business and political matters, Fall escaped one common form of calumny. Even during all the vituperation when he was the whipping boy for the cumulative sins of the Harding administration, the kind of "woman stories" that plague President Harding's memory were not used against Fall.

No longer enamored of owning a Kentucky farm, Fall now looked around for other possibilities of fame and fortune. The mines of Mexico seemed promising, and so he left from Clarksville late in 1883 on a prospecting tour south of the border. He rode on horseback through eight states of that republic, finally stopping at Nieves in the state of Zacatecas. There he worked as a practical miner and as a timberman, mucker, and mining foreman. While serving his apprenticeship, he became skilled in the operation of the hoist and the pump. He sorted ore, constructed roads, sharpened drills, and learned how to set timbers in a wet shaft to make it safe for workers. Besides gaining first-hand knowledge of mining operations, Fall apparently acquired a small financial interest in some Mexican properties, although he did not retain these investments long. He had purchased Spanish grammar books and a dictionary before crossing the border at Laredo. While in Zacatecas, he began to pick up a "working knowledge" of Spanish, a language that would later serve him well in bilingual New Mexico politics. Equally important, this experience marked the beginning of his lifelong fascination with both Mexico and mining.

Early in May 1884 Fall returned to the United States on the Mexican Central Railway's first regular passenger train from Mexico City to El Paso, Texas. After a restful, contemplative period at Clarksville and across the Red River in Arkansas, where he did some leisurely farming and reading while engaged in improving family properties, he again tried his luck at mining. This time, accompanied by his bachelor brother-in-law, Joe Morgan, Fall set out prospecting along the border near El Paso, and then in the mountains of southern New Mexico. At Silver City they loaded a lone burro with the food and equipment required for an extended exploration of the adjacent mining regions. Finally, in the early spring of 1886, they landed, weary and broke, at the booming, brawling mining camp of Kingston in the Black Range, so named for the dark growth of piñons and other pines covering its rough slopes and canyons. About 125 miles long and not more than twelve miles wide at any point, the Black Range has several peaks that soar eight thousand to ten thousand feet. Most of the streams flow east toward the Rio Grande, although many sink beneath the desolate wastelands long before they reach it. Fall's adventures in the rugged Black Range mining district are among the most significant and fabled of his life. It was at Kingston that he encountered a fellow prospector, Edward L. Doheny, who later struck it rich in oil and as a part of the Teapot Dome affair sent Secretary of the Interior Fall a little black bag filled with $100,000 in cash.

Fall had learned about Kingston through correspondence with an early prospector in the area, Henry W. Elliott, whose family he had known in Tennessee. The Santa Fe Railroad also had advertised the mineral wealth of the Black Range district. Kingston itself, named for the productive Iron King Mine, had been established as a town in 1882, although miners had worked the immediate area as early as the 1870s. Until then even the most hardy of prospectors had been reluctant to challenge the formidable obstacles of inadequate transportation, limited placer diggings, forbidding terrain, and especially the hostile Apache Indians. But the big silver boom at Kingston, which began in 1882, expanded in 1885, and reached its peak in 1888, drew in a population of several hundred. After 1888 the continued decline of silver punctured the boom, and during the next fifteen years the community dwindled to about sixty residents and the status of a near ghost town, which it remains today as a tourist attraction reflecting the frontier mining era. By 1904, however, the estimated total production at Kingston, nearly all silver, stood at $6,250,000, an impressive record for that metal in New Mexico.

Although developed relatively late, Kingston in its heyday was one of those legendary camps whose few spectacular strikes fostered the same get-rich-quick hopes as Sutter's Mill, the Pike's Peak gold rush, and the Comstock Lode. Often over-glamorized, especially in terms of the opportunities for great wealth, Kingston's big boom has gained much acclaim. Lillian Russell once played in the local theater, and William M. ("Sheba") Hurst, a mining promoter portrayed in Mark Twain's *Roughing It*, lies buried in the local cemetery. On the glorious Fourth of July all the mines shut down and the whole town celebrated with foot races, a burro derby, music by the Black Range Brass

Band, and several brawls, which came "as a matter of course." Kingston also had Pretty Sam's Casino saloon and dance hall, its share of gunplay and violence, unscrupulous gangs of rustlers, prostitutes, and Chinese opium dens, but, according to Fall, "none of the hurrah times of Abilene or Dodge City when they were the end of the [cattle] trail."

Since silver is not usually found in placer deposits, that is, scattered through surface sand and gravel, hard-rock underground mining prevailed around Kingston during the eighties. In fact, Fall had probably been enticed to the Black Range district by reports of such spectacular and much-publicized producers as the Bridal Chamber and Comstock mines—the latter developed by Ed Doheny's friend Charles A. Canfield. In one year the Comstock, also known as the "Great Canfield Bonanza," earned Canfield and his partners a net profit of $390,000, of which he took as his share $100,000 and moved to Los Angeles in 1887. Doheny and Canfield remained steadfast friends, and later teamed up to make history, and huge fortunes for themselves, as pioneer developers of California and Mexican oil fields.

When Fall and his brother-in-law came to Kingston, they were armed with rifles and six-shooters, which prospectors there considered as necessary as a pick. The Apache Indians, under such leaders as Victorio, Nana, and Geronimo, had terrorized the whites in southwestern New Mexico for years. Between 1879 and 1886 at least 140 whites had been killed in Sierra County (where Kingston is located) and Grant and Socorro counties. It had become "fashionable," declared a local newspaper in 1885, "to wear the hair on end." By the close of that year, another area newspaper reported, the Indians had forced many of the miners from their camps and "compelled [them] to take refuge in Kingston." Arriving on the heels of the last Apache scare in the vicinity, Fall and Morgan saw many deserted, bullet-marked miners' cabins along the way. Not until September 1886, with the surrender of Geronimo and his Chiricahua Apaches in Mexico, did the fear of Indian attacks subside in southwestern New Mexico.

Dapper and relatively well-dressed, Fall and Morgan were at first sized up as affluent gamblers by the Kingston residents. Actually the two "pilgrims" had run completely out of money. With his previous mining experience in Mexico, Fall had no trouble getting a job underground in the renowned Grey Eagle Mine on South Percha Creek, about six miles from town. This tough, dirty work of hard-rock mining had, in addition, the limitations in equipment and techniques imposed by a frontier locale. Years later Fall reminisced with a former coworker in the mine that at first, before a promotion to sorting ore, he had worn his fingers raw handling rough rocks while building a retaining wall. He continued:

> Then I mucked in the Grey Eagle tunnel and finally was set to work on the night shift, double handed, with a big fellow [called] "Box Car Jim." Jim did not fancy my being assigned to work with him in the shaft which we were sinking on the hill above the tunnel and on our first shift, while I was turning the drill, he accidentally (?) skinned both my hands as he afterwards confessed, thinking he would get rid of me and secure the aid of a more efficient miner. I said nothing, but when I had the hammer, another accident happened and Jim's hands were as badly skinned as mine. I have a scar on the apex of my cranium made by 18 inch steel falling 24 ft. through a hole in the rawhide bucket where Jim had overlooked it when I was sending up and he hoisting steel for sharpening.

While working "on the hammer" as a practical miner at a wage of $3.50 per day, Fall lived in an earthen dugout nearby.

At this time Fall became acquainted with many of the men who would later be his associates in New Mexico politics. But of all those he met at the rough-and-tumble camp, the one man destined to have the most influence in his future was Ed Doheny. In 1873, at age seventeen, Doheny had arrived at Fort Marcy (near Santa Fe) from Fort Leavenworth, Kansas, driving "a bunch of shave-tail mules" that government surveyors were to use as pack animals while marking the boundary line between Arizona and New Mexico. He was born at Fond du Lac, Wisconsin, in 1856, of a Newfoundlander mother and an Irish immigrant father. A staunch Catholic proud of his Irish heritage, the young Doheny supposedly neither smoked, drank, nor played cards. But he did get the gold fever early, and at eighteen began a lifelong career in pursuit of mineral wealth. In time he would be remembered for discovering more oil than any other man, and he eventually accumulated a fortune estimated at $100 million. For the next sixteen years, however, he toiled as a prospector, mining promoter, and mine operator, mostly in Arizona and New Mexico. His palmy days still lay ahead; sometimes he enjoyed prosperity, but often he lived a whole year on less than fifty dollars, shooting the plentiful wild game to subsist.

Doheny made many lasting friendships during this roving period of his life. Deceptively sentimental about the old days of roughing it, the ambitious, hard-driving fortune seeker later liked to recount adventures he had experienced while sleeping under the stars in the Black Range, the Tonto Basin, or at Tombstone. And companions of that time who met him afterwards often expressed gratification that they could still recognize in the famous multimillionaire oilman much of that likable young Irish American who had shared their campfires back on the southwestern mining frontier. His generosity with these old friends became common knowledge, because, as one companion of Kingston days put it, "You know Ed, he never does things by halves."

Even though the standard accounts fail to give him credit, Doheny had been a member of the party that discovered the rich vein of silver at Kingston in 1880. During nearly a decade in that vicinity, he at various times operated mines bearing such picturesque names as the Mountain Chief and the Miner's Dream. While Fall hammered a drill in the Grey Eagle Mine on South Percha Creek, Doheny was busy with several operations, including a lease a short distance away on the North Percha. Before leaving New Mexico in 1891 to make his fortune in oil, Doheny read law briefly and worked for about two years as a mining consultant and an expert court witness in Silver City, which was a part of the same judicial district, although a separate division, in which Fall became a fledgling attorney at

Las Cruces. A diminutive 120-pound dynamo with an exceptionally quick mind, the feisty Doheny supposedly had fallen down a mine shaft more than one hundred feet, breaking both legs, and had decided to study law while convalescing. Later, when charged with bribing Fall in the naval oil affair, Doheny recalled on the witness stand that they had met in Kingston and that Fall was among those who had loaned him law books to study during this recuperation. Whether or not after forty years Doheny's memory was completely accurate on this last point, the paths of the two men had at least crossed during those early days in southwestern New Mexico.

The exact nature and the length of the early Fall-Doheny relationship became a crucial issue in the criminal cases resulting from the Teapot Dome scandal. Doheny repeatedly insisted, in response to the accusation that his naval oil deals were a corrupt bargain because of the $100,000 he sent Fall in the little black bag, that the money was simply a loan to a longtime friend. He emphasized the closeness of his association with Fall back in Kingston and characterized the transfer of funds as a favor to an old pard that had no connection with Interior Secretary Fall's control over the naval petroleum reserves. Federal investigators and lawyers doubted or flatly rejected this explanation. Senate probers in the Teapot Dome inquiry thought the two men might have been only casual acquaintances at Kingston. Owen J. Roberts, a special prosecutor in the court cases, suspected that "Fall and Doheny may not even have known each other at the time, and that in any event their contacts were extremely slight." Roberts seriously considered sending a Secret Service agent to question old-timers in New Mexico about the early Fall-Doheny relationship, but it apparently was not done, nor could the government lawyers ever conclusively prove these suspicions in court.

Yet Roberts probably had the right idea about the friendship between Fall and Doheny. Quite simply, the two men worked near Kingston at the same time, but did they actually meet there and begin a close, lifelong friendship? Fall came to the Black Range camp in the early spring of 1886 and probably stayed several months, returning with his family to settle nearby at Las Cruces in October 1887. His brief, face-in-the-crowd presence at Kingston went relatively unnoticed in the community at large. Doheny, on the other hand, became a well-known and popular local figure while living in the general area the entire decade of the eighties, except for a brief mining expedition into Mexico in 1887.

If the federal lawyers had tried, they could have easily found many pioneers, still in New Mexico in the 1920s, who had known both Fall and Doheny at Kingston. In fact, *everyone* at Kingston during the boom days knew Ed Doheny, the ubiquitous, good-looking Irish American. He was a social favorite, distinguishing himself by such feats as renting a fancy dress suit all the way from El Paso for the town's big Christmas Eve dance. Fall could hardly have escaped at least hearing about Doheny at Kingston. As both men later claimed, their paths thus had first crossed in the Black Range mining district almost four decades earlier. For Roberts and the other government lawyers, however, the length of the relationship constituted only half of the question. They also had grave suspicions about the long-term closeness of the association between the two men—that is, whether they had enjoyed a strong, continuous bond of friendship from the mining camp to the little black bag. And that is the most important issue in the long association.

Mutual interest and financial involvement in revolutionary Mexico later drew Fall and Doheny together again. In 1919, as the chief congressional critic of President Wilson's Mexican policy and the chairman of a Senate subcommittee investigation, Senator Fall called Doheny to testify about his personal experiences and oil operations south of the border, where his companies had vast holdings. Doheny, by now a multimillionaire oilman, first spoke briefly of his humble beginnings as a prospector and hard-rock miner, including his Kingston days. He did not say specifically that Fall had been a part of those activities, but the two men, knowingly and with obvious pleasure, tossed local place-names back and forth. Later Fall stepped out of his subcommittee chairman's role long enough to take the stand himself and explain the extent of his own property holdings in Mexico. He freely admitted that he had many friends with much at stake in that country. "I worked for $3.50 a day on the hammer in quartz mining with Ed Doheny," he said of their time at Kingston. "I think very highly of him, and personally I would do anything possible to assist him."

Fall made an even more revealing statement soon after the 1920 election as he went to confer with his Senate colleague Warren G. Harding, the victorious presidential candidate. Fall wrote a charitable reply to Doheny's letter of contrition for remaining a loyal Democrat instead of supporting Harding. At one point Fall said, "I have always had a very warm feeling for you, while we have only met casually since the old days, and this feeling has grown as I have met you oftener in the last year or two." This highly significant letter clarifies both the nature and the length of the Fall-Doheny relationship: their common self-interest in Mexican matters caused an earlier passing acquaintance at Kingston to ripen years later into much stronger ties. On this basis the friendship was firmly established by the time Fall became interior secretary on March 4, 1921.

Fall's concise statement to Doheny following the 1920 election lends substantial credence to the government lawyers' doubts concerning the length of a close association, but a final point must not be overlooked. An embattled Doheny first tried to explain to the Senate Teapot Dome investigating committee in 1924 why the $100,000 was a loan and not a bribe, giving this emotional account:

> I had known Senator Fall for about thirty years or more. We had been old-time friends. We both worked in the same mining district in New Mexico in 1885 [1886]. In those days the Indian troubles were still on the country, and we were bound together by the same ties that men usually are, especially after they leave camp where they have lived under trying circumstances and conditions. Sometimes when men are in camp where their conditions are hard, and where the struggle for a living is precarious and the danger from the Indians is bad, they do not have a very great feeling for each

> other; but after they leave there they become warmer friends by reason of having associated under the same conditions.

No matter when the friendship actually quickened, Doheny seemed to say, its roots ran back deep into the rocky gulches of the Black Range mining district. Moreover, he as a multimillionaire had plenty of money to spare and Fall decidedly needed the loan. It was as simple as that.

For an America imbued with the frontier spirit this brand of logic had great appeal—but, unfortunately for Fall, not quite enough. One jury in 1929 was not convinced that Interior Secretary Fall had accepted the $100,000 as a loan from an old pard, instead of as a bribe from a greedy oil baron. He was convicted, sentenced to a year in prison, and fined the amount in question—$100,000. But the next year, in a separate trial with a different jury, the significance attached to a long-standing Fall-Doheny friendship going back to Kingston probably had great influence in winning an acquittal for Doheny, who was charged with giving a bribe to Fall in the same exchange of money. In short, the jury that acquitted Doheny of bribery in 1930 seemed to believe his explanation of the loan, based largely on the "Code of the West" involving generosity to an old pard, while this same version had not saved Fall from a bribery conviction at the hands of another jury in 1929. These two contradictory verdicts, relying on similar evidence, remain as one of the mysteries of Teapot Dome.

Actually the early mining-camp relationship of the two men had little or no bearing on the Doheny loan—or the money payment from oilman Harry F. Sinclair, which will be described later. Probably the truth is that they met at Kingston but their casual, elbow-brushing fellowship there, laced with the common experience of hardship and danger, lapsed until Fall arose as the Senate champion of American property rights in Mexico. In all likelihood, Fall and Doheny were not close friends at Kingston, nor were they close until many years afterwards.

Just as Fall's role in the Senate created the friendship as such, the election of his colleague Harding as president strengthened the bonds, and raised the stakes. Doheny sent the $100,000 largely because he believed that Fall had represented well the cause of American business enterprise in the Senate, especially regarding Mexico; he could be expected to do even more in the cabinet, and deserved some kind of extra consideration for these valuable services. As the oilman told the Teapot Dome panel, candidly acknowledging Fall's work as head of the Senate Mexican affairs inquiry as a major reason for the loan, "Yes sir; being the American with more property in Mexico than any other American, I was more interested in that investigation." Opportunism on both sides formed an important characteristic of the Fall-Doheny friendship, as often happens in even the best of human relationships. But they did develop a genuine fondness for each other, in part because, as Doheny put it, if two men have known the camaraderie of the campfire, "they become warmer friends by reason of having associated under the same conditions." Presumably this might be true even for two separate frontier campfires.

After spending several months at Kingston, Albert Fall decided to give up prospecting and mining for the time being, when he concluded that other pursuits would provide a more dependable income for his growing family. Having earned enough money to get home, he and his brother-in-law made their way south along the Rio Grande and back into Texas, where his wife had remained. It was on this return trip that he first noticed the attractions of the Mesilla Valley above El Paso. On his arrival in Clarksville, he waxed as enthusiastic about its beauties as a "real estate prospectus," describing it to his wife as "the garden of the world." Emma's chronic cough, probably caused by tuberculosis, would undoubtedly benefit from the dry, sunny climate. On top of that, the Mesilla Valley looked like a land of opportunity for a young man with as much nerve as ambition. So Albert Fall made plans to return to New Mexico and settle down at Las Cruces.

CHAPTER 2

Fighting the Devil with Fire

SEVERAL months before leaving the Harding cabinet in 1923, Albert B. Fall wrote his wife, "I have led a very strenuous life—the life of a pioneer in a Western country, in the wide-open days." With better luck this might have been his epitaph. Until the Teapot Dome scandal hopelessly tainted his reputation, the marked impression Fall had left on the public mind during his eleven years in national politics was of a romanticized westerner. At the peak of his influence as secretary of the interior, the newspapers usually associated him with mining, ranching, and the wide-open spaces. His black, broad-brimmed Stetson hat became his trademark. He was known for his combative nature, his bronzed complexion, and his soft drawl, which actually was more Kentuckian than western. The rumor got around that he always carried a gun and was not afraid to use it. His erect posture suggested that he "had spent much time in the saddle." He was described as a "fighting man" whose life stirred up memories of Buffalo Bill, with "the sort of eyes that one learned to beware of in the early frontier days as indicating a man who could take care of himself in almost any sort of company."

Secretary Fall seemed to be a self-made man in every sense of the term. His big ranch, located at Three Rivers, New Mexico, helped confirm this image, especially with easterners. Starry-eyed city folk enamored of the West were forever writing him about getting a job as a cowboy, or wanting to send an ailing or erring son to the ranch for restitution. Appropriately Fall loved horses and, for that matter, any kind of fine-blooded stock. Every year he attended the Kentucky Derby, and a close friend once declared, "I think if he was in his grave and you mentioned a race horse he would jump right up and ask about it." Early on, this self-made man with infinite faith in his own creation had learned to do things in the grand style expected of western nabobs who never worried about little obstacles getting in their way. His son's wedding was hailed as one of the brilliant social events of 1909 in middle Tennessee when the entire Fall family arrived at the bride's hometown of Fayetteville in copper king William C. Greene's private railroad car, the *Verde*, with its two black servants. Out in New Mexico, Fall ordered a big red National automobile with special forty-two-inch wheels so his driver, who was experienced in racecar competition, could take him cross-country over the roadless desert expanses without regard for sand and dry washes.

In appearance, too, Fall vaguely resembled Buffalo Bill, or perhaps a grim Mark Twain. Not a tall man, although often described as being so, he stood about five feet ten inches in height. Spare of physique, with a narrow, almost aesthetic face and hawkish, sometimes piercing, gray-brown eyes, he habitually clenched a cigar, cigarette in long holder, or pipe in a firm mouth under a heavy, drooping mustache. His hair, originally black but almost white when he left the cabinet, was swept back in long loose waves behind his ears in the old senatorial style. Fall often donned a flowing black cape, a garment commonly worn by the upper classes in Mexico, where he acquired the habit. Otherwise, his attire had become fairly conventional by the time he served in the Harding cabinet. Pictures at the ranch with his favorite horse show him wearing leggings, not cowboy boots.

Back in late-nineteenth-century frontier New Mexico Fall had seemed the embodiment of the southern gentleman turned western empire builder as he crossed the dusty streets or sauntered down the boardwalks of Las Cruces, immaculately dressed, and usually wearing the lawyer's Prince Albert coat. He carried a cane, which some unwary opponents soon learned he could brandish like a sword. Remarkably handsome as a young man, he had a special preference for starched white linen and carried himself with an erectness that harmonized perfectly with the cloth's rigidity. Frequently in those early days he might be seen drinking with his cohorts in saloons—the political clubs of the territory—and although he later expressed some public sympathy for the prohibition cause, he never advocated it in practice. In fact, he was known as a drinking man, or one with "wet proclivities," and his wife sometimes admonished him to follow moderation in this respect.

Not surprisingly, Interior Secretary Fall liked to relax by reading western adventure stories, probably because they reminded him of his own early experiences. And through a long friendship with author Eugene Manlove Rhodes, Fall actually appeared as a character in frontier fiction. Rhodes gained a national reputation using the land and people of southern New Mexico in his fourteen novels and sixty short stories. At least two other western authors, Florence Finch Kelley, who wrote *With Hoops of Steel* in 1900, and Eugene Cunningham, who turned out popular westerns for over thirty years, also based plots on events surrounding Fall's early life.

In the hallowed halls of the United States Senate, Fall often skewered opposing colleagues during floor debates, leaving them angry and vengeful. As interior secretary, he was no gentler with opponents or less tolerant of criticism. An advocate of undefiled national parks, who had confronted him in the Interior Department, left his office muttering in indignation:

> Mr. Fall can be very winning when he chooses. His forceful, picturesque personality carries far, and he uses it to the limit in gaining his objectives. His speech is fast, his manner is impetuous, and he becomes instantly aggressive at opposition. At these times his powerful face clouds to sternness, he sits forward in his chair, and pounds his statements home with gesticulation; or he throws his head back till he faces the ceiling while roaring with laughter at his opponent's replies. He does not argue, because he does not listen. He controls absolutely the attention of all hearers, and deeply impresses many with his impetuous advocacy and assertion.

On the other hand, Secretary Fall inspired genuine liking and admiration in many of his Interior associates, partly because "he talked as straight to pestiferous politicians seeking favors as to any subordinate." As one of his bureau chiefs recalled: "Fall was certainly a man of ability. He was a fighter who gave and took hard blows. I think that, and party politics, was the major cause of opposition to him rather than any special jealousy. I was fond of him but to be fair we must remember that his code was that of the frontier and frontier politics."

Fall had forged his political code back in New Mexico after leaving the Kingston mines and moving to Las Cruces. By personal inclination as well as necessity, he had earned the reputation of a hard, uncompromising fighter, and his life from that time on became one pitched battle after another. Of magnetic personality and eloquent, a social favorite, he had a talent for making fiercely loyal allies and implacable foes. He was often a vindictive antagonist, but, according to an opposition Las Cruces newspaper, "with the courtesy of a brave man." Eugene Manlove Rhodes, who saw in Fall "the quality to be loved," wrote in the *Saturday Evening Post* in 1911: "He has no acquaintances. Every New Mexican is either his steadfast friend or his bitter enemy; and they are all his admirers."

Absolutely fearless and with an explosive temper, Fall took direct action or spoke candidly if he wanted to rebuke an opponent—or correct an ally. He played poker with a passion, preferably for high stakes. Sometimes this penchant might surface unexpectedly, as when he frankly belittled the abilities of a local politician, and concluded, "You will excuse the 'poker' terms which I have used, but the game of politics is so much like a game of poker that these terms, it strikes me, are most appropriate." Even when he assumed the role of peacemaker, said the *Santa Fe New Mexican* in 1910, he usually harmonized "with a sword, with a bludgeon, rather than with soft words and caresses." As a man of action, ambitious for power and thoroughly political, Fall was always irked by the routine duties of public office, but seldom by politics itself. "You nearly always did talk [politics] when you were around Judge Fall," a family member recalled.

The place that shaped Fall's image as a romanticized westerner, and his political code as well, was Dona Ana County, which straddled the Rio Grande in southern New Mexico Territory. It was a land of sapphire blue skies and jagged purple mountains. A shimmering expanse of crystallized gypsum, called the White Sands, just south of where the first atomic bomb was later exploded, cast a desert hue over the entire countryside. In the midst of this stark terrain along the Rio Grande, the Mesilla Valley formed a thin, green oasis. Adjacent to the river was Las Cruces, the county seat and largest town (about two thousand in 1887) in this flourishing agricultural, mining, and stock-raising region. Nourished by old Mexican *acequias*, or irrigation canals, which siphoned off the Rio Grande's muddy waters, the otherwise arid lands blossomed with orchards, vineyards, alfalfa fields, and grain and vegetable acreages. In 1881 the Santa Fe Railroad had completed its line from Albuquerque to El Paso, linking Las Cruces with the rest of the nation. By the time Fall arrived in 1887, the Mesilla Valley was enjoying a full-scale boom.

But the principal business of Las Cruces and Dona Ana County was neither agriculture nor the railroad—but politics. The people, of whom a majority were Hispanic Americans, had a religious zeal for partisan activity, and almost every community event had some political significance. In fact, according to Fall, there existed in New Mexico as a whole "more politics to the square inch . . . than Tammany Hall has ever known." Through its aggressive leaders Dona Ana County habitually tried to dominate every territorial convention or contest, both Republican and Democratic. The county itself became notorious for its partisan battles, which sometimes resulted in mass demonstrations and bloodshed. In 1871 a bloody riot erupted in the town of Mesilla when separate parades supporting the two rival candidates for congressional delegate collided on the plaza, leaving nine persons dead and forty or fifty others with serious wounds. The bitter personal feuds stemming from quarrels over elections dragged on for years, sometimes punctuated by six-shooter duels in the streets or other public places, or by murders from ambush in more secluded locales.

This part of New Mexico, bordering Mexico and near the Gadsden Purchase of 1853—the last piece of contiguous territory annexed by the United States—was under the political control of a few "American," or Anglo American, bosses, who maintained power by sharing the offices and spoils with prominent Hispanics who cooperated in their intrigues. At every election a furor arose over the illegal voter registration of Mexican nationals and the duping of Hispanic citizens on the intricacies of balloting. To provide the winning margin, the Anglo bosses resorted to high-handed intimidation, bribery, vote-buying, ballot-box stuffing and miscounting, and staged riots. On the night before an election party workers customarily primed unsuspecting residents with liquor, held them in a well-guarded corral "as if they were a bunch of steers," and then herded them to the polls the next morning. Both parties used such "corral tactics" openly, and it became a competitive sport to dispatch a henchman, technically known as an "emissary," who secretly infiltrated the opposition's guarded corral the night before the election and enticed away as many potential voters as a higher bribe or more whiskey could buy. As an alternative strategy, one side might flush the other party's captives from the corral and scatter them into the mesquite thickets surrounding the town.

One local editor, who had often witnessed these perversions of the democratic system, claimed, "The money spent for whiskey and votes by the politicians of Las Cruces in the late election would have built an adequate system of water works for the town, put the streets in decent condition and planted rows of trees along every important street." The opposition newspaper went even further, blaming the retarded development of the community on the constant "state of ferment" about who would fill county offices and the overpowering interest of the citizenry in this "absorbing theme." In every election old political wounds were torn open, heated personal quarrels ensued, and the prominent civic leaders most needed to promote progress were rendered incapable of uniting.

In this tumultuous setting A. B. Fall (he was not usually styled Albert B. Fall until he became a United States senator) served his apprenticeship and cut his teeth on partisan rivalry.

He was no reformer, and there is little indication that conditions improved because of his presence. In fact, an unfriendly editor said that he only stirred up more "strife and array." Furthermore, "When the blessed Redeemer uttered that great humanitarian doctrine, 'Blessed are the peace makers [*sic*],' he evidently did not refer to A. B. Fall." Instead of cleansing Dona Ana affairs, he mastered all the Machiavellian techniques and maneuvers. In time, after carefully assembling his arsenal and changing parties, he became the political power of southern New Mexico, and ultimately of the entire state. And when Fall became a cabinet officer, the distinctive brand of Dona Ana County partisan combat still marked his style.

Fall lost little time in making a place for himself after he arrived at Las Cruces in October 1887 and his family joined him in the Commercial Hotel a month later. The early influence of his religious and scholarly grandfather, Philip Slater Fall, apparently first led him to open a book-and-stationery store, but he soon turned to real estate and land sales. Barely scraping by and plagued by debts, he also experimented briefly with the cultivation of Kentucky white burley tobacco. While his wife rested and soaked up the healthful sunshine to heal her lungs, her unmarried brother, the faithful Joe Morgan, cared for the two young children and cooked for the family. Soon after moving all of them into a small adobe house, Fall took up the pursuit of politics and law. In fact, as an unsympathetic editor complained, he was not around "long enough to change his shirt" before becoming a candidate for the territorial legislature.

Las Cruces offered many opportunities as a center of government: the county seat, the third judicial district court, the United States land office, and other agencies. A close friend observed that Albert Fall was not by nature "one of those ordinary individuals, who drop into the life of a community without a ripple or disturbance." Moreover, as a young family man intent on getting ahead, he could hardly have escaped an active role in public affairs, for the measure of success in Dona Ana County was political attainment. Nor was there any serious question about which party he would choose. For a Kentuckian and southerner, the only option possible was the "Democracy," the party of the Solid South.

This natural alignment caused great difficulty for Fall. In the years since the Civil War, territorial New Mexico, as well as other western territories, had acquired a Republican veneer because the national administration in Washington filled most of the influential public offices by appointment. Nonresident aspirants from the East often obtained these plums, subjecting the sun-drenched southwestern province to, as Fall described it, "a mild form of carpetbag government." With a steady stream of Republican presidents from 1861 to 1885, territorial Democrats found it hard, if not impossible, to secure either cherished positions or recognition. Moreover, an entrenched, quasi-Republican machine called the "Santa Fe Ring" fed on the national government, exercising substantial sway throughout New Mexico. Based on mutual cooperation for specific objectives and projects, which changed and evolved, this nebulous organization had first achieved notoriety in the early 1870s with Anglo American squabbling over possession of the Maxwell Land Grant.

The Santa Fe Ring encompassed several lesser territorial rings and branches in various county-seat towns such as Las Cruces. Although Republicans, Masons, and prominent Santa Fe lawyers tended to dominate the syndicate, some conspicuously powerful Democrats were "members" as well to ensure ascendancy no matter which way the elections went. The ring tried to command, usually with success, the territorial legislature and the lone delegate to Congress, federal appointments, county elections, lucrative government contracts and land decisions, and, when necessary, the courts. Even so, the Santa Fe Ring, although composed of individuals with common political and economic goals, never had a fixed membership or the tight-knit, ironfisted organizational structure of contemporary rings in eastern cities and states.

At the head of this territorial syndicate stood big, bluff Thomas B. Catron of Santa Fe, the Republican boss of New Mexico politics for a generation prior to 1896. The ring's most important guardian in Washington was Stephen B. Elkins. Once Catron's Santa Fe law partner and collaborator in acquiring vast acreages from the old Spanish and Mexican land grants, Elkins had left the territory in 1877 to become a cabinet member and a powerful United States senator from West Virginia. Through a combination of legal and political skills he had amassed a private empire in New Mexico of some 1,711,764 acres of land, besides banking and mining investments, and had further advanced his fortunes by marrying the daughter of wealthy and influential Senator Henry Gassaway Davis of West Virginia.

By the 1880s Catron, the apt protégé of Elkins, owned more land individually than anyone else in the United States, holding property in seven states and territories as well as Mexico. At one time or another he gained an interest or clear title in thirty-four land grants, totaling three million acres, and controlled another three million acres through the ownership of strategically located streams and water holes. His other investments included banking, ranching, mining, and various business interests. Both Elkins and Catron had started out in politics while living in Dona Ana County, Elkins as a representative in the territorial legislature and Catron as the local district attorney.

Albert Fall used the same springboard for his own career. For a Democrat, however, the road to success in Dona Ana County had many pitfalls, mainly because of the formidable nearby Republican opposition. At this time the local ringleader and, "practically, the political dictator," was towering William L. Rynerson, called the "Tall Sycamore of the Rio Grande" because of his great height. No stranger to violence, he had shot and killed the chief justice of the territorial supreme court twenty years before, during a showdown in a Santa Fe hotel. Besides his political connections with Tom Catron, Rynerson and another local stalwart, John H. Riley, owned ranch property and cattle jointly with the boss of the Santa Fe Ring. Riley had played a prominent role in the bloody Lincoln County War, opposing the Tunstall–McSween–Billy the Kid faction, and many believed that Rynerson and Catron had also been more than silent partners in the anti-Kid clique.

Another Dona Ana County Republican leader was Albert J. Fountain, longtime manager of the county party organization. Both he and Rynerson had come to New Mexico during the Civil War with General James H. Carleton's California Column and remained to practice law and politics in the Southwest. During an amazing career filled with danger and narrow escapes, Fountain had held political power in both Texas and New Mexico. As Texas senate majority leader and president in the early 1870s, he played a major role in the unsuccessful Republican effort to impose Radical Reconstruction on the former Confederate state. In 1870, while back home in his El Paso district, he was shot three times at point-blank range by an erstwhile Radical ally, only to avoid certain death when a bullet aimed at his chest was deflected by a pocket watch. He returned to New Mexico in 1873, settling down with his Hispanic wife in the Mesilla Valley, and again became a Republican power broker. Over the years he also distinguished himself as a militia colonel leading volunteers against hostile Apaches and as the nemesis and special prosecutor of roving rustler gangs. Several times he cheated death in abortive plots or ambushes; the main public complaint about his methods was that rustler captives too often got killed "trying to escape" before they could be legally hanged. Of the local strongmen, the vain, accomplished Colonel Fountain became Fall's most hated rival and enemy, especially after Rynerson's death in 1893.

When Albert Fall, lately a mucker in the Grey Eagle Mine at Kingston, challenged the Dona Ana County machine, it meant also that he would be pitted against Thomas B. Catron and the Santa Fe Ring. The rivalry between him and Catron, however, was not as bitter as sometimes portrayed. Although the two men were political adversaries and never really friends, even after Fall became a Republican and they were elected New Mexico's first two United States senators, Fall and Catron could work together cooperatively in legal and other matters when mutual self-interest demanded it. Even so, it is essential to remember that Fall's many years of aggressive warfare against the Santa Fe Ring and its local battalions gave form and substance to the code he later followed as a senator and cabinet member.

Quite simply, the ring system was the curse of New Mexico Territory—and represented western politics at its worst. Under territorial government, Fall once declared in a prime example of his spellbinding oratory, Dona Ana County was like a stagnant eddy in a river where "slime gathers, and froth and logs and dead leaves, and all manner of floating filth." With federal appointments, he said, "a lot of broken-down old political hacks" had accumulated there "to bask in the sun of political preferment, like the serpents stretched out on the [eddy's] dead logs." Yet, if the southwestern territory in which Fall learned his tactics was a "rotten borough," local conditions were not wholly responsible for that result. In this same era America produced the Tweed Ring, the Gas Ring, and various other corrupt rings in the East. What happened in remote New Mexico also reflected politics of the day and the inadequacies of the nation's territorial system.

Fall's first encounter with Colonel Fountain and the Dona Ana County Republican machine seemed innocent enough. In 1888, while Fall was away on a two-month buggy trip across the rugged country to Roswell near the Pecos River, a Democratic editor in Las Cruces started promoting his nomination for the territorial house of representatives. Pressed for willing candidates, the Democratic convention gladly nominated Fall, inexperienced and relatively unknown, about three days after he returned to town. Fountain, who had so far contented himself with managing affairs behind the scenes, reluctantly consented to run and save the seat for the Republicans. The colonel won by a slim margin, and thus the fateful rivalry began. Despite reports of many voting irregularities, Fall refused to contest the election. After this first defeat he never again lost an election at the polls in New Mexico.

The Republican bosses were alarmed by the apparent ambitions and potential of "this contemptible upstart," as Fountain labeled Fall. In addition, a substantial population increase in the territory during the past decade and the victory of President

Grover Cleveland in 1884 had strengthened Democratic ranks. The bosses decided to employ diplomacy. Calling on their adversary, a delegation of Republicans invited Fall to join their clique and offered him a lucrative federal appointment as an inducement. He rejected this tempting proposal, even though the bosses hinted darkly that they "were in the habit of securing what they desired," and if he did not join them, he would suffer accordingly not only in politics but particularly in a law practice. Because of the ring's power over the selection of juries, Fall added, "It was not an altogether idle warning I received, and this I learned by experience during the ensuing two years."

His natural instincts told him what to do next. He would "fight the devil with fire" and beat the Republican bosses at their own game. Before long he became a master of sulphurous phrases and political intrigue. Whenever an opportunity arose, or he created one, whether in a public gathering or private conversation, he harangued the Republicans and plotted their downfall for all he was worth.

As the most important part of his strategy, Fall cultivated the friendship and support of Hispanic people, who constituted a majority of the voters. In his law practice he accepted every Hispanic case he could get, even when there was no hope of remuneration. His knowledge of Spanish, gained earlier in Mexico, could now be put to practical use in a bilingual territory where court sessions, legislative proceedings, and public meetings of all kinds were conducted in both English and Spanish with an indispensable interpreter customarily standing beside the speaker. Moreover, he quickly learned the inner workings of the "don system" by which the aristocratic *rico* (rich man) class dominated the rest of the Hispanic population, thereby controlling that decisive block of votes. Party labels in Dona Ana County were almost meaningless. No Anglo politician could hope for real success without first making alliances with the influential *ricos*, or *patróns*, and the record shows unmistakably that Albert Fall came to have an "uncanny sway" over the Hispanic vote.

In New Mexico land and water represented the most tangible forms of wealth and influence. Later Fall would become a virtuoso in gaining the favors of the federal agencies and the state land office that dispensed coveted grazing leases with their crucial water holes, almost invariably to those of the right partisan persuasion. Not surprisingly, the future interior secretary won his first elective office, probably in 1889, on the three-member board of irrigation-canal (*acequia*) commissioners for the small Hispanic village of Dona Ana, which was on the Rio Grande a few miles above Las Cruces. Because irrigation was, as Fall once said, "the life of our people," these positions required strong and respected leaders, who were usually drawn from the community itself. The selection of Fall, an outsider, recognized his growing political prestige.

In 1890 Fall, by now the acknowledged chieftain of the revived Democrats, and proclaimed by them as "The Faithful Friend of the Mexican [Hispanic] Race," once more ran against Colonel Fountain for the territorial house. Fountain and his allies accused Fall of shamelessly exploiting the ethnic issue—a tacit admission that he had successfully invaded their domain. If this "Texas Democrat," they said, ran for office in the Lone Star State, he "would probably announce himself as the faithful friend of the Negro race—or in China as the good friend of the Chinamen." Despite a final Republican warning that Fall was "a pigmy and baby" compared to Fountain, the new Democratic leader won the election by comfortable majorities in all of the three counties of the district, Dona Ana, Grant, and Sierra. An acrimonious post-election vote recount, with Fall and Fountain acting as attorneys for their respective parties, further inflamed their rivalry. And in the territorial legislature at Santa Fe, Fall had his first direct encounter with Boss Tom Catron and the Santa Fe Ring.

With the unexpected support of a few "Independents," the Democrats had gained control of the lower house, and the ambitious newcomer Fall was chosen by his party as floor leader. The most important legislative issue was the establishment of modern public schools. Besides introducing needed reform, improved educational opportunities could advance the chances of statehood since many easterners regarded the New Mexico population as "not American but 'Greasers,' persons ignorant of our laws, manners, customs, language, and institutions." Although not primarily responsible for the bill, floor leader Fall provided substantial assistance in both framing and passing the "Paullin public school law," which laid the groundwork for the state's present public education program. In fact, an admiring editor declared, "His fight . . . on the floor of the House was so aggressive and impatient of obstruction or delays in securing its passage that it bordered on the impolitic, but . . . in the end hastened its becoming law." He and another Democratic leader also prepared and secured the enactment of legislation creating normal schools at Silver City and Las Vegas.

The Catholic hierarchy reportedly opposed the public school measure to protect its parochial institutions, but, according to Fall, the real enemy was Tom Catron, who feared increased tax levies on his extensive landholdings. When Catron, a powerful member of the upper house, or council, tried to insert several debilitating amendments, Fall and other representatives suddenly appeared in the upper chamber to monitor the proceedings and help save the bill. Even more exciting events took place outside the legislative halls. In a brazen attempt to assassinate Catron, armed riders galloped down a dark Santa Fe street one evening and fired rifle and shotgun blasts into the boss's lighted law office, narrowly missing him but severely wounding a Republican territorial senator who favored the school measure. Although never solved, the shooting incident probably stemmed from a local feud involving Catron's law practice and had no connection with the school bill. With the vote of the wounded senator, who was dramatically carried into the upper chamber on a stretcher, it barely won final approval.

In his first legislative experience Albert Fall had stood in the "front rank" among those Democrats who dominated the lower house. The *Albuquerque Morning Democrat* hailed him as "one of the very few" in the entire legislature "who had the courage to take the Grand Turk, Catron, by the beard." He had felt the biting winds of political strife in the territorial capital and had been a bystander to shooting and bloodshed. Moreover, Fall had found his natural element. From now on, no matter what his other interests might be—mining, law, or ranching—he would always make time for politics. In fact, at the next Democratic territorial convention in Santa Fe, where he was the keynote speaker, he flaunted his newly acquired prominence, denouncing the Republicans for sins both real and imagined like a seasoned veteran. He made no secret of his ultimate objectives, writing at this time, "My ambition is to see this a Democratic State, with two Democratic Senators," and leaving no doubt who one of those senators should be.

After his initiation in the territorial lower house Fall moved on to win a seat in the senate, or council, in 1892, 1896, and 1902. He was an associate justice of the New Mexico supreme court from 1893 to 1895 by appointment from President Cleveland, and briefly solicitor general, or attorney general, twice, in 1897 and again in 1907. His election as a delegate to the New Mexico constitutional convention in 1910 was followed by the distinction of becoming, as a Republican, one of the new state's first two United States senators in 1912.

In his early public career, as later, Fall often acted independently, sometimes refusing to attend party caucuses or to be bound by them. In the 1892 election, for example, he gave up the Democratic label temporarily, perhaps under the influence of Populism then sweeping through the nation's hinterlands, and ran for the territorial senate on a "nonpartisan independent county ticket," or "People's Ticket." He was always surrounded by controversy. A few years later, in 1897, during a heated legislative debate, he impulsively walked across the senate chamber from the Democratic side and slapped the face of Charles A. Spiess, a prominent Republican and Tom Catron's former law partner. Spiess took it "without a whimper." Afterwards, when the question arose about how many times Spiess had been slapped, Governor Miguel A. Otero recalled, "Fall only slapped Charles Spiess once, that was enough." During a loud argument at the New Mexico constitutional convention of

1910, he accosted an opposing delegate and drove him from the hall. Nor were these the only times he used the flat of his hand, a notorious temper, or his cane on a rival and got away with it.

From the beginning politics was a drain on Fall's meager resources, and he continually sought profit-making ventures to support his fatal indulgence. The vision of El Dorado he had first glimpsed in Mexico and at Kingston led him on a long search for mining wealth. But his law practice, not mining, first gave him the slim measure of financial success necessary to cushion his political expenses. He began practicing in Las Cruces in 1889, less than two years after arriving there, culminating a long process of reading law intermittently since his youth in Kentucky. In 1897, while territorial attorney general, he was elected president of the New Mexico Bar Association. Although a remote territory, New Mexico had no shortage of lawyers, probably because of the widely publicized windfalls of attorneys, such as Elkins and Catron, from land-grant litigation. Governor Edmund G. Ross wrote an eastern friend in 1887 that the spoils of Santa Fe Ring members had attracted so much attention that Santa Fe alone could boast "one lawyer to every ten [Anglo] Americans." The road to political greatness and financial success had been clearly marked out for Fall by the Republican opposition.

Fall became a familiar figure in southern New Mexico courtrooms as he made the rounds from Silver City in the west near Arizona to Roswell and Eddy (now Carlsbad) in the Pecos River country near the Texas line. Occasionally he also represented clients before the territorial supreme court in Santa Fe. Much of his practice involved both United States and Mexican law, as well as some aspects of international law, especially in cases regarding land titles, water and mineral rights, citizenship, and extradition. Fall made his first trip to Washington, probably in 1891 or 1892, for a hearing in which he convinced Secretary of State James G. Blaine that some fugitives from a political disturbance in Mexico were actually American citizens and should not be extradited. About this same time Colonel

Fountain and the local Republican machine started using federal antipolygamy legislation aimed at the Mormons in Utah to intimidate Hispanic voters and halt the gains made by Fall and the Democrats. Many older Hispanic couples who had neglected to obtain legal divorces from earlier mates across the border were now being prosecuted for bigamy. "Sir, it was enough to make one curse a government under which such things occur," Fall later wrote President Cleveland. Fall was the defense attorney in about 120 of these cases, and afterwards recalled that only two resulted in conviction. Later as a judge, when it became necessary to pass sentence on an elderly Hispanic couple found guilty of "living in adultery," he did so by "directing them to go back home and help one another and comfort one another as they had been doing for forty-five years."

In New Mexico, where livestock grazed over great expanses of the unfenced public domain, one of the most common criminal offenses was "brand burning," or altering brands, and "mavericking" unbranded calves. Fall estimated that he defended some five hundred persons accused of cattle rustling in one form or another and could not remember ever losing a single case. Murder trials, too, made up a large part of his early practice. Perhaps fifty of these indictments involved first-degree murder charges, with only one of them resulting in conviction. As it happened, the most spectacular case of his law career, and the most heralded event of his life besides Teapot Dome, included both rustling and murder. In the final act of the Fall-Fountain rivalry Fall served as the defense attorney for his friends who were charged with the murder of Colonel Fountain in 1896.

By the time of Fall's arrival at Las Cruces in 1887, a bloody range war was already developing between the "big" cattle interests and the "little" ranchers in southern New Mexico, largely caused by a virtual invasion of Texans. During the early 1880s drifting Texas cowboys, cattlemen, and outlaws had crowded in and contested the established order on the open range. Big Anglo ranching concerns controlled most of the good land and precious water holes not retained by the old Hispanic families. Although some bad blood existed between the Anglo and Hispanic ranchers, the Texans with their clannish ways threatened both branches of the existing range hierarchy. With the big ranchers and the intruding Texans engaged in brand-blotting, mavericking, and shooting each other's livestock, the inevitable conflict resulted in several killings. This violence continued into the 1890s, inflaming local politics for almost two decades.

Albert Fall, although he had sojourned in Texas, was hardly a Texan. It was his alliance with Oliver M. Lee and other expatriated Texans—all Democrats to the man—that brought him into the range war and its accompanying political struggle. In 1885, at age nineteen, Lee had come from Buffalo Gap, Taylor County, Texas, bringing with him some horses and a few head of cattle. He started ranching at Dog Canyon on the west side of the Sacramento Mountains overlooking the White Sands. When his partner saw the boulder-strewn canyon, he remarked, "Well, Oliver, this country is so damned sorry, I think we can stay here a long time and never be bothered by anybody else." But two things kept Lee in the range-war storm center: his determination to become a big rancher and his uncanny talent with both a rifle and a six-shooter. Muscular, ramrod-straight, gentlemanly, a prototype of the Cattle Kingdom cowboy, Oliver Lee also appeared as a character in the western stories of Eugene Manlove Rhodes. In fact, he became a legend in southern New Mexico, with Rhodes saying of him, "Lee has killed about eight men, in open warfare."

While struggling to make a place for himself, Lee quickly discovered that Republican political might was as potent on the open range as in Santa Fe or Las Cruces. By 1889 three of the same Republican bosses who dominated the Santa Fe Ring and the Dona Ana County machine—Tom Catron, William L. Rynerson, and John H. Riley, partners in the Tularosa Land and Cattle Company—also headed the adjunct "cattle ring" on the range. In an abortive indictment for one of the numerous killings on both sides, Lee and several of his friends found themselves in court facing, as part of the prosecution, both Rynerson and Colonel Fountain. As a Texas Democrat, Lee saw the absolute necessity of allying himself with a skillful legal and political Democratic strategist who could cope with the Republican bosses.

Albert Fall apparently first met Oliver Lee in 1889 when Lee came into Fall's Las Cruces law office and introduced himself. The two young men struck up a casual relationship which ripened into a lifelong brotherhood bound "with hoops of steel." Because they had the same enemies, their alliance was a natural one. For his part, Fall acted as the "inside man," tending to courthouse matters and devising strategy. Lee was the "outside man," or field marshal, who stood ready to serve as a bodyguard or muster a cavalry of armed cowboys when Fall's tactics required support.

As "attorney for a gang of Texas rustlers," Fall had added a strong contingent to his coalition. Nothing did more to reveal his magnetic personality and deftness at political maneuvering than his success in recruiting two highly incongruous groups, the resident Hispanics and the invading Texans, each resentful of the other. Yet both the lowly local folk and the haughty, aspiring Texans were underdogs—or, like Fall, the "outs"—and they fitted his plans well. He did not seek sweeping political reform but a palace revolution that would dispossess the Republican bosses and give him and his trusted followers the seats of influence.

To expand his base of power, Fall gained control in 1891 of a defunct Las Cruces weekly newspaper and renamed it the *Independent Democrat.* His father and brother, Philip, both recent arrivals in New Mexico, ostensibly ran the paper, but everyone knew who directed its editorial policy. Like most of the territory's weeklies, which were usually party organs, the *Independent Democrat* specialized in raw partisan invective written "with spades and fence rails." Its major objectives consisted of extolling the virtues of A. B. Fall and besting the local opposition journal, the *Rio Grande Republican*, in vituperative debate.

In his fight for supremacy Fall also relied on more dependable means than the power of the press. He set out to wrest control over the agencies of law and order from the Republicans. Justice in Dona Ana County was often determined, not by time-honored procedures and institutions, but by the capricious action of those who enforced the law. Juries were selected by a jury commission appointed by the district judge or his clerk. In this way the judge, a federal patronage appointee, had decisive influence over a jury's membership and its verdict. Moreover, he could unleash a corps of gun-carrying deputy United States marshals as well. Many legal matters also passed through the hands of the federally appointed district attorney and the elected county sheriff. Of great importance, the sheriff acted as the tax collector, which enhanced and enriched the office, and he commanded well-armed deputy sheriffs. The sheriff's election in Dona Ana County often became a crucial matter because it could mean jail or freedom, life or death, to many concerned people.

The 1892 election marked the beginning of a deadly struggle over who would have the upper hand in maintaining law and order. Stressing nonpartisanship, Fall won the territorial senate post for a district of five counties and carried the entire local "People's Ticket" into office on his coattails, including a new sheriff. The Republican machine, realizing the seriousness of the challenge, had sent forty hastily deputized United States marshals, headed by party stalwart William H. H. Llewellyn, to "guard" the Las Cruces polls. The Democratic champion sprang into action at once. As Fall confronted Llewellyn outside the polling place, he saw seventeen men with Springfield rifles backing up his adversary and the muzzles of double-barreled shotguns protruding from the building's windows. In no uncertain terms, Fall told Llewellyn that the marshals "must tear their badges from their coats and get out of town and stack their guns." They promptly left. One version of this incident has Fall shouting from the street, "Llewellyn, get the hell out of here with that dam'd militia inside of two minutes, or I will have you all killed." Then he supposedly pointed to the flat rooftop of a nearby adobe store where Oliver Lee and several armed cowboys were stationed. In a postmortem on the election itself, which included a Democratic victory nationally as well as the fusion triumph locally, the *Rio Grande Republican* had to admit, "We Have Met the Crafty Enemy And We Are His'n!"

The news of Fall's triumph in Dona Ana County led one newspaper to eulogize him as "probably the shrewdest politician in the territory." With the return of Grover Cleveland to the White House in 1893 he received more tangible recognition in far-off Washington. Fall was among the Democrats appointed by President Cleveland to the New Mexico supreme court. He apparently took the associate justiceship as a compromise since he went to the national capital for the presidential inauguration seeking the post of United States attorney, which was considered "a more lucrative office."

With the judgeship nomination pending in the Senate, Fall's opponents in New Mexico launched a strenuous campaign to prevent his confirmation. The Knights of Labor charged that in the last legislative session he had squelched a bill favoring railroad employees. Colonel Fountain and the Dona Ana County Republicans sent several letters to Washington accusing Fall of such extreme partisanship as to make him totally unfit for a judicial position. Boss Catron of the Santa Fe Ring pleaded with his powerful business and political ally, Stephen B. Elkins, to help stop Fall's confirmation:

> This is the very worst appointment which could have been made. He is the most offensive man in the Territory and the most venal. . . . He will only use his office for the purpose of oppressing and crippling his political enemies and filling his own pockets at their expense or at the expense of any one else from whom he can extort money. . . . You yourself still have considerable interests here and should not be subject to spoilation—as would result before such judges as this.

Fall did not lack influential friends. His claims were pressed by Senator William Lindsay of Kentucky, who had helped him get started reading law, and Augustus H. Garland, Emma Fall's relative and United States attorney general in the first Cleveland administration. Although for a time it appeared that President Cleveland might have to submit another name, the Senate finally approved Fall's nomination in April 1893.

Fall's tenure on the bench was anything but uneventful, even though for a man of action he found judicial duty routine and rather dull. Under the territorial system the five appointed New Mexico justices met annually in Santa Fe to form the supreme court, which acted as an appellate body. In these sessions Fall wrote few opinions of little significance. But the main job of an associate justice was to serve as the presiding judge of one of the district courts. Fall "rode the circuit" in the third judicial district (Sierra, Grant, and Dona Ana counties), holding sessions in the county-seat towns of Hillsboro, Silver City, and Las Cruces, and occasionally in places outside his area at the invitation of another judge. Besides having jurisdiction over territorial matters, such as homicide, rustling, and land disputes, the supreme court and the district courts were also a part of the federal judicial system and handled certain federal cases.

Because the third district included Dona Ana County, Fall's appointment was a major victory in his program to gain control of the local agencies of law and order. That is why the Republican machine fought his nomination so bitterly, and why his relatively brief tenure provided so much excitement. Temperamentally unsuited for the bench, Fall could not lay down the sword of Democratic chieftain when he became a judge; he simply added the clout of judicial power to his partisan role. In the unaccustomed situation of underdogs, Colonel Fountain and the Republicans loudly complained that Fall acted more like a political boss than a judge, frequently making speeches at party conventions and using his official position for "coercing individuals to vote the Democratic ticket." Demanding redress, the ousted Republican machine employed some ironic terminology: "Down with that Democratic ring; that 'one man ring' with Fall in the center." Throughout this barrage of criticism Judge Fall and his supporters contended that he was the victim of character assassination and that, in fact, there existed an actual plot to assassinate him.

All of these matters came to a head in the 1894 election, a wild and woolly affair even by Dona Ana County standards. Because it was one of the few important elective offices, and crucial in dispensing hands-on justice, the sheriff's position again became the storm center of the campaign. A recurrence of trouble on the range added a special note of urgency to the law and order struggle. Earlier in 1894 the big cattle ranchers had formed the Southeastern New Mexico Stock Growers' Association and hired Colonel Fountain as the organization's attorney and special prosecutor. So far Fountain had obtained convictions of twenty small-fry rustlers, of the outlaw variety, but Oliver Lee and the little ranchers knew the colonel would soon come after bigger game.

Pandemonium reigned in Las Cruces on election eve. Any attempt to label either side exclusively as heroes or villains, thus satisfying the demands of Hollywood folklore, would be the height of naïveté. One point was obvious: the winner of this contest might have an advantage for a long time to come. As a result, both factions proclaimed their righteousness and charged, for example, that the other seemed "desperately determined to appeal to the Winchester and the six-shooter." On election eve the town reeked with the fumes of free whiskey as the emissaries of both parties rushed about openly practicing the art of corral politics, rounding up Hispanic voters and herding them into enclosures or stealing them from the opposition corrals. Fights often broke out when enemy patrols happened to collide in these operations. "When the polls opened Tuesday morning," a disgusted observer declared, "the corrals began spewing forth their contents, and the spew went into the ballot box to determine who shall manage the business of the people and expend public money."

With the smell of battle in the air, Judge Fall abandoned any pretense of judicial nonpartisanship, calling for the annihilation of Colonel Fountain's Republican corps and the "complete defeat" of Boss Catron. The judge had a busy day. First, from his command post in an office adjoining Democratic headquarters, he hurried off to a polling place where he dispersed several unauthorized persons from the roped-off area surrounding the balloting booth and told the Republican sentry, or "challenger," to stop following voters into the booth itself. When the opposition sentry, according to Fall, "persisted in interrupting me in a very insolent and insulting manner," the judge advised the man to stand aside or get slapped in the mouth. The Republicans, in their version, maintained that Fall interfered with the balloting process, threatening to "mash" their sentry's "damned mouth all over his face." Whatever the case, the Republican challenger moved back. Then Fall finished his talk with the election judges and "retired outside the ropes."

That afternoon a mounted messenger rode in from the village of Dona Ana with a note telling Judge Fall that the Republicans there had crowded around the polling place and halted the voting. As Fall read the message, he saw Deputy Sheriff Ben Williams, known as a Republican agent, race off on horseback with three or four well-armed men, including one called "Diamond Dick." Upon inquiry, Fall learned that Williams had said that he "would go up and show the d——d democrats at Doña Ana how to do things." Immediately Fall and Oliver Lee climbed into the judge's buggy and followed Williams. Because of Judge Fall's influence, Lee had been appointed a deputy United States marshal and was carrying his trusty Winchester. In a greatly simplified version of the succeeding events, Fall remembered: "We went up to Doña Ana, and I, leaving Mr. Lee in the buggy, called on Mr. Williams as a peace officer to drive the crowd from the polling place—He did so." The local Republicans claimed they had stopped the voting because the Democrats had stuffed the ballot box at noon while the election judges were eating lunch in another room. At Fall's insistence the judges supposedly agreed to resume the election, leaving the main issue for later determination, and to record separately the votes cast before and after the ballot box incident. Later the Republicans contended that Fall had used armed force to obtain the certification of all of the votes, giving the Democrats a slim majority in the Dona Ana precinct.

The real crisis came that night in Las Cruces when the county commissioners, acting as a canvassing board, tried to reach a decision on the election's outcome. In the courthouse corridors a throng of Republican partisans ran head-on into a Democratic crowd. Both sides brandished six-shooters and rifles as threats and profanity rumbled over the trembling commissioners' heads. At this point Judge Fall, with his "personal body guard," Deputy Marshal Lee, made his appearance and intervened in the controversy. Following a heated debate, Fall negotiated a shaky compromise that permitted representatives from both parties "to protect" the commissioners while they concluded their tabulations. The armed mob was sent home. When the deliberations ended, the Democrats had been more adept either in vote-getting or ballot-box-stuffing since they won the lion's share of the spoils, including the coveted sheriff's office. Colonel Fountain and the Republicans contested the election, but the case dragged on in court for nearly a year and a half.

Meanwhile, with their control of the district court and the sheriff's office, not to mention the appointment of Fall's law partner, R. L. ("Deacon") Young, as district attorney, the Fall crowd had acquired a near monopoly in dispensing justice. Colonel Fountain's Republican forces, crippled politically, stood with their backs to the wall. In a startling display of cunning and resourcefulness, however, Fountain struck for the jugular vein by organizing a campaign to have Fall removed from the bench. An avalanche of letters and affidavits descended on Attorney General Richard Olney in Washington, accusing Fall of intimidation, ballot-box manipulation, and bringing disrepute to the district court. A friendly editor reported that the embattled judge made a special trip to Washington to refute the charges filed by those who could not "intimidate or assassinate" him, and therefore sought his removal. In a lengthy written defense of his actions Fall declared that it had become "the fashion" among his enemies to blame him for "every ill which Las Cruces republican flesh is heir to, and all calamities from a late frost to continued drought." But his undeniable involvement in partisan affairs made him highly vulnerable to Fountain's attack, especially since President Cleveland took a dim view of federal employees who played politics. In January 1895, under pressure, Fall submitted his letter of resignation. Ironically, considering the controversial nature of his judicial tenure, from that day on those who knew him best in New Mexico called him "Judge" Fall.

Now the political temperature had reached a boiling point. After Fall's removal as judge, both political factions went around Las Cruces heavily armed and ready for trouble. By tacit agreement Main Street, with its one-story adobe buildings, became a dividing line "as grim and impassable as a mountain barrier." The east side and its saloons, along with the town's leading barber shop (run by Fall's African American "spy," Albert Ellis), were reserved for the Democrats. The west side, where the Republican candidate for sheriff owned the principal general store, and where the Palmilla Club (a high-class saloon) was located, became the Republican domain. If Fall and Colonel Fountain started to approach each other on the street, they would veer off, or one would cross to the opposite side to avoid meeting.

For several months Fall had been saying that his life was in danger; now he seldom appeared on the streets without one of his unofficial bodyguards, either Oliver Lee or Joe Morgan, both special deputy sheriffs. Tom Tucker, a veteran of many shooting scrapes who had a reputation as "a real gunman," also helped guarantee Fall's safety. One September evening in 1895 the tense situation was suddenly punctuated with gunfire. As Fall, Morgan, and Democratic District Attorney Young stood talking in the shadows outside Young's law office on the Democratic side of Main Street, Constable Ben Williams of the Republican law establishment came walking down the same side of the street. Perhaps because the Republicans had hired Williams to stalk Fall, or for other reasons undoubtedly political in nature, either Morgan or Williams, who had a longstanding grudge, started shooting.

Morgan fired the first shot to take effect. It grazed Williams's head, badly powder-burning his face. Another shot, probably fired by Fall, passed through Williams's hat. Still another bullet, from Morgan's six-shooter at close range, shattered Williams's elbow and emerged at the shoulder, knocking him to the ground. Constable Williams, who had been returning the fire, somehow got across the street to the Republican side, shooting as he went. He backed into a saloon, shot out the lights, and was quickly cared for by his friends. Fall was not injured, but Morgan received a flesh wound in the upper arm. When a Hispanic messenger gave Emma Fall (who had long feared such a bloodletting) the false report that her husband had been killed, she began screaming hysterically and could not be calmed down, even by relatives with the real story, until Fall himself came home.

After the smoke cleared away, the Democrats claimed that Williams had been "out to get" Fall, while the Republicans stoutly maintained that the constable was the victim of a premeditated and unprovoked attack. Actually there was plenty of bad blood to go around. While still a judge, Fall had engineered the dismissal of Williams as a deputy marshal, and in the 1894 election they had tangled at Dona Ana in the contested ballot box incident. At that time Fall charged that his life "had been threatened and by this man Williams, who had a few days before shot an innocent man in the back, killing him, by 'mistake' as he claims." An unsuccessful attempt by Williams to pin an old Texas murder charge on Joe Morgan had stirred up trouble between those two. Fall and his Texan law clients especially loathed Williams for his work with Colonel Fountain as an undercover agent of the big cattlemen's association. The main cause of the shooting on Main Street, however, undoubtedly stemmed from Fall's removal as judge and growing tensions in the range warfare.

Not surprisingly, when the grand jury of sixteen Democrats and five Republicans convened, it issued two separate nuisance indictments, on matters apart from the shooting, against Fountain and Williams, and took no action against Fall and Morgan. Those charges were soon dismissed, and the red-hot rivalry shifted from Main Street to the desert lands beyond Las

Cruces. Soon after the shooting episode Colonel Fountain launched a bold new offensive in the range warfare. "I anticipate a hard contest, one perhaps to the death," he wrote the president of the cattlemen's association, but he expressed confidence in "corralling" all the wrongdoers on the range. The Texans became equally determined to resist Fountain's "purge," realizing that if he bagged Oliver Lee, the most successful of their number, the rest of them would be easy prey.

In January 1896 Fountain appeared at the historic courthouse in Lincoln, the scene of Billy the Kid's escapades in an earlier range war, where a Lincoln County grand jury obliged the colonel by handing down a total of thirty-two rustling indictments. Among the accused were Lee and a fellow Texan, William McNew, charged with the "unlawful branding and handling of cattle." What Fountain could not do at home because of Fall's adroit political and legal tactics, he had now accomplished in Lincoln County. On the third day of the 130-mile return trip to Las Cruces, Colonel Fountain and his eight-year-old son, Henry, met and talked with a friendly mail carrier at Chalk Hill near the White Sands. Three mysterious horsemen had been riding at a distance ahead of the colonel's buggy for several hours. Neither Fountain nor his son reached home, nor were they ever seen again.

Many in the excited Las Cruces citizenry quickly concluded that Colonel Fountain and his son "had been murdered by [the] cattle thieves whom he had indicted at the Lincoln county court." Oliver Lee's name headed the list of suspects, and most Republican partisans held Fall responsible, in some way, for the slayings. As a result, various investigators checked and double-checked Fall's every move on that fateful day. His enemies, and they were many and powerful, left no scrap of evidence unturned in trying to place some of the guilt on him, but without success.

Fall had spent most of the day at Sunol, or Black Mountain Camp, twenty-five miles from Las Cruces on the eastern slopes of the San Andres Mountains, where he had established a second home near his ambitious mining venture there, which was nearing the peak of its development. Because of those expanded operations, Fall had gone to "Gold Camp" frequently in recent weeks, sometimes staying for several days. But his detractors, disregarding this well-known information, chose to emphasize the location of Sunol on a wide bench overlooking Chalk Hill, only seven miles to the east. To them it seemed inconceivable that Fall could be so close to the tragedy without having a hand in it. Later, when Governor William T. Thornton called in the famous Pinkerton Detective Agency to work on the Fountain case, one of the detectives summed up this viewpoint: "I am thoroughly satisfied that Judge Fall was not at Chalk Hill, but I am not satisfied that he was not a party to the conspiracy. There is certainly a master hand in this whole affair, and the great legal point would be the proper disposition or disposal of these bodies so that they could [not] be found." If Fall had been involved in the "conspiracy," the Pinkerton operative asserted, he could have easily kept an eye on events at Chalk Hill by using field glasses. Although the detective wanted to throw Fall in jail as an accomplice, he could never produce the evidence necessary to do so.

Fall himself publicly ridiculed the way his political adversaries and the Pinkertons jumped to such hasty conclusions. A Pinkerton who finally managed to interview Fall and Lee together found the Democratic chieftain friendly and talkative. Frankly admitting that he had not liked Fountain "any more than he did a snake," Fall said that he knew one of the colonel's sons had accused him of masterminding the murders. When asked to recount his movements that day, he laughed and did so, but prohibited any questioning of his client, Lee. "I have told you what I would not tell another damn man in this town about where I spent my time on that Saturday," he declared. In another interview Fall told the detective "how this affair was all politics and that certain people only wanted a chance to kill Oliver Lee."

The Fountain case soon brought Fall into sharp conflict with the territorial Democratic elite, causing his first notable alienation from the party. Democratic Governor Thornton, seeing New Mexico's widespread lawlessness and numerous political assassinations as an obstacle to statehood, had a keen interest in the Fountain murders. In quick succession Thornton took three decisive steps, all of which undercut Fall's eroding base of power. First, he arranged a meeting in neutral El Paso between Democratic and Republican leaders, including Fall. This resulted in the hiring of Pat Garrett, the famous nemesis of Billy the Kid, as a special investigator in the Fountain case. Then the governor also brought in the Pinkertons. As a final blow, Thornton ended Fall's legal delaying tactics for the contested 1894 sheriff's election by pressuring the new judge to settle the matter. The judge declared the Republican candidate the rightful sheriff of Dona Ana County. Now the Democrats, including Oliver Lee and his Texan friends, had only Fall as an attorney for their protection.

Undaunted by such reverses, Fall ran for the territorial senate in 1896. Governor Thornton vigorously opposed his election. The Fountain case also became the main issue in Dona Ana County. Fall failed to carry the county, but he won in the district as a whole by only 300 votes out of the 3,800 cast. In Santa Fe he tried to adjust the unfavorable law enforcement balance by getting the Democratic territorial secretary, and interim governor, to appoint him territorial attorney general. This ploy failed when President William McKinley's newly named governor, Miguel A. Otero, soon replaced Fall and other Democratic appointees with Republicans.

Meanwhile back in Dona Ana County, Pat Garrett, duly elected sheriff in 1896, plodded along for two years in the Fountain case before formally charging Oliver Lee and two other Texans, William McNew and James R. Gililland, with the crime. Fifteen years before, Garrett, then sheriff of Lincoln County, had surprised Billy the Kid in a darkened room at Fort Sumner and shot him dead. With this much-heralded event in mind, Oliver Lee proclaimed that he would never surrender tamely to Garrett and suffer the same fate, and he went "on the dodge."

Strangely enough, soon after Fall's forced resignation as judge his relationship with Boss Tom Catron took a more amicable turn. In spite of their strong partisan differences, the two lawyers had worked together in some routine legal matters and discovered a narrow ground of understanding, no doubt based mainly on professional necessity. Then, according to Catron's biographer, Victor Westphall, the Republican boss entered "one of the most difficult periods of his career." He and his law partner, Charles A. Spiess, were charged with unprofessional conduct stemming from the notorious Borrego case, in which they had vigorously, but unsuccessfully, tried to save from the gallows four men accused of murdering the ex-sheriff of Santa Fe County. Fall offered Catron his services as one of the defense attorneys in the disbarment case, saying in strangely ingratiating tones: "In this matter, I am not only an attorney but your *friend*—and this I say to no man unless I mean it. I want you to understand that if, as to say—I have to get out of a sick bed to go to Santa Fe, there will be no hesitation." Catron gladly accepted Fall's help.

Keeping his promise, Fall worked almost as hard to save Catron's professional life as he would have to protect a Texan indicted for rustling. When the territorial supreme court ruled in Catron's favor, the Republican boss readily gave Fall much of the credit. "Hereafter it will be my pleasure and give me great satisfaction to be known on all occasions as your friend," Catron said, adding: "Should I at any time be able to serve you, I wish it to be understood that you must command. Whatever I can do for you in any manner whatever, is at your disposal." In spite of such declarations of friendship, Fall and Catron remained political rivals and never enjoyed any real comradeship. As the disbarment case and later events showed, however, territorial New Mexico's renowned partisan feuds sometimes involved a great deal of phony public posturing.

While Oliver Lee was safely on the dodge, the Spanish-American War revealed another wrinkle in political accommodation. The war also gave Fall a new opportunity to satisfy his restless ambition. In April 1898 the first call for New Mexico volunteers raised a sizable number of Rough Riders for Theodore Roosevelt's eventual command. A second call, which reached New Mexico two months later, authorized the enlistment of four companies for the First Territorial United States Volunteer Infantry Regiment, also made up of troops from Arizona, Oklahoma Territory, and Indian Territory. Customarily Republican Governor Otero would have named only faithful party members as the four company commanders. Enamored with visions of statehood, however, Governor Otero faced the unnerving prospect that Company D at Las Cruces would fail to make its quota of enlistees, thereby besmirching the patriotism of New Mexico. Otero had already promised the captaincy to a Republican stalwart when it became painfully obvious to him that only one man, the dynamic Albert Fall, could fill up the company's ranks and save the territory's honor. Although Fall wanted the commission in the worst way, the local Republican leaders would almost certainly balk at giving their hated adversary increased political prestige through military glory.

To the contrary, even before Governor Otero came to Las Cruces for the swearing-in of Company D, the Republican bosses realized that by endorsing Fall's captaincy they could get rid of him—at least for the next election, and perhaps for good if the fortunes of war were kind. In fact, they tried to hedge their bets by proposing that Fall should have the commission only if he agreed never to return to the territory. But when Otero arrived in town, he supposedly told the local Republican leaders that he would not appoint any man who was "unfit to reside in New Mexico." As the governor left the conference, he met Fall waiting outside in the street and gave him the good news about his commission. Fall "took off his hat and jumped for joy," Otero recalled, and ran "every step of the way" to the Company D encampment. A few days later when the fledgling soldiers departed in flag-decked railroad coaches, "No handsomer man was seen than Capt. A. B. Fall in his new uniform."

Governor Otero's protestations notwithstanding, some sort of implicit, if not explicit, understanding about Fall's future residency and political activity probably led to his captaincy. Even though the governor's main concern was a full-strength

Company D, he undoubtedly shared the Republican machine's desire to get rid of Fall. In fact, all manner of Republicans seemed happy at this prospect, including Tom Catron, who worked closely with Otero to get the cooperation of the local bosses. Nor can the possibility of Fall's acquiescence in such a bargain be overlooked, especially since he was hounded by debts, as usual, which made him receptive to new opportunities for financial advancement. Some kind of deal is strongly suggested by the exceptionally cordial correspondence between Fall and Catron during this period. The two had discovered a narrow base of cordiality in Catron's disbarment case, even though they remained political and courtroom foes. While in military service, Fall obtained a $100 loan from Catron to move his family back to Clarksville, Texas, from Las Cruces, since he was "closing up matters there as fast as possible." Two months later Catron's son, John, a lieutenant in another New Mexico volunteer company, got into difficulty with a superior officer and was threatened with a court martial. While Fall gave the young man legal advice, Tom Catron used political influence to get his son transferred to Fall's unit. With this accomplished, Catron implored Fall to keep a fatherly eye on his new junior officer.

More specifically, Fall wrote Catron from Georgia, in November 1898 after the war ended, saying that his company would probably be sent to Cuba by the first of the year, and adding, "I want to prepare for business there in any line which may offer inducements." He asked the Republican boss for letters of introduction and recommendation to prominent persons in Cuba, "specifying what you know of me as a man, and as a lawyer." In addition, he wanted Catron to request Senator Stephen B. Elkins and other nationally known politicians to write similar letters. Fall apparently envisioned a career for himself in Cuba modeled after Catron's and Elkins's earlier legal achievements in New Mexico that had made both of them large landholders and wealthy men. He wrote: "I want letters which will help me in making the proper acquaintances and getting the best foothold. I am bearing in mind our talk on the train in reference to land grants, as well as the general idea of opening a law office in Habana[,] Matanzas or some other place. My at least partial knowledge of Spanish will be of considerable assistance. . . . I propose to make some money if there is an opening, & want to get in with the best people." Perhaps the "talk on the train," only mentioned here, involved nothing more on Catron's part than seasoned advice to the young lawyer who had assisted him in the disbarment case. In all probability, however, the new relationship between Fall and Catron fully revealed the Republican scheme to exile a troublesome enemy, and showed that Fall himself had been consciously and willingly drawn into the plan.

If Captain Fall had actually gone to Cuba, there would be less reason for conjecture. He worked hard at it, but got no closer to the Caribbean than, in his words, "the peanut fields of Georgia," where the New Mexico volunteers were still in training at Camp Churchman, near Albany, when the war ended. Through a friendship with Brigadier General J. P. Sanger of the New Jersey volunteers, who became the commanding general of the Matanzas district in Cuba, Fall barely missed fulfilling his desire. General Sanger had officially requested Fall's assignment to his staff, as military commandant of the city of Matanzas, and Fall was awaiting orders to go, when the War Department mustered out his company on February 11, 1899. Although he never reached Cuba, or gained the military glory that so enhanced the political fortunes of many New Mexicans who served with Theodore Roosevelt's Rough Riders, Fall did meet President McKinley before returning to Las Cruces. Governor Otero took him and three other New Mexico officers to the White House and introduced them to the president, and later to the secretary of war.

As it turned out, then, Albert Fall stayed away from New Mexico only seven months, returning to Las Cruces about March 1, 1899. The local Republican bosses had to be satisfied with his absence for the 1898 campaign alone, which was not nearly long enough to please them. But he was hardly the same A. B. Fall. It was rumored that he would move to El Paso and establish a law practice there. Perhaps his military experience had opened new vistas and ambitions for him, or perhaps it all went back to his appointment as captain. Whatever the case, Fall resolutely searched for new business opportunities in the years immediately following the war and gradually abandoned his role as a fiery Democratic chieftain. In fact, he brushed aside bipartisan overtures to run for territorial delegate in 1900, saying that he had entered the army to get out of politics, and adding that he had lost time, money, and friends because of past partisan activity. These were strange words indeed for one who had perfected the art of "fighting the devil with fire."

Regardless of this apparent watershed in his life, Albert Fall could not ignore one major piece of unfinished political business. At long last the Fountain murder case was about to reach its climax. Oliver Lee had stayed in hiding during Fall's army hitch, but the creation of a new county, named after Governor Otero, now facilitated his surrender and trial outside Sheriff Pat Garrett's jurisdiction. Since the spot where Colonel Fountain and his son disappeared was in the newly formed Otero County, the authorities in Dona Ana County no longer controlled the case. This chain of events undoubtedly received Fall's approval. Some historical accounts even maintain that he engineered the new county's formation to save his friend, but Fall had not returned from the army when the territorial legislature passed the measure, arriving back in Las Cruces about two weeks before Lee gave himself up. Actually the main architect of Otero County was Fall's sometime law partner, W. A. Hawkins, who sought to benefit his client, Charles B. Eddy, the railroad promoter. Eddy was building the El Paso and Northeastern Railroad through the area and wanted to hold the sway over local affairs that a new county would offer him.

After three years of political maneuvering the Fountain case finally went to trial in May 1899 at the neutral site of Hillsboro, with Lee and fellow Texan James R. Gililland as the accused murderers. This bustling Black Range mining town was only seven miles down the Middle Percha Creek from Kingston, where Fall had met Edward L. Doheny thirteen years before.

By now a cause célèbre throughout the Southwest, the long-awaited trial attracted "fully 500" spectators, creating a circus atmosphere in the little mountain town, which normally had a population of two hundred. The unusually large number of six attorneys, four of them prominent territorial politicians, participated in the renowned proceedings. Fall, as chief defense counsel in one of the greatest court battles ever waged in New Mexico, had come a long way since his days as a mucker in the nearby Grey Eagle Mine. Two special prosecutors, William B. Childers of Albuquerque, a leading Democrat hired by the Masonic Order (of which Fountain was a member), and Thomas B. Catron of Santa Fe, who had volunteered his services free of charge, joined the district attorney in presenting the case for the territory. Besides Fall and another area lawyer, the defense team also included Harvey B. Fergusson of Albuquerque, a highly respected former Democratic congressional delegate whose political prominence accentuated the partisan implications of the trial. Any previous truce between Fall and Catron was now forgotten. For months Catron had spared no expense in following up every lead that might help him send Oliver Lee to the gallows. Fall was equally determined that Lee would go free. In short, both men wanted a favorable verdict not only to claim victory in the broader issues of Fountain's death but as a matter of personal reputation as well.

For eighteen days, including several night sessions, the prosecutors and the defense attorneys hammered away at seventy-five witnesses, as a Spanish-speaking interpreter valiantly kept pace for the benefit of those jurymen who did not understand English. The prosecution's dramatic decision to charge the two defendants only with the murder of Colonel Fountain's son, little Henry, allowed Fall to display the full range of his courtroom talents. At times he was the homey country lawyer with a soothing voice, who peered over his spectacles and scratched his head as if he shared the jury's perplexity in the complicated proceedings. Then again he became tough and harsh, harassing witnesses and entangling them in their own statements, as he did with a university professor's expert testimony on blood samples. Or he might be the political zealot on the stump, expressing scorn and righteous indignation at the story of a witness or the feeble arguments of his opponents. He left no heartstrings unplucked. One day a little girl about the same age as the murdered Henry Fountain ran up to the front of the courtroom and with obvious delight pinned a pretty bouquet of spring flowers on Oliver Lee's coat. She was Fall's daughter. Likewise, Lee's saintly, silver-haired mother swore on the witness stand that her son had been at his ranch, sixty-five miles from the scene of the crime, when Colonel Fountain and his son disappeared.

By all odds the high point of the trial came when Fall made his spectacular closing argument, which removed any lingering doubt about the outcome. So far an "occasional tilt" between Fall and Catron had enlivened the proceedings. Now Fall took off the kid gloves. With his hands resting on the jury railing, he began in a low voice and gradually built up both the pitch and the emotional content. Fall charged that Oliver Lee was the victim of a foul conspiracy conjured up by powerful and unscrupulous members of the Santa Fe Ring and the Dona Ana County machine. Then he named Boss Catron, the district attorney, and the presiding judge as participants in the plot. Pounding his gavel furiously, the judge jumped to his feet, saying, "Mr. Fall, unless you withdraw your remarks about this court from the jury immediately I shall send you to jail for contempt." Fall replied coolly: "Your honor will not send me to jail for contempt until I am through addressing this jury. When I finish my argument you may do whatever you wish." The judge did not pursue the matter. In a closing appeal Fall told the jury: "Our defense is an alibi, clearly proven. You would not hang a yellow dog on the evidence that has been presented here, much less two men."

Despite the judge's outraged efforts to maintain order, pro-onged applause swept the courtroom when Fall took his seat. Tom Catron's impressive closing argument, nearly three hours long, seemed anticlimactic. It was eleven-thirty at night when the jury went out, expecting to finish its work the next morning.

Fall insisted that it render a verdict before going to bed. After deliberating for eight minutes in the jury room, the members had their verdict: "Not Guilty." Expressing agreement, a throng of spectators milled about cheering and clapping. The bodies of Fountain and his son were never found, and, although rumors and theories about who committed the crime multiplied with time, no one else ever stood trial for the two murders. Years later Fall, by then a United States senator, was asked by a publisher for his recollections on the Fountain affair. He replied that it would be a mistake to "rake up the old story" because, of the "hundreds of people arrayed upon one side or the other, not only in a political but a personal feud," most of them were still alive. "The old animosities have been buried," he said, "and we must let them lie."

Besides the much-publicized Fountain affair, Fall acted as a defense attorney in two other sensational southwestern murder cases. Previously, in 1896, he had helped defend Constable John Selman of El Paso, who was charged with foul play in killing John Wesley Hardin, the notorious Texas badman reputed to have up to forty notches on his gun. Selman had shot a supposedly reformed Hardin while the ex-outlaw stood relaxing at the bar in El Paso's Acme Saloon. The main issue in the trial was whether the fatal bullet had entered the back of Hardin's head and come out through the eye or vice versa—that is, the all-important question of whether Hardin had actually seen Selman or was shot from behind in cold blood. Although not Selman's principal attorney, Fall did assist local lawyers in the defense. Family tradition even has him taking the jury to the Acme Saloon to prove his imaginative argument that Selman actually fired in self-defense, even if Hardin was hit in the back of the head, because the two adversaries saw each other in a mirror above the bar as both stood facing it. The trial ended in a hung jury, and Selman too was gunned down a few months later.

But this hardly concluded the case. In the trial Fall told the jury that anyone who killed a gunman like John Wesley Hardin, who had a "reputation for deluging the earth with gore," should be acquitted automatically. Hardin's nephew, Mannen Clements, became so outraged by this statement and the trial's outcome that he swore to get even. Shortly after his second unsuccessful attempt to shoot Fall, both times in El Paso's Coney Island Saloon (described as the hangout of "all the uncaged convicts of the West"), Clements himself was killed in that bar by an unknown assailant. Probably the bartender fired through a towel while seeming to dry glasses and then dropped the gun into the sink's soapy water. He was tried and acquitted of Clements's death.

The mysterious killing of Pat Garrett in 1908 occasioned another famous murder case in which Fall represented an accused assassin with a plea of self-defense. This episode stirred melancholy comparisons with the Fountain affair, especially since it embraced a land and livestock dispute and the possibility of a conspiracy. Renowned as the "Slayer of Billy the Kid," Garrett had suffered a devastating loss of reputation in the Fountain case. After the disappointing acquittal of Oliver Lee, he was appointed collector of customs at El Paso, but he lost the post in 1905 and returned to southern New Mexico, where he settled down on a small ranch near Las Cruces. At fifty-eight, his glory was past. Frustrated and deeply in debt, he gambled and drank too much, often growing quarrelsome and menacing. One controversy over his ranch and debts involved a neighboring Texan rancher who was Oliver Lee's shirttail relation, W. W. Cox, and who reportedly wanted Garrett's land. In February 1908, on the road to Las Cruces, Garrett died as he himself had often predicted—with his boots on. Wayne Brazel, who leased Garrett's spread as a goat pasture, rode into town and surrendered, claiming that he had shot the famous ex-lawman in self-defense during an argument over use of the land.

Fall and his family knew and liked the thirty-one-year-old Brazel. In Fall's relations with Garrett, he and the former sheriff had struck up a half-hearted friendship after the Fountain trial. In one instance they had joint interest in a Mexican mining venture. After Garrett returned to Dona Ana County, he sometimes borrowed money from Fall, usually to promote livestock deals. On one occasion Fall sent him fifty dollars because, he wrote, "[I] suppose you are broke as usual." There was in this remark the casual contempt Fall reserved for those no longer of any importance.

Several puzzling questions suggested that Garrett had been "foully murdered" in a conspiracy, or "pre-arranged affair," to get rid of him as a public nuisance and take over his land. Brazel, regarded by all who knew him as "the most harmless of men," had readily confessed to the killing, but a more unlikely vanquisher of the famed sheriff could hardly be imagined. Then, according to informed sources, the first of two shots had hit Garrett in the back of the head, and the second one in the chest, with the distinct possibility that the second bullet could only have been fired after the ex-lawman was lying on the ground. In fact, the most convincing version has Brazel shooting in self-defense when Garrett drew a shotgun on him, while at about the same time someone else, probably a hired gun named Jim Miller, fired in ambush from the opposite direction, inflicting another wound. The conspiracy theory was bolstered by Miller's criminal record, and indeed a year later an Oklahoma mob lynched him for blasting a former marshal with a double-barreled shotgun. In fact, Garrett had many enemies who wanted to see him dead, but, as for his disputed ranch, Fall's Texan law client, W. W. Cox, took possession of it for the debt Garrett owed him.

The unsensational murder trial in April 1909 lasted only one day and drew relatively little public attention. Fall simply argued that Brazel had fired in self-defense. Oddly enough, the only witness to the Garrett shooting was not called to testify. Even the prosecution seemed anxious to close the matter, and the jury took only fifteen minutes to deliver a verdict of not guilty. Brazel and his friends celebrated the acquittal with a barbecue hosted by Cox at his ranch. Writing Eugene Manlove Rhodes about the trial, Fall recounted Garrett's recent series of drunken brawls in Las Cruces, and he concluded, "Everybody was afraid that he was going to kill someone and a sigh of relief went up when he was finally killed."

Whether or not there was a conspiracy, or any connection with the Fountain case, Pat Garrett's death was an anticlimax for the savage partisan rivalry and range warfare of the 1890s in southern New Mexico. As the attorney for the Texan cattlemen, Fall had masterminded the strategic political planning and fancy legal footwork for the winning side. The victory was at once his finest and one of his darkest hours. He had battled successfully for the underdogs against powerful enemies, for the little ranchers against the big ones and their mighty livestock association, for the dispossessed Democrats against the entrenched Republican machine. Oliver Lee and his Texan friends now occupied the spring-fed valleys of the San Andres and Sacramento mountains as well as the sparse grasslands below. They became prosperous and respectable. For the rest of his life, however, Fall's name would be associated with bloodshed and violence, mainly because of his shadowy complicity in the Fountain affair.

But this much is clear: Fall had learned how government could be made to serve one's own needs and the special interests of friends. He had also mastered the Machiavellian tactics necessary to survive and excel in New Mexico politics. Historian Richard Maxwell Brown contends that post–Civil War New Mexico Territory may have been "the only place in America where assassination became an integral part of the political system." In that bloody environment survival was what counted—a reality that Albert Fall never forgot.

CHAPTER 3

Corporation Man

WHEN Albert Fall won a United States Senate seat in 1912, crusading Denver journalist George Creel wrote that Fall was a "'safe and sane' corporation attorney" who would follow the dictates of the special interests. This simplified portrayal struck at the heart of the new senator's lifelong dilemma. Fall had two grand passions in life—politics and making a fortune. Politics had become an obsession with him, a stage where he could dramatize himself and gain the recognition and power he craved. A friend of many years later lamented that Fall could have distinguished himself in almost any field, acquired great wealth, and died with his honor intact, but "he just couldn't stay out of politics. That was his great weakness." Over the years Fall struggled with whether to remain in politics or get out and devote his energies entirely to his law practice and business operations. It is important to remember that when he entered the Senate he had not made enough money to support this political indulgence and still have the financial security he wanted.

Actually Fall's alliance with corporate enterprise, as well as his love of politics, repeatedly brought him back into the thick of partisan activity because the economic philosophy he embraced, and those most favored by it, could best be served by a powerful voice in government. Twice he made the firm decision to leave politics behind, first at the time of his Spanish-American War captaincy and later, about 1917, toward the end of his first full term in the Senate. In both instances he relented only after much soul-searching and the enticing entreaties of friends. Finally he made the break, but it was too late. As he left President

Harding's cabinet in 1923, he had already laid plans to catch up on the time public office holding had taken away from the acquisition of wealth for himself and a legacy for his family. These well-calculated plans involving financial arrangements and employment with oil millionaires Doheny and Sinclair brought his downfall.

Fall's law practice first opened his eyes to the wonders of the corporate world and started him on the road toward achieving, in the words of Eugene Manlove Rhodes, the rank of "brevet-captain of industry." Off and on for many years, beginning in 1892, he was associated with W. A. Hawkins in loosely arranged law partnerships that sometimes included other attorneys. After the Spanish-American War, Fall formed one of these intermittent partnerships with Hawkins, John Franklin, and Leigh Clark, with the main office in El Paso. Later he worked with other lawyers in El Paso, particularly A. N. Walthall and his son, Harris, and expanded his practice through arrangements with attorneys in Las Cruces and Deming, New Mexico, and Clifton, Arizona.

From the beginning many of his cases concerned land titles, mining laws, and water rights, especially irrigation issues arising from conflicts between the individualistic Anglo American common-law system of riparian rights and the ancient Spanish-Mexican communal doctrine. These small-scale engagements only served as warm-ups for the major campaigns when Fall and Hawkins pooled their talents. In fact, it was Hawkins who ushered Fall into the corporate arena. As counsel for large railroad, mining, and development enterprises, Hawkins reputedly "thought in terms of corporations by day, [and] dreamed of them at night," eventually becoming one of the most effective corporation lawyers in the Southwest. He sharpened his legal skills with former New Yorker Charles B. Eddy, a cattle rancher turned developer, who was among the most persuasive and successful promoters ever in New Mexico. In 1889 Eddy induced James J. Hagerman, who had already made a fortune in mining and railroads, to join him in a grandiose irrigation endeavor along the Pecos River between Roswell and the Texas line. Together Eddy and Hagerman founded the Pecos Irrigation and Improvement Company and built the Pecos Valley Railway.

In the mid-1890s, when personal disagreements and financial reverses caused Eddy and Hagerman to go their separate ways, Hawkins moved his office to El Paso with Eddy and continued as his general counsel. Later he had an important role in helping Eddy build the El Paso and Northeastern Railroad to meet the Rock Island line at Santa Rosa, New Mexico. He remained as an attorney with Phelps, Dodge and Co., the copper mining behemoth, when it bought Eddy's railroad in 1905, and then with the Southern Pacific Railroad when it acquired the trackage in 1924.

Many of these heady corporate activities included Fall in one way or another. For the Pecos Valley project Fall and Hawkins, working together, "investigated practically every irrigation enterprise within the United States" on such issues as water use, the construction of dams, and the impounding of reservoirs on the public domain. In a separate undertaking the two young lawyers also had a major role in the tangled legal affairs of the Rio Grande Dam and Irrigation Company, a promotional scheme that included Dr. Nathan S. Boyd and a group of British investors. Boyd had successfully petitioned the Interior Department for rights-of-way to construct a dam at Elephant Butte on the Rio Grande and a series of smaller dams and canals farther downstream. Construction was started in 1896, but El Paso, having plans of its own for an international dam and irrigation reservoir, blocked Boyd's project. Finally, after lengthy litigation and the inauguration of a national reclamation program in 1902, Boyd lost his franchise. The Reclamation Service completed the building of Elephant Butte Dam in 1916, creating the world's largest artificial reservoir.

Such large-scale endeavors helped form Albert Fall's economic philosophy and his views on natural resources use. In the Pecos Valley and the Elephant Butte projects Fall first encountered what he considered the ignorance and limited vision of federal bureaucrats on western needs. Interior Department officials seemed to think, in the case of the Pecos Valley proposal, that western developers "should find a sink hole and stop up the bottom and puddle the sides with clay, so as to make a larger duck pond," rather than create the necessary reservoir covering seventy square miles. His frustration increased with the complex Elephant Butte controversy, which involved the New Mexico territorial government, the Interior and State departments, and various congressional committees, as well as international relations between the United States and Mexico. Along with Hawkins, Fall took part in the extensive lobbying and court action that included two appeals to the United States Supreme Court.

Throughout Fall's career in territorial, state, and national politics W. A. Hawkins remained his most enduring link with the corporate world. In various election campaigns Fall stoutly maintained that he had never drawn a salary from either the Eddy-Hagerman companies or from Eddy's later corporate ventures but had only given assistance to Hawkins personally. Nor had he ever received a retainer or salary from any railroad corporation in New Mexico, even when Hawkins was on its payroll. According to their arrangement, Fall said, he took care of the general practice and accepted no cases against the industrial concerns represented by Hawkins. In the process opportunities for fat fees and other substantial remuneration came Fall's way. He served the Southern Pacific in litigation between it and Phelps Dodge when the mining corporation built a coal-hauling railroad line from its smelter at Douglas, Arizona, to a junction with the Santa Fe at Deming, New Mexico. The Southern Pacific offered him the "attorneyship" for company business in New Mexico and El Paso, but he refused it. The ambitious, freewheeling Fall had nothing against the Southern Pacific; he wanted a more promising opportunity for quick wealth.

Fall's political opponents were openly skeptical about his protestations of only "limited" or "indirect" connections with corporations in New Mexico. Nothing did more to convince them of his alliance with corporate power than the "Hawkins Bill." Passed by the territorial legislature in 1903, this act favored the railroads and was instigated by them. By a carefully laid plan Fall and Hawkins became the midwives who breathed life into this protective measure.

In the 1902 election the law partners had forsaken their practice briefly to gain redress by other means. Once again, as he had last done in 1896, Fall ran successfully for the territorial council, or senate, as did Hawkins, who at the time was general counsel for Eddy's El Paso and Northeastern Railroad but retained his voting residence in Alamogordo. Fall and Hawkins quickly remedied the difficulties of Charles B. Eddy, whose railroad faced economic hard times because of some near ruinous damage suits and its expensive program to acquire a satisfactory water supply. Nearly all of the damage cases had been filed in Texas courts, usually El Paso, or the courts of neighboring Colorado—states where railroad companies such as Eddy's "universally and uniformly [got] it where 'Katie wears the necklace.'" New Mexico juries, on the other hand, customarily were "either more friendly disposed towards the railroads, or more easily handled by railroad attorneys." The Hawkins Bill—the brainchild of Hawkins but backed with equal enthusiasm by Fall—eliminated the practice in damage cases of "shopping around" for a favorable court outside New Mexico. It required the injured person in any suit for damages sustained in the territory, whether a worker or a passenger traveling through on a train, to present the case only in New Mexico courts. Although railroads were the main beneficiaries of this act, other corporations such as mining concerns also gained a protective advantage.

With remarkable single-mindedness Fall and Hawkins had gone to Santa Fe and rammed the measure through the legislature over a gubernatorial veto. Widely criticized, the Hawkins Bill as a whole then stood without precedent in any state or territory. It remained in effect five years until repealed by Congress under the reserved powers allowing the national body to nullify territorial legislation. During the congressional debate on repeal, it was denounced as "the most remarkable piece of legislation ever enacted," and one which must have been written in a railroad office. A committee report declared that it should have been called "An act to prevent persons receiving injuries through the carelessness of railroads and other corporations in the Territory of New Mexico from recovering any damages therefor." By the time of its nullification the Hawkins Bill had saved the railroads in New Mexico a great deal of money at the expense of injured workers and other aggrieved plaintiffs.

Organized labor in the territory, mainly the railroad workers, had already decided that it had no friend in Albert Fall. When President Cleveland nominated him as a judge in 1893, the Knights of Labor and other workingmen's organizations vigorously opposed the appointment and mounted a campaign to prevent his confirmation. In fact, the Knights in New Mexico had condemned Fall as "their most formidable enemy" and "an enemy of the rights of every working man." Their main complaint at that time involved his stand favoring railroad companies in the past legislative session, particularly on a defeated labor-backed bill concerning accident liability and workers' compensation. Now the Hawkins Bill only reaffirmed labor's worst fears about Fall, with railroad trainmen being especially enraged.

Although Hawkins had initiated Fall into corporate law circles, it was Fall the seasoned political strategist who had guided the neophyte Hawkins and the bill bearing his name through the partisan thicket at Santa Fe. The resounding majority by which the territorial legislature overrode the governor's veto of the Hawkins Bill testified to the power of Fall's persuasive skills: eleven to one in the upper house, and twenty-one to three in the lower house. Hawkins had entered the 1902 legislative race for the specific purpose of helping his principal employer, Eddy, and he never again sought elective office. For the rest of his life he continued to accumulate accolades as the consummate corporation lawyer. Because Fall remained in politics, he had to bear the public stigma of the Hawkins Bill. As Eugene Manlove Rhodes observed in 1905, "Judge Fall is now on the mourner's bench for backsliding [because] he came nearly writing 'Ichabod' on a self-erected tombstone when he joined hands with Hawkins two years ago." Fall himself would later lament, "That is one of the acts—I do not mean the only one—of mine in a public capacity of which I am ashamed."

The rise of progressivism nationally, with its emphasis on conservation of the natural resources and its condemnation of monopolistic corporate control, placed Albert Fall's emerging economic philosophy in bold relief. When conservation leader Gifford Pinchot declared that the power of monopolies was "infinitely more potent" in the West than the East, he might have had New Mexico in mind. That territory in the early twentieth century existed, according to Fall, as a "corporation country," or, by the testimony of other competent observers, as "the worst corporation-ridden country and political-machine country . . . in this American Union," with its public affairs "run entirely by gang politicians and corporate interests." Just as he had done in partisan rivalry with the Santa Fe Ring and the Dona Ana County machine, Fall set out to master the system and enjoy its fruits, not to reform it. To him it was not only inevitable but desirable that outside interests such as the Santa Fe and Southern Pacific railroads, Phelps, Dodge and Co., and the Chino Copper Company should have a free hand in exploiting New Mexico's resources. Testifying before a congressional statehood committee in 1911, he said that New Mexico was "a corporation Territory [and] must be from the nature of things" because its future development depended on outside investment.

In 1918, at the time of Fall's Senate reelection, he had an opportunity to explain his fully matured economic views, especially the role of "aggregate capital which operates always through what is known as a corporation." In New Mexico, he said, no individual investor could open the coal mines, build the railroads to transport the coal, or adequately utilize the other resources such as timber and water. Then he summarized his personal philosophy: "Believing as I do, I have always assisted in every way possible in securing capital for investment in such enterprises and I shall continue to do so whenever possible. I have [long] believed that the laws of New Mexico should protect such capital and should be so enforced as to offer an inducement for its investment." Almost as an afterthought, he added that the people, of course, might maintain control over these great concentrations of private investment through taxation and public commissions. In unformed, sparsely populated New Mexico, where growth and prosperity claimed the highest priority, this philosophy drew widespread approval, as evidenced by Fall's popularity in politics.

Actually Fall's most formative experience with big business came not through his law partnership with W. A. Hawkins, nor in railroad and irrigation enterprises inside the United States, but in massive mining operations across the southwestern border in Mexico. Although his name is unalterably associated with Teapot Dome oil, mining always remained Fall's real passion. For years in New Mexico he acquired claims, did his own prospecting and occasionally staked other prospectors, and invested in speculative ventures, always hoping to strike it rich. When Fall became interior secretary, he still had interests in various New Mexico mining properties, but he undoubtedly lost more money in them than he ever made. Mexico was a far different story. After the Spanish-American War, while seeking new financial and political horizons, Fall acquired some undeveloped mining properties in northern Mexico. "I spent a great deal of time, both alone and in company with [a partner, Samuel N. Dedrick]," he said later, "camping out, prospecting, and mining throughout the Sierra Madres along the line of Sonora and Chihuahua." These seemingly obscure holdings and others like them, as it turned out, catapulted Fall into the big-league corporate realm of a multimillion-dollar industrial empire.

On a trip to New York City to seek financial backing, probably in the summer of 1904, Fall met William C. Greene, the "Copper King of Cananea," for a discussion of Fall's Mexican mining properties and some promising development projects he had in mind. It was not an accidental meeting; in fact, the two men may have known each other earlier along the southwestern border. Greene now took a keen interest in Fall's Mexican holdings, and he liked Fall and his way of thinking even more. When Fall left New York, he joined the promoter at St. Louis for a train trip to Greene's Cananea operations in the Mexican state of Sonora. In a matter of days Greene hired Fall as his personal attorney, later making him a partner in some big Mexican ventures as well. For several years thereafter Fall would be known as "Colonel Greene's lawyer." In fact, legal and business affairs south of the border claimed most of Fall's attention from mid-1904 until his Senate election early in 1912.

In "Colonel Bill" Greene, who personified the extension of the exploitative United States frontier into Mexico, Fall found a perfect match for his own acquisitive philosophy and restless ambition. Two distinguishing traits marked Greene's style: a grandiose vision and the natural gambler's ability to risk everything and win the pot. His background was much like Fall's. Born in Wisconsin and raised in New York State, Greene went west as a youth and worked at several things, including prospector and miner, before settling down in the San Pedro Valley near Tombstone, Arizona. In an argument over water rights with a neighboring rancher, which resulted in a dynamited dam and the drowning of Greene's young daughter, Greene shot and killed his adversary just outside the OK Corral at Tombstone. He was tried and acquitted.

Meanwhile, like Fall, Greene had been prospecting and buying up claims across the border in Mexico, particularly on the eastern slopes of the nearby Cananea Mountains. By 1899 these activities had laid the groundwork for his New York–backed Cananea Consolidated Copper Company (the "4 C's"), which became his operations unit in Mexico. As a superb gambler and swashbuckling western promoter, Colonel Bill Greene had captivated eastern financial circles while attracting capital for his ambitious projects. After tackling Wall Street, the "Cowboy Capitalist" sought new worlds to conquer. By 1906 he controlled a $100 million Mexican empire that encompassed mining operations, ranches, railroads, and timberlands. All the while the copper barons in the United States, several of whom had helped finance Greene's meteoric rise, never stopped plotting to take over his properties.

Fall joined up with Greene during an especially expansive stage of the copper magnate's career. The two decades from 1890 to 1910 were a golden age of American mining in

Mexico, with dictator Porfirio Díaz's openhanded policies in full swing to attract foreign capital. Greene stood in the front rank of these American developers in Sonora and Chihuahua, the two largest Mexican states. Although not directly connected with Greene's better-known copper-mining ventures at Cananea, Fall took an important role in the intrepid promoter's "most ambitious enterprise," the Greene Gold-Silver Company. Formed in 1902 to operate abandoned gold and silver mines scattered over two or three million acres in Sonora and Chihuahua, this concern eventually had stock valued at $25 million. At the beginning of their association, Fall transferred most of his own Mexican holdings to Greene Gold-Silver, receiving stock in return. And he soon became the company's vice president and general counsel.

In 1904, shortly after going with Greene, Fall helped organize the Sierra Madre Land and Lumber Company. Greene wanted his own supply of lumber and mine timbers instead of importing them at great expense from the United States. Working with a Mexican senator, Fall made an agreement with one Telesforo Garcia of Mexico City for about two million acres of timberlands in Chihuahua. He turned the contract over to Greene, who used it in founding Sierra Madre Land and Lumber, giving Fall stock and bonds in exchange and a decisive hand in developing the property. Giant sawmills with the latest machinery soon went to work producing trainloads of lumber. To haul the timber and help tie his empire together, Greene bought the Rio Grande, Sierra Madre and Pacific Railroad, which ran from Juarez (across the Rio Grande from El Paso) to Casas Grandes and Terrazas in northern Chihuahua. He then started planning track extensions in all directions. Fall had a hand in acquiring the railroad and in its subsequent construction projects, serving as vice president and general counsel for the lumber company and as attorney for the rail line. Later he was also president and general counsel of what he called "a little two-by-four road," the Sierra Madre and Pacific Railroad, a branch line Greene organized to build from Casas Grandes on south to Madera.

Greene became enmeshed in innumerable lawsuits and always had a large corps of attorneys on his payroll. But two lawyers, Fall and Norton Chase, were his confidants as well as key players in his operations. Wall Street attorney Chase, whose nephew, Clarence C. Chase, married Fall's eldest daughter, Alexina, took care of Colonel Bill's political and financial problems in New York City, Washington, and Mexico City. As Greene's personal lawyer, Fall had some knowledge of all the promoter's Mexican ventures. The El Paso newspapers referred to him as the "organizer" and "general manager" of Colonel Bill's Chihuahua properties. Fall himself later described his role to President Woodrow Wilson: "While not interested with Greene at Cananea, I was his partner elsewhere, and was his personal legal advisor." During his hitch with the mining magnate, however, Fall regarded himself as more of a businessman than an attorney. He maintained luxurious offices in El Paso, New York City, and Concheño and other points in Mexico. Sometimes he spent seven or eight months shuttling continually in and out of Mexico. He also spent long periods of time in New York, usually staying at the Waldorf Astoria Hotel.

Fall had a staff of seven Mexican lawyers and at times eight thousand laborers under his supervision. Henry O. Flipper, the first African American graduate of West Point (1877) and an accomplished engineer and linguist, became his "right hand man and advisor" in Mexico (and was to work for him later in other capacities). "I . . . knew the common Mexican," Fall once wrote President Wilson, "from practical experience with him in the mountain camps, on the trail, in the construction and operation of railroads, saw-mills, etc.; and . . . the high-class Mexican in the Courts [and in government circles]." Besides purely business activities, his legal and political responsibilities included forging agreements with both the state and national governments in Mexico. These duties gave him intimate first-hand experience in Mexican law, politics, and society, as well as friendships with dozens of influential Mexicans, including Porfirio Díaz himself and General Luis Terrazas of Chihuahua, who had the largest single landholding in all of Mexico. Of the old dictator, Fall later remarked, "I knew Mr. Díaz personally very well, and am proud to say that I had his friendship and his very material assistance in the various enterprises with which I was connected."

Colonel Bill Greene, a big, openhearted man, delighted in loaning money or giving jobs to his old friends and in surrounding himself with boon companions. In the best sense of the term, Albert Fall had the knack of being a crony, whether of Greene in Mexico or of Warren G. Harding in the United States Senate. Without minimizing Fall's considerable political and legal skills, this quality was the basis for his relationship with Greene. Like Fall, Greene thought a forest wilderness should be utilized by sawmills and mines, not preserved, and that remote river valleys should be harnessed for hydroelectric power and tapped for irrigation, not viewed only as scenic wonders. Both men loved fine, spirited horses, good whiskey, and gambling for big money. Their common addiction to poker often helped them pass the long hours and lighten the pocketbooks of eastern capitalists they escorted around Mexico in Greene's private railroad cars, first the *Oceanic* and later the *Verde* (the promoter's name in Spanish).

Nor did Greene and Fall believe in limiting the "big game" to the poker table, as shown in their El Paso "Street Car War" of 1905. Booming and bustling El Paso served as the main American entrepôt for Greene's activities in Chihuahua. In addition, the promoter purchased the nearby Federal Smelter, acquired an old tin mine in the vicinity, and announced his intention to build a new railroad across northern Sonora and Chihuahua that would connect El Paso with his Cananea operations. In gratitude the city's business and civic leaders staged a grand dinner honoring "Colonel W. C. Greene, the Cecil Rhodes of America," with Fall as a featured speaker.

The final link in Greene's proposed Cananea–El Paso rail connection would reach across the Rio Grande between Juarez and El Paso's new Union Depot, where it would hook up with the United States railroad network. To close this gap, Fall started a bold invasion of El Paso aimed at capturing access to its depot. In April 1905 he secured from the city council a street-railway franchise and quickly hired several hundred workers to start laying ties and rails rushed over from Greene's railroad yards in Juarez. Several problems stalled and finally killed this audacious project. First and foremost, the powerful Boston utility firm of Stone and Webster already had an operating electric streetcar franchise in El Paso and did not welcome potential competition. Second, Fall's franchise specified that only streetcars could use those city lines, not trains—a small problem that he could work out later. Then, to reach the depot, his laborers had to build across property of a decidedly hostile Santa Fe Railroad.

The actual "war" began when Stone and Webster started constructing more trackage of its own to counteract the raiding force. Downtown hotel guests began complaining that they could not sleep at night for the around-the-clock hammering and clanging, while worried citizens pled with local officials to halt the pandemonium before the city was wrecked. Mob action and bloodshed seemed a real possibility when Fall's workers went out on strike after a reduction in wages from $1.50 to $1.00 a day for unskilled laborers. Before the strike could be settled, rumors arose of a meeting in Fall's El Paso law office in which Stone and Webster made a deal for Greene's street-railway company to withdraw. In July the promoter's men tore out their ties and tracks and took them back to Juarez; Greene never completed the Cananea–El Paso rail connection. The whole story of the "Street Car War" has never been revealed. Probably Greene and Fall, in a corporate poker game, hoped to draw to a straight and fill, with rail access to the Union Depot as their main objective. Another version, although hardly credible, makes the entire project a personal squeeze play by Fall from which he received a $30,000 under-the-table payoff from Stone and Webster to back away. Regardless, the strategy and execution of the streetcar campaign closely resembled the roughshod tactics Fall had learned in Dona Ana County politics.

Nothing pleased Colonel Bill Greene more than lavish spending. Also in 1905, he and Fall led some thirty eastern financiers, politicians, and socialites to the Sierra Madre back country for the colonel's famous "$10,000 Hunting Trip." Fall reportedly avoided certain death during a wounded mountain lion's attack by first bashing it in the mouth with a rifle butt and then shooting it with his six-shooter. As a memento of the great hunt, Greene took back to New York City for a pet an orphaned bear cub, naming it "Tom Lawson" after the flamboyant Boston financier who had conducted Wall Street bear raids on copper stocks. Ironically such raids and other financial pressures on Greene's enterprises had just begun. In fact, the swashbuckling promoter's economic downfall happened even faster than his spectacular rise. First, in the summer of 1906, a bloody strike of Cananea workers influenced by the radical Mexican Liberal party shook his interlocking empire. The Panic of 1907 and ill health compounded Greene's troubles, and he simply ran out of money. When the dust settled, his more sophisticated rivals in the Rockefeller–Amalgamated Copper crowd, in particular Thomas F. Cole and John D. Ryan, had closed in and scooped up the main elements of his domain. Eventually Greene's Cananea operations became an integral part of the imperious Anaconda Copper Company. At his death in 1911 "all" Greene had left was his 800,000-acre cattle ranch along the Arizona-Sonora border.

Albert Fall's own stake in Mexico, as a matter of course, suffered severe damage because of the Greene debacle. On July 12, 1906, disturbed by the promoter's reckless conduct of business affairs, Fall "quit Mexico," selling what he could of his company interests and severing his connections with Greene's disintegrating enterprises, but staying on as the hard-pressed mining magnate's personal attorney. From 1907 to 1909 he worked at a feverish pace trying to salvage as much as possible for Greene and his family. He continued these efforts into 1910, and after Greene's death in 1911 had a hand in settling the estate. As a result of these activities, he acquired an interest in some potentially valuable Mexican mining properties.

Fall's participation in settling the affairs of the Greene Gold-Silver Company proved to be the most fruitful for him. In

1920, testifying before the Senate Mexican Affairs Subcommittee, which he headed, Fall stated:

> In winding up his [Greene's] business affairs I became personally interested in certain mining claims in the district of Jesus Maria de Ocampo in the State of Chihuahua. I disposed of those interests for his account and mine and that of a large number of Mexican creditors, to an American syndicate, [which] formed what is known as the Sierra Mines Co. (Ltd.). So, disposing of my interests [,] I received $75,000 par value of stock of the company. I yet have that stock in my possession. That is my only interest in Mexico of any kind or character.

About the same time Fall wrote a Senate colleague that he would gladly sell this stock "for $7,500, or . . . I will entertain any bid under that sum." Despite such protestations, Fall retained several other potentially valuable mining investments in Mexico, particularly at Concheño in partnership with the Cleveland steel industrialist Price McKinney, who held title to the properties in his name alone. These holdings with McKinney represented cash investments of several hundred thousand dollars.

The most money Fall ever made came through his association with Colonel Bill Greene. Early in 1904, before going with the promoter, he had tried unsuccessfully to get a loan for mining machinery from his erstwhile political enemy, Tom Catron. By 1907 Fall was probably making about $35,000 a year as Greene's attorney (a tidy sum at that time), and he may have profited as much as $300,000 to $500,000 from selling his own company interests and settling the bankrupt mining magnate's affairs. Embittered creditors, stockholders, and unpaid employees complained that he had "trimmed" both them and Greene while filling his own pockets. But C. L. Sonnichsen, Greene's biographer, contends that Fall "did a remarkable job" with the ruins and "raised an amazing amount of money" to help pay off the debts. In fact, Fall showed a special concern for the promoter's widow and six young children, addressing her in letters as "My Dear Sister Mary." She wrote Fall in 1914, "I want to assure you of my very great appreciation for the interest you have taken in the welfare of the children as well as my own."

In terms of Fall's own destiny one point is more important than all the others. He came close to making his fortune with Greene, but fell short. Before and after this one big streak of luck he faced one financial difficulty after another. Even the modest affluence he gained through the Greene enterprises proved to be ephemeral. By 1913 he would write a family member, "I am very hard up for cash, in fact, have not been so severely cramped for a great many years."

Besides the collapse of Greene's empire, the Mexican Revolution of the 1910s also had a disastrous effect on Fall's fortunes. His remaining Mexican properties were largely undeveloped, burdened with indebtedness, and subject to onerous taxation and caretaker expenses, so that they fared poorly during the protracted revolutionary chaos. Both his Mexican and American investments, which he had hoped to bolster with further earnings from Mexico, soon gobbled up the money he made with Greene. This was especially true of the newly acquired New Mexico ranch at Three Rivers. Fall told a New Mexico businessman in 1912 that he had derived no appreciable money from Mexico for two years, continuing: "All my investments practically, with the exception of some Bank stock in El Paso, are at the present time, and for a long time past have been, absolutely non-productive, while my heavy expense is continuous. The result is that I am in debt instead of having any available funds." The ranch survived as his principal financial hope. In 1918, less than three years before entering the Harding cabinet, Fall wrote a son-in-law that the Three Rivers spread was his only reliable source of income. He did not expect to make any money in Mexico in the future.

Fall's Mexican experience, although ultimately unprofitable financially, became the single most important influence in his political career. Dona Ana County partisan wars had shaped his style, but Mexico determined his later life. As Colonel Bill Greene's partner, he joined the ranks of western empire builders and rubbed elbows with prominent eastern financiers and national political figures. His reputation as a corporation man now took on new dimensions. He first tasted the real fruits of corporate wealth south of the border, only to suffer substantial property losses in the Mexican Revolution. Significantly some historians identify the Cananea strike of Greene's Mexican mine workers in 1906 as the opening shots of the revolution. Like Greene, who blamed the strike on a conspiracy between the Mexican Liberal party and the United States–based Western Federation of Miners, Fall became an implacable foe of all radical agitators and red revolutionaries, in Mexico or elsewhere. Such intimate knowledge of Mexican affairs would make him the Senate expert on that revolutionary land at a time when Mexico was a major diplomatic problem for the United States. In this later role he also forged the fateful friendship with oilman Edward L. Doheny, who had started developing Mexican oil fields near Tampico a few years before Fall allied himself with Greene.

Although the money to buy Fall's New Mexico ranch came from his Greene connections, the acquisition itself was actually made possible by his alliance with the Texan ranchers. He had first seen Patrick Coghlan's historic spread 125 miles north of El Paso in 1888 while on a cross-country buggy trip from Las Cruces to the Pecos Valley. According to family tradition, he described it to his wife as "the prettiest spot I ever saw," and vowed to own it someday. Coghlan, a tall fiery, red-bearded Irish immigrant, ran his extensive holdings like a feudal domain, serving as middleman for cattle rustled by Billy the Kid's gang in the Texas Panhandle. Because of lingering drought and the court costs for his rustling and murder trials, he became heavily indebted to Oliver Lee and Lee's shirttail Texan relative, W. W. Cox.

At this point Fall, already Lee's defense attorney in the Fountain murder case, entered the picture in a decisive role. As the lawyer for Coghlan's new creditors, he initiated foreclosure proceedings. The case dragged on in the courts for more than eight years before its conclusion in October 1905 when the final decree designated Coghlan's property as security for his debt. For once Fall had enough money, from his work with Greene, to make his long-standing wish come true. He had already obtained a one-third part, and soon after the judge's decision he bought out the other two creditors, Lee and Cox. Their stern Texan folkways required Lee and Cox to fight to the death anyone who tried to seize crucial land or water, but always to make room for kin and allies. The ease with which Fall acquired the coveted Coghlan ranch only confirmed his adoption into the Texan clan. He took possession in 1906 and almost immediately began extensive renovation and expansion projects.

Located a few miles east of the White Sands, the ranch stretched into the rough western foothills and scarred canyons of towering twelve-thousand-foot Sierra Blanca, the highest peak in southern New Mexico. Actually the main depression resembles a verdant amphitheater, or basin, roughly shaped like an old-fashioned palm-leaf fan, with three mountain streams joining to form the narrow Tres Ritos (more correctly "Tres Rios"), or Three Rivers, Valley. Its deep fertile soil and plentiful water, peach and apple orchards, neat irrigated fields, and giant cottonwoods made the valley an oasis. The old headquarters ranch house, with its three-foot-thick adobe walls, served as the nucleus for the sprawling, two-story, southern-style manor house built by Fall. In this showplace of southern New Mexico he reigned as lord of a ranching fiefdom, surrounded by family, cowboys and hired help, and frequent guests. In the next fifteen years he lavished an estimated $175,000 on developing and expanding the spread until by 1921 it encompassed more than 750,000 acres in combined operations with his son-in-law Mahlon T. Everhart.

About the same time Albert Fall took over the Three Rivers property, and before the old Coghlan ranch house was renovated, Emma Fall sketched a floor plan, employed professional architects and interior designers, and oversaw the construction of their large home on El Paso's exclusive Golden Hill Terrace. The imposing red-brick, two-story, white-columned structure of southern colonial design—befitting a Kentuckian turned western empire builder—provided a magnificent view of the city and the Rio Grande below with Mexico stretching out beyond. Built solidly to withstand the prevailing southwesterly winds, the spacious mansion featured a wine cellar, fireplaces in most of the rooms, downstairs floors of parquet, and woodwork and a staircase of splendid oak. At Fall's insistence the ceilings between the two main floors contained six inches of sand as soundproofing so that household noise would not disturb him in his ground-floor library. With a fire burning in the reception hall's huge fireplace, candles gleaming in the silver and crystal candelabra, and the illumination through a large Tiffany glass window, Christmas parties and other festive occasions in the Fall home became leading social events on the El Paso social calendar.

Fall's Three Rivers ranch and the El Paso home seemed to be the perfect solution for a man who had strong personal and political ties in New Mexico, but whose law practice and business affairs were now centered in the Texas city. This happy situation had its liabilities mainly because of "Mrs. Fall's house in El Paso," as Fall called it. Political opponents soon accused him of living in Texas and playing his politics in New Mexico. Later one New Mexico newspaper described him as a "Prominent El Paso barrister and financier, now representing New Mexico in the United States senate," while another dubbed him "the honorable third senator from Texas." Moreover, although his majestic New Mexico ranch and the El Paso mansion represented the trappings of wealth, Fall did not have the enduring income to match them.

While involved with the Greene enterprises in Mexico, and supposedly on political furlough, Albert Fall astounded his partisan allies and enemies alike by switching to the Republican party. Several other prominent New Mexico Democrats made the same change of party affiliation during the pre-statehood period, but no other crossover caused so much surprised indignation. After all, Fall had been "one of the most uncompromising of democratic partisans ever identified with the political history" of New Mexico, or, even worse, "the most rabid and intense Democrat in the whole Southwest." Yet the exact time when he became a Republican and was no longer a Democrat is difficult to determine, largely because of his gradual metamorphosis and his temporary preoccupation with Mexican operations.

Actually in the territorial senate election of 1896 Fall made his last real stand as the Democratic champion of Dona Ana County. After the Spanish-American War, as his law practice became more involved with corporate interests, he steadily gravitated toward the Republican fold. For the territorial senate race of 1902, which opened the way for the Hawkins Bill, Fall was nominated by both the Democrats and the Republicans of Dona Ana County. He told his Las Cruces constituents after the legislative session, "My opinions are always Democratic," but then he qualified that by adding, "I am not blinded by partisanship and never expect to be again." Then, in 1904, soon after joining Greene's Mexican companies, he voted the Republican ticket for the first time, even casting his ballot for the unsavory congressional Delegate William H. ("Bull") Andrews.

Fall's admiration for Theodore Roosevelt contributed to the transition. In fact, he was known for a long time as a "Roosevelt Republican," or sometimes as a "Roosevelt Democrat." He met Roosevelt in 1899 at the first Rough Riders' reunion, held in Las Vegas, New Mexico, and then in 1901 conferred with him in the White House on territorial politics shortly after Roosevelt became president following the assassination of William McKinley. In 1904, when the Rough Rider ran for president in his "own right," Fall huddled privately on strategy with New Mexico Republican leaders and toyed with the possibility of making some speeches for their cause, but only because of his "personal feeling for the President." After the election he wrote Roosevelt that he had cast a Republican ballot for the first time because of his regard for the colonel, who "represented true Democratic principles" as Fall understood them. He also assured Roosevelt that he would work for the selection of delegates to the next Republican national convention who would support the Rough Rider's program. True to his word, Fall himself attended the Chicago convention of 1908 where, at Roosevelt's insistence, William Howard Taft received the Republican nomination. Like the Fall-Doheny relationship, Fall's later close association with Roosevelt would be determined by their common stand on events in Mexico.

Territorial conditions also made Fall's political conversion easier. In 1897 President McKinley appointed as governor a young, vigorous, well-educated Hispanic patrician, Miguel A. Otero, who promptly implemented hardfisted party reorganization and modernization policies that made him master of New Mexico politics during his nine years in office. The "Governor's Ring," based on loyalty to Otero, replaced the old Santa Fe Ring headed by Tom Catron. Although the territorial party remained subservient to the national Republican "Old Guard," and Catron survived with enough power to secure a Senate seat after statehood, the new order offered opportunity to promising young leaders. Albert Fall did not have to endure the humiliation of joining a party dominated by his old rival Boss Catron, but instead could ally himself with a different Republican organization.

Other changes swept across New Mexico as it entered the twentieth century. Historian Howard R. Lamar has observed that the two decades between 1880 and 1900 brought major developments to the territory, stimulated by national railroad connections, "which modified her economy, affected her native culture, modernized her government, and laid the basis for her admission to the Union in 1912." Yet the Republicans continued to dominate New Mexico politics until the time of statehood; success for an aspiring office seeker, particularly with a coveted United States Senate seat in mind, plainly lay in the Grand Old Party. In this context Fall's party switch could be viewed as blatant opportunism since he never made a secret of expecting to become a senator when New Mexico gained statehood. Toward the end of his life when asked about it, he just smiled and replied, "I knew when to change horses." But his pragmatism, important as it was, hardly provided a sufficient explanation. The switch was mainly an expression of his economic philosophy. While a cabinet member, Fall gave this account of why he became a Republican: "First: I believed that the conduct of Governmental affairs was largely a business proposition, and—Second, I believed that of the two parties the Republican Party was the most effective instrument for the administration of Governmental business." In those terms his new partisan affiliation was a logical step for a budding corporation man.

Now Fall could humorously boast that his diverse political experience, "on both sides or . . . with 'both gangs,'" gave him a distinct advantage. Many territorial Republicans received the news of his conversion with dismay or outright hostility, but they could do nothing about it. His effectiveness as a forceful campaigner alone, not to mention his new-found wealth in Mexico, made him an attractive recruit. Republican leaders soon understood why their Democratic counterparts had long complained about Fall's egotism, self-righteousness, and freewheeling independence. As historian William A. Keleher points out, Albert Fall "by sheer bluff and personality" almost immediately moved into Republican leadership councils where he dominated party affairs for years. Although always something of a maverick, he soon began blasting the Democrats as energetically as he had the Republicans.

In 1907, after three years of semiretirement from frontline politics, Fall formally announced his new party affiliation by serving briefly as territorial attorney general under his friend Republican Governor George Curry, also a former Democrat. President Roosevelt selected Curry, one of his Rough Rider captains, to reconcile the warring Republican factions in New Mexico and keep the party in power until statehood. This task made Curry's army duty with Roosevelt in Cuba and his subsequent assignments in the Philippines—as police chief of Manila and military governor of Samar Province—seem almost routine. Besides Republican factionalism, the two previous governors had been overindulgent with corporations in highly questionable public land transferrals. In fact, conservationists charged that the special interests had moved into the territory "and taken the whole face of the earth out there." Now a full-scale scandal targeting prominent Republican officials seemed about to break.

One of these so-called "Tall Timber Cases" involved the Pennsylvania Development Company, an enterprise backed by Pennsylvania politicians and capitalists whose resident agent was gruff, barrel-chested William H. ("Bull") Andrews. Once Matthew S. Quay and Boies Penrose's lieutenant in Pennsylvania politics, Bull now doubled as New Mexico's congressional delegate. Andrews and his associates, skirting the legislative restriction limiting certain public land sales to 160 acres for each person or corporation, acquired thousands of acres of timberland by getting their employees to file individual land applications. In another land maneuver a Phelps Dodge subsidiary, the Alamogordo Lumber Company, had used similar methods to obtain 23,500 acres of timberland in the Sacramento Mountains several years before Phelps Dodge assumed its ownership. Phelps Dodge itself was also under suspicion for the means by which it had acquired valuable coal lands in northwestern New Mexico.

Fall took a special interest in the charges against Phelps Dodge, particularly those aimed at the Alamogordo Lumber Company, because his erstwhile law partner, W. A. Hawkins, handled the latter concern's legal affairs. In March 1907 he and Hawkins spent a week in Santa Fe lobbying the legislature and conferring with Republican leaders on the land-fraud accusations. About that same time he heard confidentially from Rough Rider sources of Roosevelt's desire to name Curry as governor. Learning also of Curry's reluctance to accept the appointment because of personal finances, Fall urged his friend to take the position and promised him generous financial assistance in doing so. "I am in a better condition, financially, than you have ever known me," confided Fall, who had recently acquired the Three Rivers ranch with income from Greene's crumbling empire. Both he and Hawkins were convinced, Fall told the prospective governor, that Curry was the best man for the job.

Although President Roosevelt wanted the land fraud mess cleaned up, he also needed party harmony in New Mexico. In addition, about half of the Rough Riders had been New Mexicans, and some of them were ensnared in the land intrigue. As for ex–Rough Rider Curry, the president considered him to be "straight as a string" and "one of the very best men I know anywhere"—just the kind who could restore order in Santa Fe. In times past Albert Fall had been Curry's political mentor and financial benefactor, as he would continue to be while Curry was governor and for years afterwards. For different reasons, then, Curry's appointment served the purposes of both Roosevelt and Fall. Not surprisingly, after a conference with the president at Oyster Bay, New York, Curry appealed to Fall to accept, if "only for a month or two," an appointment as territorial attorney general. Moreover, the new governor said, "I am depending on you more than anyone else for advice and help and know that I will receive it." Although Roosevelt did not know Fall well yet, he approved of his selection, referring to him as "a very competent New Mexico man."

On August 8 Curry arrived in Santa Fe for his inauguration after traveling across the territory with a large group of friends in the *Ahumada*, a private railroad car borrowed by Fall from Colonel Bill Greene. Among the pictured celebrants were lean, scholarly W. A. Hawkins, wearing a soft cap in contrast to the predominant Stetson hats, and Albert Fall, looking intense and sure of his ability to sway people and events. The most sensational part of the inaugural ceremony was not the new governor's short speech but the long, bombastic "address of welcome" delivered by Fall in behalf of the New Mexico citizenry. Always the firebrand, he now "singed the hide off" the numerous special agents from the Interior and Justice departments who had invaded the territory to search out land-fraud graft and corruption. Many New Mexicans resented this bureaucratic intrusion into territorial affairs, and particularly then because any adverse publicity would undoubtedly hinder the touch-and-go struggle for statehood.

Echoing those public sentiments, Fall sailed into the federal investigators, who, he said with a straight face, had outrageously branded forward-looking corporate messengers of prosperity like Bull Andrews as grafters when everyone knew that New Mexico had less graft than any other commonwealth. Did the territory need "a guardian sent from Washington"? he asked. "Fellow citizens, Theodore Roosevelt knows better, and he has sent George Curry to New Mexico, and the other fellows [federal investigators] will go pretty quick!" This bold assumption to speak the president's mind received general approval in New Mexico, but it raised some eyebrows elsewhere. Roosevelt could not restrain his indignation when he wrote Governor Curry that Fall's appointment should be terminated as soon as possible because his "very unfortunate remarks" had "hopelessly impaired his usefulness as Attorney General." In response Curry offered to resign, citing the interference of the federal investigators as his main reason. Only the president's assurance of complete confidence, as well as his promise to bridle the agents and back Fall's retention in office for the time being, prevented Curry from quitting.

Although Fall's days in office were numbered, by his own agreement to serve only until Curry got his "feet on the ground" as well as by the displeasure of the White House, he opened a strident campaign to rid New Mexico of the outside investigators. By now these officials had uncovered what they regarded as widespread fraud in public-land transactions, had initiated civil and criminal suits against several corporations and individuals, and seemed intent on sending prominent Republicans to prison. While representing the territory in some of the land cases, Fall sniped bitterly, and often abusively, at the federal agents. Appalled by the attorney general's roughshod treatment, the investigators complained that their lives were in danger.

One incensed Interior Department agent reported to Washington on an encounter he had with Fall during a rail trip from Santa Fe to Silver City for a court hearing involving Holm O. Bursum, who stood accused of mishandling funds while territorial prison warden. Fall, who represented the territory in the case and was drinking "more or less heavily," introduced Bursum as "Honest Old Abe," and informed the Interior agent that he would find the former warden "an all right fellow and not a damn thief as you fellows back in Washington think." During a train delay, a group of lawyers and officials on both sides of the Bursum case went to a hotel barroom where they ate dinner and discussed a recent decision in the timberland litigation. At one point a very agitated Fall, "perceptibly under the influence of liquor," told the federal agent that he considered it "the most damn fool opinion he had ever heard," losing his temper and cursing the presiding judge. Then Fall said to the attorney for the timber company, also a member of the dinner group, that he would authorize the lumber concern to cut the rest of the trees in question regardless of the judge's restraining order. The extreme informality of the hearing the next day in Silver City proved equally distressing for the federal official, not to mention Bursum's eventual exoneration.

Fall, viewing the agents with contempt as third-rate bureaucratic clerks, relished the challenge to outmaneuver them. He stood on familiar political ground; they were uninitiated and outclassed. In a letter to the president he denounced the federal investigators and offered to confront them in the White House. Although Roosevelt turned down this offer, he, too, had grave doubts about the agents, who failed to realize, he said, that New Mexicans had "wholly different ideals from those, say, of Salem, Massachusetts." This kind of wisdom would soon cause Roosevelt to end the land fraud controversy. After gathering additional information on Fall's and Curry's complaints, the president held a series of meetings with federal and territorial officials in which he arranged a compromise that would remove the investigators and protect his beloved Rough Riders. The Justice Department, acknowledging that its agents had uncovered insufficient evidence to convict either the territorial officers or the purchasers in the land deals, agreed to drop most of the criminal indictments but insisted on continuing civil action to recover the land. Before the president completed this bargain, Fall had resigned as attorney general. He had served about four months, but he was happy with the results.

Largely because of Fall's skillful orchestration, the land fraud episode faded away with only a whimper. Again he and Hawkins had worked together effectively as corporate troubleshooters. The federal agents departed. True, Phelps, Dodge and Co. did have to relinquish title to all the contested coal lands, but Fall kept tracking the Alamogordo Lumber Company timberlands case until it was finally dismissed in 1912. No one went to jail, and the party split more or less healed. New Mexico had avoided a major detour on the road to statehood. Governor Curry's close friendship with President Roosevelt had been important, but Curry's political mentor, Albert Fall, had worked his magic as well. In one fell swoop Fall had saved the Phelps Dodge bacon and helped advance New Mexico's chances of admission, while also neatly enhancing his own public popularity and clout in the Republican party.

For the first time, the Republican party's national platform of 1908 made the unequivocal promise of immediate admission for Arizona and New Mexico as separate states. Beginning in 1849, only a year after its annexation by the United States, more than fifty New Mexico statehood bills had been introduced in Congress without success. Delegates had met in five spontaneous constitutional conventions, and had written four abortive state constitutions. Two persistently negative views in the East had always crushed these efforts. First, New Mexico reputedly consisted of uninhabitable desert lands, and, second, a majority of its people (those of Hispanic descent) were supposedly unfit for self-government because of poor education, lack of familiarity with the English language, and ignorance of the American political system. Of late, the image of New Mexico as a corrupt, boss-ridden, corporation-dominated province had also gained widespread acceptance. Not since the pre–Civil War slavery period had a territory faced such formidable obstacles to statehood. But with the election of President William Howard Taft and a Republican-controlled Congress in 1908, it seemed at long last that the dream might actually come true.

Albert Fall's part in answering the questions and satisfying the doubts about New Mexico's eligibility for statehood proved to be one of his most significant political contributions. As early as 1893 he had attended a statehood convention in Albuquerque, and more recently he had gone to Washington with delegations or as a freelance operator to lobby for admission. Yet his most celebrated action in the statehood movement, in 1909, when the Republicans had yet to fulfill their platform promises, appeared not only to hinder admission prospects but to doom his own political hopes as well.

In the first year of his administration President Taft made a thirteen-thousand-mile tour of the country. On his way to the Mexican border at El Paso for a meeting with Mexico's tottering dictator, Porfirio Díaz, Taft stopped off at Albuquerque. Many in the record crowd attending the territorial fair thought the president showed insufficient enthusiasm for immediate statehood in a brief afternoon speech when he emphasized the necessity of a "safe and sane constitution." That evening sixty-five dignitaries gathered in the Alvarado Hotel for a sumptuous banquet to curry the president's favor. Every detail was carefully planned. The dinner menu, considered to be "the most perfect ever served here," included bluepoint oysters from the Atlantic Coast. An orchestra concealed behind a mass of palms played at appropriate intervals throughout the evening. The speakers, selected from both political parties, judiciously advertised the cultural and political achievements of New Mexico, interspersing discreet pleas for admission with lavish praise of Taft. Everyone expected Albert Fall, in the final clinching speech honoring "Our Guest," to present "one of the eloquent, gracious addresses for which he was noted." A shocked audience heard just the opposite.

Explosive and unpredictable as usual, Fall delivered a face-to-face verbal attack on the one person who held the fate of statehood in his hands, the president of the United States. Others might "kowtow and bend [the] knee" before the "Republican anointed," Fall later explained, but he felt insulted by the long history of broken promises and Taft's apparent insincerity on immediate admission. And he said as much to the president. New Mexico had a "right" to a place in the Union, he contended, dating back to early pledges confirmed in the Treaty of Guadalupe Hidalgo of 1848. Moreover, the recent Republican platform constituted a "contract" for immediate statehood. At this point Fall aired some party dirty linen by revealing a deal made at the 1908 convention. Republican leaders had given promises of admission in exchange for the crucial votes of territorial delegations, which were needed to sidetrack labor leader Samuel Gompers's strong anti-injunction plank and substitute a watered-down version instead. With such pledges on record, Fall said, New Mexicans "might possibly be able to give more weight" to what he implied were Taft's inconclusive assurances. From beginning to end the speech challenged the president to put up or shut up on statehood.

A hush of dismay and disbelief settled over the crowd. Although not scheduled to respond, President Taft arose immediately to answer this surprising affront to presidential dignity. First, he rebuked Fall and at the same time reassured New Mexicans of his support on admission. Smiling, he told the story of an obtrusive lawyer who insisted on presenting his argument in court even after a sympathetic judge said it was unnecessary. When the trial ended, the judge told the attorney, "I have heard your argument, and I am still in favor of your cause, in spite of it." Fall might question his "sincerity and good will," said the president, but "a man cannot do more than promise and then try and carry it out." Actually Fall's revelation of the internal party fight over the injunction issue seemed to upset Taft even more than the charges of a weak-kneed stand on statehood. With sharpness in his voice, obviously meant to dispel rumors of his complicity in killing the Gompers plank, the president declared that the union version never had any real chance of adoption and indicated his sympathy for labor's plight. The blue-ribbon audience had listened to Fall's speech in stunned amazement; Taft's impromptu talk drew several rounds of cheers and applause.

Members of the president's entourage were enraged, but Taft wrote his wife, almost gleefully, about the rebuke of Fall:

> He seemed to be a man who likes to cultivate notoriety by saying something rude and out of the ordinary rules of

> courtesy, and I had to take him and spank him, which I think I did pretty successfully—at least everybody in the party seemed to think so, and it set him down where he ought to be politically. He has had aspirations for the Senate, upon the inauguration of statehood, but I don't think those aspirations are likely to be gratified.

Most of the territorial leaders left the banquet convinced that Fall had done serious damage to the statehood cause, and had just signed his own political death warrant to boot. A leading Albuquerque newspaper, speaking for "all the decent people of New Mexico," predicted Fall's immediate political demise and apologized to President Taft for the "wanton insults" of a man who was "a de facto citizen of the state of Texas, and merely a parasite on the skirts of this territory." The culprit himself, although smarting under all the criticism, made no apologies.

The dire predictions of Fall's political doom and his derailment of statehood proved to be dead wrong. Although it took a while for party leaders to calm down, his foolhardy courage in standing up to the president helped make him a popular hero with New Mexicans frustrated by the many delays on admission. Fall continued his efforts as a leader of the statehood movement. President Taft, apparently holding no serious grudges, soon sent a message to Congress recommending admission and promptly signed the enabling act for New Mexico in 1910.

Guided by his cautious judgelike instincts, Taft had repeatedly warned both New Mexicans and Arizonians to prepare "safe and sane" constitutions. He realized his fondest hopes in the case of New Mexico. The constitutional convention held at Santa Fe in the fall of 1910 produced a document described at the time as "a model of conservatism," or even "wholly reactionary." The land-grant lobby, sheep and cattle ranchers, and mining and railroad interests dominated the proceedings. Despite the Progressive Movement then sweeping across the country, the New Mexico delegates barely acknowledged direct legislation reform with a watered-down referendum, practically ignored woman's suffrage and prohibition, and gave no real force to monopoly control and regulation of big business. In

Arizona, on the other hand, the convention devised a constitution "bursting out all over" with the most-cherished progressive ideals, even recall of judges, causing Taft to threaten a veto of admission until this offensive provision was removed.

The New Mexico convention of one hundred delegates—seventy-one Republicans, twenty-eight Democrats, and one lone Socialist—turned into the kind of no-holds-barred, winner-take-all partisan fight for which the territory was renowned. As a member of the Republican majority's "coterie of six," which virtually ruled the convention and wrote the constitution as it pleased, Albert Fall became a chief architect of New Mexico statehood. This dominant elite included Republican veterans, such as deposed boss Tom Catron, as well as rising new party leaders, such as Fall. Through ironclad control of the committee system the coterie of six had all committee reports submitted to the Republican caucus for approval before going to the floor for a speedy vote. As a result, heated debate even on the most controversial issues brought few changes. The minority Democrats were relegated to a mere gadfly status.

Even though rigidly structured, the convention got its share of emotional fireworks. Fall, then "in his best fighting condition," created some of the excitement by making sarcastic and provocative comments in floor debates. Knowing well his volatile nature, Fall's wife and youngest daughter, Jouett, sat conspicuously in the visitor's area where they could face the hotheaded partisan and keep an eye on him. Nevertheless, during a sizzling exchange with Jacob S. Crist, a respected Democratic delegate who often quoted Shakespeare, Fall attacked his oratorical opponent either with scathing words or more convincing means. One observer remembered that Fall wore a gun, "as was his habit." Others recalled only a terrific verbal onslaught, bared fists, and a great deal of commotion. Regardless, Crist left the convention and did not return.

Like the other members of the coterie of six, Fall served as chairman of a major committee—the Committee on the Legislative Department. Through his hands passed the ill-fated progressive measures for popular control of government, such as the initiative and recall. Afterwards, under fire, he readily admitted that he did not fight for these reforms. The referendum finally written into the New Mexico constitution had so many exempt categories of legislation that it was practically toothless. Despite the convention's abysmal record on progressivism, in large part attributable to him, Fall maintained that he definitely favored the initiative, direct election of senators, and similar measures. Many continued to regard him as a progressive, mainly because of his well-known admiration of Theodore Roosevelt.

Fall also served as a member, but not chairman, of the Public Lands Committee, which placed few constitutional encumbrances on the state land board and its commissioner in distributing, by sale and lease, New Mexico's thirteen-million-acre legacy from the federal public domain. Regarded by many as a spokesman for the livestock industry, Fall later claimed to have written the brief, vague land article. In the years ahead this generous policy would benefit him and other ranchers immeasurably. As a member of the Judiciary Committee, Fall helped fashion the new state's court system, and he voluntarily aided the Corporations Committee in the creation of a weak corporation commission without effective enforcement powers over railroads, public utilities, and other business enterprises. Probably the convention's most admirable achievement was the ironclad protection it gave to the voting and educational rights of Hispanics, who made up about one-third of the delegates and were usually a Republican mainstay. Although little opposition arose to these provisions, Fall reportedly had a major role in formulating them. His personal handiwork in those parts of the constitution, and others, is difficult to identify, especially because the Republican hierarchy imposed a gag rule limiting roll-call votes and refused to keep a verbatim record of the proceedings. But even the abbreviated minutes clearly indicate the ramrod role he played through his frequent amendments, proposals, and parliamentary maneuvers.

Nothing better reflects the extreme partisanship of the convention than the expert job of gerrymandering legislative districts done by the Apportionment Committee, of which Fall was a member. In the first election of state officials in 1911, although the Democrats won about half of the statewide offices, including the governorship, the Republicans still managed to gain control of the legislature by a two-thirds majority. Of all the provisions he helped place in the constitution, the legislative apportionment plan had the most influence on his own political future. Lacking the popular election of United States senators, New Mexico had to rely on its Republican-dominated legislature to make the first selections, which guaranteed that two Republicans would be chosen. With gerrymandered apportionment the Republican "gang," according to progressive Republican Bronson Cutting, "expected to keep themselves in power for all times." Moreover, by making it almost impossible to amend the constitution, the Republicans hoped to render their convention handiwork permanent and unalterable. In these grandiose expectations they had finally gone too far.

Eager for statehood at all costs, New Mexico voters approved the conservative constitution by an overwhelming majority. Fall, who made an extensive speaking tour urging adoption, now emerged as the document's most effective defender in gaining approval by the president and Congress. With other New Mexicans he spent about four months in Washington, from early March through June 1911, intermittently tending to personal business affairs principally in New York City. Not only did he lobby among influential members of Congress and the cabinet, he also took statehood problems to the White House, where he had several conversations with President Taft. In hearings before a House committee Fall squared off against Harvey B. Fergusson and other New Mexico Democrats, who came to air their views on the constitution and relive "every partisan fight that has taken place in New Mexico within the last 10 or 15 years." Parrying charges by the Democrats that he was a "corporation man" and largely responsible for the "corporation-ridden and corporation-written" constitution, Fall maintained that the New Mexico convention had only taken the president's advice and produced a "safe and sane" document to assure statehood. Fergusson and his allies got some satisfaction, however, when Congress approved New Mexico statehood but stipulated that the people must be given an opportunity to vote on whether they wanted an easier constitutional amending process.

The first election of state officials in November 1911 proved to be disastrous for the overconfident Republican party. Despite the urgent warnings of Fall and one or two other leaders, the Republican organization strongly opposed the congressionally mandated "Blue Ballot" amendment (so named because it was printed on a separate ballot tinted blue), which simplified the amendment process. The Democrats, joined by progressive Republicans, formed a "Fusion Ticket" that favored the amendment, which easily carried. Thus they won an upset victory at the polls. Besides claiming the governorship, the Democrats and their allies elected one of the two congressmen and about half of the other statewide officials. New Mexico voters wanted statehood but apparently realized that the rigid amendment provision was intended to protect the special interests, and they resented it.

In a life of one pitched battle after another, Fall's election to the Senate ranked as one of his hardest fights. Eugene Manlove Rhodes had helped promote his candidacy by writing a clever article for the *Saturday Evening Post* of May 6, 1911. Fall deserved a Senate "toga," said the western author, because he was "by far the most suitable man for the place—one to whom New Mexicans may justly point with pride, or whom they may view with alarm, according to their several bents." The magazine article, which had aroused widespread comment and entered into the congressional debates on statehood, presented Fall as a public figure worthy of national consideration. From the outset the "favorites in the betting world" for the two Senate seats included Fall, Tom Catron, and Bull Andrews. It seemed almost certain—as certain as anything could be in fickle New Mexico politics—that Fall would be one of those chosen by the Republican-controlled state legislature. His new-found financial resources, his popularity, and his service to the party in the Tall Timber Cases, the constitutional convention, and the final stages of the statehood movement, seemed to assure his success. Few in the state could compete with him as a campaigner before a crowd of people. Since the selection process was confined to the legislature, however, it became one of the greatest contests of backroom power brokering in New Mexico history.

Former congressional Delegate Andrews, who had already spent a fortune promoting his Senate aspirations, appeared to have a big head start. Among his powerful Pennsylvania backers, the late Matthew S. Quay had called Andrews "the greatest lobbyist in the world," and Senator Boies Penrose had only recently told President Taft that he expected the Bull to have one of the Senate seats. As for deposed Boss Catron, his power might have waned, but he desperately wanted a "toga" and was "probably still the most unscrupulous man in the Southwest." It would be no simple task for Fall to match wits and resources with those two battle-seasoned giants. Other problems also clouded the political horizon. The increasingly influential progressive camp, according to transplanted New Yorker Bronson Cutting, regarded Fall warily as "Rich & able," with "a most plausible personality & a considerable following," but the "most dangerous man of the bunch." Fall wrote Eugene Manlove Rhodes that, although public sentiment was "practically unanimous for me as one of the Senators," there was no general agreement on another candidate.

Even before the legislature met, disturbing rumors had reached far-off Washington. President Taft received the unwelcome news that national committeeman Solomon Luna was "leaning toward" Fall's candidacy. "Now, my dear Mr. Luna," the president solemnly warned, "this will not do, for in my judgment Fall would not come up to the standard which you yourself set." Ex-President Theodore Roosevelt, who heard that the senatorial selection would be tainted with corruption, wrote one of his Rough Riders (now a state representative) reminding him of the recent election scandal in West Virginia and urging his former comrade to vigilantly guard against a recurrence in New Mexico. Once the legislature convened in

March 1912, both Taft and Roosevelt had even more cause for alarm.

Most of the gossip about outright vote buying involved the manipulations of Bull Andrews. Before the constitutional convention Andrews reportedly had tried to run Fall out of the Republican party by offering large sums of money to prevent his election as a delegate, thus eliminating him from the political scene and as a Senate rival. The assertion by a Denver newspaper that Fall came to Santa Fe with $90,000 to spend for his election in the legislature seems unlikely, as does a later rumor that he had $40,000 available for that purpose. In February he did obtain a secured loan of $30,000 from a New York bank, but whether he used all or part of this money for political activity, or on Mexican mining properties and his Three Rivers ranch, is unclear. Just before the legislature convened he wrote Eugene Manlove Rhodes implying that Andrews was spending lavishly to line up legislators, and adding, "I have absolutely refused to consider for a moment the expenditure of any money to secure the vote of any member." He had made "quite an active canvass" of Republican legislators, and had paid out some money to newspapers and for sending backers to various parts of the state to sample his strength, "but not to secure any pledges for my support." It is impossible to determine from the myriad of charges and countercharges how much Fall, Andrews, or Catron actually spent, or how he spent it, even though rumors of corruption persisted long after the balloting in the legislature ended.

Clearly the wily Bull Andrews posed the greatest threat to both Fall's and Catron's hopes. Andrews had on his side eastern money, powerful national backers, and impressive political cunning accumulated during thirty-five years of high-level partisan maneuvering in Pennsylvania and New Mexico. On the other hand, his steamroller tactics had caused public consternation, and he had attracted a number of implacable enemies, chief among them being Albert Fall. The upcoming Senate contest would decide whether Fall or Andrews had the bare-knuckles political skills to knock out the other and survive.

The body blow to Andrews's hopes was delivered in Room 44 of the Palace Hotel in Santa Fe, the same hotel in which Fall maintained campaign headquarters. As the legislators gathered, rumors started circulating that enough of the seventy-three members (twenty-eight of them Hispanics, nearly all Republicans) had pledged their votes for a combination of Andrews and a Hispanic candidate to jeopardize Fall's campaign. Four Hispanic house members, supposedly committed to the Bull, approached Fall and offered their support for a slate of him and a Hispanic. After Fall left the conference, the four legislators then reportedly told his staunch backer, Elfego Baca, that they would vote two times for Fall for $500 apiece and would stay with him to the end for $1,250 each. When Baca questioned the "nefariousness of their offer," they retorted that "the fellows at Washington [Congress] would make $50,000 at one fell swoop in perhaps a sugar [tariff] or some other deal."

After conferring with Republican chairman Venceslao Jaramillo, Fall set a trap for the four Andrews legislators. Baca, a celebrated gunman later immortalized in a Walt Disney television series as "an authentic hero of the Old West," invited the four to Room 44 and asked them if they still intended to vote for Andrews, to which two replied that they did. Baca then took a large roll of bills from his pocket, saying casually that "he had more money than he knew what to do with." He counted out four separate stacks of $500 each on a table and told the four legislators to help themselves if they would vote for Fall. Talking loudly all the while, he then "made a signal by clapping his hands," and suddenly three other Hispanics, including chairman Jaramillo and a state mounted policeman, burst into the room from their hiding place in the bathroom. The state policeman confiscated the money and arrested the four would-be bribe-takers on the spot. Blank forms of resignation from the legislature were thrust before them, which they signed, and all four were hauled off to jail. A subsequent legislative investigation filed no damaging charges against anybody, and exonerated and reinstated the four house members, but only after it was too late for them to participate in the first round of senatorial voting.

Meanwhile Fall stayed discreetly in the background, receiving much favorable publicity as the protector of public morals who had helped expose a corrupt conspiracy. The four accused legislators, who denied any guilt, contended that Baca had approached them about voting for Fall and then had shoved money into their hands. They had signed the resignations while in "great fear of bodily harm." Baca afterwards reminded Fall of the thing "which I did by the instructions of the State Executive Committee." Undoubtedly the Republican hierarchy, either collectively or as individuals, had a hand in the Room 44 plot, and in a secret meeting a few nights later in Andrews's home. The details of the second gathering went unrecorded, but party chieftains reportedly threatened the Bull, who had at last run out of money, with bankruptcy by leaving him to shoulder his many debts alone if he did not withdraw from the race, which he promptly agreed to do.

Fall and Andrews had been the leading candidates, with Catron as a strong contender, but the mutual antipathy of the front-runners made a combination between them impossible and left the door open for Catron. Now with the removal of Andrews, the legislature could name Fall and Catron as New Mexico's first two United States senators, which was done on March 28. It was the eighth ballot. To Hispanic kingpin Solomon Luna, more than any other person, both of the new senators owed their success. Luna had steadfastly supported Fall and Catron until the factious Republicans were brought into line.

The ceremony marking Fall's entry into the Senate cooled any feeling of triumph he gained from his defeat of Bull Andrews. To keep a sequence of staggered terms, the Senate parliamentarian used a lottery for the two New Mexico senators and their Arizona counterparts. Fall drew the slip giving him the shortest term of all, to end March 4, 1913, a scant eleven months away. He would soon have to endure another tumultuous election contest before he was securely seated in the Senate. Fall and his backers decided to force an early reelection before Andrews could resurrect his Senate hopes or other aspirants could gather strength. Even if the Bull could not win, he was determined to defeat Fall and avenge his earlier humiliation. Several attempts by the legislature to reelect Fall met with failure, largely because of Andrews's stalling tactics in the lower house. Finally, in June 1912, a wrathful Senator Fall, who had struck a tradeoff deal with President Taft for mutual support, arrived in Santa Fe from Washington with the startling announcement that the president had vacated all federal appointments made in New Mexico Territory while Andrews was delegate, even postmasterships, and had placed the new patronage in Fall's hands. The "terror stricken" legislators realized that unless they cooperated with the new boss, "they would no longer be on the band wagon."

Two days later a submissive state senate, which had just voted for Fall's reelection, convened in an extraordinary evening session for the avowed purpose of considering "The Medical Bill." The recalcitrant lower house had reaffirmed its earlier decision not to ballot on the United States Senate seat until the next session in January 1913. But seventeen house members, in a stratagem inaugurated by Fall himself, suddenly appeared in the senate chamber. The sergeant-at-arms quickly locked the door, and, over the protests of the presiding officer, the two groups formed a joint assembly. In the balloting that followed Fall received all thirty-two votes cast for the Senate term ending in 1919. Eight Democratic state senators and one stray Democratic house member, "who got caught in the room and could not get out," refused to vote.

The real fireworks came the next day in the house chamber, where "pandemonium reigned supreme" during nearly three hours of "both fistic and verbal combats." Finally realizing that "Andrews was done for," house members rescinded their earlier action to postpone a ballot and voted twenty-five to two in favor of Fall's reelection, with twenty-two abstentions. Immediately thereafter the senate combined with the house in another joint assembly. Amidst the "wildest of scenes" yet in a legislative session "chiefly characterized by wild scenes," with ink stands, fists, and profane epithets filling the air, Fall was reelected for the second time in twenty-four hours. It was not an ordeal for the fainthearted or for genteel folk. Indeed, Emma Fall, observing this last parliamentary melee as a spectator, became hysterical and had to be helped out of the hall.

With Fall conspicuously present in Santa Fe, it was obvious who had masterminded the blunt tactics smashing Andrews's last desperate attempt for a senatorship. The unfriendly *Albuquerque Morning Journal*, decrying the use of "strong arm methods" and "open threats of violence," questioned the legality of Fall's reelection. "No man should want to be senator so badly," stated the newspaper, "that he would permit his friends to resort to such means to secure an alleged election." Democratic Governor William C. McDonald, on the advice of his legal counselor, refused to certify the legislature's decision. For several months it appeared that the United States Senate might have to make the final ruling on the future status of Fall's membership. But the long, acrimonious controversy ended in January 1913 when the New Mexico legislature decisively repeated the rump session's action of the previous summer. Some diehards still would not give up. Bronson Cutting, the sensitive young progressive Republican, believed that several powerful Republican leaders had used "unfair means" to obtain Fall's election, especially by staging a "frame up" in Room 44. Cutting spent several thousand dollars hiring the Burns Detective Agency to prove collusion and bring about Fall's removal from the Senate, but the investigation produced a mass of inconclusive evidence.

Once again, through bold strategy and sheer bluff, Fall had mastered the governmental process and rammed through a personal objective over strong, entrenched opposition. He had proven himself qualified, at least by demanding New Mexico standards, to assume a more exalted political role. Now he could plunge into national and international affairs with the assurance that his Senate tenure would last long enough to give his opinions some significance. As for Bull Andrews, his glory had departed; he was no match for the gutfighter who had first learned to vanquish the devil with fire in Dona Ana County. Andrews had spent ten years in New Mexico waging a costly, well-calculated campaign to win a Senate seat. Too far along in years to attempt a comeback in Pennsylvania politics, rejected by powerful friends such as Senator Penrose, and infirm in spirit, the Bull died at Carlsbad in 1919, penniless and forgotten.

Another old adversary suffered a slightly less dismal political fate at Fall's hands. In the Senate Fall quickly became a more prominent figure than his colleague, Tom Catron, for whom he developed an open disdain, often belittling Catron's performance in correspondence with state Republican leaders. At the end of Catron's first term Fall blocked his colleague's renomination in the state Republican convention of 1916 and handpicked a replacement candidate. It was a fitting conclusion to Fall's old fight against Boss Catron and the Santa Fe Ring. In retrospect, however, there is a great irony in his triumphs over both Andrews and Catron, and especially the utter despair brought to the Bull's fondest hopes. The end of Fall's own career and his last days would be even more painful.

CHAPTER 4

Riding with Roosevelt

AFTER the Teapot Dome scandal President Harding's perfidious attorney general, Harry M. Daugherty, tried to distance himself from his fallen cabinet colleague, Albert Fall, by saying that they were never "chums" because Fall had been a "distinguished Progressive," while Daugherty had always remained a faithful Republican. Fall's record did not support Daugherty's assertion, either in New Mexico politics or in the Senate, and certainly not as interior secretary. Fall never sympathized with the reform program of the Progressive Movement. Yet, when he entered the Senate in 1912, one eastern newspaper, labeling him a leader of the progressive Republicans in New Mexico, curiously stated, "Senator Fall is a progressive, though he balks at the recall of judges and is not altogether enamored of the modern substitutes for representative government." As a new member of the Harding cabinet in 1921, he was described in the East as "one of the 'honey bees' of American politics," having "'sipped' the delights of Democratic, Progressive and straight-goods Republican petals with full enjoyment of all." Soon after entering the Senate, Fall himself accurately characterized his political stance by saying, "I may not be progressive enough for some progressives, and not stand-pat enough for some stand-patters, but I yield to no man in my loyalty to the republican party." Above all else, he was a militant partisan warrior.

The political pundits in New Mexico had no illusions about where Fall stood. Bronson Cutting, the wealthy newcomer and close personal friend of Theodore Roosevelt, bought the venerable *Santa Fe New Mexican* in the summer of 1912 and made it the first Progressive daily in the state. The newspaper referred to Fall's senatorial reelection as "a temporary triumph of reactionary politics," and then observed: "There has been some talk about Judge Fall being a Progressive. Up to the present time he has shown no tendency to identify himself with the Progressive organization." Fall's penchant for spectacular independent action and his well-known esteem for Roosevelt were the main reasons for his undeserved progressive reputation. Although he abhorred most of Roosevelt's domestic policies, especially conservation, and shunned the Bull Moose revolt in 1912, he always admired the colorful, energetic Roosevelt. After the Rough Rider left the White House and Fall was in the Senate, the New Mexico senator became an adviser and spokesman for Roosevelt on Mexican affairs and nominated him for the presidency in the Republican national convention of 1916. This later relationship was based, however, not on progressive ideals, but on their common stand for the protection of American rights in revolution-torn Mexico.

An uninstructed New Mexico delegation to the 1912 Republican national convention, besides appealing to progressive elements, gave Senator Fall a club to hold over the head of President Taft, who needed every delegate vote he could muster to withstand Roosevelt's challenge for the presidential nomination. In fact, Taft's plight provided Fall with enough bargaining power to make the deal in which the president vacated all federal appointments in New Mexico and turned over the new patronage to Fall, thereby guaranteeing his Senate reelection. Naturally this all-important concession was not one-sided. As Fall wrote a confidant in New Mexico: "I have a thorough understanding with the President and we will act together in all matters. I have stated to him as I have to Roosevelt's friends, that I could not follow or support the latter in the campaign which he is making against Taft." In particular, although he was "a strong friend" of the Rough Rider, Fall told the president that he disagreed with Roosevelt on such "wild ideas" as the recall of judicial decisions. In response, Taft expressed his gratification for Fall's attitude since Taft had believed that "I would fight him and that I was erratic and dangerous." An Albuquerque newspaper, noting Fall's sudden loss of enthusiasm for Roosevelt, sagely observed, "Politics make strange bed fellows, as is shown by the fact that Judge Fall and President Taft are now in the same political bed."

With the final decision on his Senate reelection still hanging fire, Albert Fall sat on the sidelines during the 1912 national conventions and the ensuing three-way presidential campaign involving Taft, the Republican; Roosevelt, the Progressive or "Bull Moose"; and Woodrow Wilson, the Democratic candidate. He gave muffled support to bumbling "Old Taft" and called Roosevelt "the greatest statesman of the age" just often enough to get the attention of the Progressives. In fact, Fall later told the Rough Rider, he chaired the state Republican convention and made a few speeches during the campaign, always refusing either to mention Taft by name or advocate his election. Only Fall's private correspondence at the time revealed exactly where he stood. To a sympathetic journalist, he wrote in August 1912 that Gifford Pinchot and other Progressives backing Roosevelt were "the worst enemies" imaginable for the West because their conservation program, if carried out, "would convert the Western settlers into a lot of peasants." He declared to trusted followers that both Taft and his campaign were utterly hopeless and that the president had "no more idea of politics than . . . 'a mule,'" adding that the administration's conservation policies were almost as bad as those in Roosevelt's platform. Not surprisingly, least of all to Senator Fall who had done little to prevent it, Wilson won in New Mexico by a comfortable plurality. The Rough Rider, disappointed by his last-place showing there as well as Fall's waffling, stoutly disavowed the rumor that he had asked Progressive legislators to support his professed admirer's ongoing senatorial reelection bid. Their close working relationship still lay ahead.

Meanwhile Fall had started making his mark in the Senate. A tabulation of the approximately sixty measures he introduced during his nine-year senatorial career and the pitifully few that survived committee action and a floor vote would hardly explain the impressive prominence he achieved. Nor did any monumental bill bear his name. For years a member of the minority party, he had little opportunity to distinguish himself as a legislative leader. Yet he managed to become an important member of the Senate, eventually gaining a seat on the prestigious Foreign Relations Committee. Mexican affairs were always Fall's great passion. He emerged as a well-known national figure in that role, and as an outspoken critic of President Wilson's foreign policy, including the Treaty of Versailles, often lambasting the president in pointedly personal Senate speeches. Legislation dealing with public lands, national forests, mineral resources, Indian reservations, and similar issues also drew his close attention. As a member of the Public Lands Committee's "western crowd," he was scorned by the conservationists and he regarded them with equal contempt.

In the Senate, Albert Fall the westerner, versatile and urbane, won the friendship and respect of such Republican leaders as Henry Cabot Lodge, Elihu Root, and William E. Borah. He had a special camaraderie with the polished James W. Wadsworth, Jr., of New York, who had managed a Texas ranch. Among the Democrats his best friend was Marcus A. Smith of Arizona, also originally a Kentuckian and one of the most popular raconteurs in Congress. After 1914 Fall's wife and youngest daughter, Jouett, were seldom with him in Washington. He lived the "hotel life" in a small apartment where various "chums" dropped in to play poker, have some drinks, and trade stories. Cleveland industrialist Price McKinney, who often made large loans to Fall, and Senator John W. Weeks of Massachusetts were among those frequently on hand. By 1919–20, when Fall and Warren G. Harding of Ohio served together on the Senate Foreign Relations Committee, the future president also sometimes joined the poker group.

Regarded by his colleagues as intelligent, determined, and a hard worker, Fall was especially admired for his expertise on current conditions in Mexico, as well as his erudite understanding of that country's history. To some of his fellow senators, however, he showed a darker side. He was vain and thin-skinned, they thought, and too often bristled at criticism. Paraphrasing Kipling, Fall moaned in one Senate debate, "I have learned to hear the words I have spoken twisted by others to make a trap for fools." He seemed to enjoy dwelling on the ignorance of easterners about western conditions and lecturing them on the finer points of land law and water rights. Often austere and arrogant in floor debate, the New Mexican exuded righteous anger and bitter discontent—about a benighted federal bureaucracy, the trials and disappointments faced by elective officeholders, or the inroads of "bolshevism" at home and abroad—and ruthlessly overrode any opposition. While waving a menacing finger, "as if to pierce the body of his opponent," he would lacerate instead the adversary's argument "with sharp sentences." He seldom gave a "set" or prepared speech, preferring to rely on brief notes and a pile of documents, papers, and reports as he presented his roving, rapid-fire remarks in loose syntax. Although a strident partisan, he marched to an independent drummer and often refused to vote blindly with the Republican bloc.

In his maiden speech on May 15, 1912, Fall came out swinging against the federal conservation program with a "states' rights" approach popular in the West. Demanding that the western states receive the same benefits from the natural resources as the older states had enjoyed, he proposed that Congress initiate an alternative to national conservation by transferring to the State of New Mexico management but not outright ownership of the forest reserves within its boundaries. Only by this arrangement, Fall said, would enterprising settlers get fair treatment on grazing permits, land leases, and access to timber.

> These are the facts, Senators. The conservation of the natural resources in New Mexico means a restriction upon the individual; means that he must not acquire a homestead in the most habitable portion of the State; and means that upon such forest reserves and Indian reserves the gentle bear, the mountain lion, and the timber wolf are conserved, so that they may attack [the settler's] herds, his cattle, and his sheep. That is conservation in New Mexico.

He also emphasized one of his favorite themes—use of the natural resources for immediate western development. Even if a "'malefactor of great wealth'" had stolen all ten million acres of forest reserves in New Mexico, Fall declared, it would be more desirable than the present system. The timber would be cut; railroads, wagon roads, and sawmills would be built; people would be employed; "and little thrifty cities would grow up all over New Mexico, if we could use our forests." His brand of conservation, he always made clear, called for "the actual development of natural resources," which gave "men their start and stake in the world" and allowed the country "to progress, to go forward." He concluded his maiden speech with the fervent hope that Congress would soon abolish the Interior Department as well as the Bureau of Indian Affairs, both of which he would administer nine years later as interior secretary.

In these frank comments Fall revealed his hostility not only to national conservation but also to the citified bureaucrats sent out west to run the program. These greenhorn "clerks," he claimed, were often so ignorant of practical affairs that they "do not know a cow when they see one and think a sheep is a predatory animal." Much of this animosity came from Fall's personal experience in dealing with local federal officials about the operations of his Three Rivers ranch, which bordered national forest lands and the Mescalero Apache Indian Reservation. Grazing permits and water rights were a constant source of irritation for him. Fall wanted federal employees, as he later made clear, who understood that the Forest Service and the General Land Office "should be friendly" to those using the public lands, "rather than to consider any man attempting to develop our country as a thief."

In one acrimonious incident shortly before he entered the Senate, Fall had secured grazing permits for twenty-five hundred of his sheep (the maximum allowed one owner) to graze on the Lincoln National Forest. When he conveyed ownership of another four thousand sheep to his son and an employee, the Forest Service ruled the "ostensible transfer" to be a subterfuge and refused to issue additional permits. Enraged and threatening retaliation through his Washington connections, Fall wrote the local forest supervisor, "Just such action as yours in this case is what has caused the antagonism of the people of the West against the Administration of the Forest Service by [officials] who have not apparently any common sense, and who only desire to put settlers and others to as much trouble as possible." This episode came back to haunt him several years later when as interior secretary he was locked in battle with the conservationists over transferring the national forests to his control.

Senator Fall continued to criticize federal conservation at every opportunity, with problems on his Three Rivers ranch often providing a reference point for these attacks. By all odds his pet natural-resources crusade called for the donation or cession of the public domain (all of the remaining vacant, unappropriated, and unreserved federal lands) to the states where these holdings were located. Such a massive grant would have amounted to twenty-seven million acres in New Mexico alone. In almost every session he introduced some kind of bill or amendment designed to accomplish this mission. As he wrote toward the end of his senatorial career, "I have for years, in speeches in Congress and out of it, and through means of proposed legislation, expressed my conviction that the public lands in the public land states should be turned over to the states for educational, drainage [and irrigation], public roads and like purposes." The Wilson administration invariably opposed and squelched all of these proposals.

Refusing to admit defeat, Fall stealthily maneuvered to obtain legislation that would provide "an entering wedge" through one of these alternatives: classifying only the most marginal lands for donation, ceding an area equal to the Indian reservations and national forests in the affected states, requiring the states to split any income from land sales or leases fifty-fifty with the federal reclamation fund, or greatly expanding the opportunities for individual 640-acre homesteads. One of Fall's proudest accomplishments was his "Soldier's Homestead Amendment" to a World War I draft bill. The amendment liberalized mineral and public-land entries and suspended homestead residence requirements for those conscripted. He also worked especially hard to obtain a limited land grant to pay for construction of Elephant Butte Dam on the Rio Grande in New Mexico, which the federal government eventually built but by other means.

Fall often argued that national conservation denied the equality of the newer western states, such as Arizona and New Mexico, by keeping the vast federal holdings out of private hands and thus off the tax rolls. "You leave us no taxable property," he told the Senate in an obvious exaggeration. An approaching crisis in state revenues, Fall said half seriously in 1914, would soon force New Mexico to become a national park or part of an Indian reservation so it could receive federal assistance. In short, he believed that all public lands should be "turned back to the people" as quickly as possible, including national forests and other federal reserves. "Never so long as I am here or have a vote anywhere else," he declared in his inaugural Senate speech, "will I vote to reserve the public lands of the United States from the individual citizens of the United States."

It would be a mistake to regard Fall as a lone Don Quixote attacking conservation windmills. Probably a sizable majority of his constituents back home in New Mexico, which contained the third largest federal landholding among the eleven western states, heartily agreed with his stand. Many western governors, state legislators and members of Congress, and editors also shared his views. In the Senate itself Weldon B. Heyburn of Idaho, John F. Shafroth of Colorado, and Clarence D. Clark of Wyoming gained more prominence than Fall as leaders of the states' rights faction. Traditionally the West had placed the top priority on exploiting the land for opportunity, farm and ranch homes, timber and mineral riches, and special amenities such as transportation improvements. The movement to donate the public domain to the states had a long, honorable history going back at least to the sectional struggles of the Jacksonian period. By the early twentieth century a showdown had arisen between the forces advocating continuation of the old settlement and development process and the increasing number of influential individuals and groups believing that the public's inalienable stake in the remaining resources must be saved. For Fall and others with his economic philosophy the conservationists had introduced a shocking new idea by maintaining that protection of the environment also required increased federal regulation of private business. Nothing else in the enemy arsenal was more alarming than this dangerous threat to rugged individualism, a cherished western trait.

It was a losing fight. The conservationists seemed to win all the important battles. In 1902 the national reclamation program became the last massive development enterprise to be financed by public land sales. The opponents of federal conservation were plainly out of step with a rising national trend, and Fall's contradictory position sometimes caused him public embarrassment. During his maiden Senate speech of 1912, he was chided by a Democratic colleague who asked how he could reconcile his well-known admiration for Roosevelt with such harsh criticism of the former president's "strongest and most dominant policy." Fall nimbly replied that he could "admire a man as a great man" but still disagree with some of his ideas. By the time he became interior secretary, Fall had moderated his views on donation of the entire public domain to the states, although he continued to advocate disposing of selected federally held lands for a variety of national projects, such as the construction of roads and the payment of a soldier's bonus.

The main reason for Fall's change of heart was a brace of conservationist victories in 1920, the General Leasing Act and the Federal Water Power Act, and not an apparent loss of faith in the states' rights doctrine. Before the United States entered World War I, the Supreme Court had ruled decisively that the federal government held exclusive jurisdiction over its public lands and could charge a rental fee for their use. This landmark confirmation of national authority sounded the death knell for the states' rights anticonservationist crusade in the West and made possible a leasing plan as a compromise between federal reservation policies and state control. After the war Congress formalized a leasing system for public holdings that enriched the western states while maintaining the national role. The General Leasing Act authorized leases on most public lands bearing coal, phosphates, and sodium as well as gas, oil shale, and oil. The Federal Water Power Act created the Federal Power Commission to issue long-term licenses to private interests for water-power development on public lands, thus striking a compromise in a lengthy controversy over another vital western resource. Both acts provided that 37.5 percent of the royalties and fees went to the individual state where a transaction took place, with the federal reclamation fund, which benefitted mostly western states, receiving about 50 percent of the receipts and the general treasury the rest.

For westerners such as Fall the legislation of 1920, with its payoffs to the states, seemed like a moral victory. But the two measures were actually a major conservationist triumph, the culmination of a twenty-year campaign to establish a permanent federal trusteeship over the natural resources, not temporary ownership until their inevitable disposal. Gifford Pinchot and his allies readily recognized the General Leasing Act as "the end of a long struggle" and the fulfillment "of a major part of Roosevelt's conservation program."

Fall's role in the 1920 legislation was not in any way decisive, although he did by now serve on the Senate Public Lands Committee. In fact, one of the main reasons a leasing act had been delayed so long, some of his colleagues correctly believed, was the opposition of western senators, such as Fall, who held out to the bitter end for alienation of the public lands. Of the two measures, he and his New Mexico constituents probably had greater interest in the General Leasing Act, with its stipulations for mining, but Fall himself also paid close attention to the formulation of provisions on oil and water-power development.

In the Senate debates on mineral leasing Fall said that he preferred something like the old Placer Law, which conveyed outright ownership to the claimant after discovery. He would vote for the present bill, however, since the bureaucratic conservationists had succeeded "in fastening upon the people of the United States their theories of governmental reservation and control of our underground riches." During the Senate discussion of the bill, he paid tribute to private oil operators as great risk-takers and railed against government development of the natural resources. Oil did not just "spout from the ground," he observed, but was the product of initiative and industry, which Americans as individuals possessed in greater abundance than any other people. Fall was thoroughly familiar with the final measure, including the restrictions on drilling the naval oil reserves, and he served on the conference committee that worked out the differences between the Senate and House versions. Yet he was too busy, with the fight against the Treaty of Versailles but mainly with his Mexican affairs investigation, to concentrate unduly on the leasing legislation that would later cause him so much grief.

Senator Fall's record on other progressive objectives was somewhat mixed. He dutifully supported constitutional amendments on the direct election of senators, prohibition, and woman's suffrage but opposed the Underwood-Simmons Tariff, which implemented taxes on personal and corporate incomes, and the Clayton Anti-Trust Act, with its strictures on trusts and monopolies. His attitude toward Indians and Indian lands was an essential part of his obsession with defeating the federal conservation program and with donating the public domain to the states, thereby making possible the unrestricted development of the West. In fact, his crusade had more success in this respect than elsewhere. He thought he knew about Indians, and believed he had their best interests at heart, even though his early impressions of them probably had a lasting effect. As he told his Senate colleagues in 1913: "[W]hen I originally went to New Mexico the first town that I went into was Silver City, and as I got off the train . . . one of the first things I saw was an American holding in his hand the bleeding scalp of a woman who had been killed by [an Apache] within a mile of the courthouse of Silver City that afternoon. The Indian who scalped her had been shot." Actually he did know one group of Indians well, the Mescalero Apaches, whose lands adjoined his Three Rivers ranch on the east. As the Mescaleros discovered, their influential neighbor had his own views about the use of their land, water, and timber.

The New Mexico legislature had called on Congress in 1912 to abolish Indian reservations. Although Senator Fall never succeeded in accomplishing this ambitious goal, he did manage to halt the creation of additional Indian holdings in the public domain. Soon after entering the Senate, he conferred with President Taft and federal officials about stopping the practice of enlarging reservations in New Mexico and Arizona, in this case the Jicarilla Apache boundaries in northwestern New Mexico, by taking lands from the public domain through executive order. Indeed, Fall wanted to throw open large portions of the reservations that he thought could be put to better use by white settlers. With the help of Senators Marcus A. Smith and Henry F. Ashurst, both Arizona Democrats, he obtained legislation in 1918 giving only Congress the authority to establish new reservations or expand them. This measure was especially burdensome for landless Indians, who had often found relief through presidential action but now had to depend on an unsympathetic Congress. Capitalizing on the industrial demands of World War I, Fall and other western senators also won approval to make executive-order reservations available for metal mining.

Among Fall's most cherished legislative objectives involving Indian holdings was the creation of a national park on the western part of the Mescalero reservation next to his ranch, a project originally advanced in Congress by territorial Delegate William H. ("Bull") Andrews. Fall also envisioned another national park at Elephant Butte on the Rio Grande and a road for tourists connecting the two facilities. Four times between 1912 and 1916 he introduced bills to establish the two parks, but to no avail. In the face of these rebuffs Fall temporarily shelved both of his national park proposals, only to resurrect them amid heated controversy when he became interior secretary.

Not surprisingly, Fall's ranch figured prominently in his private business relations with the Mescalero Apaches. Moreover, it cast him in his worst role, as a stereotypical, grasping western land baron. Overshadowed by his combined interests of about 750,000 acres, the mountainous and forested Mescalero reservation, established by executive order in 1873, covered 474,000 acres and by 1921 had 628 inhabitants. This population included 187 Indians or their descendants, mostly exiled Chiricahua Apache followers of Geronimo and Nana, who had been returned to the Southwest from Fort Sill, Oklahoma, in 1913. Senator Fall had strenuously objected to welcoming these Chiricahuas back to New Mexico, "where they themselves and their fathers made the ground run red with the blood of Americans, descendants of whom are yet living around the Mescalero Reserve."

Whatever his personal sentiments, Fall's comprehensive master plan for development of the Three Rivers Valley required the cooperation of the Mescaleros, or at least favorable agreements with the Bureau of Indian Affairs. These precious waters, which originated in the reservation on Sierra Blanca, ran southwestward past his ranch house before disappearing in the sands of the Tularosa Basin, for a total distance of only about thirty-five miles. His continued success as a western empire builder, in the spirit if not on the scale of Colonel Bill Greene's Mexican exploits, depended on capturing the scanty flow of the rivers in the mountains and diverting it to his holdings far below, where it could be used in a variety of well-coordinated projects.

As early as 1910, before his Senate election, Fall had worked out a contract with the local Indian agent by which he obtained much of the Three Rivers water but enough was guaranteed for irrigation to the three Indian families living along the banks, who farmed small acreages. Through his former law partner, railroad attorney W. A. Hawkins, he later made a five-year contract with the El Paso and Southwestern Railroad, owned by Phelps, Dodge and Co., to supply its gypsum-fouled locomotive boilers with 75,000 gallons of pure mountain water per day. In return Fall received from the railroad $2,700 annually and a construction subsidy of $17,400. He then completed a concrete dam in the stream's solid-rock mountain canyon and an "impervious conduit" of pipelines and concrete ditches running downstream to his ranch and eventually to the Three Rivers train station. Twice thereafter, in 1917 and 1920, Fall renegotiated his agreement with the EP & SW for larger sums.

Besides irrigation of the fertile bottomland fields and orchards on his ranch, a reliable water supply, Fall thought, would assure his promotion of a Three Rivers townsite surrounding the El Paso and Southwestern station. He already owned the townsite land as well as the Three Rivers Trading Company—a general store and post office. On the basis of his good water he proposed that the railroad move its division headquarters to the Three Rivers real estate venture, offering to donate land for switching tracks, maintenance shops and other structures, and residential lots for the employees. With the tourist trade from the pending Mescalero national park, and the prospect of business from a nearby national Indian tubercular sanitarium, which the federal government was planning (but never built), Three Rivers could become not only an important rail center but the area's major town. The EP & SW, however, decided against relocating its divisional facilities, which doomed Fall's ambitious townsite development project.

Meanwhile trouble had arisen between the customarily cooperative Mescaleros and their influential neighbor over water distribution and grazing rights. Besides asking questions about Fall's share of the flow, the Indians sometimes diverted water from his storage reservoirs and sold it to the nearby Harris-Brownfield ranch or let it run away down dry arroyos. At one point relations became so strained that he had to hire an Indian leader, Shanta Boy, at ten dollars a month to keep the Mescalero farmers from wasting irrigation water at night. The Indians also leased their fields and pastures to the Harris-Brownfield spread while balking at a lease renewal with Fall's cattle operations for reservation grazing rights. Successive Mescalero agents had advanced a plan, which required congressional support, to sell Indian timber and use the money to purchase a large tribal cattle herd. As one of the area ranchers who leased the Indian range, Senator Fall never approved of this visionary project, although he did give it fainthearted backing in 1920 when the difficulty arose over renewing his reservation grazing rights. At that time the hard-pressed superintendent warned the Mescaleros that their hopes for a better life depended on Fall's support and their cooperation with him. This was good advice, for their powerful neighbor would soon be the presidential cabinet officer with full charge over Indian affairs.

The creation of Fall's landed empire had brought him into conflict with not only the Mescalero Apaches but also their white friends, namely the Indian Rights Association, a national advocacy organization that had identified him as an enemy and henceforth would watch him closely. In fact, his difficulties with the Indian farmers, he became convinced, were inspired by outside influences such as the IRA. Otherwise, as Fall himself saw his dealings with the Mescaleros, he had a strong legal claim to the water of Three Rivers Creek but shared it instead of resorting to lengthy court action. Fall's soured relations with the Mescaleros made it obvious to him, however, that the one missing, and essential, piece of land necessary to round out his empire was the Harris-Brownfield ranch, a three-thousand-acre spread strategically located to threaten control of the Three Rivers headwaters. When he left the Senate in 1921, the future possession of the Harris-Brownfield property remained a major concern, especially because he was too broke to buy it if the owners decided to put it on the market.

During the flurry of early Wilsonian progressive legislation, Fall wrote a New Mexico friend in August 1914 that "the Democrats had charged themselves entirely with [the] legislative responsibility," leaving the minority Republican senators "who had business away" free to take long absences from Washington or tend to other matters. Even so, he told another confidant, "I never worked in my life as hard as I have been working, particularly during the last few months." Besides staying busy in morning and evening committee sessions, he studied the labyrinthine Senate system and carefully cultivated strategic friendships. Mainly, the Democratic monopoly of power allowed Fall to concentrate on answering the avalanche of telegrams and letters from all over the country that followed his Senate speeches about conditions in revolution-torn Mexico, and to give addresses in several eastern cities on United States relations with that troubled land. In his first year the freshman senator from a new, politically inconsequential western state was rapidly gaining a national reputation.

Fall's timing was perfect. In diplomacy, and economically as well, neighboring Mexico was the most important country for the United States in all Latin America. About a year before Fall entered the Senate, Porfirio Díaz, the aged Mexican dictator, had been ousted by a revolution and exiled to Europe. Under Díaz foreigners had controlled almost 70 percent of Mexico's wealth, with Americans alone possessing nearly 45 percent, valued at an estimated $1 billion. Suspicion of intruding United States corporations, especially the oil companies, and fear that foreign influence was undermining traditional values had aroused many of the revolutionary leaders to action. A popular saying expressed those sentiments: "Mexico is the mother of foreigners and the stepmother of Mexicans." And, "Mexico for the Mexicans" became a battle cry.

The ensuing turmoil, which spawned rampant anti-foreigner feelings, a succession of Mexican presidents, and prolonged internecine fighting led by competing warlords, greatly alarmed Americans with investments in Mexico and the fifty thousand United States citizens living there. American property losses and deaths mounted as the civil strife continued. Except for World War I and its aftermath, tumultuous relations with Mexico posed the most serious problem in United States diplomacy between 1910 and the early 1920s. These revolutionary upheavals, as explained earlier, threatened Fall's own holdings south of the border, creating considerable hardship in his personal financial affairs. Moreover, it must not be forgotten that he represented a border state and received many letters from constituents and others living in that area demanding retaliation for the revolutionary destruction and bloodshed that spilled over into American territory.

No other senator could match Fall's combination of long firsthand experience in Mexico, his scholarly knowledge of its laws, history, and culture, and his connections with prominent Mexican politicians and businessmen. When he took his Senate seat, a Washington newspaper commented that he was probably "better acquainted with the real conditions" in Mexico than anyone else in the United States government. With uncharacteristic modesty, Fall told President Wilson that because of his business activities and systematic reading, "I am somewhat better informed upon Mexican matters than are many other members of Congress." Indeed, his library contained "every history of Mexico, even including the old original Spanish works." His Senate colleagues quickly acknowledged him as the in-house authority on Mexican matters, and his strident views on the protracted controversy with Mexico brought him more public attention than any other issue until the Teapot Dome scandal. Even though the domestic battle over conservation alone might seem to explain Teapot Dome, Fall's involvement in the oil scandal began years before with his consuming attachment to American business objectives below the Rio Grande.

What Albert Fall really wanted in Mexico throughout his Senate tenure, despite his public statements, was military intervention by the United States. As early as August 1913 he confided to his former law partner W. A. Hawkins:

> You and I know that force is necessary in Mexico. Whenever I suggested it, I have been abused as a jingo wanting to bring on war, while my purpose has been to avoid just such condition as I believe will be brought about in a very short time. I have lost hope of doing anything, however, to assist in any other solution of the difficulty than an invasion of Mexico by force.

Fall's considered opinion changed slightly thereafter, in the means but not the ends, to accommodate shifting circumstances south of the border. Publicly he sometimes sugarcoated the issue by reiterating his opposition to outright war, which would be unnecessary anyway, he often added, because the Mexican people would welcome American troops to restore order in their unhappy land. With Cuba under the Platt

Amendment after the Spanish-American War as a model, he on occasion called for the United States to establish a protectorate over Mexico, or at least over such strategic parts as its northern states. In this context he might advocate interposition instead of intervention. Upon the invitation of the Mexican people and with their cooperation, as he explained this first concept, United States land and naval forces would be interposed to restore peace and order, withdrawing as soon as a functioning constitutional government went into operation.

The most noticeable shift in Fall's Mexican strategy came at the time of World War I. As the conflict approached, he invoked the Monroe Doctrine, warning that America faced the real possibility of fighting "a foreign war" in Mexico against Imperial Germany and also Japan, with precious oil and the Panama Canal at stake. He remained surprisingly quiet in public about Mexico after the United States entered the hostilities, saying later that he did not want to embarrass the Wilson administration in its handling of the European war. Following the armistice, "indirect" intervention increasingly became one of his favorite tactics. By revoking and withholding diplomatic recognition, and applying pressure internationally, Fall maintained, the United States could discredit the Mexican regime and encourage certain revolutionary elements within that country to stage a rebellion. The new government would not receive recognition until it guaranteed by treaty the security of American lives and property.

Twice the United States tilted toward full-scale military intervention, but each time drew back after a limited foray. In 1914 the United States Navy, following an affront by local Mexican officials at Tampico, bombarded and temporarily occupied the port of Vera Cruz. Then for several months in 1916 General John J. Pershing led a 10,000-man punitive expedition, consisting of cavalry, armored vehicles, and airplanes, deep into northern Mexico in futile pursuit of revolutionary warlord Francisco ("Pancho") Villa, whose troops had sacked the border town of Columbus, New Mexico, killing seventeen Americans. Neither of these abortive ventures met Fall's specifications for major surgical action. In the wake of the Tampico incident President Wilson stressed the necessity of avoiding outright war with Mexico. Reacting to outcries of rage from his constituents along the Rio Grande, Fall exclaimed emotionally in the Senate, "My God, . . . if war is horrible, what is the appearance of this kind of peace?" After Villa's raid on Columbus, in Fall's own state, the senator advocated full-scale intervention and introduced an unsuccessful resolution authorizing the recruitment of a 500,000-man army to perform the task.

Several other senators as well as prominent government officials, including at times Secretary of State Robert Lansing, supported military intervention in Mexico, but none of them with Fall's enduring intensity. Some of these national figures believed that the principles of the Mexican Revolution, although admirable, had been ignored by the selfish squabbling warlords. Albert Fall suffered no such illusions. Although always expressing friendship for the Mexican people themselves, he regarded both the revolution and its leaders as illicit, unmitigated abominations. For him the only solution, which would require supervision by the United States, was the resurrection of the Porfirio Díaz era with its dependable security for life and property and its welcome mat at the door for foreign investors. His efforts were directed to that end, but the steadfast opposition of two successive American presidents, one a Republican, Taft, and the other a Democrat, Wilson, stymied Fall's hopes to restore the Porfirian system.

Beginning with his first Senate speech on the Mexican situation in July 1912, Fall lambasted Republican President Taft as harshly as he later criticized Democratic President Wilson. Taft's cowardly approach amounted to "absolute apathy," the senator declared, and lacked the steel-willed resolve required to safeguard America's vital interests "in the so-called Republic of Mexico." The solution was simple: Fall called for an ultimatum telling the regime of Francisco I. Madero that the "killing and destruction of property must cease in Mexico" within a prescribed time. Although denying any desire for all-out armed intervention or war, he admitted, nevertheless, that he would favor sending an army of 200,000 men if it became "necessary to protect one American citizen in Mexico or anywhere else." Furious about Fall's charges, President Taft rejected this warlike strategy, but later conferred with the New Mexican on conditions along the border, especially the difficulties faced by Americans who owned mining property in Chihuahua.

Fall's appointment in August 1912 to a special Senate subcommittee to investigate American corporate influence in the Mexican Revolution indicated his rising prominence as an expert on the subject. Although not a member of the parent Foreign Relations Committee, he was added to the subcommittee by the Senate's unanimous consent, an unusual step, and became its most relentless investigator. He and the panel chairman, Senator William Alden Smith of Michigan, conducted the hearings held outside of Washington—in beleaguered El Paso, where Fall was welcomed like a conquering hero, and in Los Angeles, San Diego, New Orleans, and other places near the border.

In the beginning Fall, because of his involvement in Mexican mining, was highly suspicious of the American oil companies and their role in overthrowing his cherished Díaz regime. He made his own personal investigation of allegations that corporations based in the United States, principally Standard Oil of New Jersey and its subsidiary in Mexico, the Waters-Pierce Oil Company, had financed the Madero rebellion. His sources of information, he boasted in the Senate, far excelled those of the State Department, but he "would not dare to name" them publicly. Finally satisfying himself, he cleared the American businessmen of guilt—and apparently he was right. The corporations, declared Fall, "did nothing more than to protect and promote their interests in a legitimate way, and . . . should be exculpated of the charge that they incited or promoted the revolution against the Díaz government."

Just as the subcommittee proceedings were ending, General Victoriano Huerta toppled the Madero presidency, leaving the investigation in limbo and blunting its effects. Fall's conclusions on revolutionary finances, however, stirred great excitement in Mexico, where accusations arose that an unnamed United

States senator with large Mexican investments, obviously Fall, had supposedly sent a $200,000 check and arranged for a dynamite shipment to a rebel leader in Chihuahua. In a newspaper refutation, Fall admitted his mining interests but stressed his deep concern over the pillaging and savagery in Mexico, saying philosophically, "A man may have a heart, . . . though he possesses a silver or even a gold mine." Similarly sensational charges continued to make the headlines throughout his political career, causing him to issue repeated explanations of his Mexican financial holdings and denials of his complicity in various revolutionary activities.

For the first year of the Wilson administration Fall refrained from open criticism of the new president's Mexican policy and instead concentrated his wrath on the inept Huerta regime, which he considered incapable of bringing law and order to Mexico. He had no sympathy with Wilson's moralistic "watchful waiting," but did approve of continuing Taft's nonrecognition stance for the Huerta government, thinking it would expedite United States intervention. Gradually Fall decided that the president's vacillation was no better than Taft's "weak, imbecilic, and pusillanimous" diplomacy. In fact, the Democrats had only "'fiddled while Mexico burned.'" In March 1914, just before the Tampico crisis and with more reports of civilian bloodshed along the border, Fall opened a barrage of criticism on Wilson's Mexican program that would continue intermittently for the next seven years. His bid for a major role in determining foreign policy increased significantly when he joined forces with his political idol, Theodore Roosevelt, who was making a comeback as a Republican power after a dalliance with the Progressive party in 1912.

On the face of it, the Roosevelt-Fall alliance seemed the most unlikely combination imaginable, unless one considered the Rough Rider's hopes for regaining the presidency in 1916. Sensing the decline of fervor for domestic reform, Roosevelt focused his strategy on the two most important foreign policy issues of the day, the European war and the Mexican turmoil. Despite glaring differences on domestic programs, particularly conservation, Roosevelt needed Fall and his expertise on Mexico almost as much as Fall needed Roosevelt for his influence in shaping public opinion. The senator was the kind of decisive, rugged "outdoor man" with colorful frontier exploits that appealed to Roosevelt. But so far their attraction for each other had been one-sided, based on Fall's admiration for the Rough Rider colonel. Now their association became a genuine working friendship. "It was a strange friendship indeed for the crusader of 1912," biographer George E. Mowry has written, "but . . . Roosevelt was setting out on strange paths." To Fall, who would accompany the colonel on those paths to the bitter end, their relationship was a natural consequence of his relentless efforts to become a vital force on the national scene. Fall was not by disposition a follower, but the legendary hero of San Juan Hill happened to be among the few men he would gladly accept as a commander.

Senate Republican kingpin Henry Cabot Lodge, who had already teamed up with Fall on the Mexican issue, actually launched the Roosevelt-Fall alliance. In December 1914 Lodge suggested to his longtime friend Roosevelt that the colonel should write an article about the outrages against American women and children in Mexico. He also sent the Rough Rider one of Fall's Senate speeches describing the grisly details. Not surprisingly, Roosevelt was already a harsh critic of Wilson's Mexican policy, which he believed betrayed "the interest and honor of America." By the time the colonel's account, based largely on Fall's speech, appeared in the March 1915 *Metropolitan Magazine*, their political alliance had taken shape. In the article, entitled "The Sound of Laughter and of Playing Children Has Been Stilled in Mexico," Roosevelt quoted liberally from Fall's Senate comments on the brutal killing of Americans, adding that "every American citizen" should read the speech. Although poles apart on progressive domestic reform, Fall and Roosevelt were kindred spirits on Big Stick diplomacy for Latin America.

In January 1916, at the request of several Republican senators, Fall introduced a Senate resolution, which received unanimous approval, asking the Wilson administration a series of probing questions about the Mexican situation. The Senate Republican leadership intended for Fall's questions to open a general assault on Wilson's foreign policy for the 1916 election, but Pancho Villa's border raids and the Pershing expedition put this strategy on hold—except for Roosevelt and Fall. They wanted to unleash a massive offensive against President Wilson and Mexico as well. Fall became extremely "worked up," as he wrote his wife, over Villa's attack on Columbus. Immediately after the raid he called for the creation of a 500,000-man army to occupy Mexico and protect American lives and property, open the major rail lines, and restore a constitutional government. Earlier he had advocated a similar force, not to annex Mexico, he emphasized, but to keep it "in a peaceful condition as a buffer state between this country and the Latin American Republics to the south of it." Then, on the heels of General Pershing's troops and with Roosevelt cheering him on, Senator Fall hurried to the embattled southwestern border, where he became a roving minister plenipotentiary. His objective was to goad the Wilson administration into expanded intervention. The Pershing expedition, he correctly predicted, would only "make a mess of things" by concentrating American wrath on just one of the several revolutionary troublemakers, and thus would draw the resentment of the Mexican people.

With his customary rambunctious energy Fall conducted a quick nine-hundred-mile round-trip inspection by automobile of border trouble spots between El Paso, Texas, and Nogales, Arizona. In El Paso he said of the Pershing incursion, "[I]f we don't do it right this time we will have to later," hinting darkly that the United States might have to safeguard the Monroe Doctrine by fighting a victorious German army in Mexico if the European war ended badly. From Douglas, Arizona, Fall sent to Washington the panic-stricken plea he had received from a local resident: "Help us, if you can, before it is too late." The telegram was read before the Senate, setting off a prearranged partisan debate on the Mexican situation. Although a siege mentality prevailed along the border, Fall informed a Senate colleague, he did not anticipate an attack on El Paso, except possibly by Villa in the "Indian fashion" employed for the Columbus raid. Fall assured his colleague that he was "in constant communication" with American informants in both countries and with Mexicans of the different factions, including some of President Venustiano Carranza's "paid spies" inside the United States.

Fall's frequent reports to Republican senators back in Washington and his provocative statements to the press, often disparaging Wilson's limited intervention, drew a quick response from the president. "[S]inister and unscrupulous influences" along the southwestern border, Wilson declared, were conducting a "traffic in falsehood" for the benefit of certain American businessmen with large property holdings in Mexico. The president clearly implied that an interventionist plot existed, with Fall deeply involved in it, to stir up a war between the two countries. From El Paso an angry Fall demanded to know the names of the alleged conspirators, saying that his careful investigation had not discovered "any capitalistic influences" with plans "to poison the public mind regarding affairs in Mexico." The president himself must accept the blame for the present chaotic conditions, Fall insisted, because Wilson had recognized the Carranza regime, a hopelessly corrupt dictatorship that had failed to restore order and even now wanted the Pershing expedition to withdraw. If the administration pulled out the American troops without capturing Villa, Fall promised to "open up a bombardment in the Senate which will make the past revolutions in Mexico look like a sane Fourth of July celebration." In actuality few businessmen wanted outright war, and Carranza had obviously obstructed American military objectives, but Wilson chose to doubt whether Fall "even tries" to tell the truth about Mexican conditions.

After returning to Washington in mid-April 1916, Senator Fall grew strangely silent about United States–Mexican relations, which teetered dangerously near war. Wilson's accusation that sinister interests wanted open hostilities had stung Fall badly. He decided to back off and "give the administration as much rope as it wanted"—to hang itself. It was the quiet before the storm. On June 2, with the presidential nominating conventions drawing close, he began an unprecedented barrage in the Senate against Wilson's Mexican policy, particularly recognition of the Carranza government. Reminiscent of a range-war showdown, Fall assumed his favorite role and attacked the president like a lawyer arguing in court. His uncharacteristically well-prepared Senate speech, as the *New York Times* observed, was crafted as a Republican "campaign document" for the fall election.

Fall had already started consulting on campaign strategy with Senator Lodge and other Republican leaders, as well as with Roosevelt, the erstwhile Bull Moose dissident. His own carefully laid plan called for making the Mexican situation the paramount national issue and, on that basis, electing a Republican president wholeheartedly committed to the protection of American lives and property in Mexico. A realist above all else, Fall knew the odds against Roosevelt's selection as the Republican nominee, but he also knew the Rough Rider colonel would get the job done in Mexico if elected. Even if Roosevelt failed to receive the nomination, Fall believed, no other Republican could do so without the Rough Rider's blessing. Of no small importance was Fall's strong, longstanding sentimental attachment to the colonel. For his part the Rough Rider owed thanks to Fall for helping him blend his main foreign policy concern, military preparedness and the European war, with the Mexican issue for his White House bid.

Already in accord on Mexican matters, Fall and Roosevelt easily reached agreement on potential presidential candidates. On the Rough Rider's advice, Fall conferred with Senator Lodge about campaign tactics, emphasizing his intention to castigate Taft as well as Wilson for the Mexican fiasco. Lodge approved "without hesitation," and, according to Fall, the two senators decided that "no man connected with the Taft administration" should receive the Republican nomination. Roosevelt, who, for reasons of his own, had no love for the Taft crowd, cheerfully endorsed the Fall-Lodge pact by declaring it "completely conclusive" and one with which he could "absolutely agree." The second objective of the attack, of course, was the defeat of Wilson and the election of an interventionist Republican president, most logically Roosevelt.

As one benefit of this close association, Fall had the satisfaction of revealing to certain New Mexico Rough Riders, who had always galled him by glorying in their political connection with Roosevelt, the revered colonel's intimate thoughts on the most weighty national issues. Because of Fall's own reputation, however, letters from all over the country assured him that he was "the only man in official life" who understood the muddle in Mexico and knew what to do about it. "I am one of the best advertised men today in the United States," he confided to an old friend, "on account of the increasing importance of the Mexican question." He toyed briefly with the idea of getting New Mexico Republicans to instruct their convention delegation for him so that he could make a bid for the vice-presidential nomination. Ironically, with the usual factionalism at work, Fall's supporters had to beat back an attempt, based on the pretext of excluding all current officeholders, to deny his selection even as a delegate.

Pressing his campaign to force the Mexican question to the forefront, Senator Fall gave several stinging speeches in cities such as Boston, New York, and Grand Rapids. He continued to consult with Roosevelt on Mexico and the presidential race, as well as other topics, including the stalled Colombian treaty, which they both opposed. By early June 1916 it became apparent that the colonel would receive only the nomination of the battered Progressive party, which was scheduled to convene in Chicago simultaneously with the Republicans. But the Rough Rider still wanted his moment of glory in the Republican convention. This gave Fall, after only four years in the Senate, his greatest opportunity yet to capture the national spotlight.

The Republican platform of 1916 stressed foreign policy. As a member of the Resolutions Committee, Fall wrote the Monroe Doctrine plank, but the crucial statement on Mexico—exceeded in length only by the tariff plank—was a disappointment to him. His handwritten notes on hotel stationary indicate that he had an early role in formulating this declaration, but the final version, although it pledged a Republican president to "aid in restoring order and maintaining peace in Mexico" and to provide "adequate and absolute protection" for Americans and their property, fell short of promising outright intervention. Other members of the Resolutions Committee apparently insisted on toning down Fall's original draft to make the Mexican plank sound less warlike.

On the whole the convention was a dull affair with listless delegates. Senator Warren G. Harding, who became permanent chairman, delivered a platitudinous keynote address that made even his most ardent admirers wince. Only Fall's nomination speech for Roosevelt, made "at the Colonel's direct request," brought down the house. Fall assured the convention that only "one colossal figure of American manhood" could fulfill the vague Mexican plank with, he implied, its unstated threats of open-ended action. When he called Roosevelt's name, the audience in the galleries burst into shrill cheers and shouts of "Teddy! Teddy!" as some of the delegates below hissed "Throw him out!" The demonstration lasted thirty-six minutes, longer than that for any other nominee. It was good theater but of no effect. Charles Evans Hughes won the nomination with little difficulty. Roosevelt declined the Progressive party's candidacy and announced his support for Hughes. As the disappointed Rough Rider wrote his sister, "Well, the country wasn't in a heroic mood!"

Fall had taken a calculated risk that could have sidetracked his crusade on the Mexican issue. His alignment with Roosevelt, and especially the nomination speech, vexed many Republican power brokers, as later events would reveal. Other party chieftains, however, sensitive to charges of bossism in the convention, realized the necessity of allowing the colonel to show his strength. These leaders credited Fall with helping bring Roosevelt back into the fold and reuniting the party. More than any other single act, Fall's nomination speech for Roosevelt, who embodied the Bull Moose revolt, also mistakenly identified the New Mexican as a Progressive in the eyes of otherwise perceptive observers such as Harding's presidential booster, Harry Daugherty.

Beyond partisan concerns and the Mexican issue, Fall liked and admired Theodore Roosevelt. The nomination speech was the Albert Fall of Dona Ana County battles standing up for an ally even in a losing fight. One of his most-prized possessions, which he frequently quoted during the Teapot Dome infamy, was the letter of appreciation Roosevelt sent him after the convention. Thanking Fall for the speech and his "gallant fight on behalf of Americanism and humanity, and the performance of international duty," the Rough Rider concluded: "You have been the kind of public servant of whom all Americans should feel proud. I congratulate the whole country that you are in the United States Senate." After Roosevelt's death in 1919 the colonel's family remained "very fond" of Fall. The New Mexican had not been among the patriarch's inside circle of friends, family members knew, but he had gladly made the nomination speech in 1916 when most other prominent Republicans still shunned the colonel like the plague.

At first neither Roosevelt nor Fall had much enthusiasm for Hughes, the "bearded iceberg," but both gradually warmed up to him, mainly because they desperately wanted to defeat Woodrow Wilson. In the midst of another war scare Senator Fall was conducting a hot, dusty inspection tour by automobile of border military camps at El Paso and in New Mexico and Arizona when he received a request from Hughes for a conference in New York City. In late July the two men talked for forty-five minutes at the Hotel Astor. The Republican candidate was well posted on Mexican affairs, Fall reported, and eager to obtain additional pertinent information. Hughes said that his views on intervention would soon be "as well understood and fully as strong" as those of Roosevelt. Moreover, Hughes agreed with Fall's position "perfectly," although he would not at first take "too strong or radical a stand" on Mexico for fear of giving the campaign a "war-like flavor." Complying with the candidate's wishes, Fall remained in New York five days to consult with officials of the Republican National Committee.

He spent two hours sharing his ideas with the party chairman, William R. Willcox. Later, when Hughes made his speech formally accepting the nomination, he emphasized Mexican affairs as both Roosevelt and Fall had advised him to do. Thus, from the beginning, the 1916 Republican campaign gave special attention to the Mexican issue. Nothing could have pleased Fall more.

Even though Fall's favorite had lost the nomination, the senator changed horses easily because of the Mexican question's compelling importance and his indelible imprint on it. Moreover, in his talks with Hughes and Willcox he had won tacit approval for his proposal to organize a separate Mexican bureau that would operate an "educational as well as publicity" program alongside the main Republican campaign. In early September, while in New Mexico, Fall received the discouraging news that national chairman Willcox had shut down the Mexican bureau's fund-raising activities. No satisfactory reason was ever given. Fall's angry protests went unheeded and the nascent agency collapsed. Willcox was widely regarded as an inept national chairman or, according to Fall, "too nervous a man for this job, and rather too anxious to assume all authority to himself personally." It would be more accurate to say that, for a struggling Republican chairman who yearned to reunite his party, the independent Mexican bureau headed by a Roosevelt loyalist, and with its own budget, smacked too much of Bull Moose dissent. Fall's identification with Roosevelt and the nomination speech had returned to haunt him.

Disheartened and feeling his time had been "wasted so far," as he told his wife, Fall still had not the "remotest doubt" about Hughes's election. Primarily using his Senate office staff, he retrenched and started his own scaled-down Mexican bureau. He worked diligently for a Republican victory, paying his own expenses, although he was "worse than broke" and constantly scraping for money to prepare campaign material and employ private investigators. "I hope that the result of the election," he wrote Colonel Bill Greene's widow, "will be such that those having property in Mexico can see some relief in the near future." He conferred with Hughes again on the Mexican question and other issues, reporting afterwards that all his talks with the candidate were "of the most pleasant character."

Meanwhile Fall attempted to mend his political fences back home. He wanted the New Mexico Progressives, beginning with *Santa Fe New Mexican* publisher Bronson Cutting, to follow Roosevelt's example by rejoining the Republican party. To help entice Cutting back into the fold, Fall got Roosevelt to make a personal appeal for the publisher's support, especially in backing Holm O. Bursum, Fall's choice for gubernatorial nominee. The Rough Rider began by praising Fall as the one man—"with the possible exception of" Senator Miles Poindexter of Washington State (the sole bona fide Progressive party senator)—"with whom I have been able most cordially to co-operate among all of the people at Washington. He has done capital work in this Mexican business." This stratagem failed to work: Cutting soon informed Roosevelt that the Progressives were endorsing the New Mexico Democratic candidates but would support Hughes.

Fall had more luck purging the state party than uniting it, particularly in the case of Tom Catron, his senatorial colleague. Besides Catron's ineffectiveness in the Senate, their factional differences were intolerable. Most recently, at the Chicago convention, Catron's "action in opposing me in every way possible . . . , when I considered that New Mexico had been honored by my selection to make the nominating speech for Roosevelt," Fall wrote W. A. Hawkins, "left such a bitter taste in my mouth that although I have . . . forgiven Catron for worse things, I shall have nothing to do with him in the future." At the state convention in August he evened old and new scores with Catron by blocking the old boss's Senate renomination and placing his own candidate on the ticket.

During the national campaign, Fall met with Roosevelt at least three times and also sent him material on Mexico for campaign speeches, calling the colonel "the only man who can get it before the people." With some difficulty Fall and other concerned westerners persuaded Roosevelt to make a speaking tour in the West, which included two days of whistle-stop speeches in New Mexico. Fall joined the entourage at Albuquerque, where the colonel addressed a large crowd from the steps of the Alvarado Hotel, which adjoined the Santa Fe Railroad depot. Earlier Bronson Cutting, who accompanied Roosevelt across the state by train, had convinced him not to announce any position on New Mexico candidates. When Roosevelt later recanted, wiring the state chairman that every reputable man "who valued the honor and safety of the United States" should vote the straight Republican ticket, Cutting criticized the colonel's support of a corrupt state machine. In a post mortem Cutting also blamed the Rough Rider for implicating Hughes with the unsavory gang, and thus bringing Wilson's victory in New Mexico.

For a month preceding the election Fall made numerous hard-hitting speeches under the auspices of the national Republican organization, primarily in large western and midwestern cities. His highly publicized opening assault on the Wilson administration in New York City, entitled "The Truth about Mexico," set the tone for his later talks. The Republican National Committee distributed four thousand printed copies of it to newspapers, and Fall's office sent out several hundred more to individuals and organizations. These remarks at the Commonwealth Auditorium, based largely on previously unpublished documents, challenged the president to stop stalling and tell the American people the truth about conditions in Mexico. He concluded by referring to a list of 285 Americans killed in Mexico and along the border, adding that a complete tabulation would have the names of at least 500 dead Americans. Charles Evans Hughes, often sounding much like Albert Fall, also hammered the administration, concentrating on Mexican policy and Democratic bungling generally. And Roosevelt barnstormed the East and West, preaching military preparedness and American honor in the European war and Mexico.

It almost worked, but Wilson was narrowly reelected and Congress remained in Democratic hands by a slim margin. Moreover, Hughes lost in New Mexico, and the Democrats, with

Progressive support, captured most of the state offices, defeating Fall's candidates for governor and senator. In a nutshell, according to Fall, the bellicose Mexican issue collapsed for the Republicans nationally because of its unfavorable contrast with the appealing Democratic campaign slogan focused on Europe, "He kept us out of war," which decided the election. Without a Republican president sympathetic to intervention, a dejected and weary Fall had to reformulate his strategy and wait for—or create—a favorable turn of events.

Never one to sit back and wait, Senator Fall soon became entangled in an ill-advised, and potentially dangerous, personal diplomatic overture to Pancho Villa, whom he had recently called a ruthless murderer for staging the Columbus raid. Now, with the pending withdrawal of the hapless Pershing expedition, Villa emerged as the dominant figure in Chihuahua, Mexico's largest state. In January 1917, while in El Paso on business, Fall learned from a local doctor that an old friend and experienced hand in Mexico, Charles F. Hunt, lay seriously ill in the hospital and wanted to see the senator "for old times sake." At the hospital, according to Fall, Hunt offered to write a letter to Villa proposing a meeting with the senator. Villa reportedly sought such a conference, which also might involve several other prominent Americans, to bolster his cause in the United States. For his part Villa would have to disavow any actual participation in the Columbus attack and promise to protect American citizens and their property if he gained control of Chihuahua. Fall told Hunt that he had no objections to a discussion with Villa somewhere along the international line, and there the matter rested.

The trouble began when Hunt's letter to Villa fell into the hands of a special United States consular agent on the border, who, according to Fall, had long sought "something which would shut my mouth" and end his criticism of the Wilson administration. Indeed, the senator complained, the Secret Service constantly "hounded" him in the East and on trips to the Southwest, trying to uncover incriminating evidence of graft or "some nefarious scheme" involving him with "one or another faction in Mexico." The revelation of Hunt's letter was especially painful because of Fall's recent appointment to the Senate Foreign Relations Committee. To make matters worse, Mexican intelligence agents soon learned of the contents, and American newspapers publicized the letter as a blatant proposal for new revolutionary activity against the Carranza government, and perhaps for the creation of a separate republic in northern Mexico.

Fall denied any direct responsibility for the letter in statements to the press and by writing an explanation to Secretary of State Robert Lansing. Since his condemnation of Villa's tactics was so well known, the senator said, he had "no apologies to make," but would not hesitate to talk with the rebel leader or representatives of any Mexican faction, as he had often done, if they promised to respect American rights. Invariably, when speaking in his Washington office to agents of the various groups, he had told them frankly that no faction could possibly restore law and order "without the support not only financial, but forcible and diplomatic, of some outside power or influence." As for the Hunt letter, he attributed his friend's clumsy overture to an unstable physical and mental condition resulting from two paralytic strokes. Hunt, on the other hand, steadfastly asserted that Fall asked him to write the letter to Villa. Regardless, Fall's willingness to deal with Villa, through personal diplomacy or any other way, revealed his obsession as well as his frustration with the interminable Mexican problem. World events would soon distract him from this quest, but only temporarily.

CHAPTER 5

Mexico Still Beckons

AS American participation in World War I became more certain, Senator Fall's attention shifted noticeably to European affairs. He never turned his back on Mexico, yet for two years he muted his public criticism of Wilson's Mexican policy, though not of the president's leadership otherwise, and he earnestly supported the war effort. Indeed, he welcomed hostilities. In February 1917, two months before the American entry, Fall wrote a constituent that the United States probably could not stay out and that active involvement might be the best cure for widespread apathy and the people's dependence on government to solve all of their problems. Unlike those political leaders befuddled by ideological slogans and distant submarine warfare, he believed that the United States should fight Germany for its own national interest. Fall told a family member that for years he had thought that two countries, Germany and Japan, posed the greatest threat to the United States. Germany looked with envy at Latin America for colonies that would provide the natural resources required by an industrial nation and for homes for its excess population. If the kaiser won the present conflict, Fall said, the United States would inevitably collide with Germany in Mexico or South America, "and *then* we must fight her or give up the Monroe Doctrine—and all prestige on this hemisphere." If the Germans took France, he predicted in the Senate, Mexico would be next, and then Chicago, cutting "your great United States in two without the necessity of bombarding one of your Atlantic or western ports."

President Wilson's revelation of the intercepted Zimmermann telegram, in which Germany offered Mexico an alliance and the "lost territory" of Texas, New Mexico, and Arizona, only confirmed Fall's suspicions. When Democratic senators questioned Wilson's motives in the disclosure, Fall uncharacteristically defended the president, saying, "You accuse your own President of the veriest trickery and of practices to which no man of any sense of honor would resort." Likewise, he spoke for three hours favoring Wilson's proposal to arm American merchant ships. Once war came, he admonished his Senate colleagues to lay partisanship aside and join him in rallying round their commander in chief. Even so, he privately deplored the chain of circumstances bringing the country into the conflict, observing that Wilson had first sent a "strictly responsible" warning to Mexico almost identical to the later "strict accountability" message to Germany about the violation of American rights. If the president had enforced the earlier Mexican proclamation, Fall reasoned, this would have restrained the kaiser and prevented U-boat depredations such as the *Lusitania* sinking, which cost 128 American lives. In effect, he thought Wilson should have shown the same resolve with Mexico as with Germany.

Military preparedness revived Fall's association with Theodore Roosevelt after the disappointing 1916 election. Before the United States entered the war, Fall had offered to resign from the Senate and raise volunteers, something like the Texas Rangers, or mounted infantry regiments, for operations on the border. These units would consist of former sheriffs, cattlemen, and miners, who, he said, had "wiped out the various train-robbing and outlaw bands." Immediately after the declaration of war Fall once more tendered his services and then introduced an amendment to the army bill authorizing at least three cavalry regiments for protection of the border. Again he had in mind southwesterners who knew the trails, who spoke Spanish, and who were "able to take care of themselves." They would ride on tough local mounts that could forage for themselves, and "thus be entirely independent of any supplies." In an emotional appeal to the Senate he declared:

> I will guarantee that if you will give me the men I have asked for I will take 25 of them and no thousand Mexican bandits will ever massacre the people in another quiet town in New Mexico [like Columbus], because every man will sleep with his six-shooter in his hand and his rifle by his side, and when he rises he will pour from the muzzle of his gun a stream of fire which will drive back any bandit; and the bandits know it.

A separate proposal by Senator Harding, called the "Roosevelt Amendment," empowered the Rough Rider to raise a division of volunteers for his command in Europe.

Not surprisingly, in the controversy over the comparative merits of conscription and volunteers, both Roosevelt and Fall favored the volunteer forces. Moreover, Fall envisioned a rotation system of sending "practically all recruits," even the draftees, to the border for three months of field training before combat in Europe. Fall fought hard for both amendments. In a bombastic Senate speech he characterized a critical editorialist as "a moral degenerate, or at least, a political pervert," who was, "except for his absolute cowardice," a fitting "recruit for the crew of the German submarine that sank the *Lusitania*, [sending] women and babies of this country to their watery grave." Although the Senate approved Fall's border troops, the final congressional measure ignored his proposal, but did authorize the president, if he chose, to muster four volunteer divisions for European duty.

After consulting his military advisers, Wilson declined to call out the Roosevelt volunteers, electing to rely on a conscripted army trained by professionals. "I told Col. Roosevelt before the Army Bill passed," Fall wrote a friend, "that in my judgment, he would not be sent to Europe under any circumstances. This is another case in which I regret having been a true prophet." Furious over his rejection, the Rough Rider groused to Fall that Wilson had "industriously discouraged the best fighting men, has backed up the wooden-heads and incompetents, and has put a premium upon cowardice and inefficiency, until he has very seriously damaged the United States Army." Earlier Fall had forwarded a Choctaw Indian chief's request to raise a battalion for the colonel's prospective division. Roosevelt replied, "If Wilson had let me organize that division I would have jumped at the chance to have [the chief] & his Indians with me." From then on, Roosevelt's hatred of Wilson knew no bounds and he could not listen even to faint praise of the president without exploding in anger.

By and large Fall, although critical of Wilson's assumption of autocratic power at the expense of Congress, as well as the ineffective conduct of the war, faithfully voted for the administration's war-related legislation, mainly because of his fierce nationalism and uncompromising patriotism. He saw the war as both a righteous crusade and an opportunity for the nation to prove its political and economic superiority. Since this historic testing required the total commitment of every citizen, and "every sacrifice must be made, every material resource must be used" in the war's prosecution, opposition or unpatriotic views could not be tolerated. Disloyalty must be punished by draconian means. Speaking for the Espionage Act of 1917, which cracked down on dissent such as obstruction of the draft, he declared, "All rules of law are set aside in the face of national necessity, of self-preservation."

In the Senate debates preceding approval of the Sedition Act of 1918, which imposed even harsher controls on freedom of expression, Fall vented his wrath on the "Mexican bandit character" as well as the Bolshevik. "The majority of those now preaching resistance to such a law," he fumed, "should be set against the wall and shot; and with a few examples made, we should need to pass very little more legislation of this character." But he saved special scorn for the Industrial Workers of the World, accusing the left-wing American labor organization of inciting revolution in Mexico and treason at home. About the IWWs, Fall railed in the Senate:

> Why, I have heard it said here that it is better that a hundred guilty men should escape than that one innocent man should be convicted. I say to you that if it is necessary to save this country it is better that 10 innocent men should sacrifice their blood than that the country itself should not be saved.

> That is harsh doctrine, but war is harsh. You can not play with conditions as they exist now with silk gloves.

The *Nation* called the Sedition Act more extreme "than any similar legislation in force abroad—even in Prussia." For Fall the measure did not go far enough, although he voted for it. He would have added a loyalty oath for all federal employees and, in accord with Roosevelt, a ban on the mailing of printed material in German and all other foreign languages "unless accompanied by a translation."

Fall believed that the war demanded great sacrifices even from United States senators. In June 1918 he proposed to change the draft age range, then twenty-one to thirty-one, to eighteen and forty-five. His amendment drew considerable attention but failed by a 25–49 vote in the Senate, although Congress later adopted those age limits. He also tried unsuccessfully to mobilize every able-bodied man forty-five to sixty, giving the president authority to call up members of any occupation for combat or other war-related service. This last part caused Senator Boies Penrose, the powerful Pennsylvania Republican boss, to ask if the president could "tell a Senator or a Representative that he must abandon his office to which the people have elected him and pursue some other occupation?" Then almost fifty-seven, Fall replied emphatically, "I think if, in the opinion of the Commander in Chief, I can better serve the country in the trenches than in the Senate, it is my duty to go where he commands me."

By mid-July 1918, with victory in sight and the autumn elections approaching, the president's detractors in Congress had changed their attack from criticizing Wilson's conduct of the war to belittling his idealistic peace program. Previously Wilson had clarified his objectives by announcing the Fourteen Points, which included a "general association of nations" as an international peacekeeping organization. These circumstances greatly enhanced the importance of the upcoming election, particularly the choosing of senators who would help decide the ratification of a peace treaty. One of those senators facing reelection in November was Albert Fall. And he made no secret of his opposition to the softheaded peace without victory proposed by the idealistic president, who "came to the White House from a boys' school [Princeton University] via a State Governorship."

Bone-tired of public life, Fall had decided to leave the Senate when his term ended. While politicians often say they want to retire, he meant it. Soon after the war began, he had declared in a speech, "I say to you frankly and openly, Senators, the end of my present term will witness my withdrawal from public life, and I am speaking to you with all solemnity." When questioned by a trusted adviser about this statement, Fall said that the very thought of "being compelled" to remain in the Senate another six years was "absolutely abhorrent" to him, and that he could not bring himself even to consider it. His difficulty in getting favorable action on natural-resource measures and the Mexican question, he grumbled to another New Mexican, was "very wearing upon one who has been accustomed to dealing with business men in a business way and achieving results." Besides, he was greatly distressed by the sad state of his personal finances. "I have lost very much more money than I was able to lose, by neglecting my own personal business with necessary absence from New Mexico," he wrote an old friend. Then, in what would become a pervasive theme in his correspondence, he added, "I must endeavor to make up such loss as soon as I possibly can in justice to my family."

Fall also longed to return to his New Mexico ranch and fulfill his plans for developing it. Pessimistic about national conditions and "weary with work" in Washington, he wrote a daughter during the war, "I would give any thing in the world to be at Three Rivers." For a couple of years he had discussed with his partner and son-in-law, Mahlon T. Everhart, a division of their joint ranching interests so that Fall would know exactly where he stood financially and could "map out my own future" before leaving the Senate. They had invested large amounts of money in the extensive holdings, incurring heavy indebtedness, without so far realizing an appreciable profit. Regardless of any separation of their affairs, he told Everhart, investments around Three Rivers would be Fall's only source of income for his old age. "I do not expect to get anything whatsoever out of Mexico in the future," he said, "and I am a little old to start in to practice law [or enter] active business of any kind again." The choice for him was simple: "I must either get out of the Senate and devote my time to my personal affairs, or else devote all my attention to matters here [in Washington]." Fall left no doubt what he intended to do.

In a decision he regretted the rest of his life, Albert Fall relented and ran for reelection. Why Fall did so, when he seemed determined to leave public office, revealed a great deal about the man himself and later events in the Teapot Dome episode. First, there was the volatile situation back home in which the New Mexico Republican party, besides the old guard–Progressive split, remained divided geographically into a northern camp, where Tom Catron was still a force, and the southern stronghold of Fall and his allies. If Fall bowed out, his old adversary Catron might battle back into power and claim the vacated senatorial nomination. The resulting internecine fight could throw the state into the Democratic column for years to come. Such grim prospects, especially the possibility of Catron's resurrection, greatly influenced Fall's decision. Fall had purged Catron in 1916, and he meant for the old boss to stay purged. National concerns had even more weight in causing Senator Fall to change his mind. Begging him to reconsider, some of his oldest friends struck a responsive chord in Fall when they stressed patriotic duty in wartime, equating the obligation to serve another Senate term with his eagerness to emulate Teddy Roosevelt in volunteering for military service. These pleas made a deep impression on Fall, for whom flag-waving was much more than a jingoistic pastime.

The new Republican national chairman, Will H. Hays, used another argument in his urgent appeal to the reluctant candidate. After a visit to the Southwest in the spring of 1918, Hays emphasized that Fall and New Mexico could become the "arbiter of National destinies" by deciding whether the Republicans gained control of the next Congress. With the Democrats possibly assured of forty-seven senators and the Republicans with as many as forty-eight in the next session, one doubtful seat in the total of ninety-six might determine the Senate leadership. In effect, Hays and other Republican power brokers concluded that Fall was "2000 votes stronger than any other Republican candidate" in the state, and "As goes New Mexico this year, so goes beyond any question of doubt, the United States senate." To clinch his case, Hays brought along some senators when he visited Fall in Washington to remind him of one more compelling consideration. No other senator had his grasp of the Mexican situation, they told Fall, and when that question was settled, as it must be sooner or later, he should be in the Senate and a member of the Foreign Relations Committee.

By early May, under "terrific pressure," Fall had modified his position by agreeing to run if the state Republican convention "should draft me into the service." In other words, he would not refuse his country's wartime call to duty if it was "thrust upon me." But he would accept the nomination only if the state and national party hierarchies did not expect him to make an exhausting campaign or to spend one dollar of his own money. In addition, and of great importance for later events, the state leaders must pledge that he could resign in two years and name his own successor. Even these exacting conditions caused no problem because, as a New Mexico confidant assured him, "the State wants you and wants you bad and you are in a position to dictate the terms upon which you will consent to become a candidate."

Fall's corporate connections paid off handsomely in the all-important matter of guaranteeing campaign funding. In Fall's second high-powered conference with Will H. Hays, this time in the Washington home of George Harvey, the influential editor of the *North American Review*, John Hays Hammond offered to cover a large portion of the expenses. Hammond, a wealthy industrialist, had invested heavily in Mexican lands now threatened by expropriation. A few days later Cleveland steel magnate Price McKinney, Fall's associate in Mexican mining, showed up in Washington and told his friend, "We don't need Hammond; we will finance [it] ourselves." Senator John W. Weeks of Massachusetts and others also wanted to help provide the necessary campaign funds. In time things went so smoothly with the captains of industry that Fall got their backing for one of his pet projects, the purchase of the *Albuquerque Morning Journal*, long the state's leading Democratic paper. Earlier that year a Republican group headed by Holm O. Bursum had bought the *Albuquerque Evening Herald*. The addition of the *Journal*'s strong voice in the state's largest city, Fall believed, would be decisive in making New Mexico "a safe Republican state." At his urging, and with W. A. Hawkins, the Phelps Dodge railroad attorney, running interference, a consortium composed principally of McKinney, Senator Weeks and his Boston associates, and the Phelps Dodge interests raised $115,000 to buy the *Journal*. After the election Fall credited the newspaper as largely responsible for the sweeping Republican victory in New Mexico.

The corporate executives' eagerness for Fall to run and their willingness to foot the sizable bill necessary for him to win, especially the *Journal* acquisition, help give an understanding of his later Teapot Dome troubles. President Calvin Coolidge, the prophet of prosperity in the 1920s, would soon proclaim, "The business of America is business." Fall already subscribed wholeheartedly to this philosophy. As a corporation man himself, he moved easily among business tycoons and had no reluctance to ask for their support in various ways, whether in campaign funding or personal financial ventures. They knew, in turn, that he would take care of their needs in Washington, not because of their favors but because at heart he was a member of their tight-knit fraternity. In the case of the *Journal*, Fall later made a deal whereby the El Paso and Southwestern Railroad, a Phelps Dodge subsidiary, acquired outright from his Three Rivers ranch the water for its locomotives in exchange for the parent company's interest of $25,000 in the newspaper and cancellation of a $20,000 mortgage held by the EP & SW. With control also of Price McKinney's share of $27,500, he had sway over the *Journal* until its sale in 1920. Fall dealt in this style with captains of industry long before his naval oil transactions with Doheny and Sinclair. From his perspective, however, the 1918 election raised the fraternity's obligation to him because these corporate friends and others "forced me into this thing" when he had wanted to retire and tend to his personal financial affairs.

Senator Fall, still disavowing any interest in becoming a candidate, stated publicly in mid-June that he would accept his party's nomination if offered it, but would not lift a finger to get it. "I have never in my life," he confided to a close friend, "been called upon to make a decision which finally caused me as much personal regret." Now Fall could not turn back, and he soon began exercising the carte blanche on campaign strategy given him by anxious state Republican leaders. Before the nominating convention he conferred with party chieftains in Santa Fe. As an important first step, Fall and his advisers warned the incumbent Republican governor, Washington E. Lindsey, that he might be replaced on the ticket by a Hispanic candidate to assure Fall's election and a Republican Senate majority. In concert with the hierarchy, Fall handpicked the other nominees as well. In the Democratic convention, which met first, a delegate recently transplanted from Mississippi heatedly refused the services of a Hispanic interpreter, saying: "I don't want to talk to any one but Americans. I can make my meaning clear to them." The Republicans quickly capitalized on this unpardonable gaffe by emphasizing the "race issue" in their convention and making a special appeal to Hispanic voters. Not surprisingly, the party nominated Fall for senator, and Hispanics for the other two most important offices, governor and congressman.

Even before he officially accepted the nomination, Fall laid the groundwork for cooperation with the New Mexico Progressives. When he appealed to Theodore Roosevelt to solicit Progressive support for him and the state Republican ticket, the colonel was "overjoyed" at the opportunity. To one former Rough Rider, Roosevelt wrote:

> Senator Fall has made a really great record in the Senate. Every decent American, every believer in truth and courage in the conduct of our public affairs would feel that his retirement from the Senate was a natural [national?] calamity. In everything relating to our international relations he has shown a singular farsightedness and breadth of vision. I cannot speak too strongly on behalf of Senator Fall.

Fall also temporarily patched up his differences with the *Santa Fe New Mexican*, the state's only Progressive daily. With Fall on the ticket and the unprecedented party unity, as well as the combined clout of the *New Mexican* and Albuquerque's *Morning Journal* and *Evening Herald*, the Republicans could enter the campaign in high spirits.

Despite Republican optimism, Fall and his New Mexico handlers were apprehensive. For one thing, they could not forget the results of the disastrous 1916 election. Moreover, Fall had never faced a statewide popular election before. In a brutally frank analysis Charles V. Safford, chief of his Senate staff, described the problems ahead. Safford said that many New Mexicans, while conceding Fall's intellect and his influence in the Senate, believed that the senator had little in common with the average person and held himself aloof. They saw him as "cold blooded" and felt his sympathies lay with the "upper ten" and his "natural instinctive affiliation" on the side of the corporations. Because of his fine house and business affairs in El Paso, many also thought he was more interested in Texas than in the state he represented. To counteract these impressions, Safford recommended some publicity projects, including illustrated human-interest articles and a promotional motion picture. Fall flatly refused to be depicted reenacting a speech or "pretending to work" at his Senate desk. "I have never believed in pictures of this kind," he exclaimed, "and I would feel like a fool posing for either." The pictorial projects were dropped. In fact, Fall envisioned a limited campaign in which he would make only four or five major speeches in key locations across the state. As it turned out, he never gave a single speech or campaigned at all.

In the United States alone, the worldwide influenza pandemic of 1918–19 killed 550,000 people, ten times more than all of the American soldiers who died in action. Called the "Spanish flu," it seemed especially virulent among the young in their twenties and thirties. In early October 1918 John ("Jack") Morgan Fall, the senator's eldest child and only son, went as a delegate to the state Republican convention in Santa Fe, where his father was renominated by acclamation. Young Fall, thirty-three years old, became ill at the convention and on the return trip by automobile he died of the flu at Carrizozo, thirty miles from Three Rivers. The senator was at his bedside. A week later Caroline Fall Everhart, the senator's twenty-eight-year-old daughter and the wife of his ranching partner, died of the malady at Alamogordo. She had become sick while with her brother at Carrizozo. Fall took her and Jack's body to Alamogordo in a private railroad car. Both of the Fall offspring left little children, and Jack's wife was six months pregnant. The senator's wife, another daughter, and four of his grandchildren were also stricken at this time, but survived. In the weeks before the election Senator Fall frantically assisted with the care of his family at Alamogordo and helped give medicine to the afflicted living on his Three Rivers ranch, where there was no doctor and several flu victims perished. Jack Fall's widow later commented: "I don't know how Judge and Mrs. Fall lived through that. It was just the saddest thing [imaginable]."

In the midst of Fall's deep sorrow President Wilson did two things that forever embittered the senator and possibly affected the fate of the postwar peace treaty. First, the president, although earlier he had proclaimed that "politics is adjourned" for the duration, issued the emphatic "October Appeal," calling on all patriotic Americans to back his forthcoming peace mission in Europe by electing a Democratic Congress. With an armistice at hand, this urgent request, which by implication questioned Republican patriotism, met with public criticism and unleashed a tidal wave of partisan recrimination. Then, three days later, in reply to a query from New Mexico about his attitude toward Fall's candidacy, Wilson stated:

> Your question whether I would be willing to depend upon Senator Fall's support in settling our foreign relations is easily answered. I would not. He has given such repeated evidence of his entire hostility to this administration that I would be ignoring his whole course of action if I did. No one who wishes to sustain me can intelligently vote for him. If that is the issue the voters of New Mexico wish to vote upon, it is easily determined.

Ironically Fall's Socialist opponent for the Senate seat, with a dubious record of war support, had made the inquiry and received the president's answer. A charitable interpretation of this colossal blunder would be that Wilson mistakenly believed that the question came from the Democratic candidate. Whatever the case, the harsh attack on Senator Fall, especially in his time of grief, caused increased indignation in Republican circles.

The Democrats capitalized on the president's remarks by featuring them in an Albuquerque newspaper as a full-page ad depicting an American flag held by a uniformed soldier and sailor. The illustration closely resembled the official logo used in Liberty Loan fund-raising drives. "Like a bolt of lightning from a cloudless New Mexico sky," the caption read, Wilson's message had come to the voters in his characteristic style, "frank, fearless, a blow from the shoulder." In a responding full-page ad, the Republicans saw it as "a blow in the back" and "a studied insult to the loyalty of a great American [Fall]."

Theodore Roosevelt immediately sprang to Fall's defense, wiring the senator, "To a peculiar degree you embody the best American spirit and I trust that every good American will join in supporting you." When Fall replied emotionally that he would rather have the colonel's telegram than the "certificate of election," the Rough Rider came back with, "You are an American after my own heart." In another wire, released to the press, Roosevelt praised the senator's unmatched "absolutely straight American" record on Mexico and the war and assailed Wilson's crass partisanship. Fall's only public statement in the campaign—a telegram to the state Republican chairman—decried the president's "cruel and partisan appeal" and, foreshadowing the trouble ahead for Wilson, pledged never to back a "Bolsheviki-German Peace."

After Wilson's attack on Fall, according to one knowledgeable state politician, "all the sympathy went with him." Yet the president's criticism, although having some influence, was probably not decisive in the New Mexico senatorial election. Fall won by 1,872 out of the 46,812 votes cast for the two principal senatorial candidates, and the Republicans claimed every statewide office except one. Nationally the Republicans gained control of both houses of Congress, with a majority of only two seats (forty-nine to forty-seven) in the Senate. The loss of one Republican senator would have meant an evenly divided membership, throwing the deciding vote into the hands of the Democratic vice president. When President Wilson sailed for Europe to forge a peace treaty after the election, he lacked the solid support he needed at home, partly because of fewer than two thousand votes for Fall in New Mexico.

The deaths of two of his children during the 1918 campaign, coupled with Wilson's blistering attack, devastated Fall and colored his reasoning. As he told a close friend, "The ambitions of my life are gone, the future holds nothing of interest to me, I am the last of the Falls." The stress of sickness and death in his family, and his own later bout with the flu, made him indifferent about returning to action in Washington. Reluctant to run for reelection in the first place, he now believed that he owed no one for the office. He had continued at great personal sacrifice against his own wishes for the benefit of others and for the party's sake. Somehow he should be compensated for it. Many of his influential friends agreed. Edward L. Doheny, when testifying why he proffered the infamous $100,000 loan, said that the death of two grown children in 1918 had made Fall "feel that he was the victim of an untoward fate." Accordingly, the oil magnate observed, "I felt in great sympathy with him."

Gradually Fall regained his interest in Senate activities, especially Mexican affairs and the World War I peace treaty. Although he lost a powerful and revered friend when Theodore Roosevelt died early in 1919, he started forging another important, and fateful, alliance with Doheny. While Fall was gaining national political prominence, Doheny had concentrated on amassing a fortune since leaving southwestern New Mexico in 1891. Financially Doheny had been as lucky as Fall was unfortunate. At first, often with his business associate of Kingston days, Charles A. Canfield, he followed the familiar pursuits of western gold and silver mining. But the two sourdoughs soon found a new kind of El Dorado in the heart of present-day Los Angeles. From his hotel, according to local legend, Doheny noticed a passing wagon loaded with tarlike chunks of *brea*, used for heating and firing boilers, and he quickly investigated the source. Neither of the partners had oil-field experience, so they applied pick-and-shovel mining techniques to dig and timber a six-by-four-foot shaft about 145 feet deep. Sensing danger from gas emissions, Doheny finished the job by worming a sixty-foot eucalyptus tree trunk down another fifteen feet until oil started flowing into the shaft. This simple excavation, which yielded about seven barrels a day, helped establish the Los Angeles field, and in turn triggered the California petroleum industry. Doheny's energetic search for new oil fields, in concert with Canfield and other partners, also launched development of the Fullerton and Bakersfield–Kern River districts. After the Santa Fe Railroad was persuaded to burn his oil instead of coal in its locomotives, he became a millionaire and one of the country's leading oilmen.

Doheny's success in California led him to even greater heights in Mexico. The Mexican Central Railway also wanted to use oil in its locomotives. With the railroad's encouragement he and Canfield moved in 1900 into the Tampico region, where they virtually initiated the commercial petroleum industry in Mexico. Their big gusher, Juan Casiano No. 7, assumed legendary status, producing over 100,000,000 barrels of oil between 1910 and 1919. The record-breaking Cerro Azul No. 4, the world's greatest gusher until then, spouted 261,000 barrels a day until closed in and piped, and thereafter it produced a total of 85,000,000 barrels. By 1921, with the Doheny companies dominant, annual Mexican oil output would stand at 195,000,000 barrels, or about half that of the United States, making Mexico the second largest producer in the world. A marketing genius, Doheny sold the Mexican surplus around the globe through his Mexican Petroleum Company (Mexican "Pete") and Pan American Petroleum and Transport Company and their subsidiaries, which included oil lands, pipelines, refineries, railroads, a fleet of steamship tankers, and other facilities. In time he ranked with such international petroleum moguls as John D. Rockefeller of Standard Oil and Sir Henri Deterding of Royal Dutch Shell, the difference being that Doheny often found the oil himself. At his death in 1935 the hard-driving, bespectacled little fellow with the kindly blue-gray eyes and drooping mustache was credited with discovering more oil personally than anyone else and amassing a fortune estimated at $100 million.

Fall and Doheny were drawn together by worsening conditions in Mexico following World War I. With his allegiance to mining Fall had earlier suspected the American oil companies, perhaps including the Doheny interests, of financing Madero's overthrow of the Díaz government. Only through his personal sleuthing during the Senate Mexican investigation of 1912 did he satisfy himself that these suspicions were unfounded. Moreover, Doheny, as a prominent Democrat who contributed heavily to the party's national campaigns and attended dinners in the Wilson White House, was hardly a natural ally for the militantly Republican Fall. Cautious about openly encouraging armed intervention, Doheny had maintained uneasy relations with the various regimes until adoption of the Mexican Constitution of 1917 with its Article 27. This article flatly proclaimed the Mexican nation's inalienable ownership of all subsoil mineral resources and implied retroactive application of these provisions. Subsequent executive decrees specified the payment of rental fees and royalties on oil lands and reregistration of these lands as recognition of government control over mineral wealth. In addition, foreign companies had to relinquish their national status and the protection of their home governments. If the firms failed to reregister, or "manifest," their holdings, they were prohibited from drilling additional wells. Mexicans and foreigners alike could then challenge, or "denounce," the titles and claim them.

Doheny and other foreign oil operators, fearing expropriation and nationalization, raised the battle cry of resistance against what they considered an illegal system. This new crisis in United States–Mexican relations, with yet another threat of military intervention, caused Fall and Doheny to cross party lines and become fast friends more than thirty years after their passing encounter at Kingston. For the next five years the uncertainties of Article 27 would bind them together in Mexican affairs.

Republican command of Congress and its powerful committees offered real hope to the two new allies of accomplishing their objectives south of the border. In February 1919, Harold Walker, Doheny's chief Washington lobbyist on Mexican matters, observed that Fall would "soon again be speaking of Mexico" and reminded the senator of a parting message from his "dead friend Roosevelt." The Rough Rider had compared Mexico as a result of President Wilson's diplomacy with the terrible conditions "'of the Balkan Peninsula under Turkey's rule,'" concluding that the United States was "'honor bound'" to rectify the situation. Recovering slowly from the traumatic effects of family tragedy and his own case of the flu, Fall did not speak on Mexico in the Senate until June 16. Then, breaking his self-imposed two-year silence on this issue, he made it clear that he had not changed his mind about the Carranza government or the necessity of intervention.

By this time both houses of Congress were giving anxious attention to recent Mexican incursions along the border. Finally, in early August, the Senate passed unanimously a resolution authorizing a Foreign Relations subcommittee to investigate the "damages and outrages" incurred by American citizens in Mexico and to recommend what action should be taken. Senator Fall, who supported the resolution wholeheartedly but did not initiate it, was the obvious choice to head the subcommittee, which became known as the "Fall Committee." At last, after the abortive probe of 1912 and the scuttled Mexican bureau of the 1916 election, he had the authority to conduct a freewheeling inquiry and, if fortune smiled, to force his solution on the Wilson administration. These prospects made all the frustrations and criticisms he had endured for the past seven years seem worth it.

Meanwhile Fall had joined Henry Cabot Lodge and other senators, mostly Republicans, in opposing President Wilson's proposed League of Nations. Fall had not been a major critic of Wilson's wartime leadership. Now he emerged as a significant player in the fight against the president's peace plan, becoming one of the "irreconcilables," that fifteen or so senators who objected to the League in any form. With William E. Borah, the "Lion of Idaho" and the Senate's most eloquent speaker, as the "soul" of the phalanx, these "bitter-enders," known also as the "Battalion of Death," dominated the Foreign Relations Committee. They berated the president and his blueprint for peace with barrages of invective and sarcasm in the Senate, through the press, and on public speaking tours. A devout irreconcilable, Fall would have taken an even more conspicuous role in killing the Treaty of Versailles if his Mexican hearings, often held away from Washington, had not diverted so much of his attention.

Bitter hatred stemming from Wilson's attack in the 1918 election fueled Fall's opposition to the treaty. Conditioned by Dona Ana County feuds, he wanted to get revenge by striking the enemy where it hurt the most. But this was not the primary reason for his hostile stance. Nor was he an isolationist. As shown repeatedly in Mexican affairs, Fall lived by a Teddy Roosevelt brand of nationalism based on the traditional "lone wolf" American foreign policy of unilateral action and no entangling alliances. Membership in the League of Nations with its reliance on collective security, he believed, would destroy this time-honored policy, particularly the Monroe Doctrine.

Breaking all precedent for the American presidency, Wilson himself attended the Versailles Conference, where he succeeded in inserting the Covenant, or constitution, of the League into the peace treaty. In mid-February 1919, immediately after this triumph, Wilson returned to the United States briefly to take care of official duties before going back to Paris for completion of the negotiations. Upon his arrival in Washington he met in the White House with the Senate and House committees on foreign policy to explain the League. Senators Fall and Borah were conspicuously absent. As for Fall, who remained in semi-seclusion at Three Rivers, he declined the president's invitation on the grounds that Wilson should present his case publicly before a joint session of Congress, not in confidence to a small group of lawmakers. The *New York Times* speculated, however, that Fall refused to meet with the president because he could not "with grace" enter the White House after Wilson's "bitter opposition" during the 1918 election.

Just before the president's return to Paris, Senator Lodge, the incoming head of the Foreign Relations Committee, unveiled a Republican "Round Robin" condemning the League in its proposed form. By telegram from New Mexico, Fall added his name to the list, which finally included thirty-nine senators, far more than the thirty-three (one-third plus one) needed to defeat a treaty. With the Treaty of Versailles still unfinished, this ultimatum demanding the separation of the League from the peace accord both undermined Wilson's credibility abroad and threw down the gauntlet for the Senate ratification battle.

In mid-March, three months before Fall made his stand in the Senate, he revealed his objections to the League in a pair of speeches in New Mexico. He delivered the first speech in solemn tones to Albuquerque businessmen and the second, a specimen of the emotional, tub-thumping oratory for which Fall was locally renowned, to a joint session of the state legislature. Still suffering the aftereffects of a "severe attack of Spanish Influenza," he made both appearances the same day against doctor's orders. Later in the Senate his criticism would be more detailed, but it remained fundamentally the same.

In Albuquerque, Fall told the business leaders that League membership would cost the United States "untold rights of sovereignty." He might accept a high court of nations, something like the United States Supreme Court, but not an international government that could send American troops to settle petty differences between Russia and Poland. A plebiscite on whether to join the League might be a good idea, he said, but even if New Mexico voters approved it, he would resign from the Senate before doing so. "If New Mexicans expect [my Senate] vote in favor of the league under its present charter, they have made a mistake in choosing their senator, that is all."

At Santa Fe that evening, in "one of the most forceful and most convincing addresses of his career," often interrupted by wild applause and cheers, Fall presented a hour-long "careful and masterly analysis" to the legislature and an audience of five hundred in the packed state capitol galleries. In good voice despite his recent illness, and speaking rapidly "even with the interpreter," he emphasized that the League constituted, not a partisan issue, but "Americanism vs. Internationalism" and "the ultimate development" of the European balance-of-power theory. The Founding Fathers had warned Americans, specifically in Washington's Farewell Address, to avoid entangling alliances. Times had changed and the nation's fathers were long since dead, some pundits might say, but Fall had an answer for them: "Christ is dead! Is that any reason why we should forget the teachings of the Holy Nazarene! I do not believe the former president of Princeton college [Wilson] could teach those men . . . anything." Instead of preserving peace, as the president claimed, the League would embroil the United States in the squabbles of Europe and send its sons "to stand guard over the Turkish harems in Constantinople." Fall's Confederate heritage slipped out when he concluded, "I do not propose to vote to merge the bars [stripes] of our flag in the red flag of international socialism or to lose one of its stars in the chaos of international Bolshevism." The crowd cheered and gave him a standing ovation.

Fall broached a topic at Albuquerque that would later become a major concern for him in the Senate treaty fight and especially while he was interior secretary. Actually the League was not President Wilson's idea at all, he told the businessmen, but the brainchild of Great Britain, which wanted to save its empire and expand its world domination, thereby making America again "a subsidiary country to the British Isles." About this same time, as fears of a worldwide "oil famine" arose, Fall started sounding the alarm about British designs to monopolize petroleum supplies and exclude the United States from new fields abroad. Fall's Anglophobia, coupled with the highly publicized postwar oil scare, were key considerations in both his opposition to the Versailles Treaty and his decision to open the naval oil reserves for drilling.

National sentiment at first seemed to favor ratification of the treaty in some form, but the election of 1918, which gave the Republicans a slim Senate majority, empowered Senator Lodge and other League opponents to load the Foreign Relations Committee to their advantage. Then, playing for time until public opinion shifted, Lodge skillfully delayed the Senate vote by using tedious stalling tactics. Fall, already allied with Lodge through Mexican affairs and mutual regard for Theodore Roosevelt, became a point man in the attack.

In Fall's estimation the ratification issue was the most serious crisis faced by Americans since the great Civil War military battles. This conviction, as well as his trauma in the 1918 election and the unaccustomed power of majority control, made him noticeably less conciliatory, and more intensely confrontational, in dealing with opponents. Sarcastic innuendoes and sharp exchanges reminiscent of Dona Ana County politics often marked his debates with Senate adversaries. He characterized an elderly colleague's comments as the logic of someone in his "second childhood" and judged information used by Senator Gilbert M. Hitchcock, the Democratic leader, as woefully inaccurate because everything his foe had presented was outdated. When Fall counseled tolerance in floor discussions, Republican Senator Porter J. McCumber retorted that the New Mexican should take a little dose of his own "emetics." In a heated exchange, accompanied by "much loud talk and clenching of fists," Fall declared that his Republican colleague's recent speechmaking had declined "from the sublime to the ridiculous." This confrontation and others like it left several of Fall's colleagues angry and aching for revenge.

Fall ran interference for Lodge in various ways during the treaty fight. After a thorough study, article by article, of both the League Covenant and the peace treaty, he made several analytical speeches in the Senate, often citing historical examples and precedents in international law. He also demanded without success a "declaration of peace" that would have officially ended the war, thus isolating the League issue and simplifying its defeat. In a White House conference scheduled by Lodge for the Foreign Relations Committee, Fall only quizzed the president briefly about the treaty but left behind twenty written questions to be answered in writing later. Like propositions for a one-sided debate, these queries and Wilson's answers gave Fall plenty of material for critical comments on the Senate floor, including his observation that the president was "completely at sea" in comprehending the League's ramifications.

Before the White House conference Fall had called the idea a "farce." As the meeting was ending, Wilson interrupted the discussion and invited the committee to join him for lunch. Fall politely declined the invitation, using the excuse that he had arranged to meet his wife, who was ill. Taken aback, the president said, "I am sorry, Senator, that you are obliged to leave." While the other senators reportedly "stood aghast," Fall started moving toward the door. Lodge intercepted his colleague and, placing an arm around his shoulder, quietly implored him to attend the luncheon, no matter how he felt personally about Wilson. "No, sir!" Fall supposedly exclaimed, "I will do my official duty . . . , but I will not break bread with the man who treated me as this man did; with the man who sent the telegram this man did into my home state of New Mexico when members of my family were lying dead, and my people dying." He then hurried out of the White House.

Back in the Senate, Fall vigorously defended the Foreign Relations Committee's prolonged deliberations as being necessary to fully comprehend the weighty issues at stake. Then, as part of Lodge's delaying tactics, Fall sent from the committee to the Senate some thirty-eight amendments that would have deleted from the treaty those parts authorizing American participation in the various projected international commissions. These "Fall amendments," while drawing more than the portentous one-third vote margin for treaty rejections, failed mainly because they amounted to major textual changes requiring approval of all the signatory powers. But they served their purpose well since, as noted by Fall's boosters, his amendments both "caused and clarified" the ostensibly cosmetic Lodge reservations, which so crippled the treaty as to bring its demise. The president's wife, Edith Bolling Wilson, described the connection precisely. In the Republicans' grand strategy to defeat the treaty the difference between "the original Lodge-Fall amendments," as she labeled them, and the later Lodge reservations "was the difference between Tweedledum and Tweedledee."

In a decisive test on November 19, 1919, the Senate turned down the Treaty of Versailles with the Lodge reservations. Anticlimactic action on March 19, 1920, brought its final defeat. Some accounts have exaggerated the dramatic implications of Fall's conspicuous absence in both instances—especially his distinction as the *only* senator not present for the first vote—implying either negligence of duty or his contempt for Wilson as the reason. Both times, however, he was busy in the Southwest conducting the Mexican investigation, which was delayed by the protracted treaty fight. Not surprisingly, his correspondence reveals that in a showdown he, as an unflinching irreconcilable, would have voted against the treaty with or without the Lodge reservations.

Both Lodge and Wilson have been blamed for keeping the United States out of the League of Nations—the Senate leader for concocting the disabling reservations and the president for refusing to accept substantial modifications to the treaty. Fall believed that Wilson, not Lodge and the Republican party, should claim most of the credit for killing the pact. If the president had agreed to Lodge's reservations, he reasoned, the small band of irreconcilables standing alone could hardly have prevented ratification. As for his own part, Fall proudly accepted a large share of the responsibility. To the end of his days he considered this victorious battle to safeguard the nation's sovereignty as his greatest legislative contribution. A seasoned veteran of political warfare, Fall knew that the monumental Democratic rout made him fair game for retaliation. "Nothing is so intense as the partisanship of defeat," journalist Lincoln Colcord wrote of Wilson's thwarted hopes. Many of Fall's treaty adversaries, remembering his rough treatment, thought he received his just desserts when Teapot Dome came along.

The concurrent treaty battle and Mexican investigation hearings, as well as other demanding Senate business, created a frenzied schedule for Fall. Although still suffering respiratory distress, he seemed to thrive on the twelve- and eighteen-hour days. Just before the Foreign Relations Committee submitted its crucial report containing his treaty amendments, Fall started examining Mexican-affairs witnesses in Washington. Through the fall and winter into the next spring the subcommittee questioned 257 persons and collected almost 3,500 printed pages of evidence, mostly in hearings held in the southwestern cities of El Paso, San Antonio, Tucson, San Diego, and Los Angeles, as well as some border towns. From the beginning the objectives were never in doubt. Fall intended to repudiate Wilson's Mexican policy once and for all by revealing the atrocities and abuses suffered by Americans in Mexico and along the border. Military intervention loomed as a distinct possibility for the subcommittee's primary recommendation.

Besides Fall as chairman, the three-member panel included Frank B. Brandegee of Connecticut, a like-minded Republican and fellow irreconcilable, and Marcus A. Smith of Arizona, Fall's best friend among Senate Democrats and a hard-liner on Mexico. The bipartisan staff consisted of experienced Washington bureaucrats and veteran government investigators from the Southwest who shared Fall's views. But like the inquiry's clear-cut objectives, it was obvious throughout the proceedings who was in command. As one southwestern newspaper observed, "Senator A. B. Fall of New Mexico is the committee." Indeed, one disgruntled subcommittee staffer would later complain that Fall's "egotistical" domination of the investigation ruined its effects.

Most of the witnesses were selected for their qualifications to expose the outrages involving American lives and property, but the testimony of necessity had an appearance of balance. In fact, an early public outcry about the subcommittee's mission focused on Fall's Mexican property holdings and the influence of the oil companies in the investigation. Dismissing the questions about his fitness to head the inquiry because of Mexican oil connections, Fall bristled as he wrote a fellow Republican senator legalistically that he had never been involved "in any way, form or manner whatsoever," financially or as an attorney, in any Mexican oil company.

Some of the sharpest criticism came from the Protestant churches with missionaries in Mexico, the religious and liberal press, and organizations such as the League of Free Nations Association, which promoted international peace and friendship. Representatives of these groups usually testified that conditions were improving in Mexico and spoke of an interventionist plot headed by the oil companies and backed by American political elements, including the Fall subcommittee. Reacting angrily to these accusations, Fall often badgered critical witnesses to admit that they had only circumstantial evidence or personal impressions of an interventionist conspiracy. When one belligerent witness charged that Fall's appointment to lead the investigation was "strong circumstantial evidence" of such a scheme, the chairman exploded with indignation. Even though rumors about an interventionist plot and the smell of oil continued to surround the investigation, those called to testify usually sang more in harmony with Fall's objectives.

The hearings for the first time put the newly established Fall-Doheny alliance on public display. Accordingly one of the most congenial sessions occurred when the oil tycoon took the stand as the star witness. Chairman Fall and the famous industrialist bantered back and forth about their common experiences on the southwestern mining frontier. Then Doheny recounted his pioneering accomplishments in the oil fields of California and Mexico, emphasizing his troubles with the various Mexican regimes but especially under Carranza and Article 27. Later in the investigation Fall left the presiding role and gave testimony denying that he wanted intervention because of his own financial interests in Mexico, which he enumerated. Obviously smarting from newspaper criticism of his motives and the oil companies' influence in the inquiry, he once again declared tersely: "I never owned a dollar of oil stock in my life. I never represented an oil company in Mexico." Significantly, in light of their newfound friendship, he specifically expressed his high esteem for Doheny, saying, "I would do anything possible to assist him." Fall quickly added, however, that he had a similar regard for many of his American and Mexican acquaintances with investments below the Rio Grande. In hindsight nothing else in the Mexican-affairs investigation had more importance than the revelation, for the public record, of the Fall-Doheny friendship, which was so closely examined in the Teapot Dome scandal and the subsequent court action.

Other representatives of the oil industry also received a warm welcome from the subcommittee. Unlike their grilling of unsympathetic witnesses, the senators might coach these employees to make statements discrediting the Carranza government and the rumored interventionist conspiracy. But the petroleum corporations played a more crucial role behind the scenes. Several months before the hearings began, Doheny and other American business executives, representing several branches of industry, not oil alone, formed the National Association for the Protection of American Rights in Mexico (NAPARM) as a public-relations and lobbying instrument. Bankrolled largely by big oil concerns, this organization not only publicized Fall's investigation but also acted as its unofficial administrative arm by providing inside information, amenable witnesses (sometimes paying their expenses), and pressure on the Wilson administration.

One of the most effective operatives for big oil was Harold Walker, the Doheny attorney and lobbyist, who as his boss's alter ego plied Fall with advice and tips on strategy. Independent oilman William F. Buckley, although at odds with NAPARM, became Fall's special confidant and a self-appointed legman for the subcommittee. Several high-level State Department officials, including Ambassador to Mexico Henry P. Fletcher and members of the Mexican division, cheerfully cooperated as well, usually through sub rosa means. Buckley once declared that the investigation, "which was brought about largely through the influence of the oil companies, in which the oil companies have taken such a prominent part, and in which they have such a vital interest," deserved the unflagging support of the industry. Although not all of the companies complied, the venturesome subcommittee's activities depended heavily on the backing and services of big oil.

For good reason most of these contributions remained hidden from public view. Actually Doheny's willingness to take the stand was somewhat unusual among the cautious petroleum executives, who feared retaliation against their Mexican operations by the Carranza regime. And none of those who did appear, including Doheny, advocated full-scale military intervention. With the subcommittee's consent Buckley, who jumped at the chance to testify but rejected armed intervention, spent $5,000 of his own money on a private investigator who went to Tampico to round up a hundred or so American "colonists" and oil-field workers as witnesses. According to Buckley's plan, the oil corporations would send this group by ship to Washington, perhaps furnishing a tanker vessel for transportation, and would pay the witnesses' extra expenses over the government's $3 per diem. The companies would also guarantee a job for the employees after they testified.

Despite the best efforts of Buckley, his investigator, and chairman Fall, the big oil concerns reneged on an agreement to sponsor this scheme. For his part Carranza used the carrot and the stick by temporarily easing drilling restrictions but announcing that any Americans leaving Mexico as witnesses could not return. Even when an unsuspecting Gulf Oil Company superintendent visiting San Antonio from Mexico was handed a subcommittee subpoena, the man claimed that he was too ill to make the trip to Washington. He was later observed in the hotel lobby in apparent good health. Sorely disappointed, Buckley lashed out at those oil executives who had done so much to initiate the investigation but, unlike him, would not openly take part in it.

The tempestuous hearings conducted by Senator Fall near the southwestern border, where revolutionary activities had seethed for a decade, exposed more raw nerves than the sessions in Washington. Now the small-time American refugee farmers and merchants got a chance to tell their pitiful stories. Southwesterners from the ranches and towns along the international boundary also testified about the outrages they had endured. Most of the large corporations would cooperate with any Mexican government, regardless of its stand on social and political change, if it would guarantee foreign property holdings and eschew enforcement of Article 27. But the fifteen thousand expelled American farmers, some of whom had seen their wives and daughters ravaged, took a different view of things. With little political clout and less money for bribing Mexican functionaries, they regarded Fall as a champion, their best hope for justice and restitution. Like Fall, they wanted to obliterate the entire revolution and restore the Díaz era. Despite his alignment with the oil companies, Fall had a heartfelt sympathy for these disappointed "little people," who agreed with his Mexican policy more enthusiastically than did the business tycoons.

Fall always claimed to have a better intelligence network than the State Department. At this time he probably did. Besides information from the oil companies and his own "personal agents and private correspondents," including some Carrancista officials, he now had access to intelligence reports of the State and Justice departments, the Secret Service, and the army, making him the "clearing house" for information. In addition, he made a practice of talking to every prominent Mexican who sought him out, regardless of any faction to which the person belonged.

One of the most spectacular intelligence discoveries made during the investigation was the Carranza regime's alleged connection with the so-called "Plan of San Diego," a conspiracy to foment revolutions across the southwestern United States that would permit Mexico to regain the Mexican cession territory. Another startling revelation concerned a rumored plot by Mexican consular officials in the United States to assassinate subcommittee chairman Fall. Back in the days of Dona Ana County range warfare, he had gained the reputation of being absolutely fearless in the face of personal danger. Years later, according to a close friend, he always stuck a big pearl-handled, long-barreled Colt .45 in the seat cushions of his chauffeured automobile while traveling in New Mexico. Fall also kept a pistol in his Senate office desk in Washington. Rumors of an impending assassination attempt had also arisen during the previous Mexican investigation of 1912. In those earlier hearings, probably at El Paso, he reportedly pulled out a large gun and quietly laid it on the table in front of him, thus discouraging the would-be assassin. If the latest threat on his life had actually materialized, and it did not, Fall undoubtedly would have been ready for it.

Prior to the hearings in the Southwest, United States–Mexico relations had again reached a boiling point, and war now seemed more probable than ever before. In early November 1919 the Carranza government, ignoring State Department protests, dispatched troops to shut down American oil wells drilled without permits. Then a sensational incident escalated the controversy to the brink of hostilities. William O. Jenkins, an American textile manufacturer and land speculator who doubled as the United States consular agent in Puebla, Mexico, was robbed and kidnaped by rebel forces. When Jenkins was released after a $150,000 ransom and returned to Puebla, the local government arrested him, charging that he had conspired with the rebels in his own kidnaping to discredit the Carranza regime, and then had perjured himself in his statements about the abduction. Secretary of State Robert Lansing demanded the immediate release of Jenkins. The Carranza government would not comply, and the two countries edged closer to a rupture of diplomatic relations than at any time since before World War I.

President Wilson, who had painfully avoided full-scale intervention through numerous other crises, lay desperately ill and reportedly was near death in the White House. He had collapsed during a western speaking tour in support of the Versailles Treaty and, on his return to Washington, had suffered a massive stroke that paralyzed his left side. His real condition was shrouded in secrecy, but since he was incapacitated, the nation's affairs were adrift. Senator Fall, always a man of action, saw his chance to take control of Mexican policy and, perhaps in the process, depose his archenemy, the president. Summoned back to Washington by Senate colleagues, he dropped his preparations for the subcommittee hearings and departed from the Southwest immediately after the wedding of his youngest daughter at Three Rivers. On December 3, after consulting with Secretary of State Lansing and key senators, Fall introduced a brash concurrent resolution calling on the president to withdraw recognition and sever diplomatic relations with "the pretended government of Carranza." For good measure he added another bombshell by commenting that his subcommittee had obtained incontrovertible evidence that Mexican consular agents all over the United States were "deliberately stirring revolutionary troubles" and engaging in "Bolshevik propaganda" with Carranza's endorsement.

When the Foreign Relations Committee met to consider Fall's resolution, an appearance by Ambassador Fletcher set off a heated discussion about Wilson's condition. Senator Hitchcock, the Democratic leader, said that the president was fully in command of the Mexican situation, and Fall argued that Wilson knew little if anything about this problem because of his sickness. In the afternoon when Secretary Lansing asked the committee to soften the resolution, Fall exploded with anger and threatened to "wash his hands" of the subcommittee investigation unless his colleagues approved the proposal immediately without alteration. Lansing told the senators, under Fall's questioning, that he had not talked with the president about the resolution or about Mexican affairs generally since Wilson's illness. This startling admission was conclusive for Fall and his friends. Because of the Jenkins incident, the country stood at the brink of war, yet the nation's leader was apparently too sick to shoulder his responsibilities in the crisis. Under these circumstances, the Republican majority decided, it was the committee's duty to send a two-member delegation to the White House, where it would inform the president about the precarious Mexican situation and ascertain his views on the Fall resolution. Fall was an obvious selection; Hitchcock objected to the mission but agreed to go as the Democratic member.

One skeptic observed that the whole affair "was only an excuse for Fall to get into the White House, feel Wilson's pulse, and report that he was too ill to transact public business." Undoubtedly Fall yearned to discredit the president and see him removed from office. At the very least he wanted to force the acceptance of his resolution and bring the Carranza regime's downfall before the opportunity presented by the Jenkins case disappeared.

With surprising speed, especially since the Foreign Relations Committee may not have expected approval of its demand to visit Wilson's sickroom, the White House consented to receive the "smelling committee," as Wilson later called it, on the afternoon of December 5. Admiral Cary T. Grayson, the presidential physician, took Fall and Hitchcock upstairs in the elevator to the president's bedroom, where they were greeted by Wilson's wife. Immediately after the conference Fall mentioned to reporters that she shook hands with both of them. Nearly twenty years later Edith Bolling Wilson wrote in her memoirs that the New Mexican "entered the room looking like a regular Uriah Heap [*sic*], 'washing his hands with invisible soap in imperceptible water.'" And, she added, "I had taken the precaution to carry a pad and pencil so I would not have to shake hands with him." Whatever the case on hand shaking, Mrs. Wilson kept busy during the interview taking sketchy longhand notes.

Now what would the two main antagonists say to each other? Fall was known as the president's "worst enemy," for his animus in Mexican affairs and the Versailles Treaty fight.

Wilson's Calvinistic judgment of opponents, like the wrath of God, was legendary. From Fall's viewpoint the situation was a reversal of the 1918 election when Wilson had attacked him as the senator's family members lay dead or at death's door. Albert Fall had fixed his white-hot hatred on many adversaries, but he reserved a special loathing for the otherworldly president whose sickroom he had just entered.

Breaking the ice, Wilson welcomed the visitors pleasantly and shook their hands with his unaffected right hand. His paralyzed left hand was carefully tucked under the covers. Senator Hitchcock, who assumed a bystander role, reported several years later in a telegram: "Fall, who supposed President Wilson's right arm was paralyzed[,] was amazed when [the] President held up his right arm and shook [the] Senator's hand. Fall was further obviously surprised when Wilson motioned [the] Senator to a seat by the bed and carried on a brilliant dialogue with him punctuated by jokes and stories." Although the patient had sat in a wheelchair during the morning, he was now propped up in bed with pillows to conserve his strength. He was wearing a brown sweater. For the next forty minutes, with the two senators seated at the bedside and Mrs. Wilson across from them, pencil poised, Fall did most of the talking and Wilson mostly listened.

Fall began in a conciliatory tone, exhibiting only respect and none of the disdain he harbored for the president. "I hope you will consider me sincere—I have been praying for you sir. [And] I hope you will forget any fight [we have had]." Mrs. Wilson's on-the-spot notes do not indicate any response from her husband. In her memoirs she has him replying facetiously, "Which way, Senator?" Another more far-fetched account reports Wilson as punning, "Pray, don't!" Fall then spoke at length about the background events justifying the introduction of his resolution and the findings of his Mexican Affairs Subcommittee, all of which, he maintained, necessitated the conference with the president. To his surprise, Fall discovered that Wilson had some understanding of the Jenkins case and the resolution—actually from written material he had received just before the interview. The dramatic climax, or, as Hitchcock put it, the "bombshell thrown in at the psychological moment," came when Admiral Grayson interrupted Fall's remarks to announce that Secretary Lansing had just telephoned the news of Consular Agent Jenkins's release from prison. Fall resumed his discussion, but the freeing of Jenkins by the Carranza government temporarily relieved the tension in United States–Mexico relations that had brought the two senators to the White House.

After Fall concluded, the president said that the Mexican crisis was far too serious for him to make any hasty decisions. He promised to consider a memorandum, which Fall agreed to prepare, elaborating on the information presented in the meeting. Then, Wilson said, he would send his views on the Fall resolution, and possibly the entire Mexican situation, to the Foreign Relations Committee. The president closed the historic sickroom conference by telling a couple of funny stories, one of them involving the mythical Mr. Hennessy's observation that the United States had to take Mexico because it was "so contagious to us."

When the two senators emerged from the White House, reporters crowded around them seeking news about Wilson's health. By previous arrangement Hitchcock spoke first, giving a positive picture of the president's condition. Then the journalists turned to Fall. No matter how respectful he had seemed in the sick man's room, what would one of Wilson's harshest critics tell the American people about their president's mental and physical health? The reporters, raising their primary concern first, asked if the president seemed mentally "capable of handling the Mexican situation?" Fall replied: "In my opinion, Mr. Wilson is perfectly capable of handling the situation. He seemed to me to be in excellent trim, both mentally and physically, for a man who has been in bed for ten weeks. Of course, I am not an expert, but that's how it appeared to me." For two months the public, Congress, and most top government officials had anxiously waited for such authoritative firsthand news. Unwittingly the smelling committee had dispelled the dark rumors concerning the president's sanity and infirmities and squashed the crusade to remove him from office.

The conference thus turned into a Republican blunder and a triumph for Wilson, although it could have become a catastrophe for him. In actuality his health was so precarious, and remained so until his term ended, that the interview might have gone either way. Although the smelling committee mission embittered the president, it also helped make a martyr of him. The general impression spread that Fall, after more or less forcing his way into the White House, had charged into the sickroom and impetuously pulled back the bedclothes to see for himself the condition of the stricken Wilson. This inaccurate version of the much-publicized incident would cause Fall trouble for years.

The release of Jenkins and Fall's rosy statement about Wilson's health doomed the Mexican resolution. As agreed, the New Mexican sent a fifteen-page memorandum on Mexico to the White House that very evening. In his reply three days later Wilson stated his opposition to the Fall resolution, sharply rebuking the Senate for attempting to give unsolicited advice to the president on foreign policy. Within half a hour after Wilson's letter arrived, Senator Lodge announced that the Fall resolution was dead. Fall had been kicked in the "slats," as one Democratic senator described it. On the other hand, the crisis precipitated by the Jenkins incident was a mere interlude in Mexican affairs. Since the larger issues remained unresolved, he would have other opportunities to make his case.

Mexican affairs and the Versailles Treaty remained intertwined in the hostility between Senator Fall and President Wilson. The treaty's first rejection by the Senate, in which Fall played a major role, had occurred two weeks before the smelling committee visit, and its final defeat came in March 1920 while the senator was lambasting the Wilson administration during the Mexican investigation hearings in Los Angeles. The results of the inquiry, according to Fall's strategy, would deliver the coup de grace to the president's entire foreign policy. In late May he submitted the massive subcommittee findings, which the Senate accepted without debate. His report, with a list of 587 Americans killed in Mexico and along the border, demanded the protection of American lives and property, the withholding of recognition from any Mexican government pending a treaty that guaranteed American rights and the arbitration of all claims, and intervention by a United States army and navy "police force" if Mexico refused to accept these conditions.

Even before Fall finished compiling the 2,225,000–word report, the culmination of his eight years in the Senate, the news arrived from Mexico that General Alvaro Obregón had overthrown the Carranza regime. This unexpected turn of events, which the senator attributed to his subcommittee's denunciation of Carranza, gave Fall the upper hand, or at least a veto power, in United States–Mexico relations. Because of his objections, the Senate had already stalled the appointment of a new ambassador to the Carranza government. Indeed, this show of partisan strength, and the president's lingering physical incapacitation, indicated that recognition of the new Mexican regime would be highly unlikely except on Fall's terms.

The State Department became less cooperative after the smelling committee episode, but Fall still conferred occasionally with the new secretary of state, Bainbridge Colby, and his aides, not only on Mexico but also on the proposed Colombian treaty, whose fate rested with another subcommittee headed by Fall. His triumph was marred, however, by a threatened defection of the big oil operators, who wanted to settle their misunderstandings privately with the new Mexican government. He informed the oilmen and other business tycoons, including Doheny, of his unswerving opposition to such a course. Only official diplomatic action, he warned, would bring the desired solution with Mexico. Oil lobbyist Harold Walker, when reporting to Doheny on this matter, reminded his boss, "Fall has been our one best friend and our one best bet and I believe his advice should be given great consideration." For the time being the oil companies backed off, but only temporarily. The possibility of a private accommodation between American businessmen and the new regime continued to jeopardize Fall's hard-line position.

Although Fall had no inkling then, the last nine months of the Wilson administration, from the Mexican investigation report to Warren G. Harding's inauguration as president, would be the peak of his political career. While fighting the devil with fire since his Senate reelection in 1918, he had made many enemies in the high-stakes Versailles Treaty fight, the freewheeling Mexican investigation, and the audacious smelling committee mission. During his Senate years he had vociferously opposed the policies of two United States presidents and four Mexican presidents, drawing much criticism in the process. On the other hand, as champion of the big oil companies with interests in Mexico, he had gained some very powerful new friends, who would profoundly affect his future. Above all else, of course, his passion for Mexico had come into sharp focus in the Mexican subcommittee inquiry. Only then, and not back in the Kingston mining days, did he and Edward L. Doheny become close allies. Later, when the Teapot Dome scandal broke, Doheny commented on his fateful $100,000 loan in the light of Fall's incalculable contribution in the Mexican investigation: "Yes, sir, I considered myself under a great obligation, both on account of friendship and on account of the service he had rendered our company and other companies."

A large number of Theodore Roosevelt's Rough Riders in the Spanish-American War came from New Mexico, but Fall was not one of them. As captain in the First Territorial Volunteer Infantry, he saw only stateside duty. Later, while a United States senator, Fall became closely associated with Roosevelt on foreign policy issues. (Courtesy of Emadair Chase Jones)

Emma Morgan Fall (*seated at front*) and the couple's daughters, Jouett, Alexina, and Caroline, posed in Washington in 1913, shortly after Fall's election to the Senate. (Harris & Ewing photograph, courtesy of Emadair Chase Jones)

In the Senate, Fall gained public recognition primarily for his unswerving stand on the protection of American lives and property in revolution-torn Mexico, often advocating armed intervention by the United States. He also was known as an irreconcilable, or bitter opponent, of President Woodrow Wilson's proposed League of Nations. In this newspaper cartoon Fall is portrayed in 1914 with two other prominent proponents of Mexican intervention, newspaper publisher William Randolph Hearst and Senator Boies Penrose of Pennsylvania. (Bushnell in the *Bisbee (Arizona) Daily Review*)

In 1918 senators on both sides of the momentous debate over the Treaty of Versailles and the League of Nations gathered on the steps of the Capitol. Fall stands somewhat apart in the middle near the top, while his friend Henry Cabot Lodge poses down the steps in the front rank. (Courtesy U.S. Senate Historical Office)

The Harding cabinet: *left to right, front row*, Secretary of War John W. Weeks, Secretary of the Treasury Andrew W. Mellon, Secretary of State Charles Evans Hughes, President Harding, Vice President Coolidge, Secretary of the Navy Edwin L. Denby; *back row*, Interior Secretary Fall, Postmaster General Will H. Hays, Attorney General Harry M. Daugherty, Secretary of Agriculture Henry C. Wallace, Secretary of Commerce Herbert C. Hoover, Secretary of Labor James J. Davis. (Courtesy of the Library of Congress)

The Teapot Dome oil field and the scandal got their names from Teapot Rock, located thirty-five miles north of Casper, Wyoming. This early photograph shows the little sandstone butte with a long finger of rock resembling a teapot's spout, which was knocked off by a tornado in 1962. (Courtesy of UPI/Corbis-Bettmann)

Although not chairman of the Senate Teapot Dome investigation committee, Senator Thomas J. Walsh of Montana planned and directed the inquiry. Stern and austere, with a western background similar to Fall's, Walsh was considered the ablest constitutional lawyer in the Senate. He conducted the hearings like a trial on official morality, not of the legal and geological technicalities alone. (Courtesy of UPI/Corbis-Bettmann.)

Carl C. Magee, a flamboyant, crusading Albuquerque newspaper editor, was the key figure among the New Mexico witnesses who came to Washington and gave damaging testimony before the Teapot Dome committee about Fall's financial affairs. Magee later became editor of the *Oklahoma News* of Oklahoma City and also invented the parking meter. (Courtesy of the Center for Southwest Research, General Library, University of New Mexico, Neg. 000-284-0002)

Fall and oil magnate Edward L. Doheny (*right*) formed a happy trio with Frank J. Hogan (*center*), their chief defense attorney, immediately after their acquittal in 1926 in Washington on charges of conspiracy to defraud the federal government. Fall and Doheny had probably first met forty years before at Kingston in the Black Range mining district of New Mexico. (Courtesy Underwood & Underwood/Corbis-Bettmann)

Among the numerous character witnesses who came to Washington from New Mexico to testify for Fall in his 1929 bribery trial were, *left to right, front row*, Felipe Lucero (former sheriff of Dona Ana County), Gene Baird (rancher), Robert Geronimo (son of Apache chief Geronimo), the Reverend Hunter Lewis (Episcopal minister, Mesilla Park); *second row*, Oliver Lee (Fall's longtime rancher friend from range-war days), Albert Burch (Fall's namesake) and his wife, George Curry (former territorial governor and congressman), Mark B. Thompson (one of Fall's attorneys); and, *in the back*, probably Judge J. L. Lawson of Alamogordo. (Courtesy of Emadair Chase Jones)

In April 1934 Albert Fall gave his last public address at the dedication of the White Sands National Monument near Alamogordo. It was an emotional event for him and his many old friends in the audience. Judge J. L. Lawson (*center with megaphone*) introduced Fall (the stooped figure, on Lawson's left) for the speech. (Photograph by Almeron Newman, courtesy of Emadair Chase Jones)

The Teapot Dome scandal left a legacy often cited in history textbooks and election campaigns, as well as other, more bizarre reminders. The original owner of the Teapot Dome gas station near Zillah, Washington, supposedly became so infuriated by the scandal that, in protest, he built this teapot-shaped service station in the early 1920s. Listed in the National Register of Historic Places, the station is still in operation. (Courtesy of the Office of Archaeology and Historic Preservation, Washington State Department of Community Development)

CHAPTER 6

Kicker in the Cabinet

IN one of his last cabinet meetings Woodrow Wilson quoted a newspaperman who knew Warren G. Harding well as saying that the incoming president "had good intentions & good character—all he lacked was 'mentality.'" Whatever his shortcomings, Harding had a sentimental nature, and a superstitious streak as well, which helped determine the fate of his friend Albert Fall. The two men had known each other, casually at first, ever since Harding came to the Senate in 1915. During their membership together on the Foreign Relations Committee, they established a firm friendship. They were seated near each other in the Senate chamber, where, according to Harry Daugherty, Harding "early grew to admire the striking qualities of Fall's strong mind." Later Fall reminisced: "Over a period of years a group of us senators had associated socially three or four evenings a week—always at homes of those in the group who kept house, because, primarily, the object of these gatherings was to get good home cooking. After these dinners we would play poker, always breaking up, by agreement, exactly at midnight." They spent many pleasant evenings together in this potluck, deuces-wild, whiskey-and-soda fellowship where they got to know each other on "Albert" and "Warren" terms.

At one of these home cooking–poker parties, Fall recalled, he predicted Harding's presidential nomination. Harding was impressed by his friend's "political foresight," especially when the prophecy came true: "He seemed to feel I might be 'lucky' for him—for he was guided to a great extent by instinctive intuitions—and he told me he wanted me around him, which in view of the turn of certain subsequent events in which whatever 'fame' I may have achieved as a cabinet officer turned suddenly to notoriety, shows how ironically intuitions can sometimes develop. Particularly in politics." Moreover, Harding thought Fall was "a star of a fellow," made of the right stuff and "very much on the square," and "a very good and dependable friend." Their friendship lasted until President Harding's death midway through his first term in 1923. Significantly the future first lady, Florence Kling Harding (the formidable "Duchess"), also considered Albert Fall to be "the real salt of the earth."

Despite Fall's prophecy, he apparently gave his genial Senate colleague's early presidential aspirations little serious encouragement. Most New Mexico Republican leaders favored General Leonard Wood for the nomination because of his service in the southwestern Indian-white warfare of the 1880s and his role as the original Rough Rider commander. But Senator Fall sent out mixed signals. Although his "personal choice" was Harding, he told one of the Ohioan's promoters in January 1920, he had earlier become "rather outspoken" in expressing his support for Wood as the nominee. In May, during "a very pleasant talk" with Wood, he assured the general that his nomination would be "perfectly satisfactory." He doubted, however, if the general would be the nominee, and considered Harding as "practically out of it." Even though the Republican candidate would "very likely be elected," Fall wrote his wife, national party kingpins seemed "absolutely at sea" about who would emerge as their standard-bearer. Actually Fall, swamped by the completion of his Mexican-affairs investigation and other pressing Senate duties, paid little attention to the competing presidential hopefuls or, he said, "to politics at all."

An unexpected rebuff by a contentious New Mexico Republican party in March 1920 resulted in Fall's refusal to serve as a delegate to the national convention in Chicago. With the muddled presidential race favoring a dark-horse candidate, he adamantly insisted on an uninstructed delegation as the wisest deployment of the state's measly six votes. Some local party leaders thought he really wanted the prestige of a favorite-son designation for bargaining purposes, while others believed he was for Harding, and still others, including some close friends, thought that he favored Wood. For once, without Fall's presence and stern countenance, the Republicans assembled at Santa Fe ignored his wishes and instructed their delegation for General Wood. Since he had vowed to boycott an instructed contingent, New Mexico's famous senator was automatically frozen out. An angry Fall blamed his hitherto trusty field agent, national committeeman Holm O. Bursum, now under the spell of Wood booster Frank Hitchcock, for this embarrassing affront. Later, when at Chicago Bursum persisted in holding the New Mexico delegates in line for Wood until after Harding had clearly won the nomination, Fall became even more infuriated. The split in Fall's long-standing political partnership with Bursum continued to widen, causing more factionalism in the fragmented state Republican party and also trouble for Fall on the national scene.

Senator Fall stayed in Washington wrapping up his Mexican-inquiry report while the Republican strategists, inhaling the congested atmosphere of smoke-filled rooms, nominated Harding as their presidential candidate. Copies of his proposed plank on Mexico, about half of which appeared in the final platform, were taken to Chicago by Senator Lodge and others. Again, as in 1916, party leaders balked at Fall's belligerent demand for the use of arms "in such measure and volume as to avoid war," but pledged to withhold recognition until Mexico agreed to protect American lives and property and settle legitimate claims. In its broader aspects, contrary to popular belief, the 1920 Republican convention was "leaderless" and "headless" and not bossed by a Senate cabal or an old-guard clique, all of which played into the hands of dark-horse candidate Harding. Nor did "smoke-filled room" conspirators force Harding on the delegates, much less make a corrupt deal with greedy oil barons for Fall's appointment as interior secretary and the plundering of the naval petroleum reserves. In truth, after the leading candidates fought to a standoff, Harding remained as the "Available Man" or "Second McKinley" from Ohio (the latter-day "Mother of Presidents") who offered an antidote for sticky Wilsonian idealism.

When Harding returned to Washington from Chicago and, in a jovial mood, went to his Senate office, Albert Fall was one of the first senators invited for an intimate talk. At about this time, probably during the conference itself, the Republican nominee asked Fall to serve as a campaign adviser. Despite his growing disillusionment with politics, Fall could not turn down this request—and the opportunity it presented. But first, Fall told Harding, he must mend his precarious health and some political fences in New Mexico, where his ironfisted "harmonizing" was needed to squelch rampant Republican factionalism and ensure a presidential election victory in the state. By late summer, with Fall still in New Mexico, Harding became insistent on having his "counsel and advice." He wrote from the front-porch campaign headquarters in Marion, Ohio, "Really, I very much need to be surrounded by some of the friends whom I trust most fully [especially] through some of the anxious moments of speech preparation and determination of foreign policy." Before Fall could report for national duty with Harding, he had to employ, according to New Mexico newspaper accounts, "his usual delicate technique" and "every art known to the politician," as well as his newly acquired prestige as the presidential candidate's confidant, to hammer out an acceptable state ticket.

Fall finally joined Harding's campaign in late September, as a "confidential 'scout,'" rendering "what service I could to him quietly." He met the candidate, who at the urging of party leaders had abandoned the front porch for a speaking tour, at Baltimore, and he continued with him by special train until they returned to Marion. On the trip, following a mysterious track-switching incident in West Virginia, Fall insisted on acting as a security guard, like a western stagecoach "shotgun," getting off and patrolling at every stop. While a guest in Harding's home for three days, according to Fall, he drafted no more than "a paragraph here and there" of the candidate's speeches. Nor did he do any speaking himself nationally. As a confidential scout, he conferred with leading Republicans on campaign matters, in one instance helping soothe the disaffection of fellow irreconcilable Senator Borah caused by Harding's wobbling on the League of Nations. He also kept a close watch on Mexican affairs, through private meetings with both Mexican agents and influential Americans, and attended the Southern Tariff Conference in New Orleans as Harding's unofficial representative. Besides counseling the candidate on foreign policy, particularly concerning Latin America and the League, he advised Harding on such domestic issues as reclamation, water power, and public lands.

Fall's high-level activities were interrupted by continuing dissension in New Mexico Republican ranks, which necessitated his return to circle the wagons and "save the State for Harding." An alliance of progressive Republicans and Democrats, led by Bronson Cutting of the *Santa Fe New Mexican*, had launched disruptive attacks against the "corporation bosses," namely the "Heavenly Twins" of industry, Fall and W. A. Hawkins. Having become an issue himself, Fall traveled night and day, by automobile on primitive roads, across the sparsely settled prairies and mountains, covering as many as four hundred miles and giving nine speeches in two days. Whenever the opportunity arose, he engaged in heated debates, which he always thoroughly enjoyed.

The overall campaign in a state with isolated rural communities and a mixed ethnic population, which required bilingual speakers and literature printed in Spanish and English, had serious financial problems. In one appeal Fall asked national party chairman Will Hays "to mention the necessities" to certain wealthy benefactors, including "Mr. Sinclair, of the Sinclair Oil Company, with whom some of my personal friends are more or less intimately associated." Such outside money helped save the day. Moreover, Wall Street betting odds, which favored Harding by two to one in July, steadily soared to the recorded high for a presidential race of ten to one by election day. In New Mexico, probably as much because of the national Republican tide as Fall's campaigning, both Harding and the state ticket won by impressive majorities. It was Albert Fall's last stand as the political boss of New Mexico, as painful events would soon reveal.

After the election Harding, with a large entourage of friends and reporters in tow, began a long vacation tour that started on the Texas Gulf Coast. By invitation Senator Fall paid his respects at Brownsville. He cheerfully joined the poker games in newspaper owner Edward B. McLean's private railroad car, but Mexican affairs were uppermost on his mind. In fact, he had brought along Elias L. Torres, supposedly the personal representative both of the outgoing Mexican foreign minister and of President-elect Obregón. Torres bore an invitation asking the American president-elect to attend the inauguration of his counterpart in Mexico City on December 1 and to bring Fall with him.

For months Fall had been holding court for a parade of Mexican agents, telling them all that, as stipulated in his investigation report, recognition must be preceded by written guarantees. Even before the election American businessmen in Mexico City had tried to arrange a meeting between Fall and Obregón at El Paso, but the senator's campaign duties in the East prevented it. Now, with Fall's newfound prestige as President-elect Harding's confidant, everyone with a stake south of the border, it seemed, was clamoring to get his ear. After taking Torres to see Harding, Fall announced that although the president-elect could not make the trip to Mexico City, he would go. When Fall departed for El Paso, intending to board a special train there for the Mexican capital, he carried a personal letter from Harding to Obregón. It began, "I am asking my friend and colleague . . . to attend your inauguration and express to you my felicitations and good wishes." In a positive reference to recognition Harding concluded that he was confident "a new era of helpful relationship [lies ahead] in which the people of both nations may truly rejoice." Fall never delivered this optimistic message; he got no farther with it than El Paso.

The aborted trip revealed not only the instability and factionalism in Mexico but also the hatred and distrust many Mexican officials had for Fall. First, a statement attributed to Obregón categorically denied that Torres represented the general. Then, Roberto V. Pesquiera, the Mexican "confidential agent" in Washington recently rebuffed on recognition by the Wilson administration, brusquely commanded all Mexican border consuls not to visé Fall's passport. Pesquiera, smarting from his diplomatic failure, probably struck back at Fall because of the Senate subcommittee's interventionist stance. From Mexico City came word that prominent Mexicans feared Fall's presence would cause "embarrassing or disagreeable incidents by irresponsible persons," perhaps even an attempted assassination of the controversial senator, thereby ruining hopes for recognition. Fall himself, reportedly "astonished" by the exclusion order, blamed the fiasco on a factional row between Pesquiera and the lame-duck Mexican foreign minister. A flurry of rumors, denials, and frantic apologies emanated from Mexico. Shrugging them off, Fall left El Paso, not for a dangerous mission to Mexico City but with Price McKinney, his industrialist friend and partner in Mexican mining, for a chummy outing in Arizona. "The matter has not annoyed me at all," he declared, "except to further disgust me with any attempt to help Mexico."

Senator Fall had suffered a stinging affront, but it could have been much worse. A dogmatic Fall in Mexico City, speaking ex cathedra among proud Mexicans celebrating the swearing-in of their new president, could have damaged the chances of diplomatic reconciliation and seriously embarrassed Harding, who had good-naturedly approved the risky venture. But Fall's influence showed no signs of eclipse. A few weeks before Harding took office, Fall wrote an American oil executive, "So long as I have anything to do with the Mexican question no Government in Mexico will be recognized, with my consent, which government does not first enter into a written agreement [consistent with the investigation report]." About the same time Harding wrote his friend, "I have always believed that you knew this [Mexican] situation as well as anyone within my acquaintance and, frankly, I am on guard whenever anybody else talks to me about matters relating to that country." It seemed certain that Fall would have a dominant hand in shaping the new administration's Mexican policy.

Edward L. Doheny, as well as several other prominent American businessmen and politicians, was also invited to

Obregón's inauguration, but he backed out on the advice of his fellow oil producers. Doheny had provided his wholehearted cooperation to Fall during the Mexican-affairs investigation. Now his Washington lobbyist, Harold Walker, tightened the watch on the State Department lest it falter on recognition. Likewise, Walker increased his liaison duties with Fall, conveying his employer's views and other inside information from the oil corporations. The personal relationship between Fall and Doheny also quickened, especially after the presidential election. During the campaign, in which Doheny as a faithful Democrat had "thought it best to remain regular," they met and talked about Mexico at least once in New York City. After the Republican victory the oil magnate wrote apologetically, "It is in sackcloth and ashes that I come to your feet to beg forgiveness and admission among the ranks of the sane people of the Country." He praised both Fall's fight against the League of Nations and the "very dignified, well-poised campaign of Senator Harding." Fall accepted this gesture of atonement and injected that significant observation about the longevity of their friendship: even though they had "only met casually since the old days," he had always held "a very warm feeling" for Doheny, which had grown "in the last year or two" as they met more often.

As an additional peace offering, Doheny tendered the use of his large yacht, the *Casiana* (named after his great Mexican gusher), for Harding's pre-inauguration vacation cruise. Fall diligently pursued this prospect, but Harding declined with thanks, having already accepted a United Fruit Company steamer for his voyage between New Orleans and the Canal Zone. Then Fall himself considered taking the yacht, either accompanied by Doheny or not, for a long-planned Latin-American fact-finding cruise to Puerto Rico, Cuba, Colombia, and elsewhere as time allowed. Although this excursion never materialized, Fall discussed it with Harold Walker and, he told his wife, would suggest it to Doheny, as he had "no hesitancy in asking him for any favor." Later Doheny, signing himself "Your old friend," asked Fall to exert his "great influence" with the president-elect to secure a cabinet appointment as treasury secretary for George M. Reynolds, a Chicago banker. Fall complied, but without success. By the time Harding had entered the White House, the Fall-Doheny friendship, begun as a casual fellowship in the frontier mining camp of Kingston but solidly forged less than two years before during the Mexican-affairs investigation, had become a well-lubricated political vehicle.

From the presidential election until the inauguration, Senator Fall continued to act as a confidential scout for Harding. After a leisurely ocean cruise the president-elect came to Washington as a guest in Edward B. McLean's palatial home, "Friendship." Soon so many senators were congregating in the mansion's drawing room that it resembled the Senate chamber. Harding assigned Fall to the "special mission" of consulting with Elihu Root on delicate issues involving the League of Nations and an international court. Old-line Republicans concerned with social propriety were already shaking their heads over the Hardings' attraction to Ned McLean and his wife, the former Evalyn Walsh (owner of the fabled Hope Diamond), who had gained notoriety in Washington by spending their inherited wealth on social climbing and an extravagant lifestyle. Fall liked the McLeans and struck up a warm relationship with them that lasted through the Teapot Dome tribulations. In fact, they now invited him to stay with them until he left the city for the Christmas holidays in New Mexico, and they gave him an expensive gift for the Three Rivers ranch—a prized stallion, "Uncle White." While in the Harding cabinet, Fall would spend many pleasant evenings at Friendship attending dinner parties and playing poker.

Once back home in Marion, Harding began conferring with the "best minds" on foreign policy commitments, principally the League, which he had carefully avoided during the campaign. Among this select group was Fall, who detoured through Ohio on his way to the Southwest for Christmas. The two friends had a long talk and then walked arm in arm to meet the newspaper reporters, who eagerly waited to hear what avowed irreconcilable Fall would say. Harding began jovially: "I have brought you a living sacrifice. I myself will withdraw if my presence is embarrassing." There was a chorus of "Not at all, not at all," whereupon the president-elect said: "Now, Albert, talk as much as you please. I am here only constructively." Fall could still "see no good" in the Versailles Treaty or the League, he told the reporters, but he predicted the convening of "a new great congress of nations," this time in Washington, which would produce an international association to promote peace and also safeguard American sovereignty. When asked if Harding, who stood nearby, was coming around to a similar position, Fall replied, "That is certainly my opinion."

Newspaper accounts, portraying Fall as "closer to Harding, socially and politically, than any other" senator, placed great importance on his remarks. If anyone should know the president-elect's mind, one reporter wrote, it was Fall, "who worked and played with him during the six years they were together in the Senate." Probably Harding staged the press interview, with Fall as his spokesman, to dispel the suspicions of some Republican senators that he was warming up to the League. When inaugurated, Harding declared that the United States would not enter the League "by the side door, back door, or cellar door," but he did sponsor the Washington Disarmament Conference of 1921–22, as an international bulwark against war, as Fall had predicted.

About the time of Fall's visit to Marion the press started speculating that Harding would name him to the cabinet as either secretary of state or secretary of the interior. Strangely enough, for one driven by ambition all his life, Fall faced a dilemma. He had been resolved, since his reelection in 1918, not to serve out his six-year Senate term. Shortly before Harding's nomination Fall had written his wife, "I am more and more disgusted with politics as the game is played, and determined to get out of it as soon as my sense of duty will permit me to do so." Because of the "open secret" of Fall's desire to leave the Senate, the *Albuquerque Morning Journal* commented, local opinion was divided on whether he would join the Harding cabinet "for awhile" or reenter private business in New York City and El Paso "at once." His chronic poor health and the detrimental effect of politics on his financial affairs, the newspaper stated, indicated a return to business, although a cabinet offer might lure him away briefly.

Whenever they met, Harding insisted that Fall should be one of his cabinet members, mentioning, Fall told political confidants, a couple of possible positions, neither of which was interior secretary. Then, in January 1921, Harding, an inveterate traveler, combined business and relaxation in the sun on a Florida houseboat cruise with his "social group," including Ned McLean, Harry Daugherty, the ubiquitous Ohio hanger-on Jess Smith, and other boon companions. After some urging from the president-elect, Fall arrived later from Washington to join this jolly crew. Two days later Harding, emphasizing the need for Fall "as one of his official advisers," offered him the interior secretary post. As for the significance Harding placed on the office, Fall wrote his wife in a remarkable letter: "He thinks that the Interior Department, is second only to the State Department in importance and that there is more opportunity for graft and scandal connected with the disposition of public lands &c, than there could be in any other Department and he wants a man who is thoroughly familiar with the business and one he can rely upon as thoroughly honest, etc etc." He agonized for three days and finally accepted.

Even though Fall had difficulty expressing "all that I feel about it," he confided to his wife, "I am now trying to look upon the bright side and see the compensations which may offer themselves in that position." There was no hint he meant monetary returns or that he had a foreboding about the future. For years, however, a large framed picture of Harding and his Florida houseboat companions hung above the fireplace of the exclusive Cocolobo Club on Caesar's Island near Miami, a port once frequented by the infamous pirate "Black Caesar." Some superstitious observers later noticed a strange shadow over Fall and another, but less noticeable, over future Attorney General Harry Daugherty, and regarded this picture as a prophecy.

Undoubtedly Fall would have shown more enthusiasm if he had obtained the cabinet position with direct influence over

Mexican affairs. His wife once declared that she had heard him say he would rather be secretary of state than president. Harding probably did consider his friend for that appointment, and Fall, despite later protestations, wanted the job. Fall may have realized before Harding that it was politically impossible. Reminiscing about their talk in Harding's Senate office immediately after the nomination, Fall recalled that his colleague summoned him by telephone: "I hastened down the hall. . . . And then—before I realized what he was saying: 'I want you to be my secretary of state! I'm going to be elected.'" Fall reacted in amazement: "'It simply isn't feasible, Warren,' I said. 'You can't afford to make a man from a little inland state like New Mexico your secretary of state.'" Because of tradition and political reality, Fall reminded his friend, the appointment belonged to a populous eastern state, such as New York, which had thrown crucial delegate support behind Harding in the convention. For some time after that Harding "repeatedly returned to the subject" with Fall, and he felt out several party leaders as well. He at least toyed with the idea until a month or so after the election when prominent Republicans "raised such a row" in private protests that he dropped it.

Even as his own chances faded away, Fall tried to keep a hand in the selection of the secretary of state. His choice was Republican elder statesman Elihu Root, for whom Harding had no enthusiasm because of, according to Fall, "a sort of 'spiritual incompatibility'" between them. Charles Evans Hughes received the prized appointment, Fall believed, because he was the most logical New Yorker after Root. Even so, "a persistent rumor" in Washington said that Hughes would hold the State Department portfolio not as a permanent assignment but only until an opportunity arose for Harding to appoint him to the Supreme Court. When this occurred, perhaps in only a few months, Fall was expected to move from Interior to the State Department.

Senator Fall advised Harding on other cabinet selections with more success. In particular, he liked to take substantial credit for the appointment of Secretary of Commerce Herbert Hoover, who would later, as president, refuse to spare him from prison for his oil transgressions. Of all those Harding considered for the cabinet, none drew more intense hostility than Hoover. For most old-guard Republicans, understandably wary of this rising new star, Hoover gave them "gooseflesh." Progressives such as Gifford Pinchot and Senator Hiram Johnson were likewise horrified at the prospect. But Fall saw Hoover as a popular choice and "a very valuable Cabinet member." He did detect major pockets of opposition, namely Ned McLean and William Randolph Hearst, who despised Hoover as a rival newspaper owner. Especially troublesome was the bad blood between McLean, publisher of the *Washington Post*, and Hoover, who owned the *Washington Herald*, over a coveted Associated Press franchise.

Harding was equally determined to have Hoover in the cabinet, although exactly which department, he wrote an admirer, caused him "more concern than any others under consideration." According to Hoover, he had the choice of the Interior or Commerce posts and chose Commerce because of its importance in the postwar economy. In fact, Harding never actually offered Hoover the more esteemed Interior position, which he preferred, but decided to give him the less important Commerce slot despite the bitter opposition to any appointment for Hoover. The solution came in what Fall termed "the biggest political 'trade'" of the cabinet-making process, involving powerful Republican senators who distrusted Hoover but insisted on having billionaire Andrew Mellon for treasury secretary. Fall acted as an intermediary, he maintained, in helping work out a compromise—"Mellon and Hoover or no Mellon." Early in the campaign Harding had pledged to appoint a westerner as interior secretary. Both Fall and Californian Hoover met this requirement, but whereas Fall's nomination would sail through the Senate, Hoover's appointment even to the lowly Commerce role might run into serious opposition. In this political context Fall was just the right man for the Interior job.

Meanwhile trouble was brewing back in New Mexico over the naming of Fall's Senate replacement. His selection for the Interior post soon became common knowledge, but Harding wanted no public announcements made on cabinet nominees as yet. This restriction placed Fall in an extremely awkward situation. When agreeing to run for reelection in 1918, he had exacted from the state party hierarchy the promise that he could resign from the Senate in two years and pick his own successor. After Harding's victory in 1920 Fall talked twice with Republican Governor Merritt C. Mechem about a senatorial replacement in case he took a cabinet position, and he thought they had reached a firm understanding on those who were acceptable. Holm O. Bursum, Mechem's political mentor and until recently Fall's trusted ally, had made it known that he expected the governor to give him the vacant Senate seat. When, to the surprise of many, Fall quietly informed Republican insiders of his unswerving opposition to Bursum's selection, divided party leaders squared off for what the *Santa Fe New Mexican* called "The grandest little old political battle staged in New Mexico for many years."

The split between Fall and Bursum, whose names had been synonymous with Republican "bossism" since territorial days, arose from recent events. Most conspicuously, in Fall's opinion, Bursum had cast his lot with national Republican kingmaker Frank Hitchcock and defied Fall's wishes for an uninstructed delegation to the 1920 national convention. In addition, Bursum as national committeeman had taken control of $47,000 in state campaign funds, about half of which had been raised by Fall himself; he handed out $40,000 personally, leaving $7,000 for distribution through regular party channels. Now Bursum and his crafty handler, Hitchcock, wanted to rule New Mexico, which Albert Fall would not tolerate without a fight. And Fall had another objection to Bursum as his successor. New Mexico should send someone to Washington, he commented sarcastically, who could "eat in the Senate restaurant, knowing the proper respective functions of a knife and fork," and otherwise "associate with his colleagues upon terms of social as well as intellectual equality"—attributes he did not ascribe to Bursum.

In short, Fall had notified Governor Mechem to expect his resignation, but had said nothing about it publicly because of

Harding's ban on cabinet announcements. Sworn to secrecy on the Interior post, he was prevented from fighting Bursum openly over a nonexistent Senate vacancy. As Bursum gained support, one hope remained to stem the tide. If President-elect Harding publicly confirmed his friend's selection as interior secretary, Fall would be free to stop Bursum's campaign dead in its tracks. In Washington, according to Fall, a swamped Harry Daugherty instructed him to send a telegram over Daugherty's name to Harding in Florida recommending an announcement of the embattled senator's cabinet designation. Still not ready for such publicity, Harding rejected the idea. Later Daugherty used this incident as an example of Fall's duplicity, saying that the telegram was sent without his permission. In actuality, though, Harding replied to Daugherty, who referred to "my telegram" when relaying the response to Fall.

Next Fall tried to reverse his field by informing New Mexico Republicans that any action on their part would be premature because he might not resign from the Senate. This maneuver gained a little time and prevented a party endorsement before Harding's inauguration. Once Fall was installed in the Interior Department, however, Governor Mechem soon gave Bursum the Senate seat. This defeat damaged Fall's prestige at the very beginning of his cabinet service. In his preoccupation with international affairs he had neglected New Mexico politics and lost his home power base, with serious consequences for his influence in the Harding administration. Moreover, the split between Fall and Bursum signaled the collapse of the Republican machine formed in the late territorial period. In September 1921, despite Fall's continued opposition, Bursum won a special election to complete the unexpired Senate term. He was defeated in 1924 for the regular six-year term, but by then Fall, bogged down in the Teapot Dome scandal, had far more serious worries.

Despite his problems back home, New Mexico's first cabinet member took office in a blaze of glory. In sharp contrast with the subdued inaugural ceremonies, the new president, as his first official act, made an unprecedented surprise visit to the

Senate chamber, less than a hour after taking the oath of office, to present his cabinet appointments in person. Standing beside Vice President Calvin Coolidge on the rostrum, Harding read the names aloud, starting with Fall's, and was greeted warmly by his former Senate colleagues as he entered and left the chamber. Since Senator Lodge, the majority leader, had already polled the relevant committees, the entire cabinet was confirmed without any objection voiced, in record time—less than ten minutes. Open opposition to Hoover's appointment as commerce secretary, although widely rumored beforehand, failed to materialize.

Albert Fall, who had yet to resign from the Senate, sat in his regular seat during President Harding's dramatic appearance. A spontaneous round of applause arose when the president read his name. After Harding left, Fall stood up and, in the midst of cheering, submitted his resignation. Then some horseplay ensued as the senators, facing toward him "as one man," started shouting, "Get out" and "You are no longer one of us," until Senator Lodge came to Fall's rescue by proposing his immediate confirmation. Lodge's motion passed unanimously, "to the accompaniment of a thunder of applause," and the new interior secretary, smiling broadly, hurried out the Republican exit. "On that day," journalist Mark Sullivan recalled, "Democrats as well as Republicans were his friends and well-wishers."

Generally Fall was considered qualified for the job, but his selection stirred much less enthusiasm in some quarters than it had in the Senate. The liberal *New Republic* called him and Daugherty "unspeakably bad appointments." Not surprisingly, there was "much uneasiness among Mexicans," who assumed that Fall, not Hughes, would determine the new administration's Mexican policy on such matters as recognition and intervention. "To us Fall smells of petroleum," a leading Mexican newspaper declared, "and we already know what that means among Yankee politicians." Conservationists and Indian-rights advocates also voiced apprehension. In the West, Fall's past arose to haunt him when some pioneers remembered his reputation as "an old time gun toter" in Dona Ana County.

Sunset magazine portrayed him as "an unreconstructed, frankly acknowledged standpatter whose power has its roots in the old-style domination of corporations in New Mexico politics," one who found "wise conservation of natural resources . . . hateful to his every instinct." But most westerners seemed to feel they had a friend in the new interior secretary. One prominent western Democratic senator wrote Fall of his "very great gratification" since the Interior position was "scarcely second in importance to that of the presidency, so far as the material interests of the people of [my] State are concerned." Ironically the senator was Thomas J. Walsh of Montana, who would bring Fall to disgrace in the Teapot Dome investigation.

Fall should have turned a deaf ear to Harding's offer of a cabinet position. Impulsive and restive, almost paranoid about opposition or criticism, he had never been at ease as a public servant. By nature a rebel, he became the "kicker" in the cabinet during the next two years: "It got so I was expected to make objections. Most of the rest of them were more reserved. I wish now that I had been, too. For every time I kicked about something I made an enemy, and in later years all these little disaffections piled up against me. As we say out west, I spoke too many times when I should have been listening." His life had consisted of one pitched battle after another, and now he was constantly in conflict with fellow cabinet members and other administration officials as well as several public figures and groups outside the government. Although possessing charismatic leadership ability, he lacked the temperament for the job. Long years of political warfare in New Mexico and the Senate had made Fall, according to one national columnist, "a fighter and an individualist," or something "like the star football player who can't somehow harmonize his play with the rest of the team." Another journalist, using more appropriate terms, commented that Harding had placed "a tamed Buffalo Bill type of man" in charge of the Interior Department.

An early warning of Fall's decline sounded back in New Mexico when he lost an important battle to his Senate successor, Holm O. Bursum, over control of the local federal patronage, most of which Fall had planned to hand out. Despite Fall's vigorous protests and his predictions of Bursum's certain defeat, President Harding swung control of the state's patronage to Bursum except for federal appointments emanating from the Interior Department. Another bitter pill for the interior secretary to swallow came when Bursum won the September special election by 5,515 votes, a margin three times greater than Fall's in 1918. Moreover, by July 1922 New Mexico's first cabinet officer was complaining that for the past eighteen months the state Republican party had "displayed no desire to follow my advice nor even to ask it," but instead had "placed its destinies in other hands than mine." When his prestige started sinking, Fall had written his wife testily, "Thank God, I am in a way to get out of politics and I shall do it at the earliest possible moment."

In the realm of international affairs Fall's cabinet career began more smoothly, particularly in the case of the Colombian treaty's ratification. Proud of building the Panama Canal, Theodore Roosevelt had bristled at any hint of his complicity in the separation of Panama from Colombia. Besides mutual abhorrence of President Wilson's Mexican policy, Fall and the Rough Rider had quickly found common ground in their opposition to the Wilson administration's pending "blackmail treaty" (the Thomson-Urrutia Treaty, negotiated in 1914), which proposed to give an apology and a $25 million indemnity to Colombia. Senator Lodge and other Roosevelt defenders, including Fall, stalled ratification until after the Republicans gained control of the Senate in 1919. Suddenly American diplomacy showed newfound interest in more friendly relations with Colombia. Roosevelt's death earlier that year offered one explanation for the different tack, but the main reason was the postwar "world oil crisis"—that is, the gnawing fear that Great Britain would secure a virtual monopoly of the world's limited petroleum reserves.

As "oil entered diplomacy," Senator Fall became a barometer of this changed international order, undergoing what some considered a "conversion" experience. Known as a staunch protector of Roosevelt's reputation, he emerged in a new role as the outspoken advocate of American petroleum interests in Colombia. In mid-1919, just after the Senate removed the treaty's offensive apology clause but left the $25 million indemnity intact, the Colombian president issued a restrictive petroleum decree similar to those in Mexico. In Fall's thinking the Colombian problem now became identical to the Mexican dilemma, and, in fact, he attributed Bogota's obstinacy to the work of Mexican diplomats and propagandists. As chairman of the Foreign Relations subcommittee responsible for the treaty, he proposed a "petroleum amendment" that would have provided the same kind of ironclad guarantees for American property rights as he also sought in Mexico. Columbia was more compliant than Mexico, however, and soon enacted new oil legislation potentially favorable to American companies. Fall's subcommittee, assured of Bogota's "good faith," sent the treaty to the Senate in June 1920. There, because of impending adjournment, it reposed until after the presidential election. If Mexico would only follow the example set by Colombia, Fall lamented, the problems between the United States and its next-door neighbor would vanish.

Fall would have managed the Colombian treaty's ratification in the Senate if his cabinet appointment had not intervened. While with Harding in Marion following the election, he stressed the urgency of approval and encouraged the president-elect to call for speedy Senate action even before the inauguration. Five days after taking office, Harding asked for prompt passage of the seven-year-old agreement. From the Interior Department Fall wrote Senator Lodge, "I very much regret that I cannot be side by side with you in this fight, as I have so much enjoyed being with you in other fights which we have gone through together under your able leadership." The majority leader replied, "I shall miss you sorely in the debate as indeed I miss you constantly in the Senate." Although on the sidelines, Fall supplied Lodge with technical information from the departmental files now at his command as well as long quotations from Roosevelt's letters to him implying that the colonel would favor the present treaty version if he could speak from the grave.

Despite lengthy discussion on the sanctity of Roosevelt's reputation and the "complete somersault" of the Republican leadership, the Colombian treaty without the apology clause won Senate approval a scant six weeks after Harding took office by a vote of sixty-nine to nineteen. Pledges by both Lodge and Fall that ratification would lead to an even more important Colombian treaty of amity and commerce never materialized. For the moment, however, the new administration hoped to use the present pact "to lay the foundation for better Latin-American relations." Fall's role in the ratification seemed to indicate that he would also guide Harding's Mexican policy as the "Secretary of International Interior Affairs."

With Mexico, however, Fall could not deliver an easy diplomatic solution. In fact, even the triumph with Colombia backfired in a cabinet feud between him and Secretary of State Charles Evans Hughes, who as the Republican presidential candidate in 1916 had so eagerly sought Fall's advice. Hughes cheerfully endorsed the Colombian treaty, but he resented Fall's role in its ratification, particularly when the interior secretary's statements to Senator Lodge about Great Britain's exclusionary international oil operations in Mexico and elsewhere brought an official protest from the British ambassador. This initial rift between the two cabinet officers carried over into Mexican affairs, which became their main battleground. Fall's assumption that he would be President Harding's mentor on Latin America, especially Mexico, was the main reason he had accepted a cabinet appointment. After all the frustrating years of his single-minded devotion to this cause, he was determined to crown his public career with a diplomatic victory that would restore Porfirian tranquility in Mexico and assure his own rightful place in history. Only the most gifted of prophets, and certainly not Fall himself, could have foreseen that he would be chiefly remembered for his policy affecting the little-known naval oil reserves instead of his role in Mexican affairs.

Under these circumstances Fall's clash with Secretary Hughes was inevitable. Ambitious, highly sensitive, and conscientious, the bewhiskered Hughes was determined to run the State Department without interference. No greater contrast in personalities could be imagined. Hughes abhorred the loquacious interior secretary's cabinet discourses on foreign affairs, attributing them to "vanity and mental indigestion." Harding had promised Hughes a free hand in all aspects of foreign policy, which obviously included the Mexican issue. One of the inflexible cabinet members had to bend or there would be serious trouble in the new president's official family. Someone once observed that Hughes could be easily defeated at poker but never at chess. Unfortunately for Fall, a superb poker player, the dealer's choice was chess.

Fall began to realize that he would have a limited role as a presidential foreign-policy adviser when Harding deferred to Hughes on the British complaints stemming from the Colombian treaty. At the same time Fall had increasing difficulty even getting a hearing before the stony-faced secretary of state, who refused to open any doors willingly. Indeed, he slammed one shut when the death of Chief Justice Edward D. White, in May 1921, renewed predictions of Hughes's selection for the Supreme Court at the earliest opportunity, clearing the way for Fall's elevation to the State Department. Plainly irritated, Hughes scotched these rumors by signaling Harding that he would regard a judicial appointment now as a vote of no confidence in his performance as secretary of state. Hughes also reduced Fall's influence in Mexican affairs by emphasizing the use of established diplomatic channels, not private informants and self-appointed agents, such as those making up Fall's intelligence network. Yet another early indication of Fall's declining diplomatic fortunes came from a former Mexican Affairs Subcommittee staffer, who reported the very cold shoulder he had received at the State Department when Secretary Hughes abruptly left him "standing alone, feeling like a fool on a fool's errand." Fall was beginning to get the same feeling.

Ironically, despite their cabinet rivalry, Fall and Hughes held similar views on Mexico. The bearded secretary of state and onetime Supreme Court justice, whose concept of his office was narrow and legalistic, had a strong concern for American property rights. Although desiring a good-neighbor policy in Latin America, he also sought an open door for petroleum development around the world, leading the British to nickname him the "Secretary for Oil." But, unlike Fall, Hughes believed in a type of intervention, or what he called "nonbelligerent interposition," that depended on diplomatic pressure, not the threat of military action. Closer to Fall's thinking, he insisted that the Obregón regime, as a requirement for recognition, must sign a treaty guaranteeing American property rights acquired in Mexico before the Constitution of 1917 and Article 27. In May 1921 Hughes revealed the administration's Mexican policy by sending the Obregón government a treaty draft that included most of the Fall subcommittee's stipulations. Obregón resisted these demands for another two years.

Meanwhile Interior Secretary Fall managed to keep abreast of Mexican affairs through his crumbling intelligence system and such personal contacts in the oil companies as William F. Buckley and Doheny's lobbyist, Harold Walker. With the encouragement of Hughes, whose diplomatic overtures had stalled, American oilmen went to Mexico City in the summer of 1921. There they negotiated a private agreement with the Obregón government for a temporary reduction of petroleum export taxes. A coalition of American bankers headed by Thomas W. Lamont of J. P. Morgan and Company worked out a repayment plan for the Mexican national debt. Both Edward L. Doheny and Harry F. Sinclair, who also had operations in Mexico, were members of the oil delegation. Doheny tried to assure Fall that the oilmen's mission had not compromised the hard-line agenda of the Mexican Affairs Subcommittee, but the interior secretary could take little comfort from this news, nor in a second pilgrimage by American petroleum magnates the next year.

By early 1923 Hughes, with American bankers and oil companies acting as diplomatic brokers, had prompted the formation of a joint commission to break the recognition impasse. The United States and Mexican commissioners, meeting in Mexico City from May into August, drew up the Bucareli agreements in which Mexico pledged to pay for expropriated agricultural lands, uphold the "positive acts" doctrine safeguarding rights to oil lands acquired prior to Article 27, and cooperate in establishing two commissions to consider all claims. Although only informal accords, not a binding protocol or treaty, the Bucareli agreements cleared the way for recognition, which the United States extended to the Obregón regime on August 31, 1923, six months after Fall's resignation from the cabinet. Hughes had accepted half a loaf. Contrary to the admonitions of Fall, who insisted on binding guarantees from Mexico, the accords depended almost entirely on good faith. The Bucareli understanding did end the long diplomatic crisis spawned by revolutionary turmoil, but it was soon disregarded by Mexico, which eventually expropriated foreign oil holdings in 1938.

Long before recognition, Doheny, the fabled "Oil King of Mexico," had abandoned Fall's exacting standards and compromised with the Mexican government. Shortly after the Bucareli agreements he loaned the Obregón regime $5,000,000, and his Mexican Petroleum Company invested an additional $9,500,000 in Mexico. Then, in 1925, perhaps seeing the expropriation handwriting on the wall, Doheny began selling his Mexican properties to Standard Oil of Indiana, while retaining his California petroleum holdings. In the end Fall's long crusade for American property rights in Mexico seemed futile, but his efforts were not overlooked by such American investors as Doheny and Sinclair. When he obtained, while interior secretary, more than $400,000 from the two wealthy oilmen, they were, in large part, showing their appreciation for Fall's stand on Mexican issues.

Besides Fall's differences with Secretary of State Hughes, another row in the Harding administration occurred when Fall lambasted Harry Daugherty after the attorney general's surprise action in obtaining a sweeping federal court injunction to break the railroad strike of 1922. Proud of his constitutional expertise,

Fall had helped Daugherty prepare a legal opinion on the concurrent coal strike, but he was not consulted on the railroad restraining order and considered much of it unconstitutional. At the next cabinet meeting, threatening to resign, he told President Harding that the injunction left all of them open to public ridicule and that Daugherty "should be reprimanded right here." As he grew angrier, Fall recalled, he shouted at the attorney general, "You don't know any law, and you can't learn any." The president closed the discussion abruptly by stating his approval of the injunction with the most objectionable sections deleted, and by sternly telling Fall to see him after the meeting. Once they were alone, Harding said: "I wish you wouldn't 'ride' the attorney general like that. You are too hard on him. I don't want to hear any more outbursts about resigning, either." Fall apologized to the president and continued to have a fairly good relationship with Daugherty while they served together in the cabinet.

The Interior Department alone, with its sometimes contradictory emphases on conservation and development, or public works, had enough built-in problems to frustrate Fall. The secretary's official headquarters, in the "biggest permanent office building in Washington," symbolized his far-reaching responsibilities. Resembling "a great salon in a beautiful home," his commodious office quarters were adorned with redwood from Yosemite, majestic Indian faces filigreed on huge glass sheets, and militant stuffed Alaskan eagles perched as if ready to take flight. President Taft described the Interior Department as "the 'lumber room' of the government, into which we put everything that we don't know how to classify." It was a conglomeration of bureaus and agencies, from the General Land Office to the Bureau of Education, with a multitude of troubles. The Geological Survey, which emphasized pure science and research, had to justify its existence to a business-minded Congress. Mind-boggling difficulties regarding land claims and tribal government, unsolved for decades, plagued the Bureau of Indian Affairs. The Reclamation Service, shackled with a failed self-financing system for federal irrigation projects, faced attacks from every side. Critics of the General Land Office charged it with careless management and wanton disposal of the public domain, and demanded a return to the standards of Theodore Roosevelt's day. On and on, the list of headaches seemed endless.

Interior was also ensnared in several long-standing jurisdictional conflicts with other executive departments. Usually these interdepartmental feuds involved conservation of the natural resources. By 1921 the conservation program launched by President Theodore Roosevelt, ably assisted by his forestry chief, Gifford Pinchot, had reached a climax, with the federal government empowered to manage and regulate resource development ranging from the forests to mineral deposits. At this moment of triumph Warren G. Harding was elected president, followed by the shocking news of Fall's cabinet appointment. Pinchot declared to a friend: "Fall has been steadily on the wrong side of the Conservation question, although not one of the leaders. On the record, it would have been possible to pick a worse man for Secretary of the Interior, but not altogether easy." He ended a similar assessment with the warning "Trouble ahead." Secretary Fall and the conservationists were on a collision course from the beginning.

To further complicate matters, the new Republican administration had promised a far-reaching reorganization of the federal bureaucracy. The 1920 platform, glorifying efficiency and economy in government, called for a "thorough investigation" of the executive departments, "with a view to securing consolidation" as well as "a more business-like distribution of functions." In his inaugural address Harding enthusiastically endorsed these objectives. By the time Harding took office, Congress had already established the Joint Committee on Reorganization composed of three members from each house. Because of the president's "peculiar interest" in reorganization, Congress asked him to appoint a personal representative to work with the committee. Harding selected an able progressive Republican from Ohio, Walter F. Brown, who as the committee chairman began the much-ballyhooed, but ill-fated, task of devising a reorganization plan acceptable to the president, the cabinet, and Congress. The

Republican predilection for businesslike government operations remained a major political theme throughout the 1920s.

It would be difficult to exaggerate the importance of the Harding administration's realignment program in the events leading to the Teapot Dome scandal. This ambitious initiative unlocked Pandora's box by declaring open season for empire building by all cabinet officers. For Secretary Fall, who eagerly embraced the proposed shuffling of federal bureaus, it became the main rationale in his objectives for the Interior Department, whether in gaining control of the national forests or the naval oil reserves. Not surprisingly, most of his cabinet colleagues jealously guarded their own domains, thereby embroiling him in more controversy. Fall's personal ambition and his freewheeling economic philosophy, particularly on the role of private enterprise in resource development, always cloud any assessment of his official actions. For an understanding of his motives, however, Fall's cabinet career must be placed in the context of the Republican reorganization crusade. All too often his attempts to win jurisdictional battles have been characterized as nothing more than avaricious grabs for personal aggrandizement, rather than the efforts of a dutiful cabinet head fighting in the high-stakes interdepartmental competition. In comparison, Commerce Secretary Hoover was a more ambitious, and more successful, empire builder than Fall, but through skillful maneuvering avoided public controversy.

Fall assumed his new assignment with customary vigor. No other cabinet post, except secretary of state, was more to his taste. From long experience as a rancher, farmer, mining investor, and western senator, he knew the Interior Department and how he wanted to run it. Although not keen on administrative chores, he could wade through a great amount of paperwork quickly because, according to Bronson Cutting, he possessed "an amazing mind [and] could take any document, glance at it in an instant or two, and master every detail of it!" Besides a notorious temper, other observers noted, he had "the courage of his convictions," made a decision quickly, and having reached it was "difficult to sway." First and foremost, he was determined to make Interior the Department of Natural Resources, the unchallenged federal agency for management and development of the national patrimony. As an unabashed apostle of the "come-and-get-it traditions of the young West," he intended to fight the devil with fire and turn the clock back on the conservationists. This retrospective approach, it should be remembered, was consistent with President Harding's campaign pledge of "a return to normalcy," which had helped garner a landslide record 60.2 percent of the popular vote.

By far Fall's most heated cabinet controversy arose over his crusade, in the spirit of government reorganization, to transfer the Forest Service from the Agriculture Department to Interior and his proposed development plan for the natural resources of Alaska Territory. In this confrontation he clashed head-on with Agriculture Secretary Henry C. Wallace, a shrewd red-headed Iowa newspaper editor with the disposition of "a natural-born gamecock." Of the two semiofficial social sets around Harding—the poker players and the golfers—Wallace had informal access to the president on the golf course. Among Wallace's main supporters were Gifford Pinchot and the forestry conservation movement. Pinchot had backed his longtime friend for the cabinet and considered Wallace to be its "best appointment." Thus when Fall tried to move the national forests out of the Agriculture Department, where Pinchot had carefully lodged them, he had to fight not only the hardfisted agriculture secretary but also a battle-seasoned army of conservationists. This dedicated corps—influential public figures, skilled lobbyists, and accomplished propagandists with a string of sympathetic newspapers at their command—had stood at Armageddon for years battling all those who threatened Roosevelt-Pinchot ideals. They often tried offenders in the court of public opinion, as a previous interior secretary, Richard A. Ballinger, had discovered to his dismay. Fall's failure to recognize the power of the conservationists proved to be a fatal mistake.

Secretary Fall's conservation troubles began when he plunged ahead with his own reorganization scheme even though Harding's overall realignment program was floundering. Impatient and determined, he formulated a comprehensive set of "development policies" for the Interior Department. Then, about three months after taking office, Fall started implementing these policies, and his reorganization agenda, when he acquired control of the naval petroleum reserves from the Navy Department. The transfer was approved by Navy Secretary Edwin L. Denby and authorized by President Harding in an executive order, not by an act of Congress. It was announced in the newspapers and drew little immediate attention. But the transfer did alert the conservationists, who started tracking Fall and questioning his intentions. Like hounds after a timber wolf, they followed his trail, which began at the naval oil reserves, then forked up north to the forests of Alaska, and in the end switched back to the naval reserves again. The first real excitement of the chase came in Alaska.

In speeches and interviews Fall explained how his development policies would unlock the nation's bounties for immediate benefits, not hoard them for some distant future. "All natural resources should be made as easy of access as possible to the present generation," he declared. "Man can not exhaust the resources of nature and never will." Often he titillated an audience by saying confidently that the riches of Alaska alone, "now lying dormant," could solve most of postwar America's economic problems. For example, he told economy-minded citizens, the untapped northern wealth, "if properly handled," could pay off the burdensome war debt and provide veterans with both pensions and a bonus without exacting a cent of taxation. He was particularly impressed by the possibilities for development of Alaska's vast coalfields, unlimited petroleum reserves, and "wonderful forests." Fall pointed out that Alaska, although a potential El Dorado, remained in the economic doldrums, an object of concern for Washington officialdom. Indeed, after several conferences with Fall, Harding began asking, "What's the matter with Alaska?" and looking to his interior secretary for the answer. Then the president reportedly told Fall "to go ahead and carry out the program which both are convinced will mean a greater Alaska."

Secretary Fall stood ready to tackle the Alaska problem right away. He believed that the greatest handicap shackling the territory—the barrier to its development and progress—was federal bureaucracy and red tape. Five cabinet departments, with some thirty-eight bureaus, exercised control there, causing inevitable conflict and confusion. There was "just one way to develop Alaska," as he saw it, "and that is to vest absolute authority in a single head, and that supreme authority must be the President himself." Once the consolidation occurred, Fall obviously believed, the president should place the administration of Alaska's natural resources under the interior secretary. Drawing on similar proposals in the Wilson administration, he started initiating bills for an ambitious federally sponsored development plan in Alaska that would offer attractive inducements to private enterprise. Under Fall's recommendations the interior secretary, with a revolving fund of $5 million, would build sawmills, paper factories, smelters, railroads, and other facilities and operate them until they could be sold or leased to private investors. Oil exploration and drilling, as well as mining, would be encouraged on public lands. With this pump-priming infusion of state socialism, the Republican interior secretary seemed to say, Alaska would enjoy a boom even greater than the gold rushes, and the nation as a whole would share the economic windfall.

Rambunctious as ever, Fall rushed ahead even though he realized that his Alaska program was loaded with dynamite. The other cabinet heads with jurisdiction there would hardly capitulate without putting up a fight. In addition, the specter of the Ballinger-Pinchot controversy of 1909–10, in which Pinchot had accused Interior Secretary Ballinger of giving away Alaskan coal land claims to private enterprise, still hovered over the Interior Department, tarnishing its conservation image. The key to success for Fall's plan, however, lay in the national forests of Alaska. If all of the territory's development activities were placed under one administrative head, as Fall wanted, the national forests there would certainly be included. Just as logically, in his mind, where the Alaska timberlands went, the rest of the national forest lands should also be lodged administratively. In short, Fall's government reorganization scheme for Alaska would get the ball rolling for transferring the entire National Forest Service from the Agriculture Department to the Interior Department.

This apparent interdepartmental raid and personal power grab by Fall had a long history, going back before 1905 when Interior, which previously controlled the "forest reserves," lost them to Agriculture. Interior never became reconciled to its loss. Successive interior secretaries, regardless of party, struggled and conspired to regain the timberlands. And since the national forests symbolized the conservation movement, this long-standing feud epitomized the bitter rivalry between the two departments for dominance in managing the nation's resources. Now Secretary Fall, a veteran of Dona Ana County political wars, got his turn to battle Interior's traditional foe.

Agricultural Secretary Wallace responded to Fall's challenge cautiously. Remembering the Ballinger-Pinchot affair's divisive effects on the Taft administration, he hoped to avoid a similar upheaval in Harding's cabinet. But Pinchot and his conservation warriors had no official ties to restrain them. Through his watchdog in Washington, attorney Harry A. Slattery, Pinchot had kept tabs on Fall since the naval oil transfer. Now he became thoroughly alarmed because, as Slattery observed, the inclusion of the Alaska timberlands in Fall's development scheme "means everything." Clearly the interior secretary wanted charge of Alaska's forests and the entire Forest Service—that was an anathema in itself—and Fall wanted control of the forests as a means to begin massive exploitation of all of the northern territory's vast resources, a prospect that made the Ballinger-Pinchot episode seem like child's play. Pinchot decided that he must stop Fall in Alaska to save not only his beloved national forests but the overall conservation movement as well.

After two long conferences with Secretary Fall and another with President Harding, Pinchot sent out a call to arms for conservationists: "Fall has made up his mind to get the [Forest] Service, and Harding is on the fence." With Slattery lending expert assistance, Pinchot proceeded to try the interior secretary in the court of public opinion, just as he had done with Secretary Ballinger a decade earlier. It was known among the Pinchotites as the "Fall war." Personal pleas went out to prominent conservationists; thousands of form letters were mailed to organizations and the "friends of forestry." Soon leading newspapers and periodicals began lambasting Secretary Fall and his proposed Forest Service transfer. Prone to depict his opponents as crooks and villains, Pinchot roasted Fall unmercifully as a foe of conservation, a friend of the exploiter, and the archetypical livestock baron who lusted after national-forest grazing rights in the West. Later Pinchot's crusader suspicions proved to be right in Fall's naval oil transactions. In the forest transfer fight, however, he was guided mainly by a conditioned reaction against the Interior Department, which he simply did not trust. If the mythical Johnny Appleseed had somehow become interior secretary, "Sir Galahad of the Woodlands" Pinchot would undoubtedly have fought just as hard to prevent a forest transfer.

Secretary Fall, who had never ducked a fight in his life, fumed under the mounting criticism until he could stand it no longer. Then, bristling with indignation, he tried to even the score. In a series of news releases and press conferences he emphasized Harding's government reorganization campaign and characterized the Pinchotites as "parlor socialists and impractical economists" who feared a loss of prestige if necessary realignment occurred. He had not "the remotest thought" of overturning forest conservation policy if the Forest Service came under his jurisdiction. His "sole purpose" was the coordination of federal activities to solve the problems of Alaska, "an empire of incalculable riches" that was inflicted with "too much bureaucracy." For the sake of progress the territory must be opened up to private enterprise and individuals such as veterans of the recent war.

The conservationists had Fall on the run even before Agriculture Secretary Wallace "got his fighting clothes on." Once in action, Wallace stressed the disadvantages of the forest transfer and concentrated on defeating Fall's proposal not in the public arena but inside the administration. Soon the two cabinet officers were locked in open controversy and exchanging brickbats. Fall reportedly asked President Harding to stop the "vicious propaganda" coming out of the Agriculture Department. By mid-March 1922 the interdepartmental argument, producing rumors of a cabinet crisis and Fall's resignation, had landed in Harding's lap. Fall wrote former Secretary Ballinger that he had warned the president and the cabinet that he would open up Alaska and not let it "rust" even if this caused another uproar like the Ballinger-Pinchot affair. In April he told a family member of "a long and very satisfactory conference" in which Harding promised to "get actively behind my development policies," including federal pump priming in Alaska. Fall made no mention of the forest transfer, saying only that the president gave assurances of "confidence in my judgment and his determination to back me to the limit."

In the end Harding failed to honor this commitment, although at first he undoubtedly wanted to do so. Alaskan development and the forest transfer became inextricably entwined, creating an explosive political issue. The Pinchotites, backed by aroused public opinion, then succeeded in killing Fall's proposals. In late summer 1922 Fall conceded defeat. Even though the Reorganization Committee chairman favored the forest transfer, Fall wrote W. A. Hawkins, Alaska realignment was bogged down. "Whether it will ever be carried out or not I don't know," he said, "and insofar as I am personally concerned don't care." He had done his duty, forcefully presenting the Interior Department's case and his own convictions, and would go no further. Later the taint of Teapot Dome on the Interior Department ruined its chances of ever acquiring the Forest Service and delayed the "opening up" of Alaska for another fifty years.

Another confrontation between Fall and Wallace flared up in the Federal Power Commission. Once again Secretary Fall became the kicker, stirring up a controversy and drawing President Harding into it. The membership of the FPC, a new federal agency created by the Water Power Act of 1920 to provide a unified government policy for water power development, consisted of Fall, Wallace, and Secretary of War John W. Weeks (chairman), as heads of their departments. Fall considered FPC Executive Secretary O. C. Merrill, a former Forest Service chief engineer, to be an undercover agent for Wallace in Agriculture's conspiracy to take over resource-management functions properly belonging to Interior.

The fiercest disagreement between Fall and Merrill arose over the Girand case, in which Merrill recommended FPC approval of a proposed private power project on the Colorado River. Fall not only blocked the Girand application but also insisted that "no construction of any kind should be allowed upon the Colorado, except under United States Governmental ownership and control." This stand by the faithful protector of private enterprise seemed incredible, especially since the Girand project had strong backing from western mining interests. The explanation was simple. First, federal control would facilitate an agreement with Mexico on the Colorado's disputed international waters, which Fall's Mexican Affairs Subcommittee had demanded as a condition of recognition. More important, Fall was promoting his development program for the Interior Department, whose Reclamation Service had its own plans for construction of the gigantic Boulder Canyon project.

Indeed, Secretary Fall had already submitted to Congress the Fall-Davis Report (acclaimed as the "Bible of the Colorado River"), which recommended that the federal government build the highest dam in the world at or near Boulder Canyon, about ninety miles downstream from the Girand site. An "All-American Canal" from the lower Colorado to California's Imperial Valley would help complete this comprehensive blueprint, which promised flood control, increased irrigation, and the huge amounts of hydroelectric power needed to pay for the great dam. Although the Fall-Davis Report was mostly the work of Arthur Powell Davis, director of the Reclamation Service, Fall eagerly endorsed the prospectus and held hearings in support of it. The monumental river project, with its potential for growth and progress, appealed to his western pride and fitted neatly into his Interior development policies. As in the case of Alaska, he believed that taming the Colorado "could never be successfully solved by any other agency than . . . the federal government." Moreover, congressional approval of the Fall-Davis Report would assure Interior and its Reclamation Service a dominant role not only on the Colorado but, as a consequence, in the multipurpose projects envisioned for other river basins as well.

Fighting the devil with fire, Fall went to his friend in the White House and asked for Merrill's head and, for good measure, reconstitution of the FPC as an appellate body. Harding, although willing to support a restructuring of the FPC, balked at the removal of Merrill for fear of offending Secretary Wallace and escalating the already red-hot Fall-Wallace rivalry into a cabinet showdown. Fall had to settle for the cabinet's agreement that no construction would be allowed on the Colorado until Congress made a decision on the Fall-Davis Report, which was eventually embodied in the Boulder Canyon Project Act of 1928.

Meanwhile the press reported yet another "deadly quarrel" in Harding's official family, this time between Fall and Commerce Secretary Hoover. The rumored controversy involved the president's appointment of Hoover to the Colorado River Commission, a body authorized by Congress to draw up a seven-state compact for the division of Colorado River waters. Supposedly, Fall wanted the assignment himself and was bitterly disappointed when Harding ignored his wishes. In truth, Fall, who intended to stay in the cabinet only a year or so, could not assume the longterm commitment required of members of the Colorado River Commission. As an unabashed Hoover admirer, he strongly supported Hoover's selection, and his recommendation was one of the main reasons that Harding gave the commerce secretary the job. The newspapers, however, hailed Hoover's choice as another indication of Fall's deteriorating relationship with Harding, even though Hoover himself took the initiative in trying to quash this rumor. In this notable instance, then, although their fictional clash caused embarrassment for Fall and Hoover, Fall had acted as Harding's trusted adviser and not as the kicker in the cabinet.

The Boulder Canyon project, envisioned in the Fall-Davis Report, became a conservation landmark. It was the first large-scale federal enterprise based on the multipurpose objectives of flood control, irrigation, and hydroelectric power, and as such it set the precedent for comprehensive resource planning. In this new conservation era the Reclamation Service (renamed the Bureau of Reclamation in 1923) enjoyed the dominant role Secretary Fall demanded for it. Hoover's long association with the project, especially the Colorado River Compact that apportioned the waters, resulted in the majestic dam near Boulder Canyon being named for him, although political pettiness forestalled the honor until 1947. Fall received only slight recognition for his early but important part in the river's development. For instance, a 1924 Democratic campaign pamphlet accused the Coolidge administration of attempting to block the Boulder Canyon project in favor of private power. Even Fall with his black oil sins, the tract stated, had not tried to turn over the Colorado to the "Power Trust" and "*give away power rights worth a thousand Teapot Domes.*"

The reverberations of the Fall-Wallace warfare seemed endless, as is illustrated by the rivalry between Interior's National Park Service and Agriculture's National Forest Service. Worldly, utilitarian Pinchotites scoffed at the conservation concept of aesthetic preservation represented by the "sentimental nature lovers" who fought to establish the competing Park Service in 1916. In the 1920s a bitter interagency struggle surfaced when the Park Service sought command of recreation in the national forests, and the Forest Service, which began placing more emphasis on recreational use and wilderness protection, responded by trying to absorb the parks. Secretary Fall, who believed that outdoor recreation "should be all under one head," stepped into this ongoing controversy and, extolling government reorganization, called on Congress to give the Park Service control of recreational facilities in all of the national woodlands. This particular contest remained a standoff while Fall was in office, but, as stated by historian Donald C. Swain, the Park Service "emerged from the 1920's as the main competitor of the Forest Service in the race for conservation leadership."

For Park Service officials, who feared "routine annihilation" from the Harding administration, Secretary Fall was a pleasant surprise. At first Parks Director Stephen T. Mather, who had dedicated his life and considerable personal fortune to this cause, thought Fall's appointment meant "the crash of falling trees and the sound of distant dam construction." To Mather's amazement, Fall told him in their first conference to expect no major changes in either policy or personnel. As in the case of the Colorado River, the secretary indicated a sympathy for "necessary" development in the parks, but only by the federal government, not by the states or private enterprise. Consequently, after an inspection tour of the western parks in Mather's company, Fall opposed Democratic Senator Thomas J. Walsh's bill to dam the outlet of Lake Yellowstone, killed a scheme to cut the rim of Lake Tahoe for a federal reclamation project in Nevada, and condemned Republican Senator Ralph H. Cameron's promotional efforts for his own private interests in the Grand Canyon.

On the other hand, Secretary Fall's deviation from fundamental park philosophy sometimes alarmed Mather. National parks, the faithful believed, should possess the uniqueness and majestic grandeur of Yellowstone, Mount Rainier, Yosemite, or the Grand Canyon. To the horror of Mather and his staff, the new interior secretary became the chief advocate of a contradictory monstrosity—an "All-Year National Park" or, as quickly nicknamed by its critics, "All-Over-the-Map" park or "Mexican freckles." This proposal resurrected one of Fall's old dreams, unfulfilled in the Senate, for a national park in southern New Mexico. As the All-Year National Park, the expanded version featured a federal highway network connecting a dozen widely scattered locations, including part of the Mescalero Apache Indian Reservation, lands around Elephant Butte reservoir on the Rio Grande, the White Sands, and the Malpais lava beds in the Tularosa Basin. In keeping with Fall's long-held views, but contradicting preservation canons, the prospective park would be subject to mining and mineral leasing, hunting, grazing, timber cutting, and hydroelectric and irrigation development. Fall also proposed that the federal government sell 10 percent of the public domain to pay for road construction in the West, such as the highway between Elephant Butte and the Mescalero reservation.

The All-Year Park project had widespread civic support in El Paso and southern New Mexico, but it was Fall's handiwork and he took command of the drive to obtain congressional approval. Murmurs of protest arising from the Mescalero reservation subsided after Fall himself talked to the Indians and then quietly dispatched to New Mexico a trusted former superintendent, now employed by Harry Sinclair, who also explained the advantages of the new arrangement. Parks Director Mather remained unconvinced. Forging ahead, the interior secretary temporarily patched up his differences with Senator Bursum, who sneaked the All-Year Park bill through a busy Senate in July 1922.

The Senate approval awakened the aesthetic preservationist defenders of the national parks and, not unlike the Pinchotite forest propaganda corps, they unleashed an unmerciful assault on Fall and his park plan. With Mather sidelined by illness, this publicity onslaught was led by his influential friends, particularly Robert Sterling Yard, a former *New York Herald* editor who was now head of an advocacy network, the National Parks Association. Yard, a more extreme preservation purist than Mather, attacked Secretary Fall as "the greatest danger that our National Parks System has yet encountered." First he blasted Fall's New Mexico project as substandard, and then he took aim at the interior secretary's more comprehensive idea of adding numerous public campgrounds throughout the national parks. As strident crusader Yard discovered in a face-to-face encounter, Fall was "a very dangerous fighter," mainly because of "his extraordinary individualism and precipitancy," which made him think "his own solution of any problem [was] the only rational one." This confrontation, instead of repulsing Yard and the aesthetic preservationists, merely encouraged them to redouble their efforts.

Once again Fall ran head-on into a major element of the conservation movement, and once more he went down to defeat. Despite his vigorous support, the All-Year National Park bill died in a House committee. That the far-ranging project formed a disjointed horseshoe around Fall's Three Rivers ranch did not help his case. This raucous row further embittered the crusty yet thin-skinned interior secretary on the fortunes of public office. Many of the radical preservationists wrote Fall off as having "no conception of national park standards," but he should not be judged by the All-Year Park alone. Mather nursed no serious grievances against him and refused to believe that bribery was involved in the Teapot Dome affair. Likewise, Mather's successor, Horace M. Albright, observed that Secretary Fall "must go down in history as a strong friend of the National Parks." Significantly Fall's proletarian proposal for more public camping and recreational facilities, in tune with the rising tide of tourism, and to some extent his concept of widely scattered locations, were later employed in the national parks system. Moreover, all the incongruous parts of his All-Year Park, except the Mescalero reservation, eventually became state or federal recreation or conservation sites—most notably the White Sands National Monument near Alamogordo and Elephant Butte on the Rio Grande, now New Mexico's largest and most popular state park.

The All-Year Park proposal, although involving a two-thousand-acre cession from the Mescalero reservation, drew more fire from guardians of the national parks than from Indian rights advocates. When Secretary Fall turned his attention to Navajo and Pueblo lands, however, he collided with a rising wave of Indian policy reform that would culminate during the New Deal. The Navajo reservation included portions established both by presidential executive order and by treaty. About the time Fall took office, droves of oil company representatives were drawn to the Four Corners area by the discovery of gas and possibilities of finding oil on the executive-order portion of the reservation near Farmington, New Mexico. In June 1922 he issued an administrative decision classifying all executive-order reservations as public lands that were temporarily placed in Indian hands and therefore open to oil and gas exploration under the General Leasing Act of 1920. This meant that the state involved, the reclamation fund, and the federal treasury would split production royalties, but the Indians would not have a share. About 9 million acres of the 22 million acres of Indian lands affected by this ruling lay in the Navajo reservation.

An abusive whirlwind of criticism hit the interior secretary. Herbert Welsh, executive secretary of the Indian Rights Association, regarded the decision as "revolutionary" and a breach of his uneasy truce with Fall. From Farmington a correspondent for the *Kansas City Star*, alluding to the Teapot Dome lease, reported that Fall was also plotting another "oil grab" in the treaty portion of the Navajo reservation. By creating a tribal council controlled by a special commissioner, the journalist charged, Fall and his "political henchmen" in New Mexico intended to circumvent the traditional Navajo decision-making process for mineral leases and thereby favor Standard Oil. In his bombastic response the interior secretary blamed disgruntled oil speculators for such "false and libelous" accusations. Critics saw Fall's ruling on the executive-order lands as a frontal assault on all Indian reservations. But he apparently had the limited primary objective of providing royalty income from the Navajo reservation for revenue-poor western states, especially New Mexico. Secondarily, of course, this episode involved his fundamental attitude toward the natural resources, and one of his main concerns as interior secretary—to open the West for development.

The Bursum Bill, which caused a much louder public outcry, originated from another nagging problem in Fall's home state. For generations New Mexicans had been moving onto Pueblo Indian lands, by either purchase or squatting, until some three thousand non-Indians (representing twelve thousand persons, mostly Hispanics) claimed property rights and at some pueblos most of the precious water rights. Earlier court action seemed to sanction these landholdings, but a Supreme Court decision in 1913 questioned their legality. With the "colonists" fighting eviction, and armed conflict a distinct possibility, the plight of the non-Indians became a major issue in New Mexico politics. Secretary Fall was determined to settle this knotty problem once and for all, and the Bursum Bill contained his solution. The final draft was prepared in Fall's Interior Department office under his supervision. In fact, critics sometimes called it the "Fall-Bursum bill." As its main provision, the measure confirmed most of the non-Indian claims and offered compensation to the Pueblo Indians in lieu land or cash. Fall maintained that the Indians had been consulted on the bill, but the Pueblos vehemently denied that it was so.

Indian rights advocates, fearing the destruction of Pueblo culture, vociferously opposed the measure and directed equally harsh criticism at Secretary Fall and Senator Bursum, its official sponsor. The prime mover in this campaign was Stella M. Atwood, a spokeswoman for the General Federation of Women's Clubs. John Collier, a young urban social worker, was hired by Atwood as the GFWC's chief publicist and field agent on Indian welfare. In November 1922, at Collier's instigation, an All-Pueblo Council convened at Santo Domingo, reportedly their first such united action since the revolt against Spanish rule in 1680. More than a hundred delegates representing twenty pueblos issued an appeal to the American people stating that the Bursum Bill would "rob us of everything which we hold dear—our lands, our customs, our traditions." The council then dispatched a seventeen-member delegation, escorted by Collier and Atwood, to the East, where the Pueblos skillfully argued their case before audiences in Chicago, New York City, and Washington. This entourage included eight Pueblo governors who carried with them the silver-headed canes of authority bestowed by President Lincoln.

In the East, Collier and Atwood busily cultivated nationwide support for the Pueblo cause. Eastern lawyers, business leaders, clergy, and teachers raised a furor; in New Mexico the artists and writers of Santa Fe and Taos, as well as Bronson Cutting's *Santa Fe New Mexican*, joined in. Behind the Bursum Bill lay the plight of two threatened groups: the Pueblos and also a large number of Hispanic and Anglo settlers within pueblo boundaries. This basic problem was obscured by the outpouring of publicity, orchestrated mainly by Collier, which branded the bill as nothing more than a land-grabbing raid on powerless Indians and a plot to obliterate their ancient way of life. As the *Washington Herald* put it, the Pueblos were "being irreparably victimized" by the "political machinations" of Secretary Fall and Senator Bursum. At one point the *New York Times* also reported that Fall, Bursum, and other prominent Republicans were "financially interested" in Pueblo lands—an erroneous charge the newspaper soon retracted.

With the Bursum Bill stalled in Congress, the Navajo and Pueblo issues remained unresolved when Secretary Fall left office in March 1923. In the Indian Oil Act of 1927, which earmarked all royalties for the Indians but permitted the states to levy a production tax, his 1922 administrative decision on oil and gas development for executive-order lands was largely reversed. The act did confirm some twenty exploration permits (most of them authorized by Fall) on the Navajo reservation as well as more than four hundred applications for permits. The rumored Standard Oil conspiracy to bilk the Navajos of their treaty oil holdings failed to materialize. In the Pueblo Lands Act of 1924, a compromise measure evolving from the Bursum Bill, the non-Indian settlers received some of the protection for their land claims that Fall and Bursum had sought. A special board established to settle disputes over titles and the compensation for lost land usually favored the non-Indian claimants.

Secretary Fall also banned Indian dancing and peyote smoking, but his most significant contribution to Indian policy came in an unexpected way. John Collier, the future New Deal Indian affairs commissioner, began his long, distinguished career with the Pueblo lands dispute. Especially after the Teapot Dome scandal erupted, Collier employed an Indian reform strategy based on a conspiracy reminiscent of the naval oil debacle. According to Collier's "devil theory," Fall had concocted a monstrous Indian land grab involving the Navajo oil and gas holdings, the Pueblo lands, and a third thrust, the failed Indian

Omnibus Bill of 1923, which would have completed the Dawes Act of 1887 by individualizing remaining tribal lands. As already explained, however, Fall's objectives in the first two matters were unrelated, even though both concerned problems in New Mexico. The Omnibus Bill, although Fall agreed with its intent, originated in a strong postwar impetus for assimilation, not from a plot devised by him. In Fall's larger western development plan he had not targeted the Indians and their lands for exploitation any more than the national forests, Alaskan resources, or the public domain. Yet Collier, in his reform crusade leading to the capstone Indian Rights Act of 1934, successfully portrayed Fall as the epitome of all the evil forces working against Indians, and he tarred the Bureau of Indian Affairs with the same brush. In short, Fall became, in Collier's words, "the indispensable villain." The scoundrel of Teapot Dome, the public seemed willing to believe, was capable of any and all transgressions.

During Albert Fall's two years in the Harding cabinet, he used the battle cry of government reorganization, under the banners of efficiency and economy, in attempts to expand the Interior Department's turf. Fall later said that he accepted a cabinet position as an easy way "to get out of politics" and public office. As the kicker in the cabinet, however, he experienced a series of disappointments, frustrations, and defeats that gradually sapped his influence even with his bosom friend President Harding. Maelstroms of criticism surrounded him because of several of his official actions, and for one who had adopted confrontation and controversy as a way of life, he bruised very easily. Making up for lost time financially had become an obsession with him. It warped his judgment and had a significant bearing on the most important decisions he ever made, as a cabinet officer or otherwise: to take almost half a million dollars from oil millionaires Doheny and Sinclair at about the same time that he leased the naval petroleum reserves to them.

CHAPTER 7

Leasing the Naval Oil Reserves

ONE of Gifford Pinchot's disciples complained bitterly that the usually invincible conservationists, "after great efforts and against terrific obstacles," had established their policy for the naval petroleum reserves only to see "its secret overthrow within one year after the present Administration took power." Once again the culprit was Interior Secretary Albert B. Fall, who had stealthily installed a new set of leasing arrangements for these government oil lands, thereby reversing a cherished conservationist accomplishment. What became for Fall the biggest battle of a life filled with heated public controversy initially appeared as only another part of his development program for the Interior Department, which also included the national forests, Alaskan resources, and Indian reservations. But the Teapot Dome scandal, resulting from his leasing of the naval reserves, reached far beyond one person's ambitions or a squabble over how to handle a parcel of the national patrimony. It also involved the Harding administration's government reorganization plans, national defense, and a world oil famine that never materialized.

In World War I the Allies "floated to victory on a wave of oil," more than 80 percent of which was furnished by the United States. As the first major conflict featuring oil-fueled machinery, the war demonstrated the importance of reliable petroleum resources to support an industrial system, whether for national defense or postwar prosperity. Soon after the armistice, despite a glutted oil market, Americans experienced "frightened doubt" when experts gloomily predicted the depletion of domestic reserves in ten or perhaps twenty years. Official reports, to make matters worse, revealed that British and Dutch concerns, in collusion with their governments, had conspired to obtain a worldwide monopoly of foreign oil reserves and exclude American companies from promising fields in the Middle East, the Dutch East Indies, and even parts of Latin America. A sharply increasing demand for petroleum products resulting from America's budding love affair with the automobile and a mechanized society exacerbated worries about an oil famine. Quite simply, the big stakes were in oil during the early 1920s. This is why Teapot Dome became the "aristocrat" of all the Harding scandals.

One major concern in the postwar oil crisis was the national imperative to guarantee adequate petroleum for the United States Navy, which had decided in 1913 to switch from coal to oil as fuel for its modern battle fleet. Similar apprehension over national security had dictated the establishment of the naval petroleum reserves earlier in the century. The key figure then was President Theodore Roosevelt, who in 1906 boldly set aside 66 million acres of public coal lands by executive order. Roosevelt's dramatic action raised a nagging question, which would be debated for years in naval oil deliberations, about the president's authority to make such withdrawals of public land by administrative action without the approval of Congress. Three successive presidents, Taft, Wilson, and Harding, followed the precedent set by Roosevelt, usually with success. In 1912 Taft, by executive order, designated nearly seventy thousand acres of lands in California for naval petroleum reserves: Elk Hills Reserve (No. 1) and Buena Vista Hills Reserve (No. 2). In 1915 Wilson added a third reserve, by selecting 9,481 acres north of Casper, Wyoming, for the Teapot Dome Reserve, and also created the first naval oil-shale reserve in Colorado in 1916. The oil lands supposedly contained proven deposits, and, as the term "reserve" indicates, they were set aside for the navy's use only in times of emergency when regular supplies might be limited. So steadfastly was this policy applied that the reserves had not been opened even for the exigencies of World War I. Harding's administrative tinkering with the three existing petroleum reserves led to the Teapot Dome scandal, but he established a fourth one of nearly twenty million acres in northern Alaska with relative ease.

To a great extent the Teapot Dome dispute dealt with conflicting interpretations of the General Leasing Act of 1920, the conservationist triumph regarding mineral leases on public lands, and another measure passed by Congress a few months later. Josephus Daniels, the Wilson administration's stubborn, controversial navy secretary, was bitterly disappointed that the leasing act left bureaucratic control over the naval petroleum reserves in the Interior Department. At his insistence the naval appropriations bill of June 4, 1920, contained a "fateful amendment" (sometimes called the "Daniels bill") empowering the navy secretary to assume management of these lands. In this capacity he was charged "to conserve, develop, use and operate the same in his discretion, directly or by contract, lease, or otherwise, and to use, store, exchange, or sell the oil and gas products thereof, and those from all royalty oil from lands in the naval reserves." For operational expenses Congress allocated a measly $500,000 from the royalties, rentals, and bonuses earned by the reserves, with the rest going to the federal treasury. Presumably if the navy needed more money for major projects, such as construction of storage facilities or pipelines, it would have to ask for additional appropriations.

Congress refused to approve one of Daniels's favorite proposals, to give the navy authority to refine its own oil. In fact, the Senate had stricken the word "refine" from an early draft of the bill and substituted the term "exchange." Another important provision retained the interior secretary's jurisdiction over those portions of the reserves with "pending claims or applications for permits or leases" under the General Leasing Act. Indeed, the interior secretary could lease to legitimate claimants the producing wells already on these lands, and the president also might, "in his discretion," permit the operators to drill additional wells in the surrounding area. This meant that the two cabinet officers and the president each had a responsibility for certain parts of the reserves. Both acts, although allowing some drilling, still identified the reserves with national defense and the navy's future needs. For the short time Secretary Daniels remained in office, he controlled their fate, resolutely keeping the navy's oil in the ground. Of great importance for Albert Fall, disgruntled western oilmen had not obtained what they wanted most—unrestricted exploitation of the reserves—and they continued to seek influential friends in government who would aid their quest.

The Harding administration counteracted the mostly British and Dutch exclusionary tactics in foreign oil fields by promoting an "open door" policy overseas. Interior Secretary Fall, showing a keen awareness of the high stakes, nationally and globally, moved quickly to facilitate this program of dollar diplomacy. As a senator, while fighting for the rights of American oilmen abroad, he had made a study of the international oil situation, gathering information from "every source" available to him. Now, with the vast files of technical data from several federal bureaus at his command, he had access to intelligence from the oil fields of the world. Increasingly his stance in international affairs would be clothed in postwar oil-crisis rhetoric, even regarding Latin America, which was always his primary concern. He now lambasted the abortive proposals for League of Nations membership as a ruse to protect the Dardanelles "so that Great Britain might forever secure free passage for the oils of Mesopotamia and Batoum."

Secretary Fall's first major accomplishment for American petroleum interests abroad came when he collaborated with Senator Lodge in ratification of the Colombian (Thomson-Urrutia) treaty with its $25 million indemnity. As explained previously (Chapter 6), the logjam on this treaty broke in the spring of 1920 after then Senator Fall received assurances about American investments "from perfectly reliable representatives in Colombia," whereupon his Foreign Relations subcommittee recommended approval. Probably Fall's main private intelligence source was James W. Flanagan, general manager of the Andian National Corporation (a Canadian subsidiary of Standard Oil of New Jersey), who came from Bogota to lobby for the long-delayed accord, thereby ensuring an oil pipeline concession for his company in Colombia. A soldier of fortune and international industrial spy for Jersey Standard's president, Walter C. Teagle, Flanagan specialized in "dirty tricks." He also possessed an impressive talent for winning friends in high places, which he now proved by teaming up with Senator Fall and another prominent treaty advocate, Colombian Minister Carlos A. Urueta. Although Fall was accused of undergoing a sudden "conversion" by Flanagan, the manipulative oilman's far-reaching influence more accurately helped the senator obtain a modus vivendi for penetration of the political tangle in Colombia.

While furnishing Senator Lodge with ammunition for the ratification fight, Secretary Fall first discounted the dead Theodore Roosevelt's opposition and then provided the main argument for the treaty. An accommodation with Colombia was imperative, he declared, to save American interests in the world oil rivalry with Great Britain. Repeatedly using the word "*crisis*," he charged in classic spread-eagle style that the British government had taken over all the big, privately owned British petroleum companies, and had either excluded Americans from many foreign fields or severely restricted their operations. As proof, he sent Lodge a diagram and an annotated map, prepared by Interior Department geologists, purportedly showing how British government-controlled concerns, such as the Royal Dutch Shell combine in Colombia and Venezuela and the Mexican Eagle ("Aguila") Company in Mexico, were rapidly gaining an upper hand. Sneering critics might question why he and Lodge had changed their minds about the treaty, Fall snorted, but the answer lay in changed international conditions, not "the dictation of some greasy oil corporation."

Fall's name often came up in the Senate debates on ratification. One Democratic skeptic attributed Lodge's change of heart to "an oil proposition that Secretary Fall had pipe-lined into this treaty." Lodge seemed to be saying, another critic charged, that the $25 million indemnity was necessary because "Secretary Fall has discovered a great deal of oil down there that the Standard Oil Co. and other companies want." Other opponents complained about blackmail by Colombia and "simply stupendous" lobbying by Americans, but conceded that the treaty was "oiled for passage" and could not be stopped.

The treaty, when ratified, was hailed in the press as the beginning of a new United States oil policy abroad. President Harding would now, predicted one eastern newspaper, "carry the American flag into the oil fields of the world to give battle to British competition." Fall's twisting of the lion's tail, particularly his much-publicized accusations about the British government's monopolistic role, drew a sharp protest from the British ambassador, who wrote Secretary of State Hughes that these charges were untrue and did "grave damage to the friendly relations between our two countries." In lengthy factual rebuttals that Fall prepared for Hughes, he admitted he had erred in saying the British government owned the Mexican Eagle Company, but stood his ground on the status of Royal Dutch Shell and the British practice of shutting out American oilmen. Overly pretentious and sometimes inaccurate in his assumptions, Fall was nonetheless right about British intentions to dominate strategically located foreign oil deposits at the expense of the United States.

The Colombian treaty did help stem the British oil tide. Because of high-pressure tactics smacking of fraud and collusion, the Colombian government accepted the document along with the indemnity and modified its petroleum laws to please the United States. Fall's cohorts, oil promoter Flanagan and former Minister Urueta, were among the treaty's chief lobbyists in Bogota. Soon afterwards, as American oil hunters marched into the surrounding jungles, Flanagan obtained Jersey Standard's long-sought pipeline concession in Colombia. Urueta became an attorney for Flanagan's company, the Jersey Standard subsidiary. By 1929 the agreement had opened the door in Colombia to American investments totaling $280 million, the greatest increase in all Latin America. Of this amount, the commitments of American petroleum companies ranked second only to loans floated on the New York Stock Exchange. For Colombia the new accord stimulated an economic boom called "the dance of the millions."

Later Fall's part in the Colombian treaty would be associated with his notorious oil sins. In 1924, when the Teapot Dome scandal revived memories of his influential role in the ratification, the Senate investigating committee attempted to uncover any Colombian "oleaginous connections" involving him. President Coolidge furnished the senators with the pertinent diplomatic correspondence, but Senator Lodge of the Foreign Relations Committee reportedly refused to cooperate. The *Chicago Tribune* sent a reporter to Bogota to investigate charges arising in the Teapot Dome probe that $5 million of the $25 million indemnity to Colombia had gone to "unnamed parties" for their part in obtaining the treaty's ratification. After examining official Colombian records, the journalist found the Bogota government "free of suspicion" and concluded that none of the indemnity paid thus far had been siphoned off in Colombia by foreigners. Although leaving open the possibility of a "slush fund" used in the Unites States, he apparently discovered no evidence that Fall received a payoff.

Secretary Fall also struck hard blows against the foreign oil threat inside the United States. As with Colombia and Mexico, the principal enemy for Fall was the Royal Dutch Shell combine, whose British and Dutch masters, according to him, intended "to exhaust the oil supplies of the United States while denying our explorers the right to prospect for oil elsewhere." This gigantic conspiracy resembled the original Standard Oil monopoly, "but increased to world magnitude." At this time the Shell combine had two major producing subsidiaries in America: the Shell Company of California and the Roxana Petroleum Corporation. Fall soon tangled with both of them. His weapon was a provision in the General Leasing Act of 1920 which authorized the interior secretary to refuse leases on public lands to any foreigner whose country discriminated against American oilmen. Using this power, he prohibited any leases on the public domain, as well as contracts or renewals on Indian lands, to foreign companies without his approval.

Then, in September 1922, Fall rejected a lease requested by Shell of California at Woodside Dome in Utah but allowed a reprieve of sixty days for the filing of "definite and positive evidence" that the British and Dutch governments had extended equal privileges to Americans. The Shell concern eventually withdrew its application. On March 3, 1923, his final full day in office, and reportedly as his last official act, he denied three leases on Creek and Cherokee Indian lands in Oklahoma to the second Shell subsidiary, Roxana Petroleum. For a parting fusillade he collaborated with a sympathetic journalist on three inflammatory newspaper articles lambasting Royal Dutch Shell. This series, which carried no byline, and a preceding news release on his Roxana decision ran on four straight days in the *New York Times*, twice on the front page. Following loud protestations by Shell, Fall's successor as interior secretary, Hubert Work, reversed the Roxana ruling on a technicality, and the Roxana company obtained the oil leases on Indian lands. Even so, Fall's exclusionary orders prevented both Roxana and Shell of California from operating on the public domain itself until 1928.

For an American public facing a fuel famine, Secretary Fall's roughshod treatment of Royal Dutch Shell vented not only postwar oil-panic anxiety but also the indignant patriotism of the day as well. The prospective petroleum crisis, and especially the rebuffs suffered by Americans in foreign oil fields, also created a widespread demand at home for tight control of all domestic deposits. In this respect the naval petroleum reserves appeared to be a veritable ace in the hole for the United States. Here the Harding administration's crusade for government reorganization, to obtain a businesslike realignment of federal bureaus, intersected the world oil situation. Without the pervasive reorganization movement Fall could not have gained control of the reserves, but with realignment in the air, and possessing supreme self-confidence, especially in his own legal ability, he assumed command of the naval oil lands with ease.

Thanks to the so-called Daniels bill, management of the naval reserves had been shifted from the interior secretary to the navy secretary. On May 31, 1921, President Harding issued an executive order transferring authority over the reserves back to the Interior Department. Unlike the General Leasing Act and the Daniels bill, both passed by Congress in 1920, the presidential order was the same instrument used by President Roosevelt when he withdrew the public coal lands, setting the precedent for creation of the naval reserves. To those uninitiated in conservation struggles, the transfer seemed like a simple transaction consistent with the administration's emphasis on bureaucratic realignment. It was announced in the press and, for the time being, drew little public attention otherwise. When an inquisitive senator questioned the executive order as a "contravention" of congressional delegation of authority in the Daniels bill, Fall replied that the new navy secretary had asked the president to make the shift, which was legal and proper under that bill as well as certain wartime legislation.

Fall and Navy Secretary Edwin L. Denby had probably initiated the transfer as early as April 1, 1921, or less than a month after Harding took office. According to Fall, Denby asked him in the White House, when they met at the cabinet room door, to take charge of the reserves because of the Navy Department's inability to deal with their grave drainage problems, while Interior possessed admirable staffing for the job in its Bureau of Mines and Geological Survey. As to the perils of leasing, Denby had commented to his official advisers: "It is full of dynamite. I don't want to have anything to do with it." Next, in a "brief conversation," the president and the two cabinet officers agreed on the transfer. From that point on Fall carried the ball. He drafted the original executive order as well as a cover letter for Denby's signature and sent them to the navy secretary for his endorsement.

Theodore Roosevelt, Jr., following in his father's footsteps as assistant navy secretary, also played a key role in the transfer. Young Roosevelt enjoyed Fall's renowned storytelling, often dining and playing poker with him at Ned McLean's elegant home. At first he considered the shift "a logical thing to do" because of all the talk about government reorganization. After a spirited discussion with naval officers familiar with the oil reserves, he changed his mind and urged his boss to cancel the transfer. Secretary Denby said impatiently that it was "too late"—the deal had already been made. Unsuccessful in this attempt, Roosevelt took his copy of the executive order to the Interior Department, where Fall rejected significant alterations submitted by the navy officers but did accept "without hesitation" an amendment that required "consultation" with the navy on any new "general policy" of drilling. Because of this added condition, Secretary Denby had to countersign all the subsequent leases and contracts, thereby, as it turned out, sharing the blame with Fall. Roosevelt, now satisfied with the safeguards given to the navy, personally delivered the amended document to Harding, who signed it. Inexplicably an explanatory letter written by Denby, which told of the naval officers' opposition to the transfer, apparently did not accompany the executive order, adding, critics believed, a sinister note to the transaction.

President Harding apparently endorsed the transfer without any other legal or documentary support than the advice of his trusted friend, Secretary Fall, who regarded an additional opinion as absolutely unnecessary. As a senator Harding had served on the Naval Affairs Committee, and now as commander in chief he faced the complexities of naval logistics that would soon surface in the Washington Disarmament Conference. Advocating government reorganization, he had told Secretary Denby that all the public lands should be under one department and that Interior was best for the job. Moreover, as Fall portrayed his friend's executive style, the president set the tone of his administration like a former newspaperman: "Harding was 'lazy!' He was an editor. He wanted the rest of us to go out like reporters, get whatever he wanted, bring it in and lay it on his desk completed—and then he would 'edit' it."

Even though Fall was a star reporter, he hardly had the beat all to himself. Secretary Denby, despite a disastrous loss of reputation in the Teapot Dome hearings, was a honest, well-intentioned cabinet officer. Elected for three terms to Congress from Michigan, Denby had served on the House Naval Affairs Committee and as a member of the Ballinger-Pinchot inquiry in 1910. Although no expert on western land issues, he was highly sensitive to the oil-drainage problem and to a modern battle fleet's need for fuel oil in seaboard storage tanks. He also approved of the government reorganization program, which seemed to justify transferring the reserves to the better-staffed Interior Department. Like Fall, Denby "had a different conception of preparedness" from that of the Pinchotite conservationists and many of his own Bureau of Engineering officers. Whereas the conservationists wanted to keep the oil in the ground, Fall and Denby believed that it should be taken out and stored in above-ground tanks near the sea for emergency use by the navy.

Albert Fall often said that he never owned a dollar's worth of oil stock in his life. His professional specialties were gold and silver mining in combination with the practice of law. Yet, as interior secretary, he assumed official responsibility for petroleum development on millions of acres of the public domain, Indian lands, and the relatively small naval reserves. Fall was determined to give priority for these domestic deposits to American oilmen who were facing exclusion overseas. Simultaneously, as signified by Harding's campaign pledge of "a return to normalcy," the fundamental relationship between government and business, imposed during the Progressive Era, had changed from trust-busting to cooperation, laying the groundwork for a partnership that scholars have called the "associational state." In the vanguard of this movement Edward L. Doheny transcended partisan politics by making campaign contributions to both major presidential candidates in 1920. During World War I, he and Harry F. Sinclair had served together on such blue-ribbon government boards as the National Petroleum War Service Committee, which gave birth to the oil industry's postwar trade association, the American Petroleum Institute. After the armistice, like other captains of industry, Doheny and Sinclair anxiously sought ways to bridge the peacetime economic turmoil. They wanted to perpetuate the cooperative relationship with government, as well as the stability and profits, of their wartime experience. In Secretary Fall they had an able, willing champion.

Many other American oilmen also competed for Fall's favors, making his job of parcelling out the domestic deposits a difficult one. Of all the federal petroleum lands under his control, the little-known naval reserves presented the most serious problems, beginning with drainage. The reserves were not compact government-owned units because of the numerous claimants clamoring for real or imagined rights. Potentially rich in oil deposits, the Elk Hills Reserve in California was threatened by drainage from adjacent private wells. The Buena Vista Hills Reserve in California, checkerboarded with private holdings, had practically ceased to exist as an emergency oil reservoir. Teapot Dome in Wyoming, with the exception of 400 of its 9,481 acres, was covered with claims, most having little validity. Even more problematic, Teapot Dome's richness remained unproven by actual drilling, although it lay adjacent to the highly productive federally owned Salt Creek field. In short, all three reserves were dotted with lands held outright or claimed by individuals or corporations. Hundreds of producing wells either within or adjoining them were contributing to drainage as they tapped the navy's emergency oil supply.

Secretary Fall inherited another problem along with the reserves. Besides their worries about an impending oil famine, United States naval leaders were nervously anticipating an imminent attack by the Japanese in the Pacific. Soon after World War I a top navy strategist reported, "It is apparent that our most probable enemy at the present time is Japan, and that differences of policy exist between the two nations which cannot be reconciled now or in the future." By terms decided in the Washington Disarmament Conference of 1921–22, the United States could increase fortifications in the Hawaiian Islands but not in the Philippines. Even before the conference, the navy's "war plans" had called for building tanks at Pearl Harbor that would hold 1.5 million gallons of fuel oil for the Pacific fleet. These plans did not originate with Secretary Fall, but he had to figure out how to get the oil and the storage tanks to hold it.

The Japanese "war scare" concerned Fall as administrator of the naval reserves, but not as much as the drainage dilemma. While only the extent of drainage from the California reserves remained in question, the experts still debated whether Teapot Dome was in real danger. After consulting Geological Survey and Bureau of Mines geological studies, several with conflicting or inconclusive findings, Fall reached the conclusion, based largely on his own mining experience, that serious leakage was occurring from Teapot Dome. Later he wrote Doheny: "[Secretary] Denby may have been actuated solely by fear of war with Japan. I was actuated: primarily, by a sense of responsibility in the matter of saving to the Navy its oils [from drainage]; and secondarily, to place the same in a form and in places where they could be utilized." Fall's priority would receive an early test.

Just before the Wilson administration ended, Navy Secretary Daniels had asked for bids to drill twenty-two wells along the eastern edge of the Elk Hills Reserve in California where new gushers on adjoining private property had caused alarming drainage. Known as "offset drilling," this procedure would supposedly minimize the underground siphoning effect of the neighboring wells. The unopened bids for drilling, including one from Doheny's Pan American Petroleum Company, landed on Fall's desk after he took control of the naval reserves. On July 12, 1921, he awarded a contract for the twenty-two wells to the Doheny concern, which had submitted the best proposal. Unlike Fall's later naval oil negotiations, this transaction drew little criticism since Daniels had originated the process, there was open competitive bidding, and Doheny clearly offered the government the highest royalty.

As the navy's agent for its petroleum reserves, Secretary Fall could not ignore the budgetary plight of the short-funded sea arm of the nation's defense, threatened by an oil famine and pinched by the economies of postwar isolationism. Actually the navy already earned millions of dollars in royalties from leases previously granted by the Wilson administration to private operators on the California reserves. Under the Daniels bill, however, all but $500,000 for operating expenses vanished into the federal treasury. The Buena Vista Hills Reserve alone, where the drainage was most serious, had produced $5,500,000 for the general fund. If the navy expected to benefit fully from the oil being taken out of its lands, it would somehow have to collect and store, or perhaps burn as fuel, the royalty oil without converting it into cash. Fall stepped forward to solve both of the navy's dilemmas—drainage and the disappearing income from royalty oil.

An Interior Department subordinate observed that Secretary Fall, with implicit faith in his own ability as a lawyer, was often contemptuous of the legal opinions of other attorneys. Unlike many lawyer-executives, he always looked for "a way to do things" instead of "all the reasons for not doing them." Or, as he wrote his wife about this time, "I am accustomed to doing things first and talking about them afterwards." Employing this pragmatic approach and the skills of a western horse trader, Fall implemented an ingenious barter system by which he exchanged the navy's royalty crude oil for refined products and the construction of above-ground steel storage tanks, thereby meeting the national defense needs. "Frankly, I thought it was a good idea," he recalled, adding, "I was a little vain about having hit upon it." To him the Daniels bill, especially its broad powers to develop, store, and exchange the production of the reserves, seemed ample enough to cover his grand scheme.

Fall's first step was the leasing on April 7, 1922, of the entire Teapot Dome Reserve in Wyoming to Harry F. Sinclair's Mammoth Oil Company, an offshoot of the Sinclair Consolidated Oil Corporation. In this quiet deal there was no public advertisement for bids and no immediate announcement of the agreement. Besides the lease, Mammoth pledged to construct a pipeline from Wyoming to the Midwest, where it would connect with the main line from the Mid-Continent field to Chicago. Fall touted his program for the reserves as a blow against monopoly, in this case Standard Oil of Indiana, which controlled the outlets from the neighboring Salt Creek field and set the prices there. The real innovation of the contract appeared in a section requiring Mammoth to pay royalties not in oil but in certificates, which the navy could exchange with the company for fuel oil, gasoline, kerosene, lubricants, and various other petroleum products at twenty-seven different seaboard points on the Atlantic and Gulf coasts and in Cuba. Or the royalty oil certificates could be traded to Mammoth for construction of storage tanks, wherever they were needed, or for cash.

Next Fall addressed the Japanese war scare in the Pacific. In exchange for the royalty crude from the California reserves, he advertised for delivery of 1.5 million barrels of fuel oil stipulated in navy war plans and for construction of storage facilities and other works, as well as the dredging of a channel, at Pearl Harbor. Unlike Doheny's strip lease for offset wells or Sinclair's lease-contract, this was not a lease for drilling but a contract to take the navy's royalty oil from existing wells as compensation for certain services rendered. Again, Doheny, representing the Pan American Petroleum and Transport Company, the parent concern of the successful strip-lease bidder, was among those submitting proposals. In fact, he filed two bids. The first one stated Doheny's offer without embellishments. His second proposal held out a tempting carrot: if given a preferential option for any future leases on the Elk Hills Reserve, Doheny promised to reduce the construction costs in his first bid by approximately $235,000. Since the government's original announcement said nothing about such a trade-off, the competing companies had not included comparable alternatives in their bids. On April 25, 1922, less than three weeks after the Sinclair deal was closed, Edward C. Finney, acting interior secretary during Fall's absence in New Mexico, and Navy Secretary Denby accepted Doheny's second proposition.

Doheny soon exercised his preferential option on the Elk Hills Reserve. When the navy's royalty oil from the California reserves proved insufficient to pay Doheny for the Pearl Harbor construction work, the government on December 11, 1922, granted him a lease to develop the rest of the eastern part of Elk Hills adjoining the offset wells. In addition, this agreement included another preferential clause authorizing his company to drill wells on the reserve's western portion when the navy was ready. Now Doheny had a controlling hand on Elk Hills and the navy would receive more royalty oil—plus other benefits. A supplemental contract was signed with the Doheny concern for building additional storage tanks and filling them with 2.7 million barrels of fuel oil at Pearl Harbor and for furnishing to the navy upon demand 4 million barrels of fuel on the Atlantic and Pacific coasts. In the sweeping lease-contract deals with Doheny and Sinclair, Fall had adroitly sidestepped the restrictions of the Daniels bill and given the navy its fuel oil without a congressional appropriation. It was all cleverly tied up in a neat package.

The negotiations with Doheny and Sinclair led to the Teapot Dome scandal, but Secretary Fall, through similarly bold, pragmatic actions, also became entangled in other acrimonious federal oil controversies. In the long-standing case involving the Honolulu Consolidated Oil Company, which claimed title to several large tracts on the Buena Vista Hills Reserve, Fall rejected the company's claims of ownership but granted it leases on more than three thousand acres of naval lands. Critics of this decision, which overrode earlier ones, pointed out that, under the General Leasing Act, the interior secretary could make leases only for producing wells, not land. Another celebrated dispute concerned Section 36 in the Elk Hills Reserve, which the State of California had sold to Standard Oil, perhaps in violation of federal law. For years this case had been tied up in bureaucratic red tape while Standard Oil pumped millions of barrels of oil from the naval reserve, reaping profits estimated at $10 million. Under the Harding administration a Justice Department official recommended an injunction against the company, but Attorney General Daugherty took no action in the matter. Secretary Fall, on the other hand, granted a hearing to Standard Oil, listened only to its arguments, and then, almost casually, dismissed the proceedings against it. Although Fall was roundly criticized for an arbitrary exercise of judicial power, his detractors produced no evidence of collusion in the Section 36 episode, nor in the Honolulu Oil case.

The Salt Creek oil field, as a different part of the public lands, also came under Fall's jurisdiction, and his solution to the problem there placed him in another storm center. Under a long-standing arrangement the United States Shipping Board bought all of the government's Salt Creek royalty oil, and then exchanged it with the Midwest Refining Company, a Standard Oil of Indiana subsidiary, for fuel oil delivered to the merchant marine on the Pacific Coast. Although the Shipping Board benefitted from the exchange, the prices it paid to the Interior Department for distribution to the federal treasury, the reclamation fund, and the State of Wyoming were not competitive. In August 1922 Fall wrote his wife that he had worried for weeks about how to get better prices for Salt Creek oil, but that his efforts "to educate" Shipping Board officials had "gotten no where." Then, with President Harding's promise of support, he refused to renew the contract with the Shipping Board and, on December 20, 1922, signed an agreement with the Sinclair Crude Oil Purchasing Company for the Salt Creek crude. This contract, as well as one with another company for royalty oil from the Cat Creek field in Montana, was awarded publicly after open bidding. Not only had he obtained better prices for the government, Fall maintained, but also a competitive market to challenge Standard Oil's supremacy in Wyoming. Indeed, the Salt Creek agreement rounded out Fall's "whole program" for the Wyoming oil fields, which began with the Teapot Dome deal, by including a provision that Sinclair would expedite completion of his pipeline to the Midwest.

The Salt Creek transaction is often confused with the Sinclair naval-reserve deal and Harding's knowledge of it. For instance, Fall wrote the president in October 1922 of the difficulties with Salt Creek oil pricing. In his reply, which is often incorrectly associated with the Teapot Dome Reserve, Harding sent these assurances: "I have had no concern about the Wyoming oil matters. I am confident you have adopted the correct policy and will carry it through in a way altogether to be approved." Even Senator Thomas J. Walsh, before the Teapot Dome inquiry, conceded that the original royalty oil arrangement with the Shipping Board had "met with violent opposition" in the West, and, accordingly, he had favored Fall's solution to the problem. The Salt Creek contract with Sinclair contained an option for renewal at the end of five years, and in 1928 Fall's successor, Interior Secretary Hubert Work, granted an extension. Later that year Attorney General John G. Sargent, hinting at fraud, declared the contract illegal because Fall had had no power to give Sinclair an option for renewal. After voiding the agreement, the federal government made a financial settlement with Sinclair.

Dissatisfaction with Secretary Fall's distribution of domestic oil deposits arose immediately, adding to the clamor in response to his ongoing confrontations over the national forests, Alaskan resources, and Indian lands. As already mentioned, only 400 of the 9,481 acres on the Teapot Dome Reserve were free of private claims and held without dispute by the navy. Fall avoided the burdensome chore of clearing the reserve's title by requiring Sinclair's Mammoth Oil Company to do the job before the contract was signed. As it happened, the Pioneer Oil and Refining Company, a subsidiary of the Midwest Refining Company (in turn a Standard Oil of Indiana offshoot), had gained control of practically all of the nebulous claims and exacted the stiff price of $1,000,000 for them—$200,000 in cash and $800,000 in oil from the prospective lease. When critics accused Sinclair of "buying off" a competitor for the Teapot Dome contract, and Fall of complicity in the deal, the oilman simply said, "I quite appreciate that a million dollars is a lot of money, but I found it necessary to pay it."

Other challenges were not as easily met. John Leo Stack, a disgruntled Denver oil lobbyist and former government investigator, had tried for years to get a lease on Teapot Dome, even joining forces with Doheny in a proposal to drill offset wells next to the Salt Creek field. Shortly before his first big naval-reserve agreement, Doheny relinquished his share in the Stack compact to Pioneer Oil for $15,000 (the amount he had spent financing Stack's efforts), thereby raising questions later about Fall's master-hand in parceling out the reserves. Thereafter neither Pioneer Oil nor Sinclair paid much attention to Stack's pretensions. Feeling that the oil company and Sinclair had "conspired together to gyp me out of my interest," Stack sought the help of some influential individual or firm to secure his "rights." In Frederick G. Bonfils and his newspaper, the *Denver Post*, Stack found both.

Stack and Bonfils agreed to share any spoils with Bonfils's partner, Harry H. Tammen, and a cooperative Wyoming attorney. Bonfils and Tammen had a long record of journalistic extortion. Immediately, in a steady barrage of editorials, feature articles, and cartoons, the *Post* started criticizing the Teapot Dome lease. One sizzling Sunday front-page article with big black headlines, "SO THE PEOPLE MAY KNOW," charged that Sinclair had received a "gift" of one of the nation's richest undeveloped oil fields "through trickery that verges, if it does not encroach, on the bounds of crime." Decrying the secrecy of the Teapot Dome transaction, the newspaper brushed aside Fall's contentions about serious drainage. For added effect, Bonfils sent copies of the *Post* to the White House, cabinet officers, and members of Congress, while Stack started legal action asking for $5 million in damages and naming Pioneer Oil and Sinclair as the principal defendants. As an ace in the hole, Bonfils sent one of his star reporters, D. F. Stackelback, down into New Mexico to make a firsthand investigation of Fall's personal affairs for possible use in future articles.

Secretary Fall soon learned of the Stack-Bonfils pact and wrote Sinclair about the *Post*'s attacks and the validity of Stack's interests. Although conceding that Stack might deserve something and should get "his just due," Fall objected to the newspaper's blatant attempts at blackmail. In their dealing "on this 'Teapot' Dome matter," he told Sinclair (obviously for use in negotiating with Stack), "there is nothing to hide; nothing to be afraid of, and full publicity, if truthful, is welcomed by myself as I am confident it will be by yourself." Fall became more edgy, and noticeably angry, when he heard from friends in New Mexico about the inquiries of the *Post* reporter, Stackelback. In the Three Rivers vicinity Stackelback had gone around to the neighboring ranches and towns asking about Fall's finances, poking into files and records, and compiling his findings into a report for Bonfils. About this time Fall was also informed, he wrote Sinclair, that if Stack and his associates failed to get satisfactory compensation, their court suit would provide "an opportunity for bringing out a whole lot of interesting stuff about the 'Teapot' Dome deal." Plainly Stackelback's snooping, Fall told a New Mexico friend, was intended "to force Sinclair to submit to blackmail through attacks on his contract [for the naval reserve]." In the end Stackelback's report never appeared in the *Post*. Bonfils testified in the Teapot Dome investigation that the information was "shocking and astounding," but he feared a libel suit if he published it.

Perhaps the crafty Denver newspaper owner had other reasons as well. After lengthy haggling, Sinclair agreed to give Stack $250,000 in cash and half the oil income from 320 acres on Teapot Dome, with the possibility of exchanging the land for $1 million later on. From then on the *Post* lost all interest in the sordid aspects of the Teapot Dome lease. Instead it carried a laudatory article in its weekly publication, *Great Divide*, on the "gripping story of the sensational rise to fame and fortune of Harry F. Sinclair, one of the most spectacular men of the present day."

The payoff to Stack and his confederates hardly ended Fall and Sinclair's troubles with the press. Another Denver newspaperman, John C. Shaffer, who published the *Rocky Mountain News*, the *Denver Times*, and several papers in the Midwest, owned some oil land next to Teapot Dome and had long sought a lease on the reserve. Although Shaffer held no investment in the Pioneer Oil Company, that concern paid him $92,500 after selling its claims to Sinclair for $1 million. In addition, Fall urged Sinclair to offer Shaffer a one-half interest in 420 acres on Teapot Dome. This appeal, although ultimately unsuccessful, prompted the publisher to write Fall, "I am very grateful to you for your interest and help in this matter."

The Hearst publications, whose consistent support of Fall began with his Senate stand on Mexico, reprinted an early

Denver Post attack on the Teapot Dome lease. Fall protested to William Randolph Hearst, offering to open his files and give "full and frank explanations" of his acts to Hearst's reporters. Explaining the Stack-Bonfils compact in detail, Fall declared, "I can establish the fact that they have suggested that I should not allow myself to be made a scapegoat, but should compel Mr. Sinclair to settle with them and stop this newspaper fight." As a result of Fall's complaint, Hearst apparently called a halt to any more such articles in his papers. Back home Carl C. Magee and his *New Mexico State Tribune* in Albuquerque continued to criticize the Teapot Dome deal, but for the time being caused Fall only minor concern.

At the height of the *Denver Post*'s assault Fall, concerned as usual about his health, wrote his wife that no one in Washington seemed to pay attention to the newspaper criticism except the few opposed to the administration or to him. Those "who know me think too little about it even to become indignant," he said. Then he confided: "I worry a little about all these things simply because they are aggravating and tend to distract attention from other matters. If I were not so busy and nervous, I would pay no attention to them at all." Another vexing problem of adverse publicity, which Fall did not mention to his wife, had arisen when he called out the marines to protect Teapot Dome.

"Colonel" James G. Darden, a close friend of Attorney General Daugherty and a court favorite of Mrs. Harding, had worked in Harding's presidential campaign and contributed a large sum to it. He and Fall were longtime enemies, going back to New Mexico territorial politics when Darden had connived with archrival Bull Andrews to prevent Fall's election to the Senate. Since Fall never forgot an old grudge, the ersatz colonel could expect no favors from the Interior Department. As it happened, Darden had a meritless 160-acre claim on Teapot Dome. Hearing gossip that the entire reserve would be leased, he arranged with the Mutual Oil Company to start drilling a well on his bogus claim, perhaps hoping to obtain the overall contract through his political influence. Probably with this in mind Darden conferred with Daugherty, who advised him to talk with Secretary Fall. The colonel, knowing Fall's "temperament" well, thought it over a few days before taking this advice, because, as he recalled, the interior secretary "was kind of peevish about anything he wanted to do, and might be . . . hardheaded." Just as Darden expected, even when he recounted his great efforts for the Republican party, Fall merely scoffed at his Teapot Dome claim. Then the two old political enemies got "a little mad," and their discussion drifted off into other matters.

For the official record Fall regarded Darden and Mutual Oil as no more than common trespassers on government property. He and Navy Secretary Denby formally ordered them off Teapot Dome, but they refused to budge. Once the Sinclair contract was made, Fall explained to a presidential aide, the course of legal action became perfectly clear. "Should some person walk into the White House and attempt to establish himself at a desk in your office," he declared, "I can not imagine your being compelled to go into the courts here to secure the ejection of such party from the Executive offices." A suit by the federal government, he had written Harding earlier, would "play into Darden's hands" and those "of possibly fifty other parties" with similarly worthless claims by tying up Teapot Dome in litigation for years. If this happened, Sinclair would relinquish his lease at once. Let Darden go to court, if he wished, not the government. In short, Fall told the president that no suit would be filed "unless you order directly to the contrary," but then added, "It is imperative that something should be done immediately." The marines as the navy's police force, he suggested, were the logical choice to remove invading trespassers from the Wyoming naval oil reserve.

Harding was reluctant to take drastic action against his friend and campaign contributor. Early on he wrote Fall: "I have my call out for an interview with Mr. Darden. If he does not comply with friendly recommendations we will immediately take steps to eject his company from the government property." According to Darden, his talk with the president went badly:

> He [Harding] said, "Jim, how about this property you think you own in Teapot Dome, or in Wyoming," [as] he put it. I said, "I don't know; I couldn't tell you. We feel naturally we own it, because we spent some money to get it." He said, "Fall doesn't think you own it. He is kicking up Jack"—no; he didn't say "kicking up Jack." He said, "He is T. N. T."

Even presidential pressure failed to convince Darden. As a last resort, he turned again to his friend Daugherty, but the attorney general could offer no help because, he said, Fall was "determined" to remove the trespassers.

In late July 1922, with the Mutual Oil Company still drilling on Teapot Dome, Fall arranged with Acting Navy Secretary Theodore Roosevelt, Jr., to send a marine detachment from Washington to evict the "squatters." Fall's personal briefing of Captain George K. Shuler, as recalled by the marine officer, had all the intensity of a Dona Ana County vendetta:

> [Secretary Fall] said that he had taken the matter up with the President that morning, and that the President did not want to take this action because an officer of the company that was trespassing was a close personal friend, and contributed to the campaign fund. And Mr. Fall told me that he had told the President that his friend was a low down S. O. B., and Mr. Fall said that the President told him that he supposed he was all that when he sent him his check, and Mr. Fall said that he told the President, "Mr. President, by God, he was." But he said the President finally consented, and that was why the marines were to go out. He said, "What would you do if they served an injunction on you, signed by a Federal judge"? I said, "Mr. Secretary, I have never seen an injunction in my life, and wouldn't know one if I saw it, and if they served one on me I would file it." He said, "I guess you will get along all right out there."

Captain Shuler performed his mission well. With four well-armed enlisted marines, several Interior Department officials, and two Casper newspapermen, he went from Casper by automobile to Darden's claim on the naval reserve. As the self-appointed commandant of Teapot Dome, because, as he later explained, "being the only representative of the Navy Department around there, . . . somebody had to be commandant," Shuler persuaded the Mutual Oil operators to cease drilling and depart peacefully. After placing a government seal on the drilling equipment, he and his men had lunch with the company's field superintendent.

This unprecedented display of naval power in landlocked Wyoming caused the state's governor and the national press to protest Fall's reliance on military action instead of the courts. Later, in the Teapot Dome investigation, Senator Walsh contended that Secretary Fall had rejected a federal suit on Darden's claim because he and Sinclair feared a court test on the legality of the Mammoth Oil contract. But for Albert Fall, nursing an old political grudge, Darden's challenge on Teapot Dome was a special case demanding the same kind of retaliation as in a New Mexico range war. And Fall must have relished sending out the marines as much as dispatching Oliver Lee and his cowboys back in the old days.

Meanwhile the Teapot Dome contract with Sinclair of April 7, 1922, although made quietly without competitive bidding, had not remained secret for long. In fact, before any public announcement and despite denials from the Interior Department, several newspapers, including the *Wall Street Journal*, publicized the lease. Protests about the absence of open bidding began pouring into Washington. The financial editor of the *Denver Post*, which had not yet started its attacks, declared that only a congressional investigation into the Teapot Dome leasing would "avert a scandal" which threatened "the oil industry in Wyoming and the administration at Washington." Several politically prominent Wyoming oilmen, the editor said, were taking steps to protect their rights. Senator John B. Kendrick, a Democrat from Wyoming, received many of these angry inquiries. When he could not get satisfactory information from the Interior and Navy departments, he introduced a Senate resolution asking Fall and Denby if negotiations for a lease were underway.

From his Three Rivers ranch Secretary Fall confirmed the awarding of the Sinclair contract, giving assurances that there was "nothing sensational" about it. No one was trying to "put over anything whatsoever," he asserted, since the program to prevent drainage had been under consideration for a year. Fall probably wanted to delay an announcement of the Teapot Dome lease until he completed the companion Doheny agreement, for tank construction at Pearl Harbor, so he could release news of the two deals simultaneously with the official disclosure of his new policy for the reserves. Now he was forced to reveal everything prematurely since the Doheny negotiations were not yet concluded. As a result, the Interior Department issued a press release on April 18 heralding the Sinclair and Doheny contracts as a new policy "for the opening of the naval oil reserve in Wyoming to private enterprise, and the operation of those already opened in California in a manner designed to assure the navy permanent storage of fuel oil above ground." Besides giving details of the Sinclair arrangement, the statement emphasized that the new program was a departure from the old one of storing the oil underground. Later Senator Walsh speculated that Fall had delayed disclosure of the Teapot Dome lease for fear that public "disapproval" of it might prevent completion of the Doheny deal. Whatever the case, a firestorm of criticism now swept through Congress and the press.

Next came a cat-and-mouse game with Senator Robert M. La Follette, the Progressive-Republican, who sided with Gifford Pinchot on conservation issues and often conferred with Pinchot's Washington agent, Harry Slattery. About a year earlier La Follette had told Slattery of confidential information from inside the Navy Department that Harding's executive order transferring the reserves to Interior was illegal. Slattery promised to check out the report with Assistant Navy Secretary Roosevelt, but young Roosevelt, although admitting his part in the executive order, "hit the ceiling" and defended Fall as a "great good friend" of his family. Later, when rumors of naval oil leases began circulating, La Follette made inquiries in the administration about the transfer. In response Fall sent him some documentation with the explanation that he could not release "full publicity" about naval oil plans because they involved "military policies." When Fall informed Harding of this episode, the president replied, "I quite approve of the manner in which you responded to his inquiry." Neither of them had much use for the gadfly Wisconsin senator, who had bickered with Theodore Roosevelt years before and opposed America's entry into World War I.

The pesky La Follette was not easily dissuaded. On the same day the Senate received official word of the Sinclair contract, he introduced a blockbuster resolution, written mostly by Slattery, calling for Secretary Fall to furnish the Senate with copies of all the leases, documents, correspondence, and related papers on the leasing of the various naval reserves. An amendment also authorized the Public Lands Committee to investigate all aspects of the naval oil leases. In the ensuing floor discussion La Follette, Kendrick, and other senators, voicing recurring themes of the forthcoming Teapot Dome scandal, condemned the new oil policy as an unwarranted departure from the previously accepted program followed by three presidents, criticized the secrecy of the Sinclair negotiations, and attacked Fall's conservation record. On April 29 the Senate passed the La Follette resolution by a vote of fifty-eight to zero, and the biggest battle of Albert Fall's tempestuous life was underway.

Secretary Fall was still at his ranch in New Mexico. By now a veteran of congressional hearings on his various departmental initiatives, he commented to the press that the public "would most thoroughly approve . . . the businesslike way" in which the navy's oil fields were being handled. He welcomed "any investigation senatorial or otherwise," Fall said, but would save his other statements for the Senate committee, adding facetiously, if it wanted him to testify. Once back in his Interior Department office, he began supervising the collection and copying of the twelve thousand pages of correspondence and documents demanded by the Senate. Then, declaring that he was sending "every possible paper, or scrap of paper," the Senate might want, Fall had the "cartload of documents," contained in mailbags, dumped in the Public Lands Committee's quarters. It was charged that he tried to overwhelm the committee with the sheer bulk of the shipment yet did not transmit all of the relevant material. These omissions, however, probably resulted from bureaucratic oversights rather than subterfuge.

At this point two statements, one made by Fall and the other by Harding, began echoing throughout the Teapot Dome controversy and would eventually help ruin Harding's historical reputation. In a lengthy report to the president, Fall justified his handling of the reserves and recalled that the new oil policy had been discussed from time to time with Harding and in cabinet meetings. Both the new program and the recent contracts with Sinclair and Doheny, he assured the president, would "redound to the credit of your administration, both in the immediate present and in the distant future." Nothing could be further from what actually happened. Then Harding, in a letter to the Senate, wrote his own political epitaph when he declared, "I think it is only fair to say [that the new naval reserve plan] was submitted to me prior to the adoption thereof, and the policy decided upon and the subsequent acts have at all times had my entire approval." From then on it was Harding's oil program as much as Fall's.

The Senate investigating committee would not begin its hearings until nearly a year and a half after the La Follette resolution was passed, and six months after Fall left the cabinet. The committee chairman, Reed Smoot of Utah, and the ranking member, Irvine L. Lenroot of Wisconsin, were both Republicans. Senator La Follette, although not a committee member, believed correctly that Smoot and Lenroot were less than sympathetic to the investigation. He and Kendrick encouraged Senator Thomas J. Walsh of Montana, a Democratic member, to take "the laboring oar" of the inquiry "and to see that it was prosecuted with vigor." Only preliminary work was done for months, even by Walsh, who before the hearings began in October 1923 spent "something more than a month" in intensive study of the facts. The Montana senator became a self-appointed prosecutor. Although actually he was nothing more than a minority-party committee member, he made most of the preparations and called all of the witnesses for the hearings. Even Walsh, however, never imagined the sensational revelations ahead.

Meanwhile, with Harding's letter to the Senate soothing public apprehension of wrongdoing, the fall midterm elections drew attention elsewhere. In Wyoming Senator Kendrick, campaigning for reelection, made the Teapot Dome transaction a major issue. Troubled Republican leaders there pleaded with Fall to come and defend his oil policy. Fall wrote Harding from New Mexico that he could not accept this invitation, or similar ones from Utah and other states, because of his wife's distress over the death of her only brother, Joe Morgan. But he emotionally pledged his loyalty to the president "so long as we both live." At Albuquerque, where he spoke for the Republican cause, Fall discussed the Teapot Dome contract for the first time publicly. "It has guaranteed to the navy greater reserves than the navy has ever had before," he said, "and has provided, without cost to the taxpayers, storage facilities for one and one-half million barrels of oil." In addition, one well on Teapot Dome was bringing the government $3,300 a day more than the royalty scale for any other oil field. Demonstrating that Fall's magic was vanishing, the 1922 election gave New Mexico Republicans their worst defeat since statehood, with the Democrats electing a senator and the lone congressman, all of the statewide officials, and, for the first time, a majority in the lower house. The president's party also suffered severe losses nationally.

In January 1923 the announcement of Secretary Fall's impending resignation from the cabinet spurred Senators Walsh and Kendrick to take an important step in the naval-oil investigation. Fall's main justification for leasing Teapot Dome, as he stated in his report to Harding and others, was the serious drainage by privately owned or leased wells in the adjoining Salt Creek field, a contention rejected by many oilmen. To determine the validity of Fall's theory, Walsh and Kendrick got the Public Lands Committee to hire two geologists, who, during the summer of 1923, would study Teapot Dome's underground structure and report on their findings. When the geologists completed their work, Walsh told the press, the inquiry would be expanded to take in other aspects of the leases.

Fall was infuriated. Several times, beginning soon after passage of the La Follette resolution, he had urged Senator Smoot and other committee members to authorize such a geological study. In fact, he had exhorted the panel, in justice to him and the president, to conduct "a full investigation" immediately or, after discussing his report and the other evidence available, announce "that no further investigation was necessary." The committee had treated him unfairly, he felt, in purposefully delaying the geological examination until after he left the Interior Department. A hasty inquiry probably would have saved Fall much grief, but as a former Senate investigator himself, he knew that the congressional mills usually ground slowly in such matters.

In Fall's last months as interior secretary another congressional action occurred to embarrass him. As a dress rehearsal for the Teapot Dome hearings, Senator La Follette's subcommittee of the Committee on Manufacturers probed into the high prices of gasoline and other petroleum products. Through the testimony of several prominent oilmen La Follette revealed some significant information about the naval reserves. J. C. Donnell of the Ohio Oil Company, which operated in Wyoming, criticized the Teapot Dome lease, maintaining that the cheapest and best storage for the navy's oil was underground in its natural reservoir. Sinclair caused some excitement when he valued his Teapot Dome holdings "at a greater amount than $100 million," although adding that it would take $60 million to $70 million to carry out the contract. Both Sinclair and Robert W. Stewart of Standard Oil of Indiana admitted that their two organizations, on a fifty-fifty basis, owned the Sinclair Crude Oil Purchasing Company, which held the Salt Creek royalty oil contract. Similarly the two giant concerns controlled the Sinclair Pipe Line Company, which was obligated to construct the connecting pipeline from Wyoming to the Midwest specified in the Teapot Dome contract. Stewart also said that the pipeline would probably have been built regardless of the naval reserve deal. These revelations, although common knowledge in petroleum circles, seemed to refute Fall's boast of breaking the Standard monopoly in Wyoming oil fields by awarding the Teapot Dome and Salt Creek contracts to Sinclair. By raising questions about Fall's oil policy, although not his integrity, the La Follette subcommittee broke ground for the full-scale Teapot Dome investigation later.

Fall had not intended to remain as interior secretary more than a year or so. Only a few months after taking office, Fall wrote his wife that President Harding was yielding too much to certain senators, especially on appointments, and making "serious mistakes." Because of cabinet protocol, he felt restricted in advising Harding except on matters involving the Interior Department. Accordingly, since his official influence was severely limited, he could be of more use to Harding outside the cabinet. And the president "certainly needs good, independent, and STRAIGHT FROM THE SHOULDER advice," Fall told his wife, "if ever a man did." Before the end of his first year there were rumors that he, as well as others, would leave the cabinet. In an uncharacteristic, and misleading, response he stated to the press: "I have not been asked to resign and I am not thinking of resigning. Like every other politician, I am going to hold on to my job." Actually Fall had resolved to leave public life as soon as possible, and Harding knew of his wishes. The president pointed out that Postmaster General Will H. Hays had already announced his intention to depart, and that another resignation so soon would suggest discord in the cabinet. At his friend's insistence Fall reluctantly stayed in the cabinet another year.

Fall's disgust with public office and political affairs only increased. Perhaps some of it resulted from his "exaggerated idea of the influence which he expected to have with the President," as the *New York Times* put it. But his battles over the national forests, Indian lands, the All-Year Park, and the naval reserves simply wore him out. In September 1922 he wrote his wife philosophically that with the biblical life span ending for him in only a decade, he had lost the optimistic enthusiasm of youth and now realized he was growing old. He wanted the last years of his life to be free of the stress and worry accompanying the political spotlight. Then he reminisced:

> In public life I expect criticism and I have had more of it possibly, than the average man. I have led a very strenuous life—the life of a pioneer in a Western country, in the wide-open days, and have subjected myself to criticism in many ways. I am accustomed to doing things first and talking about them afterwards. Any man in the Government service, who gets out of the rut, steps upon the toes of someone else and must expect to hear criticism and meet opposition.

It would take eight to ten years, he said, to make the changes he thought necessary in the Interior Department, and he did not have that much time. To a former law partner he wrote that he had accomplished everything possible in Interior without additional legislation, which seemed unlikely. The prospect of "perfunctorily" filling a bureaucratic position had no appeal to him. Consequently, Fall told a New Mexico friend, he would retire to private life permanently and never hold another office "by election or appointment."

Even a seat on the Supreme Court was not enough to sway the retiring interior secretary. Fall took inordinate pride in his legal ability, as demonstrated in his personal management of the naval reserves, and many others apparently shared his view. President Harding had the opportunity to fill four high court vacancies, an unusually large number for his relatively brief administration. Shortly before retiring, Fall wrote a friend, "I have declined the position of Associate Justice of the Supreme Court twice within the last few months." About this same time the press confirmed rumors that Harding was so anxious to keep his friend in Washington he had offered Fall a Supreme Court seat. Although these reports undoubtedly had some truth to them, Harding made a habit of flattering prominent politicians with offers of high office when he knew they would not accept them. Probably this was the case in his overtures to Fall.

On January 2, 1923, the White House announced Fall's decision to leave the cabinet on March 4. He had served as interior secretary at great financial loss, the statement said, and was returning to private business in the Southwest. In a Washington speech, considered to be his "swan song," Fall compared his impending retirement to the ecstasy of the early Christians, who were happy to die in Roman arenas because of the joys of heaven awaiting them. Like those martyrs, he said, "I confess to a grateful sense of satisfaction as I contemplate my approaching political demise." Although the public expected more of its officials than ever before, he had great confidence in the "rough justice" of popular judgments on officeholders and their actions. "Today the tendency is not only to criticize a public servant for any act of omission or commission," Fall maintained, "but to charge him personally with being actuated by ulterior motives of personal or purely selfish interest." This "soliloquy," remarkable for its confessional overtones, was printed in the *New York Times* on the day he retired, with the addition of his views on world social, economic, and political conditions.

When Fall said goodbye to his Interior Department bureau chiefs and key staff members, they presented him with a humidor in a heartfelt farewell ceremony. The future looked as bright for the sixty-one-year-old New Mexican as the cloudless horizon at his Three Rivers ranch, to which he now retreated. After an extended period of rest and relaxation he would decide what to do next. For the time being only the two geologists appointed by the Senate Public Lands Committee to study drainage were doing much on the Teapot Dome question. When they submitted their findings, the naval oil investigation might well fizzle. The appearance of the long-predicted oil shortage might also have vindicated Fall's leasing policy for the naval reserves. Within months, however, the American oil panic faded away with the discovery of rich new reserves at home, in Oklahoma, Louisiana, and California, which created a glutted market for several years.

CHAPTER 8

The Teapot Dome Investigation

IN the future, Albert Fall wrote his wife while contemplating retirement from the cabinet, he would choose only the employment that appealed the most to him and that offered the best financial security for himself and his family. "I am at the zenith of my intellectual powers," he said, "and for the next four or five years can expect dividends from my earning capacity, if I am in a field where I am untrammeled by official chains and restrictions." Before leaving office, Fall told a close friend that at least three potential employers had made him offers. One was tendered by Edward L. Doheny, who wanted him to take a key position with the oilman's Mexican interests. Another tempting bid came from investors with extensive Latin-American mining operations. And Harry F. Sinclair proposed to make Fall a part of his petroleum empire. Whichever offer he decided to accept, Fall declared, he could confidently expect to earn at least $50,000 a year. These promising prospects were good news indeed for one who had suffered repeated financial setbacks during his eleven years in national public office.

With his valuable Mexican investments gone, Fall's most substantial financial asset was his New Mexico ranch at Three Rivers. While expanding this empire in the Tularosa Basin with his son-in-law and partner Mahlon T. Everhart, he had systematically and aggressively swallowed up numerous small ranches and homesteads, often causing complaints that he was trying to "hog the country." Now forty different ranching units of varying sizes, scattered over an expanse fifty-five miles long and twenty-four to thirty-five miles wide, made up his spread. Fall did not actually own this entire area since his holdings were strategically situated so that they contained most of the water holes, giving him control of large swaths of rangeland on the federal public domain. He also leased state lands and held national forest and Indian reservation grazing permits.

The ranch was a magnificent property, meeting all the requirements of a baronial estate. Fall loved the rough rolling stretches, rocky mountain canyons, and occasional verdant valleys of his domain. Besides both purebred and range cattle, he raised horses and mules, hogs, sheep, various barnyard fowls, and sometimes hunting dogs. Streams and ponds were well stocked with fish. Deer, bear, wild turkey, and other game abounded in the foothills and mountains. Although cattle were its main business, the ranch also produced large irrigated crops of alfalfa, corn, wheat, maize and other forage feeds, as well as fruit and vegetables in abundance. Fall liked to experiment with different kinds of fruits and unusual plants, and found it especially challenging to graft improved varieties of nuts onto native trees. With his close-knit family gathered around him in his showplace southern-style ranch house, he played the role of Three Rivers patriarch like a courtly Kentucky gentleman, receiving due respect. When he entered a room, family members rose to their feet in the old southern tradition. At various times in this "one-family community," and often simultaneously, all of Fall's children and their families lived in the rambling Three Rivers ranch house or at nearby ranches.

Even though local people spoke of the "Fall ranch" and Fall himself called it "my ranch," both designations require some explanation. In 1913, while away serving in the Senate, he had attempted to place the ranch on a sound financial footing and assure its future development by consolidating most of his ranching interests with some of Everhart's holdings. In the resulting corporation, called the Tres Ritos Cattle and Land Company, Fall was president and Everhart was general manager. The merger did not include the land around the old ranch house, known as the "home place," which Fall retained and operated separately as the "Tres Ritos Ranch." Over the years he and his son-in-law carefully rounded out their spread by buying adjoining property and water holes. As a separate venture, Fall established the Thoroughbred Cattle Company when he borrowed money from his friend Price McKinney to purchase a herd of registered Hereford cattle in Kansas. All of this expansion and development required large outlays of money above the ranch corporation's profits. In the years after World War I, while one of the worst droughts ever known plagued the Southwest, the cattle market was unstable and selling prices were low. By the time of Fall's cabinet service the ranch corporation had become heavily indebted to the M. D. Thatcher Estate Company, an investment concern owned by Everhart's relatives, who also controlled the First National Bank of Pueblo, Colorado.

Fall respected Everhart's judgment in ranching matters and had a special personal regard for him, especially after the death from influenza in 1918 of his wife, Caroline, who was Fall's middle daughter. After Fall was appointed interior secretary, he placed Everhart in complete control at Three Rivers, including the home place operations. Everhart had other ranching interests in New Mexico and Colorado, and could not devote his entire attention to management of their Three Rivers affairs. Needed repairs and improvements were sometimes neglected, causing Fall considerable distress. "It [the ranch] is a constant source of annoyance," he wrote his wife in August 1922, "and my visits there are anything but pleasant." He had invested large sums of money with little return, Fall said, and continued, "I have been thought to be, and possibly properly so, a fool about . . . my ideas of running things at the ranch." Unwilling to give up his dream of becoming a successful cattle king, he believed that, when the drought ended and cattle prices revived, the ranch would become a paying proposition. His most fervent efforts to bring about its salvation began before he left the Harding administration.

In his land acquisitions Fall had fashioned his holdings into a symmetrical and fully operational ranch, with one notable exception. Known as the Harris-Brownfield ranch, or simply the Harris ranch, this strategically located tract of three thousand acres, with additional leases and grazing permits on public lands, controlled the headwaters of Three Rivers canyon, one of the main stream's three forks and a principal source of water for Fall's pastures and farmlands below. If the Harris place fell into unfriendly hands, hostile action over water rights, perhaps even a long, costly court fight, might be the result. Meanwhile, without a reliable water supply, Fall's hopes for his ranching empire would wither away. Also among the tract's attributes was an inviting hydroelectric site where he wanted to generate power for downstream wells that would irrigate his low-lying farms and orchards, thus stabilizing the supply during times of drought and intermittent seasonal flow. It was a dream he had nurtured for years. When the Harris family announced its intention to sell out, Fall had to purchase the land if he wanted to protect the value and integrity of his own holdings. Although he held an option to buy it, other prospective buyers coveted what one of the owners described as "about the best small ranch in New Mexico." For Fall it was the old story, he said, of water as "the life and substance" of ranching in the Southwest.

Fall at first tried to purchase the Harris place in partnership with Edward B. McLean, who wanted to experiment with raising race horses in high elevations. The wealthy socialite newspaper publisher eventually backed out because, Fall said, heavy income taxes and "rather extravagant family expenditures" left him nothing for such investments. Then Fall discussed a loan with his partner in Mexican mining ventures, Cleveland industrialist Price McKinney. They had met in Mexico while Fall worked for Colonel Bill Greene. Now McKinney was president of the McKinney Steel Company, one of the nation's largest independent steel producers, and a multimillionaire through his industrial, banking, and Mexican mining interests. A shrewd, even "cold-blooded," businessman, McKinney shunned the Cleveland social scene but delighted in sharing Fall's national prestige, and especially in meeting political celebrities. Both loved horse racing, and they often attended the Kentucky Derby together. McKinney made frequent trips to Washington, where he was royally entertained by his friend. In early 1922 he and his wife were among the guests, who also included the Dohenys, when Secretary and Mrs. Fall honored the Hardings with a formal dinner at the Willard Hotel. Since Fall liked the company of wealthy business tycoons, he often dropped by McKinney's beautiful Cleveland mansion or nearby country estate, Ridgemere Farm.

Over the years McKinney had often loaned Fall sums of $30,000 or more. In Fall's 1918 senatorial reelection the steel magnate put up $27,500 of the $115,000 needed to purchase the *Albuquerque Morning Journal* and offered to pay his friend's campaign expenses as well. As early as December 1920, when Fall asked about a loan to buy the Harris ranch, McKinney said that he would back him for up to $250,000 through a large Chicago bank in which the industrialist was a major stockholder. On the basis of McKinney's friendship and long record of past loans, Fall seemed assured of having the money to buy the Harris place.

In a conversation with Harold Walker, Doheny's Washington lobbyist, Secretary Fall had mentioned the Harris ranch sale while discussing how his pressing official duties left him little time to take care of personal affairs. Shortly afterwards, while the controversial naval royalty-oil exchange program was being formulated by the Navy and Interior departments, Doheny himself came to Fall's office on other business and incidentally brought up the interior secretary's ranching interests. In a general conversation about his holdings, Fall said that he intended to round them out by purchasing the Harris ranch and was working out the financial arrangements. As Fall recalled, Doheny then suggested, "Let me lend it to you." He would probably not need a loan from the oilman, Fall said. To which Doheny replied: "Well, if you do, I'll let you have it. Don't lose that ranch property for lack of money. You need it too bad for that." Doheny's generous gesture, according to Fall's favorite version of this momentous incident, had nothing to do with the naval reserves or a bribe. It resulted largely from the oilman's deep sense of gratitude to the friend who had "gone to bat" over the years for those Americans with oil holdings and other property in Mexico. "Why, if you never paid it back,"

Doheny exclaimed, "I'd still feel indebted to you for what you did down there for us."

Senator Walsh later saw a "sinister import" in the loan since it was given two days after Doheny expressed his interest in the contract, which he eventually obtained, to exchange royalty oil for the construction of Pearl Harbor storage tanks. But even though Fall's recollections may be self-serving, the naval reserves played only an incidental role in the Doheny loan. Doheny's generosity came mainly as recognition of services already rendered by Fall in Mexico.

When the Harris family decided to sell the ranch without delay, Fall, strapped for cash, had to make up his mind in a hurry. Inexplicably he did not borrow the money from Price McKinney. He attempted to communicate with McKinney, according to one dubious account, only to learn from the industrialist's Cleveland office that he was somewhere in the Thousand Islands of the St. Lawrence River and could not be reached. If this was so, McKinney's decision to take a vacation at that particular time probably changed Fall's life irreparably.

Whatever these circumstances, Fall next began a series of grievous mistakes by telephoning Doheny for a loan of $100,000, specifically asking for it in cash. For good reason, Fall recalled, he wanted cash because most of the banks in New Mexico were in receivership or threatened by it, making banking transactions by check very risky. Without hesitation Doheny instructed his son, Edward, Jr., to withdraw the money from a New York City bank and take it in a satchel, or what became known as the infamous "little black bag," to Fall in Washington. Fall received the bundle of bills in his Wardman Park Hotel apartment, counted them, and filled out a note to Doheny, leaving the interest rate blank for his friend to stipulate as he saw fit. On his way to California for reclamation hearings, Fall carried the cash "in a steel box inside a large brown grip" from Washington to El Paso, where the Harris ranch deal was concluded. He had often traveled with large cash amounts in Mexico, he remembered, once transporting $480,000 for a business transaction. Price McKinney, Fall's usual source of borrowed funds, accompanied him on the trip to El Paso and California, which raises a question about the industrialist's unavailability for a loan.

On December 5, 1921, Fall closed the Harris ranch deal, which also included a herd of cattle and some horses and mules, for $91,500. The immediate down payment of $10,000 was made in $100 bills from Fall's small metal box and counted out to the Harris heirs in the El Paso office of Fall's son-in-law, Customs Collector Clarence C. Chase. With the addition of the Harris place, Fall's ranch was now a harmonious operational unit.

The Harris ranch purchase, although necessary, only exacerbated Fall's financial situation. More ready cash was needed at Three Rivers for repairs and improvements, to repay the indebtedness to Everhart's relatives, and for some additional, smaller land acquisitions. During the same trip to the Southwest in which he closed the Harris deal, Fall found a solution for these weighty money problems through another oil magnate, Harry F. Sinclair. Significantly Fall's relationship with Sinclair was quite different from his frontier-based friendship with Doheny. Like Doheny, Sinclair had risen quickly in the oil business, starting in the new Kansas and Oklahoma fields, to become a major independent producer with assets estimated at $380 million in 1922. Also like Doheny, whose precarious oil supply depended heavily on his revolution-torn Mexican fields, Sinclair badly needed more production to feed his rapidly expanding worldwide marketing operations. After merging his holdings in 1919 to form the Sinclair Consolidated Oil Corporation, he aggressively sought both a foothold in foreign oil fields, in part because of the predicted famine in domestic production, and new sources at home. Sinclair also owned a successful stable, Rancoras, and his horse, Zev, named for his favorite lawyer, J. W. Zevely, won the Kentucky Derby in 1923. A big, bluff, bald man, he was usually congenial but also a ruthless negotiator who almost always won in anything he did.

Fall had known Zevely, but not Sinclair, for several years. As a natural basis of sociability, however, both Fall and Sinclair loved horse racing and poker, and, in fact, the oilman frequently joined the convivial White House card games. According to Fall, he had met Sinclair three or four times at the Kentucky Derby before the spring of 1921, when he arranged a conference for the Colombian minister with Sinclair, Doheny, and other American businessmen. Afterwards the oilman invited Fall to accompany him by private railroad car to the derby, but Fall declined because he had already made plans to go with Price McKinney.

In late December 1921, while Fall was at Three Rivers for Christmas, he received a telegram from his Washington office that Sinclair and Zevely wanted to confer with him at the ranch "on a very urgent and important matter." Soon after Christmas, Sinclair's private railroad car, the *Sinco*, carrying the oilman, Zevely, and their wives, pulled onto a siding at the Three Rivers station. Ostensibly Sinclair had come to request a modification of his oil lease on the Osage Indian Reservation, which Fall promptly granted, but he also asked about the prospective leasing of Teapot Dome. The oilman would have an opportunity to submit a bid, Fall assured him, when the time came.

During his visit, Sinclair apparently became enthralled with the primeval setting of Three Rivers. He and his party attended a country dance, and the oilman shot quail, a wild turkey, and a big buck deer near the Rock House, a picturesque, rambling ranch house on the Fall spread. At seven-thousand-feet elevation, this large granite-block structure, with its thirty-foot-long living room, five enormous fireplaces, and cathedral-sized windows, stood under towering Sierra Blanca. Declaring his interest in owning part of the ranch, Sinclair told Fall that the Rock House would make an ideal retreat for the Sons of Hope, his poker-playing social club of wealthy pals, and that the dry mountain air might benefit his wife's "weak lungs." At first Fall dismissed these statements as pipe dreams, attributing them to the "passing fancy" of a city dweller smitten by the great outdoors. Later, in Washington, Zevely told him: "I know you thought Sinclair was joking, or just talking, but he wants to buy part of your ranch. He thinks it would be a great place to breed race horses. . . . Sinclair's very enthusiastic about that 'rock house.'" After thinking it over, Fall decided to sell Sinclair a one-third interest in his combined operations with Everhart for

$233,000, the amount needed to pay off the ranching corporation's indebtedness and commitments, including the $100,000 loan from Doheny.

Fall later insisted that his ranch-sale conversations in Washington with Sinclair and Zevely took place after, not before, the oilman was awarded the Teapot Dome contract of April 7, 1922. Then, in May, Sinclair and Zevely completed the ranch transaction with Fall. Everhart picked up $198,000 in Liberty Bonds from Sinclair in Washington and delivered them to Fall's apartment in the Wardman Park Hotel, where they were stored temporarily in an old Senate desk. Zevely had said beforehand that the deal would involve Liberty Bonds, and Fall raised no objection to this form of payment. After Fall kept out $2,500 worth of bonds, Everhart took the rest with him to New York City, where he collected another $35,000 in bonds from Sinclair and arranged a line of credit with the oil magnate that eventually totaled about $36,000 in cash. Everhart then shipped the Liberty Bonds to Pueblo and deposited most of them for the ranch corporation. While in New York, he also paid Sinclair $1,100 by check for a shipment of livestock the oilman had sent to Three Rivers.

The sale of a one-third interest to Sinclair, which would undergo intense scrutiny in the naval oil investigation, was a good, although not exceptional, bargain for Fall. Two years earlier he and Everhart had made a similar offer to another son-in-law for $95,000, but this was before the Harris ranch and other acquisitions. Senator Walsh regarded Sinclair's payment of $233,000 as nothing but a bribe, and the story about the oilman's purchase of an interest at Three Rivers as a "shallow fable." But since Everhart was known for his personal integrity and strict business practices, his participation in every phase of the Sinclair ranching transaction tended to enhance the appearance of legitimacy.

Almost immediately, impressive changes started appearing at Three Rivers. Debts and back taxes were paid. Long-needed repairs and improvements were made. More blooded stock was added to the cattle herds. Another 6,500 acres of land adjoining the Harris ranch were purchased. The most spectacular addition was a hydroelectric project costing $53,000 that utilized the Harris water rights. Nine miles of timber poles and copper wires carried the electricity to the home place, where it powered irrigation wells, refrigeration and lighting for the main ranch house, and similar purposes. By the time Fall resigned as interior secretary his ranching empire seemed to be running smoothly.

Sinclair paid little attention to the Three Rivers ranch after buying a one-third interest in it, subsequently spending only three or four days there. After his first trip in December 1921 he did send Fall, as already mentioned, six Holstein heifers and a bull, six Duroc-Jersey hogs, and an old prize-winning race horse, Sunflash II. This livestock shipment and Fall's belated payment for the cattle and hogs became a much-discussed issue in the Teapot Dome inquiry. On a second trip to New Mexico in November 1922 Sinclair talked to Fall at the ranch about the upcoming Salt Creek royalty-oil contract and did some hunting. While returning to New York in his private railroad car, the oilman telegraphed his bid for the Salt Creek contract to the Interior Department. His offer was the one finally accepted. This trip to Three Rivers would later be regarded with suspicion because Sinclair's proposal arrived after the advertised deadline and immediately after he conferred with Secretary Fall.

When Fall left the cabinet, he fully intended to devote six months to his own affairs and relaxation before accepting any employment. His seclusion at Three Rivers lasted only about half that long. He turned down an invitation to join a delegation of oilmen on an industrial peacemaking mission to Mexico City, telling Doheny that it would be unwise so soon after his cabinet resignation. Before leaving office, Fall had learned of Sinclair's plans to develop the oil resources of Sakhalin Island, then in dispute between the Soviet Union and Japan, and that the oilman might ask him to make a trip to Japan. In May 1923 J. W. Zevely arrived at Three Rivers to discuss a trip to Europe instead of Japan, and later sent an urgent telegram requesting Fall to come to New York City prepared to sail for England, where he would meet Sinclair. In New York Fall quickly discovered that a Russian oil deal involving much more than Sakhalin was under consideration. Since the United States steadfastly refused to recognize the Soviet Union, Fall wanted to consult President Harding on the advisability of a recently resigned cabinet officer visiting that country. Moreover, Sinclair's prospective Sakhalin oil agreement reportedly stipulated that it would expire in five years without American recognition.

Harding raised no objection to the trip. Indeed, Fall recalled, "He said he would be very glad for me to go to Russia, because he was satisfied he would get the truth of Russian conditions [from me, and] he had not been able to get the true facts from any other source." Fall pledged not to approve any oil contract that required diplomatic recognition because, if it was granted, Harding would face accusations in the forthcoming presidential election of being "in partnership with Sinclair." Fall's wife, who was also at the White House, recalled that the president not only approved of the trip but also told Fall to go and make some money for himself. At the invitation of Mrs. Harding the Falls returned for lunch the next day. It was the last time Fall ever saw Harding; the following day the New Mexican sailed for England. On August 2, 1923, while returning from a trip to Alaska, the president died in San Francisco.

In London, Fall joined a large entourage of Sinclair and Barnsdall International Oil Company representatives who were negotiating with a Soviet trade official for oil concessions. Fall cautioned the group to avoid any agreement that involved foreign-owned properties expropriated by Moscow, a particularly sensitive issue because of the high-profile confiscation of Standard Oil holdings. This was good advice. Sinclair eventually obtained a contract to develop the entire Baku field, where Standard Oil and Royal Dutch Shell had residual claims, but it was revoked when the Teapot Dome scandal ruined Sinclair's chances of raising the required capital. A similar fate awaited the oilman's Russian concession on northern Sakhalin Island, which foundered in the Russo-Japanese territorial dispute and the Soviet campaign to gain United States recognition. Although Fall said that he advised against the Sakhalin contract because it was dependent on recognition within five years, he became an advocate for renewing diplomatic ties with Russia. His stand drew sharp criticism in light of the Harding administration's hostility toward the "Bolshevik menace" and the conditions of Sinclair's Sakhalin agreement. As for Sinclair's statecraft motives, he undoubtedly hoped that Fall, as a former cabinet member and the president's close friend, would impress the Soviets with the possibilities of recognition. In his frenzied worldwide quest for oil, Sinclair also supposedly gave the Persian prime minister a bribe of $275,000, or about the same amount as he invested in Fall's ranch.

While in Europe, Fall witnessed potentially earthshaking events. Traveling as Albert B. Fall, "rancher," he went from London to Berlin for more oil talks and then to Moscow, where he accompanied Sinclair, reported the *New York Times*, in an "advisory capacity." The American oil delegation, which had arrived in a chartered luxury train, was received hospitably by the Soviets, housed in a czarist palace, and wined and dined. Sinclair and his associates, who included officers of the Chase National Bank and Blair and Company, attempted to form a syndicate that would take over all of the Soviet Union's vast petroleum resources, its refineries, and its international marketing operations. "The proposed contract with Russia," Fall wrote his wife, "could have been closed had we remained in Moscow a few days longer—[and] had Sinclair himself been in a position to close it." But the Americans could not agree on terms for "so enormous a proposition." Negotiations with the Soviets had broken down on legal technicalities, Fall said, until he wrote a "letter of explanation and modification to the Russian authorities which brought matters to a crisis." Fall then urged Sinclair to take over the gigantic concession himself if his associates agreed and he could raise the necessary funds. He would stay in Europe and keep the negotiations going, Fall told Sinclair, while the oilman went to the United States and tried to arrange the financial backing.

From London, Fall wrote his wife that he would return to Moscow and conclude the contract if Sinclair succeeded with the fund-raising, which, he said, was doubtful. As it turned out, the oilman could not arrange the funding, and anyway the Soviets probably would have refused to turn over their entire petroleum industry to a single foreign oil company. Albania once offered to make Sinclair its king, which he refused, but his dream of exploiting all of Russia's oil resources, if fulfilled, would have ranked him above royalty.

Only Fall's expenses of $10,000 for the European trip were paid immediately by the consortium of American oilmen. If the gigantic concession had materialized, he would have sought additional compensation through a substantial interest in the syndicate. In addition, when Zevely came to Three Rivers to discuss the European oil venture, Fall said that he had not completed the financing for two or three small ranch acquisitions and needed to do so before he could make the trip. Zevely volunteered to advance the money for Sinclair, and, through a note made out to the attorney, Fall received $25,000 in Liberty Bonds for the land purchases. After the Teapot Dome scandal erupted, the Sinclair and Barnsdall companies belatedly paid Fall about $25,000 for his European services, which was used to liquidate this loan.

On the same day President Harding was buried at Marion, Ohio, Albert Fall returned to New York City from Europe. Fall went to Washington, where he and his wife called on Harding's widow, who was a guest of Ned and Evalyn McLean at Friendship. The United States was preparing to recognize the Obregón government of Mexico, following the Bucareli agreements. At Calvin Coolidge's request Fall conferred with the new president for three and a half hours on Mexican affairs, discussing among other things Doheny's preferences for ambassador. When Coolidge expressed "great confidence" in the oilman, Fall said that he would get an elaboration of Doheny's views by coded telegram. Probably Fall also talked with Secretary of State Charles Evans Hughes about Mexico and the Soviet Union, and the Falls were dinner guests of Commerce Secretary and Mrs. Herbert Hoover.

Despite his determination not to accept employment for several months, Fall found it increasingly difficult to relax at

Three Rivers. Soon after returning from Europe, he was called to Los Angeles by Doheny, who wanted his counsel on making a private loan of $5 million to the Obregón government. As Doheny later succinctly phrased it: "It seemed to be either to loan 10,000,000 pesos to the [Mexican] Government or lose [my property there]. On his [Fall's] advice I loaned it to the Government." The oilman left out one important part of the story. Probably in November 1923, immediately after Fall testified in the Teapot Dome investigation, he again conferred with President Coolidge in Washington on Mexican matters, and especially Doheny's loan. His account of this meeting was most revealing: "I asked Mr. Coolidge, if, having recognized the Obregón government he desired it sustained, in which event they must positively have money immediately or De la Huerta would overthrow Obregón. Mr. Coolidge said: 'He thought they wanted the Obregón government sustained, but could not guarantee the loan.'" After explaining that the loan would be repaid by remission of Doheny's Mexican oil taxes, Fall got straight to the point. Doheny wanted the president to acknowledge the loan and pledge to exert diplomatic pressure if Obregón failed to fulfill its terms. Coolidge thought the request was "a fair one" and would "cause no embarrassment to the administration." Then, and only then, Fall said, "Upon my report of the interview with the President the loan was made."

Both Fall and Doheny later tried to downplay Fall's association with the oilman at this time, claiming that it was only advisory and required no actual employment. A long trail of telegraphic exchanges on the Mexican loan, however, suggests a much deeper involvement. Fall also acted in "a confidential capacity" for Doheny's payment of $800,000 to the Vera Cruz state government to clear his oil titles there. Besides acting as an agent in Mexican affairs, he participated in the reorganization of Doheny's California oil interests held by the parent Pan American Petroleum and Transport Company. In New York City he joined Doheny and the prospective financiers in negotiations to form the Pan American Western Company, a new subsidiary requiring $20 million in stock and $15 million in bonds, which would take over the California properties. Fall later said that as early as September 1923, about the time of his first meeting with Coolidge, he had agreed to begin formal employment for Doheny starting January 1, 1924. Until then he consented to help out with the Mexican transactions and the formation of Pan American Western.

About a month after Fall first talked with President Coolidge, Senator Walsh returned to Washington from Montana and began making final preparations for the naval oil hearings. When he wrote other members of the Senate Public Lands Committee asking them to come and assist him, Walsh found that they had little enthusiasm for the investigation. Walsh had few solid leads, but he received several tantalizing tips. From the Democratic party chairman in New Mexico he learned of "recent rumors, at first taken as mere political propaganda but now accepted as being facts." Among other things, the Democratic leader claimed, Sinclair had purchased the Harris ranch for $125,000 and given it to Fall, undoubtedly in "some connection" with the Teapot Dome lease. Walsh doubted such reports about Fall's financial affairs, but did not ignore them. He started making real headway when, after a thorough study of the mass of documents sent from the Interior Department, he decided that President Harding's executive order transferring the reserves was invalid and, consequently, Fall's naval oil leases were made without authority. "Having found the whole thing a usurpation," he recalled, "I easily reached the conclusion that it was fraudulent." With this conviction fixed in his mind, Senator Walsh, acting as a prosecuting attorney, conducted the hearings like a trial in the court of public opinion.

Fall clearly won the opening round of the investigation when the committee released the findings of the two consulting geologists. Both reports supported Fall's contention that drainage by wells in the Salt Creek field was depleting the navy's oil in Teapot Dome. The potential production of Teapot Dome had been greatly overestimated, the geologists also reported, indicating that Sinclair's evaluation of the reserve at $100 million was excessive. The inquiry had "blown up," it appeared, since

Fall's critics had placed so much emphasis on the two independent geological studies, and both favored his position. One committee member publicly predicted that the investigation would end in a day or two. Like the *New York World*, many newspapers concluded that with the geologists' reports the "bottom fell out of the charges" that Senator La Follette and others had spread throughout the country. Recognizing the danger of drainage, Fall had made a favorable bargain for the government with Sinclair. Now nothing much remained of the "famous scandal." For good reason Albert Fall could look forward to his appearance before the committee with confidence, if not cocksureness.

Walsh's subsequent strategy was a simple one. Although suffering a reversal on the drainage issue, he managed to minimize the damage later with contradicting testimony from other geologists and by emphasizing the wisdom of keeping the navy's oil in the ground. He did not question that some drainage of Teapot Dome was taking place, but challenged Fall's arguments on its seriousness and the necessity of leasing. Actually Walsh's strategy did not depend on the drainage dispute, the illegality of Harding's executive order of transferral, or the lack of a public announcement soliciting bids. In fact, he realized that the leasing legislation of 1920 did not require competitive bidding. All of these considerations were only incidental to Walsh's primary objective. It was much simpler, and far more telling on public opinion, to disclose bribery, conspiracy, or secrecy, or all three, in the naval reserve transactions. Walsh's main line of attack after the geological reports was based on this assumption. And as one of Fall's subordinates in the Interior Department pointed out: "Walsh was also a honest, able, and hard working man. It was the latter which prevented his being smothered, as he one time nearly was."

The two antagonists who now confronted each other in the Teapot Dome inquiry had strikingly similar backgrounds. Both were westerners, molded and shaped in frontier environments, with western ideas about such matters as conservation and public lands. Fall had entered the Senate in 1912, and Walsh in

1913. As a senator Walsh had become an influential Wilsonian Democrat, who supported virtually all of Wilson's legislative program. Stern and often austere, he was regarded by many as the ablest constitutional lawyer in the Senate. Significantly Walsh had been a leading advocate of the Treaty of Versailles and had often tangled with the irreconcilable Fall in Senate debates on the League issue. It is impossible to say how much partisan revenge Walsh was now exacting against Fall for the treaty's defeat, but this old grudge cannot be overlooked as one of his motivations. In short, Fall was an intensely partisan Republican (although originally a Democrat) and Walsh a confirmed, partisan Democrat, but the main difference between these two men lay elsewhere. Fall, a loyal Republican gutfighter, viewed government as a sort of concurrent majority of the special interests, with himself as their minister plenipotentiary. Walsh, on the other hand, combined party fidelity with a keen legal sense and strict personal morality. A chance stroke of fate brought them together in the Teapot Dome episode, but Walsh emerged a national hero, and Fall became the archvillain of American politics in the 1920s.

If Fall could not claim unblemished conservationist credentials, neither could Walsh. In fact, Walsh's distinguished career exhibited many quirks resulting from his Democratic partisanship and strong political ambition, which sometimes smacked of opportunism, and from his role as a senator from the "copper state" of Montana. In the Senate both he and Fall were members of the "western crowd" on the Public Lands Committee, who were viewed with contempt by the Pinchotites. Walsh, with the support of other Democratic members and the "side-door assistance" of Republicans such as Fall, was regarded in 1917 as the dominant Senate voice on public land matters and a kingpin in the "looting program." During one Senate debate on opening the naval oil reserves, he had placed "very great importance" on the expert opinion of his good friend and fellow Democrat Edward L. Doheny to bolster his argument in favor of leasing. Aesthetic preservationists portrayed Walsh as an "indefatigable and unscrupulous spoilsman and enemy" of the national parks.

By the time of the Teapot Dome investigation he had emerged as a moderate, or perhaps a pragmatist, on natural resource issues. The inescapable point is that Walsh, despite his political partisanship and philosophical inconsistencies, possessed a morality as upright as the Bitterroot Range in his home state. For him the investigation was more a judgment on official rectitude than a test of conservation principles.

Fall appeared as the first witness of the inquiry. He was not subpoenaed, declaring before he left Three Rivers for Washington that he would testify only because of committee chairman Reed Smoot's request to "Please come." For two days the bombastic former interior secretary and the austere senator from Montana faced each other as Fall defended his handling of the naval reserves. Since they understood each other perfectly, it seemed altogether possible that the confrontation would result in a western standoff, and it often did. Sometimes Fall gave a crackling reply to a rather sarcastic query from Walsh. He talked easily and convincingly, often at length, about Harding's executive order, the benefits of the leases, and some of his business relations with Sinclair and Doheny since leaving office. At times he was jocular, chiding Walsh with some sly remark; then again he was angry when it seemed his integrity or judgment had been impugned. For every question he had an answer, and sometimes, momentarily turning prosecutor, he quizzed Walsh on some point. Patiently, and at times condescendingly, he explained the details of some matter at the Montana senator's insistence.

When Walsh asked why he had neglected to call for bids on the Teapot Dome lease, Fall replied without hesitation: "Business, purely. Because I knew I could make a better price without calling for bids." Other oil companies might have submitted proposals, Fall said, but there was "only one bid" he could have accepted because of the benefits offered by Sinclair. In response to further questions from Walsh about the Sinclair contract, he commented caustically: "Senator, you remind me of the difference that was stated once between the protestant and the atheist, who will take one passage from the Bible possibly and prove that it was not inspired, to say the least of it. Now, I do not mean to say that this was an inspired contract, but I am certainly willing to stand on the result." Walsh also wanted to know who had furnished the legal advice on the royalty-oil exchange agreement with Doheny for the construction work at Pearl Harbor. "The Secretary of the Interior, largely, himself," Fall answered. Several times Walsh questioned the secrecy surrounding the Teapot Dome lease. Why had the official announcement of the contract been delayed for two weeks after it was signed? The reason, Fall said, was national security. As a mere business agent in the transaction, he could not usurp the navy secretary's role and disclose plans for large military storage facilities. "It was the Navy's business," Fall commented, and he knew nothing about the brisk, furtive trading in Sinclair oil stocks during the two weeks between the signing of the Teapot Dome contract and its announcement.

In his final remarks Fall again emphasized national security. Convinced that world opinion favored disarmament, which would result in a reduction of the United States Navy, he had acted to conserve and store oil at Pearl Harbor because that would make "one-half of the battleships then on the Pacific . . . worth more than the total number under other conditions." In short, he said proudly, "the efficiency of the United States fleet in the Pacific waters to-day is more than doubled already by this policy."

Other witnesses, mostly from the Interior and Navy departments, added nothing of a spectacular nature. Just out of the hospital, Navy Secretary Denby appeared without an opportunity to consult his technical advisers or refresh his memory from pertinent documents. He had requested Fall to take charge of the naval reserves, he recalled, and then Fall had prepared the executive order of transferral and handled all the paperwork. Obviously unwell, he was sometimes doubtful and at other times could not remember routine information. Denby's dismal performance, which contrasted with Fall's emphatic self-confidence, raised serious questions about his reputation as a conscientious public servant.

A naval officer who had helped administer the oil reserves and opposed their transfer testified that Secretary Fall engineered his reassignment from Washington to the Charleston Navy Yard in South Carolina. Admiral John K. Robison, who commanded the reserves after the transfer, said that he favored the leasing program because of drainage. He recalled first hearing of the drainage threat from Doheny, whose son had served on his ship during the war. Later, when Fall confided to Robison that no acceptable bids might be submitted for the Pearl Harbor storage project, the admiral appealed to Doheny's patriotism and secured the oilman's promise of a suitable proposal. Sinclair's testimony, although unexciting, included a notable admission about his much-publicized $100 million evaluation of the oil in Teapot Dome. Although conceding that he had overestimated the reserve's potential value, the oilman denied that his mistake was calculated to cause a sharp rise in Sinclair stock prices. Sinclair said nothing about buying a one-third interest in Fall's ranch.

During the first round of hearings, the strong tribal loyalties of the Senate were noticeably at work. When Senator Fall had been named interior secretary in 1921, one of his predecessors in that office, Franklin K. Lane, had written a former subordinate, "I am glad he is from the Senate, they care for their own." While Fall and Walsh traded brickbats in the hearings, the other committee members had rarely raised any questions, except Republican Senators Smoot and Irvine L. Lenroot, who occasionally inserted leading queries and information helpful to Fall. Only Walsh seemed unsympathetic, and even he was severely criticized by fellow Democrats for letting Fall off so easily and for showing him "senatorial courtesy" in the interrogation.

Most of the press accounts also were favorable to Fall. Only a few newspapers took an early interest in the proceedings, and perhaps only one of the reporters who regularly attended the sessions, Paul Y. Anderson, a free-lance correspondent for the *St. Louis Post-Dispatch* and other papers, understood the significance of the story and covered it adequately from the beginning. When Walsh tried to stir up some interest in the inquiry, a prominent writer for periodicals replied that he would like "to go after the Teapot Dome matter," but muckraking was no longer popular with editors, who now depended on advertising by big corporations, instead of circulation, for their profits.

In early November, when the investigation was adjourned for a month, Fall's reputation and integrity were still secure. So far the probe had not successfully challenged his administration of the reserves. Some of the testimony had raised eyebrows, but the burden of proof was still on Senator Walsh. It seemed that Fall had a right to become indignant at this blatant attack on his record as a public servant. Like other Republican leaders, Fall assumed that Walsh was only out to "'pin something on the Republicans'" and, if given enough rope, he would hang himself. This misconception showed that they understood only one side of the Montana senator—his Democratic partisanship. Perhaps Fall's greatest mistake in his first appearance before the Teapot Dome committee was to underestimate Walsh. By the time he realized his error, it was too late.

Rumors of a big land deal in New Mexico continued to reach Walsh, who recalled that "sometimes it was Fall who purchased for Sinclair; again Sinclair who purchased for Fall." These vague leads revealed little until a friendly Washington newspaper editor steered Walsh to D. F. Stackelback, the *Denver Post* investigative reporter whose findings on Fall's financial affairs had been buried by publisher Frederick G. Bonfils. Stackelback could prove, the senator heard, that before the Teapot Dome lease Fall was broke but afterwards had several hundred thousand dollars. In fact, after talking with more than twenty cattlemen and public figures in New Mexico, the reporter had become convinced that Fall was about the only rancher in the state who had the money to buy additional land. All the rest were "broke or nearly so" because of the drought and slumping cattle prices. Summoned to Washington by Walsh, Stackelback brought along his written account as well as notarized documentation for Fall's purchase of the Harris ranch, for his payment in the summer of 1922 of ten-year-old delinquent taxes, and for the blooded livestock shipment from Sinclair. More important, as Walsh remembered it, the reporter also furnished the names and addresses of persons in New Mexico "who could tell of Fall's sudden rise from financial embarrassment, if not impecuniosity, to comparative affluence." Although Stackelback never testified formally before the committee, he supplied the earth-shaking evidence that Walsh needed to break open the case.

Fall expected more of the senatorial courtesy he had received earlier. He had known for several months of Walsh's efforts to gather incriminating information, but assumed that his financial affairs would not be publicized before he had a chance to explain them. Since Walsh had avoided the subject thus far, Fall thought that his analysis was correct. He did not worry even after learning from Senator Smoot about Stackelback's confidential accusations. But senatorial courtesy only went so far with Walsh. When Fall heard that Walsh was subpoenaing witnesses in New Mexico for the next round of hearings, he gloomily concluded that his former Senate colleague intended "to besmirch my character or to raise a smoke screen." Indeed, the so-called "New Mexican witnesses" who trooped to Washington when the hearings reopened gave the damaging testimony that led to the ruination of Albert Fall. And it was the appearance of Fall's fellow New Mexicans that first produced the excitement and the spectacular headlines that had so far eluded Walsh in the inquiry. In the second phase of the investigation Fall's personal affairs would be laid bare for all to see.

Senator Walsh's main objective with the New Mexico witnesses, in relation to his overall strategy, was to connect Fall's improved finances with Sinclair's visit to Three Rivers prior to the Teapot Dome lease. For this reason Carl C. Magee, the volatile editor of the *New Mexico State Tribune* in Albuquerque, became the "star witness" among those testifying from Fall's home state. Magee's appearance resulted from Stackelback's investigative probing, and, in fact, the *Denver Post* reporter, before going to Three Rivers, had received his first incriminating tips from Magee in Albuquerque. Stackelback informed Walsh about Magee and what he could be "expected to tell." As the first witness to discuss Fall's finances, Magee was a key figure in the entire investigation.

Magee had left a law practice in Tulsa and moved to New Mexico because of his wife's health. During a visit to Three Rivers early in 1920, he professed strong Republican loyalties. Fall explained that he had to sell his $25,000 interest in the *Albuquerque Morning Journal* due to dire personal financial circumstances. Magee later purchased the *Journal* for $115,000 from the consortium formed by Fall for his senatorial reelection in 1918. Although initially showing a willingness to become Fall's political protégé, Magee was "a zealot, a reformer, a John Brown of Osawatomie sort of character." A few months after buying the newspaper, he began lambasting the state Republican organization, singling out Fall for vilification as the boss of a corrupt machine, and calling for a new order. After the Senate passed the La Follette resolution authorizing the Teapot Dome investigation, the *Journal* jubilantly proclaimed: "Harry Sinclair's reported presence in New Mexico when Mr. Fall bought the Harris ranch and other property, a short time ago, may [now] receive attention. Mr. Fall was presumed to be 'hard up' at the time he is said to have paid cash for these properties. Who, if anybody, loaned him the money?" At first Magee had only seemed intent on disrupting the Republican party in New Mexico. Then, even worse, he switched parties and backed the entire Democratic ticket in 1922.

Meanwhile Magee himself had run into financial trouble. In assaulting the Republican organization, he began with the sacrosanct state land office. Before long, according to the editor, Fall came by his Albuquerque office:

> He [Fall] said, "Didn't I tell you that the public land office was organized to suit me?" I said, "Yes; I think you did tell me something like that." And I said, "It isn't organized to suit me." He said, "I want you to back away from it." And he said, "Will you do it?" And I said, "I should say not." And he said, "I am going to break you." I said, "Put on your hat and wade in; the water is fine."

After this confrontation, as Magee recalled, "I attacked him every day or in every way there was to attack him." The banks from which Magee had borrowed money to buy the *Journal* and some new equipment refused to extend his loans. Blaming Fall and other prominent Republicans for his misfortunes, he had to sell out in June 1922. He then started another Albuquerque newspaper, which became the *State Tribune*, and continued his journalistic assault. His practice of calling names in print without sufficient regard for the libel laws resulted in several stormy legal actions, which usually ended in his criminal conviction and a speedy gubernatorial pardon. Later, in a hotel lobby scuffle, his pistol shots shattered the arm of a hostile judge and accidently killed a bystander, but he was acquitted on a manslaughter charge.

In his testimony Magee told the committee that on his first visit to Three Rivers everything about the Fall ranch seemed dilapidated. Later, on a speechmaking trip in August 1923, he noticed from the main highway some conspicuous beautification, fencing, and grading improvements along the road leading to the ranch house. He also heard stories in nearby Carrizozo about the construction of electrical installations on the ranch costing thousands of dollars. Although Magee presented mostly hearsay, Senator Walsh now introduced Fall's local tax records. Between 1912 and 1922, it seemed, Fall had not paid certain property taxes; then, in June 1922, he paid all of the delinquent amounts. Later in the investigation, evidence submitted at Fall's behest showed that his disputed assessments had been tied up in court for years until finally determined in 1922, whereupon he paid them.

The other New Mexico witnesses provided additional information—and some misinformation—about the large amounts of cash involved in the Harris ranch purchase, Sinclair's first visit to Three Rivers and his livestock shipment, and the various land additions and improvements at the ranch. Despite convincing favorable explanations from some of these witnesses, the sensational revelations about Fall's improved finances, although often speculative, obscured everything else. The recurrent question had already been asked in Magee's editorial: "Who, if anybody, loaned him the money?"

After the New Mexico witnesses told their stories, some skeptics still portrayed Walsh as "a muckraker, vilifying worthy public servants," but now even his detractors had to take the investigation seriously. Not even the testimony of a "greatly outraged" Doheny, who extolled Fall's integrity, removed the spotlight of suspicion from his friend. So far Fall's work for him had been in "an advisory way" for the Mexican loan negotiations, the oilman said, but he had just as good a position waiting for Fall as he had given President Wilson's interior secretary, Franklin K. Lane. Bristling at Walsh's insinuations of unfairness to the navy, Doheny defended his Elk Hills leases and contracts, while conceding that his company would be "in bad luck" if it failed to make a $100 million profit from these arrangements. When asked by Senator Lenroot if Fall had profited "directly or indirectly" through the naval oil transactions with him, Doheny answered, "Not yet." In Sinclair's second appearance before the committee Lenroot asked him the same question. Sinclair replied, "No sir; none, unless he had received some benefits from the cattle [shipment to the ranch]." Now, according to Walsh, it was up to Fall "to tell where the money came from."

Increasingly apprehensive about the Doheny loan and Senator Walsh's partisan motivations, Albert Fall set out to stop the investigation before it went any further. He began a deceptive strategy that was, to put it mildly, a terrible blunder, by attempting to show that the money came from another source. When the New Mexico witnesses started their damaging testimony, Senator Smoot wired Fall at Three Rivers that he must come to Washington at once and refute the charges. Instead, Fall dispatched his son-in-law, Clarence C. Chase, to give an explanation of the ranch holdings and operations. If necessary, Fall told Smoot, he would testify personally after Walsh concluded his political antics.

But Chase did not go straight to Washington. Fall had written Price McKinney, the Cleveland steel magnate, asking, as he later said, "one of the best friends I ever had in the world" for a great favor that would throw Walsh off the trail. As Chase recalled it: "What Mr. Fall wanted was that Mr. McKinney would tell the committee that arrangements had been made with him to get that money. That he could have gotten it from Mr. McKinney instead of Mr. Doheny had he asked for it." McKinney had not replied to the letter. When Chase showed up in Cleveland with a similar request, McKinney candidly informed Fall's son-in-law, "I have not made him a loan and I could not say that I have." Although Fall's boon companion for twenty years, who had loaned him a total of well over $100,000, McKinney as a hardheaded businessman would not take such a great risk even for a close friend. If he had done so, his wealth, banking connections, and record of past loans to Fall might have been convincing enough to halt the investigation, at least temporarily. McKinney's refusal to honor Fall's urgent request, of all the turning points in the naval oil affair, was certainly one of the most decisive actions. It ruined Fall's counterattack and caused him to offer a much less plausible source for the money. If the Teapot Dome scandal had a shadowy mystery figure, one who might have changed its course, it was Price McKinney.

Nothing was going right for Fall. Chase went on to Washington, but, with the alternative money source eliminated, he had no reason to testify. At Senator Smoot's nervous admonition, Fall and his wife soon started a strange meandering journey by train to the East, ostensibly to tell all. He tried unsuccessfully to get McKinney to join him in Washington. Fall's bizarre journey with several detours lasted nearly three months. At Kansas City the Falls met Chase, and he doubled back to the East with them. By the time they reached Chicago, the strain began to affect Fall's precarious health; he "was broken down completely" and had to stop for a brief rest. While in Chicago, he received a telegram from Doheny imploring him to come to New York City immediately. Currently engaged in a $20 million fund-raising campaign for his new subsidiary, the Pan American Western Company, Doheny wanted to avoid bad publicity at any cost. In fact, if the committee asked him whether he had ever loaned any money to Fall, the oilman declared in their New York conference, he would answer categorically, "No!" And it would be a good idea, Doheny continued, for Fall to inform the senators that the money came from Ned McLean. Finally, however, Doheny relented and said, "Well, if you are called and put upon oath . . . , of course, you can tell the truth and tell the committee that I will surrender the contracts and leases." At this time Sinclair's lawyer, J. W. Zevely, delivered copies of the testimony in the hearings, sent from Washington by Senator Smoot, and Fall also conferred with Sinclair himself.

In Washington the Teapot Dome panel anxiously awaited Fall's appearance. From his room in the Waldorf Astoria Hotel, where he was confined with "an exceedingly bad and threatening cold," Fall wrote Senator Lenroot, the new committee chairman, that the doctor had ordered absolute rest for a few days. He regretted that "a combination of illness and other very important matters" had kept him from testifying that week, but he would clear up all the questions raised by Magee's statements when he did take the stand. Meanwhile, Fall said, he was going to Atlantic City for two or three days of healthful sea air.

At Fall's invitation Ned McLean came to the Ritz-Carlton Hotel in Atlantic City on December 20, 1923, to talk about the loan question. Dressed in a dark red smoking jacket, Fall was "in a very nervous, bad physical condition." As McLean recalled their conversation, he said:

> "Ned, you remember our check transactions of two or three years ago." I said, "I do." He said, "Will you say"—or "do you mind saying . . . that you loaned me that in cash?" And he said one thing, he said, "It has nothing to do with Harry Sinclair or Teapot Dome." And now these are his exact words: He said, "They are barking up the wrong tree. . . ." Then the result of that was I said, "Yes, I will, Senator."

Again Fall notified the committee that his health would not permit him to testify when he had hoped. "I will advise you as soon as my health is regained," he concluded.

Still not well, Fall came to Washington just before Christmas. His Wardman Park Hotel apartment became a beehive of activity. Lawyers and aides of McLean, Doheny, and Sinclair came and went giving advice, relaying information, and speculating on the attitudes of the different committee members. Senators Smoot and Lenroot visited the sick man one afternoon, but they had not come to inquire about his health. They desperately wanted Fall to defend himself and the Republican party by testifying where he had obtained the money to buy the Harris ranch. The senators became insistent. Fall replied that it might have come from any of several sources, including McLean. One of the senators, perhaps Lenroot, said that if Fall would name McLean as his benefactor, the taint of oil would be removed from the loan, and "such an answer would blow Walsh out of the water and stop the entire proceedings." Fall stubbornly declared that he would not give the committee any information at all on his personal business affairs.

On the night after Christmas other important callers came to Fall's Wardman Park apartment and found him in bed. Among them was Will H. Hays, Republican national chairman in the 1920 election and afterwards Harding's first postmaster general. Hays had reason for great concern because Sinclair had helped retire the 1920 Republican campaign debt with a donation of at least $160,000, most of it from the same group of Liberty Bonds the oilman had used to buy his interest in Fall's ranch. It was the largest single contribution by any Republican, and had been offered at about the time Senator Walsh began uncovering the damaging details of Fall's finances. The proximity of these two events led Walsh to speculate afterwards that Sinclair's generosity might have been inspired by a "dire need of friends at court." Evidently Hays was now worried lest the committee expose the Republicans' debt arrangements and somehow link them to Sinclair's money transactions with Fall, thus creating a landslide of criticism that would crush not only Fall but other prominent Republicans and the party's hopes for the 1924 presidential election as well. In short, Fall's predicament had all the makings of a Republican catastrophe.

In a long, spirited discussion that night in the Wardman Park Hotel, Hays urged Fall to end the speculation about his financial affairs. Hays said that he had talked to key members of the committee, who assured him that a letter of explanation from

Fall would end the hearings. Sinclair was there also to offer his pleas to the bedridden Fall. During the evening, Fall was probably in communication, through their representatives, with Doheny and McLean. Finally, with Hays, Sinclair, and a Sinclair attorney, G. T. Sanford, hovering over his bed, Fall dictated and signed a letter to the committee stating in detail that he had never received "one cent on account of any oil lease or upon any other account whatsoever" from Doheny or Sinclair. The money in question, for the Harris ranch purchase, had come from McLean. The next day the letter, probably delivered by Hays to Senator Lenroot, turned up as the first topic of business for the Teapot Dome panel. From Palm Beach, McLean sent word to the committee that he had indeed loaned Fall $100,000 in November 1921 on a personal note that was "absolutely unsecured." Although McLean was willing to make a written statement under oath in Florida, his attorney declared, he could not leave Palm Beach to testify in Washington because of his own ill health and illness in his family.

Fall thought he had stopped the investigation dead in its tracks. He had explained the source of his funds to buy the Harris ranch, and McLean had substantiated his story. Even a Senate committee would be reluctant to challenge the veracity of a former cabinet officer, especially when his account was so logical. Except for Senator Walsh's skepticism, Fall might have gambled and won at this point in the Teapot Dome investigation. Instead of ending his troubles, however, Fall's letter to the committee brought the critical turning point of the inquiry. McLean lacked the financial credibility of Price McKinney. As Walsh later remarked, "the knowing ones smiled incredulously at the idea of Ned McLean's having such a sum of money at hand to loan, though rich in property, or of his loaning it if he had it." When Fall and McLean subsequently turned up together in Palm Beach, Walsh followed them to the Florida resort city and pried the admission from McLean that he had not loaned $100,000 to Fall. The revelation that Fall had lied about his finances cast a sinister light on every aspect of the naval oil transactions, and the Teapot Dome scandal began spouting up.

Fall's great lie cost him everything. Just why a shrewd politician would take such a chance is unanswerable. Undoubtedly he thought it was the easiest way out, that is, it would end what he considered a politically motivated investigation. The pressure from his Republican friends and Sinclair at the Wardman Park, his western ethic of protecting a "pard," Doheny, who was in the midst of a crucial corporate fund-raising campaign, and his serious illness at the time no doubt influenced his action. Years later he characterized the letter as an attempt to avoid personal and political disaster:

> I knew perfectly well, at that time that the Democratic leaders were preparing to wage war on the Republican Administration by making charges of general dishonesty. My friend Harding was dead. The new [Coolidge] Administration would not want to be burdened with my defense. I knew that if I disclosed that Doheny had loaned me the money an avalanche of political abuse would be let loose against the Republican Administration, against Doheny and against me. I knew the power of the public press, and how it could be used under such circumstances from the floor of the Senate. I knew that under these conditions my reputation would be defamed, and that I would be unable to adequately meet in the public press the charges against me. To avoid this calamity I made the unspeakable blunder of attempting to evade the matter by an untruth. I wrote the Committee I had obtained the money from McLean. I thus made a bad matter very, very much worse.

This monumental falsehood, Fall said in retrospect, was "the only thing in the world" he regretted about the whole Teapot Dome affair "except the suffering of my poor wife and daughters." The naval oil transactions, although widely questioned, were defensible. Fall's greatest mistake, besides taking the money itself, was misleading the committee. His letter, instead of ending the inquiry before Senator Walsh discovered the real sources of Fall's affluence, opened the floodgates of political vituperation.

At Palm Beach, while Walsh was extracting McLean's admission that he had not made the $100,000 loan, the senator also played a cat-and-mouse game with Fall, who vacillated about talking to the inquisitor. According to McLean, Fall was "shot to pieces" emotionally and physically. "For the first time in my life," McLean's wife recalled, "I saw a man crumble right before my eyes." Fall's wife was always at his side, and their two married daughters arrived from the Southwest to furnish additional moral support. Fall and McLean consulted continually with a battery of lawyers and "advisers." Everyone tried to give Fall advice. From Washington came word through Attorney General Harry Daugherty, who offered his services, that President Coolidge had Fall "in mind" during this period of unjustified "embarrassment." Fall wanted to make a clean breast of it, to disclose the "absolute facts," one daughter observed, but the advisers were all making conflicting recommendations. In Fall's weakened condition the ordeal was "killing" him. He desperately sought an attorney who could provide expert legal counsel about giving testimony to Walsh, but to no avail.

Just before McLean told Walsh the truth, Fall apprised Doheny by telegram of the situation at Palm Beach: "Walsh authorized to take testimony as subcommittee. Will examine McLean and probably myself. Facts will be developed, possibly names not disclosed." Since Walsh had not expected McLean to deny making the $100,000 loan, he was "dumbfounded" by the newspaper owner's corrected story. Walsh then wrote Fall a letter saying that he would be "glad" to get either an oral or a written statement from the former cabinet officer. At first Fall indicated that he would talk to Walsh, but then changed his mind and sent him a letter that only verified McLean's latest account. Perhaps, when his health permitted, he would "desire to amplify this statement . . . for the committee at a later date." He apparently could not bring himself to break his vow of loyalty to Doheny.

Next in their bizarre travels Fall and his family entourage prepared to depart for New Orleans. Before leaving Palm Beach, however, he dictated another telegram to Doheny. Ned McLean recorded the first draft on a typewriter in his beach cottage. Doheny had to tell the committee about the loan, Fall said, and, if the oilman did not, he would do it himself. Fall also stated that he was going to New Orleans, where Doheny must meet him. McLean thought the telegram was a "classic" and showed it to C. Bascom Slemp, Coolidge's executive assistant, who, at McLean's invitation, was supposedly vacationing at Palm Beach. While discussing the message with McLean and one of Fall's daughters, Slemp made a profoundly wise observation that Fall should have made for himself earlier. Slemp could understand Fall's loyalty in shielding a friend, the presidential aide said, but Doheny would be protected by his money, and Fall must look out for himself. Between McLean's cottage and Washington there was a steady exchange of telegrams, many of them in weird codes, one of which used "Apple" for Fall's name. Through a special leased wire to McLean's *Washington Post* office, Slemp may have kept Coolidge informed about the events at Palm Beach.

By this time Albert Fall's troubles were front-page news and reporters dogged his tracks. At New Orleans, Emma Fall told the clamoring journalists that her husband was too ill to talk to them. But a resolute Fall, like the decisive, forceful, gutsy fighter of old, took command of his sinking situation and called a summit meeting. From Washington, at Fall's insistence, came Harry Sinclair's lawyer and confidant, J. W. Zevely. Two days later Doheny arrived from California, bringing with him his attorney, the Democratic power broker Gavin McNab, and Fall's former law partner, W. A. Hawkins, who had boarded the oilman's private railroad car, the *Patriot*, at El Paso. That evening in Fall's Roosevelt Hotel rooms he, Doheny, McNab, and Hawkins gathered for an important conference. Zevely, who had already been briefed by Fall, did not attend because Doheny declined to consult with him.

Fall laid two crucial issues on the table immediately. First, he said, Doheny and Sinclair should telegraph President Coolidge requesting him to initiate court action through the attorney general that would cancel all of the naval oil leases. Second, the $100,000 loan must be explained fully to the committee. McNab vetoed Fall's first proposal on legal grounds, but Doheny accepted the second one. Then McNab asked who would tell the committee about the loan. Fall said that he thought Doheny should do it, and Doheny agreed. With that crucial question settled, McNab then added a bizarre twist to the meeting. What about the note Fall had signed to secure the loan? the attorney queried. The investigating panel would surely want to see it. Since Doheny had mutilated the note by tearing off Fall's signature as a protective measure, McNab wanted Fall to make out a new form. With special ink, pen, and paper, McNab said, "no expert could tell whether a document written with it [them], or a signature made, had been written three days or three years before." Although Fall considered this a "Damned fool idea," confirming McNab's reputation as Hollywood comedian "Fatty" Arbuckle's lawyer, he dutifully complied. Doheny decided not to use this document when he testified but informed the committee that he would produce a note later. Whether "the delay was to allow the ink to ripen," Fall never learned. When Doheny did present a note, it was the original form with the signature torn off.

After the New Orleans meeting both Fall and Doheny headed for Washington to appear before the Teapot Dome panel. Now Fall had no choice; he had finally been subpoenaed to give his testimony. As a precaution against his leaving the country, two Justice Department agents and a local detective kept him under surveillance in New Orleans. Fall expected to accompany Doheny to Washington in the oilman's private railroad car, but Gavin McNab objected, saying that it would create a bad impression if they arrived together. So Fall and Sinclair's lawyer, J. W. Zevely, followed Doheny by train later. Before reaching Washington, Doheny and McNab made a last-ditch effort through another of the oilman's attorneys, William G. McAdoo, a Democratic presidential contender, to deter or stop the investigation of the loan. They also pressured Walsh. Both McAdoo and Walsh refused to cooperate, but it was too late to hinder any aspect of the cascading inquiry anyway.

Until now Senator Walsh was convinced that Fall had surreptitiously received perhaps $175,000 or $200,000 from a single source, Harry Sinclair. He had not originally considered the possibility that Doheny, too, was Fall's benefactor. The impression of Sinclair's solitary role had been strengthened by the surprising testimony of two of Theodore Roosevelt's sons, Theodore, Jr., assistant navy secretary, and his younger brother, Archie, who had just resigned from a Sinclair subsidiary. The day after Walsh's findings at Palm Beach, Archie said, Sinclair had told him to book the oilman's passage on the next ship leaving for Europe. Even more disturbing was Archie's conversation with Sinclair's private secretary, G. D. Wahlberg, who hinted that their boss, having bribed Fall, had left the country because of Walsh's Palm Beach revelations. Wahlberg was particularly worried, Archie recalled, about a payment of $68,000 to Fall's ranch foreman, for which the secretary held the canceled checks. Wahlberg had advised Archie to resign from the Sinclair concern to protect his reputation and family name.

When Wahlberg took the stand, he told a different story. Young Roosevelt had not heard him correctly when they were actually talking about a livestock shipment to Fall's ranch. "I think I referred to six or eight cows," Wahlberg stated, "and he probably understood that to mean $68,000 in some manner." This apparently lame excuse only placed more suspicion on Sinclair. Theodore, Jr., was convinced that Sinclair's secretary had been "reached" and persuaded to lie about the incident. In a later appearance Wahlberg added another explanation. During his conversation with Archie, he now recalled, two salary checks totaling $68,000 to Sinclair's "farm horse manager" (the racehorse trainer at Rancoras stable) had been lying on his desk. Evidently young Roosevelt had misunderstood him to say that the checks were "To the manager of Fall's farm."

No evidence presented in the investigation ever documented a $68,000 payment in checks to Fall, his ranch foreman, or Everhart, the ranch manager. At this time J. W. Zevely testified about Sinclair's $25,000 loan in Liberty Bonds made to Fall before the Russian trip and the $10,000 for Fall's expenses in Europe, although he failed to reveal the oilman's purchase of an interest in the Three Rivers ranch for $233,000 in Liberty Bonds. Much later, when Sinclair returned from abroad, he refused to enlighten the committee with any further information, and incurred a contempt-of-the-Senate citation. In subsequent appearances he was more forthcoming on his financial arrangements with Fall, but never mentioned $68,000 in checks sent to the Three Rivers ranch. Despite Archie's confusion over the conversation, however, Wahlberg had become justifiably apprehensive about Sinclair's Liberty Bond payments to Fall, and he had conveyed his fears, in some form, to young Roosevelt. This testimony caused an immediate furor, largely because it involved Theodore Roosevelt's sons.

When Doheny testified, Senator Walsh realized that Fall had received money not from just one but from two sources. In a crowded Senate hearing room Doheny began by reading from a prepared statement and then expanded on those comments during a lengthy cross-examination. "I wish first to inform the committee that on the 30th of November, 1921, I loaned Albert B. Fall $100,000 upon his promissory note to enable him to purchase a ranch in New Mexico," came the dramatic announcement. As one of the main reasons for the loan, Doheny emphasized a friendship going back more than thirty years to their shared hardships on the New Mexico mining frontier. Since then, said the oilman, he had prospered to the extent that $100,000 was a mere "bagatelle" to him, or "no more than $25 or $50 perhaps to the ordinary individual." As for repayment of the loan, Doheny declared, "If Mr. Fall is well enough and in good health, I expect he will enter my employ." And Fall's salary in representing the Doheny interests in Mexico would be large enough to easily allow repayment of the note in five or six years. Throughout his testimony Doheny stoutly defended his naval oil contracts and leases as good bargains for the government, offering to relinquish the Pearl Harbor project if a board of experts proved otherwise, or even if his company was only compensated for its expenditures. Doheny was asked if he thought his contracts should be returned because the loan gave him an unfair competitive advantage. "Well, if it will clear Senator Fall from any suspicion of being in collusion," he replied, "I am perfectly willing to do it." But he had not come before the committee to confess any iniquity, and simply to give the contracts back "would be a confession of wrong-doing."

Doheny's "bombshell" was the climax of the entire inquiry. Democrats as well as Republicans on the investigating panel were now of one mind. To them and the crowd that jammed the hearing room, including almost a quorum who had absented themselves from the Senate chamber, and to newspaper readers all over the country who scanned the glaring black headlines, the oil magnate's testimony stigmatized the loan as a corrupt transaction. This impression prevailed despite Doheny's stubborn assertions that no collusion was involved. Like Fall, the oilman maintained that the loan was a personal affair having nothing to do with his corporate operations.

Although anxious for Doheny to testify fully about the loan, Fall disliked several aspects of his friend's prepared statement and testimony. He blamed Gavin McNab for most of the offensive parts. For one thing, the oilman had failed to elaborate on the unlikelihood of Fall's official acts being influenced by the loan. Doheny had indeed paid the $100,000 to influence him, Fall conceded, but not in the naval oil transactions. Besides "pure friendship" and his unlimited wealth, Doheny had offered the money "through the desire to have a first call upon my services when I went out of official life." That is, with all the promising oil prospects in Mexico, Colombia, Venezuela, and elsewhere in Central America, Doheny wanted to ensure that he would command Fall's expertise in Latin-American affairs, not to mention the former interior secretary's lobbying clout in Washington. As the later hearings disclosed, the oil magnate made a hobby of hiring retired cabinet officers and paying them handsome salaries. In fact, he had employed four members of the Wilson cabinet, including ex–Treasury Secretary McAdoo, who was Wilson's son-in-law, and ex–Interior Secretary Franklin K. Lane.

The testimony of Doheny, Wahlberg, and Zevely, which revealed money going to Fall from both recipients of the naval oil contracts, brought a public clamor for corrective measures. Now everyone in Washington scrambled to climb onto the

Teapot Dome bandwagon. President Coolidge had started showing a perceptible interest in the investigation when the Roosevelt brothers took the stand. The Justice Department was watching the proceedings, Coolidge indicated, and would take action against any wrongdoing. In Congress there was a demand for legislative annulment of the Teapot Dome contract, but Senator Walsh insisted that cancellation of the oil leases belonged in the courts, and his view prevailed. Trying to stay one jump ahead of Walsh, the president announced his intention to appoint two special federal prosecutors, one from each party, who would conduct the civil and criminal litigation resulting from the investigation. Soon afterwards Congress passed the Walsh resolution, which branded the Doheny and Sinclair naval reserve arrangements as fraudulent and corrupt, and "authorized and directed" the president to initiate immediate court action to cancel the agreements and punish the guilty parties. Because of widespread distrust of Attorney General Daugherty, the Walsh resolution also provided for the presidential appointment of special prosecutors, independent of the Justice Department and confirmed by the Senate. Just as Fall had proposed at New Orleans, the government chose to settle the merits of the naval oil deals in court.

Still very ill, Fall did not appear before the committee for over a week after his arrival in Washington from New Orleans. Levi Cooke, an attorney Fall had only recently engaged, informed the panel that his client was "on the verge of a nervous breakdown" and presented statements from four physicians that Fall was too feeble to come to the hearings. The committee, or a subcommittee thereof, Cooke suggested, could question Fall in his sickroom. Senator Walsh, recalling Fall's notorious smelling-committee visit with a bedridden President Wilson, vetoed this recommendation, saying that the senators should not "intrude" on the witness. Instead the committee appointed its own medical board of three doctors, who, although finding the patient in "an anxiety state," pronounced him able to testify as specified. A subpoena was then issued ordering the former cabinet officer to appear at the hearings the next morning.

The darkest day of Albert Fall's life began as he arrived by automobile from J. W. Zevely's home, where he had been confined under medical care, to face the Teapot Dome committee, most of whom had been his Senate colleagues. He had been ill with respiratory problems and near nervous prostration for weeks. His friends in the Southwest, who remembered him as sturdy, ramrod straight of stature, and a hard fighter who in countless political and legal battles had never compromised with a foe, could hardly believe the newspaper stories from Washington that described him as "aged, broken, and sick." In the hearings that day "the morbidly curious [spectators who] crowded all approaches to the committee room and packed it to suffocation" craned their necks to get a look at the man who had become the most controversial witness "in the most sensational congressional investigation, certainly in recent years." The ten committee members, led by the chairman, Senator Lenroot, pushed their way through the crowd to a table and seated themselves. The throng parted slowly as Fall moved through it to the table. He was accompanied by his lawyer, his physician, and Mark B. Thompson, a longtime friend from New Mexico. Although he carried a cane, Fall walked steadily without using it and without assistance.

Once Fall was seated across the table from his "inquisitors," he was asked by Senator Walsh if he wished to make a statement. Reading from a typewritten manuscript, he began in a firm voice, "Mr. Chairman and gentlemen of the committee, I decline to answer the question for the following reasons and on the following grounds." The crowd, expecting some sensational revelations, stirred visibly, but the rest was anticlimactic. Fall continued in a clear voice that carried all over the large room, giving two main explanations for why he declined to testify. First, since the Senate had authorized the investigation to last only through the previous congressional session, the committee's mandate had expired and it had no right to continue the inquiry or to ask him questions. Second, in adopting the Walsh resolution, Congress had removed the naval oil issue from the committee and turned it over to the courts. Since he would be involved in future litigation, Fall said, he refused to testify on Fifth Amendment grounds of self-incrimination. In short, he would wait until his day in court, under established rules of evidence, to say anything further about his financial affairs or the leasing arrangements. Then he concluded by expressing his "full respect" for the committee and the Senate. Even if Fall, who "looked pale and feeble," had tried to testify, a former Interior Department subordinate observed, he "probably would have broken down under a hard cross examination."

Following a hasty executive session, the committee heeded Fall's admonition and asked the Senate to renew its investigative authority, which was promptly done. Some senators advocated retroactive impeachment, a contempt-of-the-Senate citation, or another appearance for Fall, but those proposals were dropped when he advised the panel that he would not waive his Fifth Amendment rights. With the traumatic experience of the investigation behind him and the uncertainty of courtroom ordeals ahead, Fall left Washington for the Southwest on February 14, 1924. After a few days in El Paso, he withdrew to the quiet of Three Rivers to lick his wounds.

Ed Doheny may have been even more stunned than Fall. Both he and Walsh were prominent Democrats and staunch Catholics of Irish descent, and the senator's relentless questioning had been an especially bitter pill for the wealthy, imperious oil tycoon to swallow. The grilling by such "political wolves" reminded him, Doheny said, "of old times in the West when one of our dogs at the mating season joined the wolves and . . . at night I could hear our own dog barking at our camp with the wolves." When quotations on his company's stock spiraled sharply downward following his testimony, and funding of the Pan American Western subsidiary was disrupted, Doheny's worst fears were confirmed. Moreover, he and Walsh had been good friends for years. Although outwardly Walsh showed little reluctance to go after a fellow Democrat, his cross-examination of Doheny, the senator declared, "was one of the most distressing duties perhaps ever imposed on me."

When the Teapot Dome scandal became a gusher following Doheny's testimony, several of Fall's former Senate colleagues were shocked that a man who had been one of them could become a fallen angel. Republican Senator Charles L. McNary of Oregon recalled his impression of Fall as a man of character, ruggedly honest and fearless, who told stories of his bravado in shooting scrapes with Mexican ruffians. "And again we find," McNary philosophized, "that the dog that bays [at] the moon is usually the one who kills the sheep." Democratic Senator Henry F. Ashurst of Arizona took a more compassionate view: "Ex-Secretary Fall is now ill and helpless. Every way he turns he is assailed by a new anguish. His career teaches us to walk humbly." But there was no compassion expressed by the austere Senator Walsh. Fall's troubles, he said, only vindicated "the wisdom of the patriarch who proclaimed centuries ago that the way of the transgressor is hard."

CHAPTER 9

The Final Crushing Blow

TEAPOT Dome was established as a symbol of political corruption, with Albert Fall as the archvillain, in the election of 1924, and the scandal reappeared as a campaign issue at four-year intervals for the next fifty years. In 1924 the Republicans, needing a scapegoat for the sins of the Harding administration, pointed smugly at prominent Democrats who had also become entwined in the naval oil controversy and settled upon Fall as the Republican to bear all the blame. The Democrats, on the other hand, realized the clout of Teapot Dome in their efforts to pin the corruption label on their opponents and, with some difficulty, nourished it through that election and the 1928 campaign as well. Even though not enough to win either contest for the Democrats, it was, nevertheless, a longterm windfall for their party. And with the aid of the extended, sensational litigation that followed the Senate investigation of Fall's oil deals, Teapot Dome remained continually in the headlines for almost a decade. Such long and concentrated attention fixed the oil controversy as the leading example of political wrongdoing until it was superseded by the Watergate scandal of the 1970s.

In the beginning the spectacular revelations made by the Teapot Dome investigating committee had been a one-sided frolic for the Democrats at the expense of the Republicans. The Democrats rejoiced because they were, as one senator self-righteously declared, as free of this iniquity as the angels in heaven. On the other hand, President Coolidge and the Republicans, having fallen heirs to the Harding scandal legacy, squirmed as their opponents derisively charged that the initials GOP now stood for "Grand Oil Party." The Republicans had broken the

Eleventh Commandment, "Thou shalt not get found out!" and the Democrats formally announced that they would make corruption the main issue of the forthcoming campaign. But apparently the Democrats overlooked until later that Edward L. Doheny, as a prominent Democrat and heavy contributor to party coffers, had been mentioned favorably as their vice-presidential nominee in 1920.

The tide began to turn when Doheny, in his third appearance before the Teapot Dome committee, indiscriminately splattered oil on fellow Democrats as well as Republicans. Again Doheny said that he had intended to hire former Interior Secretary Fall of the Harding cabinet just as he had employed members of the Wilson cabinet, including the Democratic president's son-in-law, former Treasury Secretary William G. McAdoo. For legal services involving Doheny's Mexican petroleum interests, as the oilman remembered it offhand, he had paid McAdoo an annual retainer of $50,000, or a total of $250,000 (actually a total of $150,000 since 1919). What had been a purely Republican scandal now developed Democratic liabilities as well.

Until Doheny's latest disclosure McAdoo had been the leading contender for the Democratic presidential nomination in 1924. Now McAdoo's hopes began to crumble. Doheny had not been reluctant to implicate fellow Democrats, McAdoo was convinced, because McAdoo had declined to make Senator Walsh stop the probe into Doheny's $100,000 loan to Fall. On his way from California to Washington for a hearing before the committee, McAdoo and his wife received a telegram at Albuquerque stating that her father, Woodrow Wilson, was dead. It was said, when he arrived to give his testimony, "McAdoo is coming to Washington to attend the Wilson funeral on Wednesday and his own Thursday." As a witness McAdoo asserted that he had agreed to represent the Doheny interests because the fight against the Mexican government's confiscation of Doheny's oil lands was consistent with the Wilson administration's policies. But it was also revealed that McAdoo's law firm would have received an additional fee of $900,000 if he had succeeded in getting an agreement with Mexico that would protect Doheny's Mexican oil investments. In short, McAdoo's potential fees were well over $1,000,000, whereas Fall had received only $100,000 from Doheny.

McAdoo's employment with Doheny had nothing to do with the naval oil deals, but he suffered from guilt by association anyway. The general public had difficulty understanding the difference between Fall's leasing a naval reserve for a price while a cabinet member and McAdoo's selling his legal services to the same oilman shortly after leaving the cabinet. Thus when the leading Democratic presidential candidate became entangled in the oil scandal, Republicans could shout "corruption" almost as loudly as their opponents, and the oil issue was practically neutralized. In fact, McAdoo's Democratic detractors in his own party's national convention, stressing his association with another key issue, burst into a chant whenever his name was mentioned: "Ku Klux Klan" and "Oil! Oil! Oil!" or sometimes a combination approximating a football yell, "Ku, ku, McAdoo—Oil!"

Calvin Coolidge undoubtedly would have won the 1924 presidential election even if an untainted McAdoo had been the Democratic nominee. Coolidge had unbeatable "Republican Prosperity" on his side, and the New England Puritan succeeded in dissociating himself from Teapot Dome and the other scandals, imputing all Republican sins to the dead Harding and the live Fall. It was a masterful feat. By all the rules of partisan warfare, Coolidge as the most conspicuous member of the Harding administration should have been another victim, like McAdoo, of the Teapot Dome "mudgunning." According to Fall, the naval oil contracts were discussed on "more than one occasion" in meetings of the Harding cabinet. Since Coolidge had attended these sessions as vice president, the Democrats now charged that he knew of the oil deals and should have done something about them when he became president. Although former Harding cabinet members vigorously denied that the contracts and leases were ever considered in their presence, this question arose repeatedly in 1924 and later campaigns, especially in 1928 when former Commerce Secretary Herbert Hoover ran for president. As president, Coolidge had also conferred with Fall on the Doheny loan to Mexico and other Mexican matters, and had tacitly approved the loan. He was a personal friend of Ned McLean, and his executive assistant, C. Bascom Slemp, had been on hand when Senator Walsh pursued McLean and Fall at Palm Beach. Yet the wily little New Englander evaded an untoward political fate.

Although known as "Silent Cal," Coolidge was "keen of ear, quick of eye and delicate of nostril" in the partisan arena. At first he took as little public notice as possible of the Teapot Dome investigation, while privately he consulted regularly with committee chairman Lenroot and other Republican senators about the hearings. Then, as the inquiry became a hot issue, he got the jump on Senator Walsh by appointing special counsel to prosecute the wrongdoers, thereby effectively shifting judgment of the naval oil controversy from politics to the courts. From then on his public pronouncements indicated that he was engaged in a thorough housecleaning in which the guilty would be punished, whether Republicans or Democrats. A combination of this strategy, his image of Puritan honesty, and the involvement of Doheny, McAdoo, and other prominent Democrats with the investigation helped save Coolidge. Like the biblical figures in the fiery furnace, he emerged from the Teapot Dome inferno with little more than the "smell of smoke" on him.

Similarly President Coolidge escaped the stigma of other Harding scandals and liabilities, making his victory in the 1924 election all the more amazing. Two holdover cabinet members, Navy Secretary Edwin L. Denby and Attorney General Harry M. Daugherty, came under fire as a result of the Teapot Dome inquiry. Although the president resisted congressional pressure to dismiss Denby, he gratefully accepted the navy secretary's resignation. Democratic Senator Burton K. Wheeler of Montana conducted a separate, sensational Senate inquiry into Daugherty's failure to "arrest and prosecute" Fall, Sinclair, Doheny, and others guilty of oil sins. When the attorney general refused to furnish Wheeler with Justice Department files, Coolidge demanded his resignation, and Daugherty grudgingly complied.

Rumors of irregularities and payoffs in prohibition enforcement while Daugherty ran the Justice Department, as well as conjectures about the suicide of Jess Smith, his key "Ohio Gang" operative, continued to swirl around the deposed attorney general, but at least he was no longer part of the Coolidge administration. Budding scandals involving the Veterans' Bureau, the Shipping Board, and the Alien Property Custodian also bypassed Coolidge with little damage.

Stern Charles Evans Hughes, the "bearded iceberg," expressed President Coolidge and the Republican party's apologia when he proclaimed, "Guilt is personal and corruption knows no party." In response the Democrats fumed that, inescapably, it was a Republican, Albert Fall, "who conspired against the safety of his country and sold its essential instrument of defense for 30 pieces of silver." The vilification of Fall by both major parties, and by Robert M. La Follette's third-party Progressives, continued throughout the 1924 campaign. Fall's disinheritance by the Republicans was total, and their scourging was only exceeded by the infamy heaped upon him by the Democrats. He was virtually excommunicated from his own party. As a result, the neutralized oil-scandal issue was hardly decisive in the 1924 election; other factors, such as a rising tide of prosperity, the strife-ridden Democratic party and its weak nominee, Wall Street lawyer John W. Davis, and continued public infatuation with Harding "normalcy," had far more influence on the outcome.

The 1924 election did make Albert Fall the scapegoat of the Teapot Dome scandal forevermore, for the Republicans and for the Democrats as well. Isolated and discredited, he had borne the brunt of the political denunciation at his Three Rivers ranch. During the campaign maelstrom, Doheny and Sinclair had experienced, one newspaper stated, "no particular impairment of their social freedom." Now, with court action ahead, the two oil magnates would have to stand with Fall because "No one can conspire with himself." Most of Fall's former Senate and cabinet colleagues shunned him, but Doheny wrote philosophically that, like a stained garment, they must now "put the situation in soak, and when the time comes obliterate the stain." Their plight would not be "in soak" very long.

Just before the election the first court action resulting from the Teapot Dome investigation began in Los Angeles. The federal government's two special prosecutors, Atlee Pomerene, a former Democratic senator from Ohio, and Owen J. Roberts, a little known Republican lawyer from Philadelphia, launched a civil suit to cancel Doheny's royalty-oil exchange contract for the Pearl Harbor construction work and his preferential lease on the Elk Hills Reserve. At the insistence of Doheny's attorneys, Fall grudgingly stayed at Three Rivers and did not attend these non-jury sessions. The presiding federal judge, emphasizing the $100,000 loan, declared the agreements invalid because of fraud and conspiracy, and also because Harding's executive order of transferral was illegal. In 1927 the Supreme Court affirmed this judgment, resulting in a loss of about $10 million to Doheny's company for its expenditures on the Pearl Harbor tanks, and eventually $25 million more in cash payments to the government. In separate litigation Doheny's heirs and successors had to pay an additional $8.5 million after some of his offset leases on Elk Hills were canceled in 1933.

The civil suit to cancel Sinclair's Teapot Dome contract was much more complicated because Pomerene and Roberts, during their preparations for the case, "struck upon something big," so big it made them "dizzy." In the records of western banks where Fall had accounts, the prosecutors discovered a reference to certain Liberty Bonds that were part of $3,080,000 in these securities originally held by the Continental Trading Company of Canada. This short-lived dummy corporation had been formed in 1921 by Sinclair and three other prominent American oil executives to "skim" profits from some of their companies. These funds were then converted into Liberty Bonds. From Sinclair's share of $757,000, it appeared, had come the $233,000 in bonds he gave Fall for a one-third interest in the Three Rivers ranch.

When the Teapot Dome suit began in Cheyenne in March 1925, it involved not only the old issues revealed by the Senate investigation but also the recently uncovered peculations of the shadowy Continental Trading Company. The federal prosecutors worked diligently to gather additional information, but they could establish only a circumstantial connection between Sinclair's Continental bonds and Fall. Even though lacking many of the essential details, Roberts confirmed at Cheyenne that the mysterious Canadian concern had been organized not as a conspiracy to obtain the Teapot Dome lease but to bilk the oilmen's companies. He and Pomerene received little cooperation from Continental's founders, most of whom fled abroad. Sinclair showed up at Cheyenne, but since he faced criminal charges later, he could not be compelled to testify.

Fall, who first learned of the Canadian company from the newspapers before the trial, was on hand, too, subpoenaed as a witness by the government. Although showing his age, the *New York Times* reported, he was "still the old Fall" of less trying times:

> He was still biting big, black cigars with his old-time vigor. His head was just as high as in the days when he was a Senator. He did not seek seclusion. Instead he made it a point to take all of his meals in the main dining room of the Plains Hotel and then he would mingle with the crowd in the lobby, and mornings and afternoons, all alone, he would take a constitutional through the streets.

After the federal prosecutors failed to call him to the witness stand, he left for Three Rivers without giving any indication whether he would have testified or claimed his Fifth Amendment rights. Fall said later that he wanted the truth told at Cheyenne by Mahlon T. Everhart, as well as Sinclair and himself, about the ranch deal, but the oilman refused to carry out this plan. Although Everhart admitted in his testimony that he once had $230,500 in Liberty Bonds in his possession, he declined, on the basis of self-incrimination, to answer any questions about how he got them. Without this "missing link" it was difficult for the prosecution to prove its case.

In a signal victory for Fall and Sinclair the federal judge at Cheyenne sustained the Teapot Dome agreement, maintaining that proof of fraud was lacking and that, contrary to misinformed public opinion, the transaction was "a good contract for the government." The circumstantial connection between Sinclair's Liberty Bonds and Fall, in the judge's reasoning, was "characterized as hearsay." A court of appeals, stating that "the accrual of condemnatory incidents" more than provided "the so-called missing link" between the Sinclair bonds and Fall, reversed the Cheyenne judgment and canceled the Teapot Dome arrangement. In 1927, when the Supreme Court upheld the appeals court's decision, it condemned Fall's actions in words frequently quoted thereafter to damn him. Calling his acceptance of the $233,000 in Liberty Bonds from Sinclair secretive and indefensible, it branded him "a faithless public officer." The Sinclair company, banished from Teapot Dome as a trespasser, suffered losses of about $12,500,000.

With the final Teapot Dome decision and a similar opinion in the Doheny civil case several months earlier, the courts had voided Fall's most notable oil deals and returned the naval reserves to the federal government. President Coolidge also revoked Harding's executive order and restored administration of the reserves to the Navy Department. The old policy of keeping the navy's emergency oil supply in the ground, dramatized by the spectacular charges of fraud and conspiracy, had triumphed over Fall's program based on the danger of drainage and a Pacific war scare. Only one thing might have vindicated his policy. If a full-blown oil famine had actually struck the United States, the public might have viewed Fall's actions more tolerantly. In 1924, as previously stated, the oil crisis began to disappear with the discovery of highly productive new fields at home, which created a large surplus for several years. By the late twenties few remembered that the Teapot Dome affair had been shaped by the postwar international oil crisis and by Interior Secretary Fall's determination to open domestic deposits, such as the naval reserves, to American oilmen who had faced exclusion from foreign fields.

The mystery of the Continental Trading Company and its slush fund of Liberty Bonds remained unsolved until the Teapot

Dome committee resumed its investigation in 1928, placing special emphasis on the Canadian concern's activities. Senator Walsh dropped a bombshell when he showed that Sinclair had donated $75,000 to the Republican election fund in 1920 and then, about the same time the naval oil scandal broke, "loaned" an additional $160,000 in Liberty Bonds to liquidate the party's campaign debt. The main witness was Fall's son-in-law, Mahlon T. Everhart, who, now protected against self-incrimination by a shortened statute of limitations, provided detailed information about the $233,000 in bonds paid by Sinclair for a one-third interest in the Fall ranch. Everhart also testified that Sinclair had directed him to act as trustee for the oilman's share. As a result, Sinclair's name did not appear in the ranch's corporate stock records, and, in fact, no written evidence existed that the oilman owned part of the spread. Everhart understood that Sinclair was primarily interested in the ranch for a hunting and riding club, and for raising race horses, but he admitted that the oil magnate had never started any development of this kind at Three Rivers.

For the first time the total amount Fall had received from both Doheny and Sinclair now came to light. Besides the $233,000 in Liberty Bonds, Everhart testified that Fall had also told him to ask Sinclair for a loan, or line of credit, which eventually amounted to about $36,000 in cash. These sums, together with $10,000 in traveler's checks for Fall's expenses on the European trip with Sinclair and the $25,000 loan in Liberty Bonds at that time, as well as the $100,000 loan in cash from Doheny, brought the known total from both oil magnates prior to the Teapot Dome investigation to $404,000. In addition, during the naval oil litigation, Doheny and Sinclair paid a large part of Fall's legal expenses, including his own hotel bills as well as the travel, meals, and lodging for his witnesses, and the oilmen often furnished him with lawyers, simply because Fall was financially unable to do so. Fall also received payments from Doheny for cattle trades and other personal transactions. The total of all these later expenditures by both oilmen may have amounted to $300,000.

Between the Doheny civil suit in 1924 and the Senate investigation of the Continental Trading Company in 1928, the federal prosecutors, Pomerene and Roberts, also conducted criminal cases against Fall, Doheny, and Sinclair. The prosecutors had decided to try the civil cases first, believing that cancellation of the Doheny and Sinclair contracts would make it easier to obtain criminal convictions of Fall and the two oilmen. In the criminal trials the defense attorneys hammered away at a common theme—that the naval reserve contracts, made by their clients in patriotism and good faith without any connection to personal financial affairs, had benefited the navy by bolstering national security and by alleviating the drainage problem. The prosecution, on the other hand, emphasized bribery and conspiracy to defraud the government, as well as secrecy, in the negotiations. Anticipating "grave difficulty" proving bribery, Pomerene and Roberts scheduled the conspiracy cases first. It soon became apparent in the criminal proceedings that Owen J. Roberts, later appointed to the Supreme Court, was the more forceful and skilled of the two special prosecutors.

Unlike the civil court decisions, the verdicts in the criminal cases would be rendered by juries. Fall welcomed a jury trial, he wrote Doheny, "with confidence in the results." The defense attorneys shared this view. Instead of facing only a legalistic judge, who was unimpressed by theatrics, they would also deal with everyday citizens, who might be swayed by dramatic appeals. Frank J. Hogan, Doheny's chief counsel, was a master of the art. Virtually unknown outside of Washington before Doheny retained him in 1924, Hogan became recognized nationwide for his legal talents and numbered among his clients some of America's richest men by the time the naval oil cases ended. His exceptionally keen mind and unexcelled courtroom manner set him apart from the other defense attorneys and made him more than a match for prosecutors Pomerene and Roberts. From the beginning, although Fall had his own lawyers, Hogan bore the burden of the defense in any legal action involving Fall and Doheny together. Peering through pince-nez eyeglasses, the debonair, immaculately attired Hogan conducted most of the defense examinations and cross-examinations of witnesses. In this dominant role before the jury box, according to one firsthand account, he "played with all the skill of a consummate actor upon the emotions of his jury, or dazzled them with his astounding memory for facts and his brilliant eloquence."

After several delays the Fall-Doheny conspiracy trial began in Washington in November 1926. For the first time the principal figures in the naval oil controversy were threatened with fines and jail sentences. The case was the most-heralded event thus far resulting from the Teapot Dome inquiry. One periodical went so far as to call it "the most famous political case since the impeachment of Andrew Johnson." During the pretrial proceedings *Revelry*, a novel by Samuel Hopkins Adams portraying lurid aspects of the Harding administration, had hit the market. Among the first of many such fictional exposés, it caused a national sensation, and later it became a play and a motion picture. Fearing that prospective jurors would be prejudiced by the novel because they were, as reported in the newspapers, "all reading that book, sitting up nights reading it," Hogan carefully screened jury candidates about their knowledge of its inflammatory contents.

In the courtroom Doheny's $100,000 loan came under intense scrutiny, with the oilman, as a witness, defending it on the basis of his long friendship with Fall going back to Kingston mining days. He also revealed that in the spring of 1925 Fall had transferred to him one-third of the capital stock, valued at $200,000, in the Three Rivers ranch corporation as security for the loan. Otherwise, Hogan chose to stress the Japanese war scare and Doheny's patriotic role in securing oil tanks for the navy over the drainage problems in the reserves. The testimony ended abruptly without Fall taking the stand. One reporter recalled how Fall had entered the Senate years before, "a big, powerful figure with a Western fighting mustache," looking something "like a sheriff on the stage." Now he appeared "white and broken, thin, incredibly aged. . . . Looking old, he is no longer typically Western. Old age has no locality." In his closing argument Hogan summoned the late President Harding as the "silent witness" who had approved Fall's naval oil policy. He lambasted the ghouls who had defamed Harding's name, saying, "While I live I will defend him, despite all the character assassins that attempt to invade the sanctity of his tomb and tear the shroud from his dead body!" In short, the defense maintained that just as the loan had been based on a long-standing friendship, so was the Pearl Harbor transaction based on patriotism and national defense. Three weeks after the trial began, the jury rendered a verdict of not guilty for both Fall and Doheny.

Public reaction to the decision was overwhelmingly critical. Despite a few favorable editorials, the general view of the press was, "Acquitted, but not vindicated." Federal prosecutor Atlee Pomerene felt that the jury members were the only twelve men in the country who thought Fall and Doheny were innocent. Democratic Senator Thomas J. Heflin of Alabama, who frequently delivered Senate harangues on the naval oil controversy, exclaimed, "My God, have we reached the point where criminals in high places can not be convicted in the courts of our country?" Fall himself, writing a former law partner, simply observed that the result of the trial fully justified both the loyalty of his friends and his oil actions with Doheny. The second part of this assessment was too optimistic. Although Fall and Doheny had won acquittal on the conspiracy charge, separate bribery indictments were still pending against them, and Fall still faced a conspiracy charge with Sinclair.

Because of Fall's poor health, his conspiracy trial with Sinclair did not begin for almost a year. But the legal fireworks started much earlier. In March 1927 Sinclair, who had refused to testify before the Teapot Dome committee, was convicted for contempt of the Senate, sentenced to three months in jail, and given a $500 fine. This dramatic action created an extremely unfavorable atmosphere for the Fall-Sinclair proceedings, which opened in October in Washington. And the real fireworks were still ahead.

Two weeks into the trial another sensation was added to the already spectacular Teapot Dome scandal. The federal prosecutors discovered that Sinclair had hired fifteen private detectives from the Burns International Detective Agency to shadow the jurors, apparently hoping to uncover evidence for a mistrial if the case ended in a conviction. Instead, after Pomerene and Roberts submitted their findings on Sinclair's covert activities, the judge indeed declared a mistrial but accused the oilman of jury tampering. Sinclair was subsequently convicted of criminal contempt and handed a six months' prison sentence, which, in 1929, he served concurrently with his three months' term for contempt of the Senate. William J. Burns, head of the detective agency and previously Harding's chief of the Bureau of Investigation (forerunner of the FBI), Burns's son, and a Sinclair company official also received jail sentences or fines in the jury surveillance episode. The judgment against Burns was later reversed by the Supreme Court.

Fall had no part in shadowing the jury; it was the imperious Sinclair's harebrained scheme alone. Yet, in the avalanche of public scorn following the mistrial, Fall was roasted along with Sinclair. One western newspaper stated: "Whatever they touch they stain and corrupt. They think dirty gold will buy honor. . . . Anarchists, Bolsheviki, I.W.W., and thugs are high-minded citizens in comparison." Undoubtedly furious at Sinclair's bungling intrigue, Fall regretted most the lost opportunity to refute the Teapot Dome conspiracy charges that, he said, had been "the football of politics and the delight of the muckraker for more than three years." He was ready for retrial immediately, but the federal prosecutors found this impossible to do. For reasons of health, Fall commented, he wanted to proceed quickly because he would be unable "to contend with the rigors of Washington climate during a trial in the winter." If the prosecutors forced a retrial in January, Fall said, he might have only a fifty-fifty chance of returning to New Mexico alive.

Even before the aborted proceedings Pomerene and Roberts had considered a severance, or separation, of the Fall-Sinclair conspiracy indictment because of Fall's deteriorating physical condition. The prosecutors had concluded, however, that they stood a better chance of getting a conviction if Fall and Sinclair came into court together than if the oilman was tried separately. Fall's health worsened after the mistrial, and it appeared that he would not live long enough for a retrial with Sinclair. After several postponements because of Fall's condition, Pomerene and Roberts successfully petitioned for a separate Sinclair conspiracy trial, which got underway in April 1928 in Washington.

Just before this trial began, Fall gave his testimony in a 513-page deposition at his El Paso home as he was questioned by Sinclair attorneys and federal prosecutor Atlee Pomerene. For the most part he covered familiar ground, but in greater detail, in justifying Sinclair's Teapot Dome contract: the danger of drainage, the benefits to the navy, and the involvement of Interior and Navy department subordinates in the negotiations. None of the money coming from Sinclair, he declared, had influenced his official acts. Showing that he had not lost his legendary fiery temperament, he at times took over the cross-examination and grilled Pomerene, his former Senate colleague. At one point the federal prosecutor reacted angrily, "I am not on the stand now." To which Fall shot back, "I know you are not, but I am."

At the close of the interrogation Fall said that he had not publicly discussed the oil leases because it would have been unfair to the Republican party, given the political overtones of the Senate investigation and everything that had happened since then. Near the end his personal physician, who had hovered over him and frequently ordered rest periods during the four days of questioning, began looking anxiously at the patient. "Get away, doctor, and let me alone," Fall reportedly said. "I am having more fun than in years." Although the deposition provided a personal catharsis for him, Fall was again thwarted in publicizing his case as he saw fit. In the trial itself the defense attorneys vetoed use of his deposition as evidence. Probably they decided it contained information potentially detrimental to Sinclair's cause, such as Fall's letter to the Teapot Dome committee in which he denied receiving any money from the oilman.

The main issues before the jury in the Sinclair conspiracy proceedings concerned the Liberty Bonds and the money that had passed from Sinclair to Fall. Had the oil magnate intended to influence Fall's acts as interior secretary, or had he actually purchased a one-third interest in the Fall ranch and parted with an additional $71,000 for legitimate reasons? The answer to these questions hinged on a painful rift within the Fall family. In 1927, under Senator Walsh's prodding, Congress had shortened the federal statute of limitations from six to three years. Now Fall's son-in-law, Mahlon T. Everhart, could no longer claim his Fifth Amendment protection against self-incrimination. As Everhart himself put it, he "ran out" on the family and reluctantly became the federal prosecutors' key witness, repeating the testimony about Fall's financial affairs that he had only recently given in the Senate investigation of the Continental Trading Company.

Besides these Continental revelations and Sinclair's contempt shenanigans, the Supreme Court had six months earlier upheld the court of appeals' decision canceling the Teapot Dome contract because of fraud and corruption. The Senate inquiry, still in session, continued to unearth additional devastating details about the Continental concern as the Sinclair trial drew to a close. This combination of damning accusations seemed to assure a conviction in the Sinclair case. The jury members chose to believe, however, that the oil magnate had indeed purchased an interest in the Fall ranch, and not that he had attempted to buy Fall's favor as interior secretary. In direct contrast with the civil suit nullifying the Teapot Dome deal, the jury found Sinclair not guilty of conspiracy to defraud the government, thereby supporting Fall's explanation of the oilman's payments to him as legitimate business transactions.

Again the public outcry was deafening. "The verdict was the greatest surprise Washington has had in years," reported the *New York Times.* Republican Senator George W. Norris of Nebraska repeated a theme often heard in the naval oil cases concerning "checkbook justice"—that there was one set of laws for the rich and another for the poor. "Sinclair has too much money to be convicted," Norris exclaimed. "We ought to pass a law that no man worth $100,000,000 should be tried for a crime." One of the jurors, disclosing that the panel had never been close to a guilty verdict, elaborated on a key point: "If Fall had wanted to sell the lease it seems to me that he would have gone after at least $2,000,000 and would not have accepted $233,000, as he could have gotten more." Otherwise, the outcome of the Sinclair case meant that Fall would never be tried again for conspiracy in the leasing of Teapot Dome. With Sinclair's acquittal there was no point in bringing him into court on the same charge because, simply, it takes two persons to conspire. The best bet now for the frustrated federal prosecutors lay in presenting a bribery case against Fall alone in which he was portrayed as an unfaithful and corrupt public official for accepting $100,000 from Doheny. And if Fall was convicted of accepting a bribe, then almost certainly Doheny would suffer the same fate for giving the bribe. Or so it seemed to Pomerene and Roberts.

During all the years of waiting for his day in court, Fall was usually compelled, according to a close friend, to "vegetate" at Three Rivers. It was a trying life for him, under constant denunciation by the press, Congress, and the general public, and especially so since he had "never allowed anyone to build themselves up at his expense." His diversions included reading on a wide range of subjects, with special attention to Mexico, and, when his health permitted, supervising ranching operations. Frequently guests dropped by for a visit, and lawyers representing him and the other defendants came to confer on court strategy. An old friend, western writer Eugene Manlove Rhodes, and his wife lived on the ranch or nearby for a couple of years in the late 1920s, giving the Falls agreeable company and much-needed encouragement.

As before the naval oil debacle, Fall continued to have a closer association with Doheny than with Sinclair. In fact, the two oil magnates, who had been forced into a common mold by their relationship with Fall, did not like each other. "I have known for years, and know now," Fall wrote one of his lawyers, "of the personal feeling of these two men the one for the other, and . . . it is not of a cordial nature in any respect." Whereas Fall only saw Sinclair occasionally in court or on legal business, he went to Los Angeles several times during the early litigation to confer with Doheny and his attorneys, and just to visit the oilman and his wife. He always stayed as a guest in Doheny's palatial home at 8 Chester Place, located in a private parklike area featuring tame deer, monkeys, and parrots. In April 1925 Doheny dropped by Three Rivers largely for a social call. Sinclair met with Fall in El Paso at least once, and his personal attorney, J. W. Zevely, made two trips to Three Rivers within one year, but on legal matters.

About a year and a half before the Fall-Doheny conspiracy trial of 1926 rumors began circulating of a rift between the two defendants. A lengthy interview with Doheny appearing in the *New York Times* in July 1925 seemed to confirm these reports. For seven hours in his ornate library at 8 Chester Place the oilman had told a reporter his version of the naval oil transactions. Even though Doheny insisted on giving the interview against his attorneys' advice, the lawyers did persuade him to avoid any discussion of the $100,000 loan and Fall's letter to the Senate committee saying that the money came from McLean. Doheny consistently defended Fall in his comments, but one of his attorneys informed the reporter that the disastrous letter was "the one incident in his long friendship with Mr. Fall that Mr. Doheny cannot excuse." Since both men had refrained from making public statements on the naval reserve deals, Fall was upset by the oilman's divulgence of his views outside the courtroom. And the attorney's remark infuriated him. He did not "propose to be made a 'goat' of" by such self-serving insinuations, Fall wrote his own lawyer.

Doheny was conciliatory in answering Fall's heated written protests. He had given the interview, the oil magnate explained, to obtain the one thing he wanted most, "the good opinion of the public." As one who had led "the life of a prospector," a pursuit based mainly on hope, Doheny continued, "I have not yet given up hope that public opinion may be greatly changed [about you and me], and those who have been reviled with us because of our efforts to serve the Government." Fall cooled down after some reflection, and wrote emotionally to his friend that "nothing except death could eradicate from my memory my appreciation of your friendship, as I have understood it." By this time he blamed the entire disagreement on Doheny's lawyers.

Despite such flare-ups, and what Fall believed were deliberate attempts by Doheny's attorneys to disrupt their friendship, a hearty cordiality continued between the two men. Fall sometimes complained that Doheny did not write him often enough, especially about routine developments in the naval oil litigation. It was Fall whose health and finances were ruined, who was isolated at Three Rivers, and who stood to lose the most in reputation. Little wonder that he often became troubled and despondent. Under these circumstances Doheny wrote warm encouraging letters to his friend, in an easy style with a homey philosophical tone. Some of them were masterpieces. On one occasion Doheny wrote that he refused to permit "the poisonous atmosphere" of all "the unjust attacks" to influence him. He recalled an incident years before while prospecting in Arizona's Tonto Basin in which his companion had shot a grazing deer, disemboweling it. The fatally wounded animal began desperately eating the leaves of an oak bush, not understanding that it no longer had any need for food. In the same way, Doheny said, he tried to stay busy with business affairs that no longer were of "vital concern" to him but kept his mind occupied.

Fall appreciated these letters, but he enjoyed even more the infrequent occasions when he and Doheny could talk alone without the interference of a bustling bevy of lawyers. "I am fully aware, as you are," he once confided, "that we never misunderstand one another, and one of the chief pleasures of my life is my conviction that we are mentally and otherwise in perfect accord when either the two of us or Mrs. Doheny, yourself and myself are meeting undisturbed." Although sometimes tried by fire, their friendship lasted through the vicissitudes of the naval oil cases.

As indicated by his *New York Times* interview, Doheny was keenly interested in swaying public opinion, and this was not his first attempt to do so. Before Fall's Senate Mexican-affairs investigation of 1919–20, Doheny had funded for $120,000 the Doheny Research Foundation. This early think tank, headquartered in Berkeley at the University of California, sponsored specialized studies on Mexico by a team of eighteen nationally recognized scholars and journalists, with the stated objective of improving United States–Mexico relations. Doheny also financed newspaper and monographic criticism of Wilson's Mexican policy, and engaged the services of George Creel, the wartime propaganda wizard, although they soon fell out. Not until the Senate Mexican inquiry, which first bonded his close relationship with Fall, did Doheny find a public-relations venue he could enthusiastically endorse.

During the early trials Doheny regularly wined and dined reporters at 8 Chester Place in Los Angeles, or in Washington in a posh suite of private clubrooms opposite the courthouse. He also employed a special press agent who joined him in the courtroom and distributed a steady flow of favorable releases to the newspapers. Before the Fall-Doheny conspiracy trial of 1926, Doheny made plans to get his side of the naval oil story before the public in a more dramatic way. At first he and Fall discussed the possibility of commissioning a motion picture. They consulted such Hollywood notables as Will H. Hays, Fall's former cabinet colleague and now head of filmdom's censorship office, about the technicalities of the project. Then, over lunch at 8 Chester Place, they asked Cecil B. DeMille, famous for his spectacular *The Ten Commandments* and other film successes, if he would produce a movie stressing how the naval oil transactions had actually benefited rather than harmed the nation. DeMille, impressed by Doheny's personal account of the leases and by the dramatic potential of the subject, later commented that "it would have made one of the most talked of motion pictures of the decade." He was especially fascinated by "the long history of intimacy and complete trust between Mr. Doheny and Mr. Fall, as shedding light on the informality of their financial transactions." But the New York film executives considered the proposed movie "too political and controversial," and thus too great a departure from the usual entertainment production. DeMille's contractual obligations prevented him from proceeding independently, and the picture was never made.

Next Doheny decided to sponsor the publication of a series of articles or a book. After mulling over the idea, he settled on Fall's life story as the perfect framework for presenting the oil-lease episode. A popular account of his friend's rise to prominence in national government after an exciting and colorful life on the southwestern frontier, Doheny believed, would have a tremendously favorable effect in winning over public opinion. For the task Doheny hired Mark B. Thompson of Las Cruces, who knew Fall well, was then one of his attorneys in the oil cases, and had professed literary ambitions. With the oilman furnishing the financial backing, Fall and Thompson toiled at Three Rivers with research in correspondence files, government documents, and other sources available there. From time to time Doheny made handsome payments to Thompson for his efforts. Apparently Fall also had some kind of employment arrangement with the oil magnate in the writing project and, perhaps, as an adviser on Mexican affairs as well.

Fall was jubilant, as he wrote W. A. Hawkins, at the prospect of seeing his version of the naval oil affair in print without alteration or embellishment by a sensation-seeking journalist. Although he would consider the stake of others, particularly his fellow defendants in the criminal cases, he intended to discuss, "in the most open, frank manner possible, irrespective of objections," certain crucial matters, "following boldly and frankly my own ideas alone." Throughout the summer of 1925 Doheny kept track of the research and writing in progress at Three Rivers, frequently exchanging correspondence with both Fall and Thompson. Several sections of the proposed publication appeared in rough drafts, some of which were sent to the oilman for inspection; but evidently in early 1926, for an undisclosed reason, the whole project was canceled. Frank J. Hogan and other defense attorneys received copies of an analytical history of the naval reserves, prepared largely by Fall, which they used in the litigation. In 1931, just before he went to prison for taking a bribe from Doheny, Fall collaborated with an *El Paso Times* editor in writing fifteen nationally syndicated newspaper articles that gave his side of the Teapot Dome affair. Otherwise, no extended statement of his views was published during his lifetime.

One reason Fall had wanted to publish his own story in 1925 was his belief that the various defense attorneys were unwilling to follow a legal strategy that would justify his official acts. In fact, he continually disagreed with the way the defense counsel handled the litigation. An experienced trial lawyer himself, he held definite opinions about case procedures and courtroom tactics. When he sat in on conferences among the various legal advisers, as he often did, Fall stated his views in no uncertain terms, frequently lecturing them on the finer points of jurisprudence, leasing legislation, and similar topics. After all, he had dealt with land and mineral laws most his life, while the younger men knew little about such matters except what they had learned recently in the oil cases. Despite his insistence on being consulted, however, Fall soon concluded that his advice was given little consideration.

As Fall wrote one of his lawyers, "Unfortunately, . . . I practiced law for years and this experience probably unfitted me more or less for being a good client." After a turbulent association with his first chief counsel, Henry A. Wise, a former United States attorney for New York, he replaced him after the Fall-Doheny conspiracy acquittal with Wilton J. Lambert, one of Ned McLean's legal mainstays. For the Fall-Sinclair conspiracy mistrial he employed William E. Leahy, a former Washington judge. No matter who represented him, Fall was convinced that his attorneys too often subordinated themselves and his interests to the desires of Doheny's and Sinclair's lawyers, with whom he consistently clashed. At one point he told the defense attorneys that he would argue his own case in court, no matter how unethical and unprofessional it might seem—a threat he never carried out.

Although Fall had many differences with Sinclair's legal staff, he most often found himself in conflict with Frank J. Hogan, Doheny's preeminent chief counsel. He deeply resented the apparent conviction of Doheny's legal strategist that an openly close friendship between Fall and the oilman might suggest a "continuing conspiracy." After the unsuccessful Doheny civil trial in Los Angeles he complained bitterly to Wise about several points of Hogan's courtroom tactics. Fall objected to the main defense proposition that, as he paraphrased it, "I was an old, broken-down imbecile, an object of charity, and that I really had nothing whatsoever to do with the leases." He was also disturbed that the defense failed to give the details of his confidential advisory role with Doheny for the Mexican loan negotiations and the Pan American Western Company's organization, which would have explained why he said that he had obtained the $100,000 loan from Ned McLean. Likewise, Doheny's attorneys refused to emphasize an exchange of correspondence between Interior Secretary Fall and his Bureau of Mines director, H. Foster Bain, which supposedly showed that Fall had not pressed for the Pearl Harbor storage deal. Of paramount importance, he thought the drainage issue should be given precedence over the Japanese war scare, but Hogan took the opposite approach, apparently because of its emotional effect. Generally Fall viewed most of the defense attorneys' courtroom efforts as "too round-about, too 'gorgeous,'" and lacking in "simplicity and directness."

Undoubtedly the greatest source of conflict between Fall and Hogan was the lawyer's reluctance to use Fall as a witness. Fall wanted to testify and tell his own story, especially about the misleading letter to the Teapot Dome committee concerning Doheny's loan. Despite his vociferous demands, he was never called to the stand, even though Doheny did appear as an effective witness in their criminal cases. Besides the risk of putting a defendant on the witness stand, especially one whose testimony could be impeached, or discredited, because of the letter, Hogan and the other defense lawyers, knowing Fall's fiery temper, probably feared that if he testified, as one insider put it, the federal prosecutors "would badger him till he blew up and made a mess of things." After watching Hogan in action for several years, Fall became more amenable to the skilled advocate's leadership. In 1929, when Fall went into court on a bribery charge, Doheny employed Hogan to defend his friend, and Fall readily accepted this arrangement.

Fall's most stinging criticism of the defense attorneys concerned their fat fees. For his services in the Fall-Doheny conspiracy trial, it was rumored, Hogan received a million-dollar check and a luxury automobile from Doheny. And he may have obtained a similar fee, or more, for his later legal work. Sinclair's lawyers apparently drew equally impressive compensation. In Fall's opinion these exactions amounted to "a gold digging expedition, which was without parallel." His own relatively meager funds were soon drained away by legal expenses. The income from his ranch was uncertain, and his credit was severely limited. In fact, as already pointed out, he had to allow Doheny and Sinclair to pay his court and attorney bills, even the costs of his own hotel accommodations and the travel and lodging for his witnesses. This financial dependence on the two oilmen, Fall believed, in turn subordinated his interest in the courtroom to theirs. Regardless, by the time of his bribery trial in 1929 Fall was practically insolvent.

As Fall's trial approached, although six years had passed since the Teapot Dome investigation made its first headlines, the oil leases were still a red-hot political issue. Leery of partisan implications from the start, Fall had hoped in vain that none of the cases would be tried in Washington or while Congress was in session. To his dismay, key legal actions had often come just before elections or soon afterwards. Undoubtedly, he wrote Hogan in 1930, politics had "cut a big figure in these cases," being responsible for their origination, "and almost entirely responsible for the adverse decisions which have be-set us." True to form, the election of 1928 preceded Fall's bribery proceedings by less than a year. Herbert Hoover won the presidency, but only after the Democrats denounced him as a member of the Harding gang that had fraudulently leased the naval oil reserves. Soon the bribery trial would become another milestone in a long chain of political events associated with Teapot Dome.

Fall's health had steadily deteriorated since the Fall-Sinclair mistrial in 1927. Afterwards his attorneys had informed the federal prosecutors confidentially that Fall's "heart and lungs were in such condition that in all probability he could not live more than three months at the most." Owen J. Roberts felt relieved, writing a fellow lawyer, "Personally, I am fervently praying that he may die in the meantime as I doubt whether there could be a conviction against a tottering old man who evidences in every way the senility that has overtaken him." To be near specialized medical care, Fall now spent more time in El Paso, where he was often confined to his home there. Fall told Sinclair early in 1930 that, because of his heart and lungs, he probably had "nothing to look forward to except semi-invalidism in the future." But he lived on, and the federal prosecutors, perhaps beginning to believe that he was shamming about his health, insisted that Fall stand trial in Washington for bribery in October 1929.

When Fall arrived from El Paso, suffering from bronchial pneumonia, he was accompanied by his wife, his two daughters, Jouett Elliott and Alexina Chase, and his physician. It was a pathetic scene in the courtroom. "Bent, white-haired and but a shadow of his one-time robust self," he was cared for by his doctor, a nurse, and an attendant, who carefully tucked him into a green Morris chair. When the judge entered, and everyone stood up, Fall attempted to rise but fell back into his chair. The next day he had a slight hemorrhage during the proceedings and began spitting up blood. With assistance he tottered from the room, apparently about to collapse. A three-day recess followed, and there was talk of calling off the trial.

The presiding judge selected Dr. Sterling Ruffin, once President Wilson's doctor, to examine Fall and determine the seriousness of his condition. Newspaper reports credited the ailing man's friends with saying that, for personal reasons, this particular doctor was the only one in the country Fall would not permit to enter his sickroom. Then a panel of four court-appointed physicians, as well as Fall's own doctor, stated that his life would be endangered if the proceedings continued. The federal prosecutors, asserting that the melodramatic portrayal of Fall's condition made an impartial trial impossible, called for a mistrial. Rising to the occasion, Frank J. Hogan strongly objected, saying that the prosecution had insisted on "trial by ordeal," and the defendant, "if he can drag himself here, wants to meet trial by ordeal" and not continue living with "this thing hanging over what thread there is left of his life." After the recess ended, Fall, "weak almost to the point of utter exhaustion," dramatically entered the courtroom in his wheelchair. The judge denied the prosecutors' motion of a mistrial, and the bribery case against the former interior secretary resumed.

As the proceedings unfolded, it became apparent that there was hardly any new evidence for the prosecution to present. But Pomerene and Roberts did have one big advantage they had not enjoyed before. In the conspiracy cases against Fall, Doheny, and Sinclair, all of which had resulted in acquittals, the defense attorneys had successfully argued that, since the naval oil agreements contributed to national security, the government had not been defrauded but, in fact, had benefited from these transactions. Now Fall, as the lone defendant, faced a much different charge. In effect, the jury's main responsibility was to decide whether he had been an unfaithful public servant, whether he had taken a bribe to influence his official acts, regardless of whether the government had suffered injury or received benefits because of those actions. The emphasis on this clear-cut issue—to the virtual exclusion of complicated national security matters, the drainage problem, and related technicalities—presented to the everyday-citizen jurors a moral question they could understand. Thus the narrowness of the bribery charge posed a greater danger of conviction for Fall than he or Doheny or Sinclair had faced in the earlier conspiracy trials. In addition, although the proceedings focused on Doheny's $100,000 loan, the judge allowed the federal prosecutors to submit evidence on the Liberty Bonds and the money Sinclair gave to Fall. This was only one in a series of damaging blows to the defense.

Among the New Mexicans who testified as character witnesses for Fall were Oliver Lee, his old-time ally in range warfare, and

Robert Geronimo, son of the famous Apache chief. Doheny took the stand as the heavy artillery for the defense. He claimed a long friendship with Fall and stubbornly maintained that this was the basis for his $100,000 loan, which, he pointed out, was secured by the much-publicized note with the mutilated signature. As he had previously done in the 1925 Fall-Doheny case, Doheny explained that Fall had also assigned to him one-third of the ranch corporation's capital stock as additional security for the loan.

In Hogan's closing arguments, his photographic memory and dramatic skills never sharper, the chief defense attorney portrayed Doheny as a great patriot and Fall's true friend. Surely the jurors did not think that Doheny would double-cross his old companion of frontier days. "Why, it is like asking you to believe the unbelievable," the brilliant trial lawyer intoned. It was also inconceivable, he declared, that they would sentence Fall to the penitentiary, "instead of sending the slumped form in yonder chair back to his home and family." Part of that day, all of the next, and some of the following day Hogan reasoned with the jury, concluding with his familiar plea to "send Albert B. Fall back to the sunshine and the lung-healing climate of his beloved New Mexico with your verdict of not guilty—not guilty." The appeal was so convincing that one juror dabbed her tears with a handkerchief and several people in the audience became openly misty-eyed.

Another decisive blow against the defense came in the judge's stern charge to the jury. Despite Hogan's fervent pleas, the judge said, "You have nothing whatever to do with the sunshine of New Mexico. . . . You are here to decide this case on the evidence, and nothing else." Even more damaging, perhaps, he also specifically stated that the jurors could consider the payments Fall had received from both Doheny and Sinclair on the same basis in deciding the question of bribery. They might couple their verdict with a recommendation for mercy, he added suggestively, although it would have no binding effect. After deliberating for twenty-four hours, the jury returned to the courtroom. The clerk asked, "What do you say? guilty or not guilty?" The foreman answered, "We find the defendant guilty, and with recommendation of the mercy of the Court." With these words Albert Fall became the first American cabinet officer convicted for a felony committed while in office.

Even cynical Washington had seldom witnessed the courtroom spectacle that followed the verdict. Fall slumped into the blankets that swathed him in his Morris chair and "appeared completely stunned." His wife sobbed uncontrollably for a moment and then rushed through the seething crowd to comfort her husband. One of Fall's daughters fell forward in a faint, while the other one cried hysterically. Turning ashen pale, Fall's friend and lawyer, Mark B. Thompson, slid from his chair to the floor and lay there unconscious for ten minutes. Some observers thought he was dead or dying of a heart attack. Doheny was angry. "That damn court [judge]—," he muttered, and then added, "This was not the verdict of the jury, but the verdict of the court." The suave Hogan, his customary smile missing, pointed to Thompson's crumpled form and exclaimed, "Bring back that jury and let them laugh at this, too." In the hallway several women who had attended all of the sessions shouted their disagreement with the verdict. One of them, the wife of a juror, was "screaming mad." Finally she found her husband posing for the newsreel cameras. "You miserable rat," she cried, "Come out here where I can get my hands on you." Court attendants had to quiet her. Brushing away a tear or two as his wife joined him, Fall showed no further emotion. When the excitement in the courtroom died down, he was lifted into his wheelchair, bundled in blankets, and taken out of the building by his friends.

Hogan immediately petitioned for a new trial on the grounds that the judge's jury charge was prejudicial and that Fall's financial transactions with Sinclair had no relevance for the Doheny loan. Denying Hogan's motion, the judge imposed a fine of $100,000 and imprisonment for one year on Fall. Because of the defendant's physical condition and the jury's recommendation for mercy, the judge declared, he had not levied the possible fine of $300,000 and a three-year jail sentence. As he pointed out, the forthcoming appeal automatically postponed imprisonment; otherwise, he would have suspended that part of the penalty until Fall's health improved.

At last the press was satisfied with the conclusion of a naval-oil criminal trial. "You really can convict a million dollars in These States," exulted Kansas editor William Allen White in his *Emporia Gazette.* In a long press release Fall avowed his innocence, labeling himself a faithful public servant "from my youth." Besides the judge's biased statements, he said, a determined foreman had turned the other jurors against him "by arguments that were unjust and unfair." Indeed, one of the jury members later disclosed that the "very real doubt regarding the justness of a verdict of guilty, was shown by the fact that on the first ballot nine of the twelve votes were for acquittal." He had reluctantly joined in the vote for conviction, being the last one to do so. Another juror, who reportedly begged Fall's wife for forgiveness, had favored the guilty verdict only after receiving assurances that Fall would not receive a prison sentence because of his age and health. In the past, as a trial lawyer defending a client, Fall had often played the odds with a jury and won, but not this time when it counted the most.

Another old specter had arisen during the trial when the judge named Dr. Ruffin to examine Fall. It was said that Ruffin had been attending the afflicted Woodrow Wilson in the White House during the infamous smelling committee visit of 1919 and had objected to Fall's reputed drawing back of the bed-covers to see if the president was paralyzed. Now Senator Heflin retold the mythical story as fact in the Senate, accusing Fall of attempting to cause a mistrial with faked illness:

> [T]his old criminal, Fall, . . . walked out of this Chamber down to the White House into the sick room of the stricken President and pulled the covers off of him, gazing on him like he would a stricken animal, a beast. He said around the corridors of the Capitol before he went, "I will be one of three [actually two] to go down and pull the covers off of him and look at him for myself," and he did it. Doctor Ruffin protested against such action, fearing it might result in the

> death of President Wilson, but the protest had no effect upon this criminal.

For many this version of the smelling committee episode justified Fall's fine and jail sentence. This was just what he deserved, they reasoned. If he had pulled the bedclothes off the desperately ill Wilson, showing him no mercy, why should Fall be shown mercy now even though he was old and sick?

No attempt was made during the trial to refute the bedcover-pulling myth, but immediately afterwards Fall's wife obtained the help of his erstwhile political enemy, Senator Bronson Cutting of New Mexico, who replied to Senator Heflin's accusations. Cutting proved on the Senate floor that Fall had not touched Wilson or his bed other than to shake hands with the president. He cited a letter from Dr. Ruffin in which the physician said that he was not even in the White House when the 1919 conference occurred. Admiral Cary T. Grayson, Wilson's personal doctor who was present, stated that he had witnessed no such action by Fall. Former Senator Gilbert M. Hitchcock, who had accompanied Fall to the White House, also informed Senator Cutting that the story was "absolutely false." Fall's conduct in the president's sick room was "exemplary," Hitchcock recalled, and he speculated that the erroneous account had probably started years before when someone, "speaking figuratively," had referred to the smelling committee mission. Cutting's convincing efforts at damage control discredited but did not lay to rest this old myth, which would still return to haunt Fall periodically.

Since Fall's bribery conviction had labeled the $100,000 loan as tainted money, it seemed only reasonable to assume that another jury would look at Doheny's part in the exchange the same way. But in March 1930, with the same judge presiding, the oil magnate was acquitted of giving Fall a bribe. Again the judge's charge to the jury was probably decisive, but this time in favor of the defendant. Even if Fall had a corrupt intention in accepting the $100,000, the judge implied, it did not mean that Doheny had the same intent in giving the money. Then he declared categorically:

> Did this money pass from Doheny to Fall? If it did, did it pass with a corrupt intent or with an innocent intent? When this case closes there is after all only one main question left in it, because Mr. Doheny on the stand testified that the money did pass from him, through his son, to Fall. So that after all, the question that you ladies and gentlemen have got to decide is what was in [Doheny's] mind when he did a certain thing. You have got to decide by your verdict what was in Mr. Doheny's mind at the time that this money passed.

The jury, as one wag commented, not being psychologists or mind readers, acquitted Doheny on the first ballot after deliberating only a hour. Public servant Fall was guilty of taking a $100,000 bribe, while oil millionaire Doheny was innocent of giving a bribe in the same transaction. Apparently the nation expected a higher code of ethics for its public officials than for its millionaires.

The mystery of the two paradoxical verdicts baffled most observers of that day and has continued to do so since then. Fall and Doheny were tried in the same court, with the same judge, with the same two federal prosecutors, and with much of the same evidence. Frank J. Hogan served as the chief defense counsel in both cases. Seemingly only the juries were different. As for the acquitted defendant's views, Doheny said, "I am only sorry that the same verdict might not have gone to my friend, Mr. Fall, who deserved it as much as I do." Fall commented that "truth and innocence" had triumphed, but he asked the public to answer "the puzzle" of the two different decisions. This was the same puzzle that troubled the press: "When is a $100,000 bribe not a bribe?" The Doheny verdict, according to the *Nation*, tended "to shake confidence in the operation of our law." One of the federal prosecutors, Atlee Pomerene, declared that the jury system in the District of Columbia, where both cases were tried, had "fallen down" because of lack of intelligence among the jurors available there to decide such complex cases.

Two crucial points help explain the paradoxical verdicts. First, Fall's personal financial arrangements with Sinclair, especially the ambiguities associated with the oilman's one-third interest in the Three Rivers ranch, which were admitted as evidence against Fall but had no part in the Doheny trial, showed that he had received payments from not one but two recipients of naval oil contracts. To make matters worse, he had misled the Teapot Dome committee about both money sources, most notably the Doheny loan. Second, a different federal statute from the one used against Fall was involved in the Doheny case, with the two laws emphasizing the intent of the bribe-taker, in one instance, and the bribe-giver, on the other hand. Under these circumstances it was possible for one person to be convicted and another acquitted of bribery in the same financial transaction. Moreover, Fall as a public official had sworn an oath to protect and defend the government, while Doheny as an enterprising private businessman had not done so. As Fall's longtime admirer, W. A. Hawkins, regretfully put it, no cabinet member could be exonerated for accepting that much money from someone, even a friend, seeking a government contract, especially if he had to lie to cover it up.

Otherwise, the grandfatherly Doheny, whose only son had met a tragic death, made a very appealing witness in his own behalf, whereas the proud, belligerent-looking Fall never took the stand to defend himself. A jury could hardly overlook this fact when Doheny became the key witness in Fall's trial and the defendant himself remained silent. Doheny went free "with a halo of beneficence and brotherly love about him," one periodical stated, because he convinced his jury that the $100,000 was "not so much a loan as a testimonial" made in appreciation of Fall's self-sacrificing public service, especially in Mexican affairs. Perhaps, then, the real Doheny verdict was delivered by the *New Republic*, which pronounced the oil magnate guilty before the bar of public opinion despite the jury's decision, "and largely because of that fact, the easy morality of Harding's day has disappeared."

Except for some odds and ends, including the cancellation of Doheny's Elk Hills offset leases and the financial settlements between the federal government and the two oilmen, only the appeal of Fall's conviction remained in the naval oil litigation. In June 1931 the Supreme Court refused to review the verdict, which a court of appeals had unanimously upheld. While facing imprisonment for his oil sins, Albert Fall was stigmatized with yet another transgression growing out of Teapot Dome. His accuser was no less than the president of the United States, Herbert Hoover, who gave the dedicatory address at the Harding Memorial, also in June 1931. Besides Teapot Dome and the other scandals attributed to Harding's presidency, two books appearing after his death had especially clouded Harding's reputation. *The President's Daughter*, published in 1927, was written by Nan Britton, a young woman who claimed to be the mother of Harding's illegitimate child. The other sensational account, Gaston B. Means's *The Strange Death of President Harding*, published in 1930, contained the confessions of this mendacious Justice Department agent, who asserted, among other bogus charges, that Harding had not died of natural causes but was poisoned by his wife to avoid impeachment. As a result, the dedication of Harding's imposing marble-columned tomb in Marion, resembling a Greek temple, had been repeatedly postponed until now.

President Hoover did not avoid the main issue. Speaking of Harding's last days, Hoover told of accompanying the president to Alaska immediately preceding his death in August 1923. Those on the trip had seen "a man whose soul was being seared by a great disillusionment" because of his "dim realization" that he had been betrayed by friends holding positions of public trust. Later, in court, it was proved that these men had betrayed not only Harding's friendship but their country as well. In effect, Hoover implied that Harding had died of a broken heart. No names were mentioned. Former Attorney General Harry M. Daugherty, who, because of favorable jury verdicts, had narrowly escaped Fall's distinction of becoming the first Harding cabinet officer convicted for malfeasance, sat in the audience directly behind Hoover listening to this damning indictment. But Fall was saddled with most of the guilt because his bribery conviction and pending imprisonment were then current news.

This was not the first time for such intimations. Almost immediately after Fall's bribery verdict in 1929, former President Calvin Coolidge's *Autobiography*, which had also run in serial form, appeared as a book. Coolidge had hinted that Harding's discovery of the betrayal by "some whom he had trusted" perhaps was "more that he could bear." "Silent Cal" failed to elaborate, but the timing of his comments, coming so soon after Fall's conviction, suggested to many that Coolidge was pointing the finger of blame at Fall. Even earlier, in his book *Masks in a Pageant*, published in 1928, William Allen White had recalled a clandestine conference between Harding and Fall's wife in Kansas City while the president was en route to Alaska. No one seemed to know what Emma Fall said after she dropped by unexpectedly, slipped past the reporters outside, and spent a hour "closeted" with the president in the Muelbach Hotel's presidential suite, but Harding had appeared "perturbed and anxious" as he went to deliver his speech that evening. With the benefit of hindsight White seemed to suggest some connection between this mysterious meeting and the Teapot Dome scandal that was revealed a few months later. White also told of the arrival of a long, coded message from Washington that had greatly disturbed Harding during the return cruise from Alaska. Near collapse, but withholding the contents of this dispatch, Harding had supposedly kept asking Hoover and others aboard what a hypothetical president should do when his friends had betrayed him. Several days later Harding died in San Francisco.

After Hoover's speech at the Harding Memorial, Emma Fall's secret conference with Harding in Kansas City and what she had confided to him, if anything, caused much lively speculation. She maintained that her visit had been only a prearranged social call, which included dinner with the Hardings, that she had not been alone with the president all evening, and that the naval oil leases had not been mentioned. Soon after Hoover's address Senator Arthur Capper of Kansas, who was a guest in the presidential suite that evening and from whom White supposedly obtained most of his information, publicly substantiated the main points of Emma Fall's version of the meeting, thus contradicting nearly everything attributed to him in *Masks in a Pageant*.

Judson C. Welliver, a White House speech writer and political adviser who was White's principal informant for the events of the Alaska trip, also disclaimed many of the details presented by the author. Although a communication delivered by a naval airplane caused Harding serious concern, Welliver said, he was certain that the president had not gone around asking confidants aboard what a chief executive should do when duped by his friends. He theorized that White or someone else had this confused with a serious talk between Harding and Welliver in Washington before the departure for Alaska in which the president had complained that Senator James E. Watson of Indiana and others he did not name had betrayed his confidence. Later, in his *Memoirs*, Hoover told of a troubled Harding questioning him, before the naval airplane arrived with the coded message, about what should be done concerning a potentially damaging Justice Department scandal involving Daugherty's Ohio crony the late Jess Smith. This, too, may have been the origin of White's story about Harding nervously asking what a president should do when betrayed by his friends. Significantly, however, neither Fall nor Teapot Dome appears to have been mentioned in Harding's talks with either Welliver or Hoover.

In fact, Fall and Teapot Dome had no part in Harding's death, which was caused by an acute coronary thrombosis with myocardial infarction, or a heart attack. Although the strains of the presidency probably contributed to his demise, Harding died without learning the baser aspects of the naval oil deals. At the time of Emma Fall's visit to the Muelbach Hotel and the naval airplane's delivery of the coded message, the Teapot Dome hearings had not yet started, and there was little indication that the inquiry would blossom into its sensational proportions six months later. Fall was in Europe advising Sinclair on Russian petroleum concessions. Senator Walsh, who had not started his intensive study of the naval reserve leases, was touring the Orient and then mending political fences in Montana. It is also significant that Harding's widow, the devoted "Dutchess," who was with him on the Alaska trip and until he died in San Francisco, remained cordial to the Fall family even after Teapot Dome erupted. Florence Harding went to her death in November 1924 probably believing implicitly in Albert Fall, just as her husband did.

After the Supreme Court declined to review his bribery conviction, Fall's best hope for staying out of prison was presidential clemency. President Hoover's speech at the Harding Memorial seemed to close that door, but the two men had been, in Fall's words, "rather more than friendly" while serving together in the Harding cabinet, and had remained on cordial terms afterwards. In fact, while commerce secretary, Hoover had written the departing interior secretary a heartfelt tribute in March 1923:

> This note is just by way of expressing appreciation for the many kindnesses I had at your hands during the last two years in the Cabinet. I know that the vast majority of our people feel a deep regret at your leaving the Department of the Interior. In my recollection, that Department has never had so constructive and legal a headship as you gave to it. I trust the time will come when your private affairs will enable you to return to public life as there are few men who are able to stand its stings and ire and they have got to stay with it.

Soon after Harding's death, when Fall returned from advising Sinclair on Soviet matters, Fall and his wife had dinner with the Hoovers in Washington, but the two men had no further communication after this social engagement. Four months later the naval oil scandal began. Now Fall's friends worked hard to obtain a presidential pardon for him, but without success. Even if a president facing reelection the next year wanted to do so, he could hardly grant a pardon to the only defendant convicted in a criminal case resulting directly from Teapot Dome. Hoover's comments at the Harding Memorial had made it plain that thère would be no pardon.

One other possibility remained. The District of Columbia court in which Fall was convicted could suspend his prison sentence for reasons of health. After four El Paso physicians certified that he was too ill for incarceration, the court authorized an official physical examination. Fall reported to William Beaumont General Hospital at Fort Bliss near El Paso, where for a week army doctors investigated his health. Extensive tests showed that the sixty-nine-year-old patient was suffering from severe hardening of the arteries, a chronic heart ailment, disabling arthritis (particularly in the spine), chronic but inactive tuberculosis, and pleurisy. Speaking for the government, federal prosecutor Atlee Pomerene called for Fall's commitment to prison. Frank Hogan countered that confinement in the humid East Coast climate would imperil his client's life and urged suspension of the sentence.

In denying a suspension, the judge, who found no great change in Fall's physical condition since his conviction, observed that clemency was a presidential concern, and not for the court to decide. If the defendant desired, however, the place of incarceration could be changed to "some more salubrious climate than that of Washington" by amending the sentence to make it a year plus one day, which was done. As a result, the New Mexico State Penitentiary at Santa Fe was designated for Fall's imprisonment. One of Fall's daughters regarded the judge's refusal to suspend the jail time as a death sentence for her father. Fall received the news calmly. Smoking the stump of a black cigar, he told the reporters: "Yes, gentleman, I have many friends in Santa Fe. But I hope I won't find them in the penitentiary." It was a relief, he said, to have the matter settled.

Both Republican and Democratic leaders in New Mexico urged President Hoover to grant a last-minute pardon. A petition signed by all the members of the state legislature was rushed to the White House. It was useless. On July 17, 1931, the United States marshal in New Mexico received orders to take Fall into custody and bring him to the state penitentiary. The next day a big black ambulance pulled up to Fall's El Paso home. As a large gathering of family members and friends stood watching, the former cabinet officer, dressed in pajamas and a green smoking jacket and leaning heavily on a cane, came out and was almost bodily lifted into the vehicle. On the way to Santa Fe, Fall stopped off for a day of rest at his Three Rivers ranch. The ambulance, accompanied by a caravan of cars carrying relatives, friends, and reporters, arrived at New Mexico's ancient capital on July 20. The penitentiary gates swung open momentarily, and the ambulance went directly to the prison hospital and delivered its occupant. Years before, Albert Fall, "one of the stormiest figures who ever added excitement to American politics," had come to Santa Fe to serve in the territory's legislature and its highest court. Here he had played a dominant role in drafting the state constitution and had been elected to the United States Senate. In the summer of 1931, at Santa Fe, he became convict 6991.

Lengthy civil litigation had forced Doheny and Sinclair to return the naval oil reserves to the government. As an incidental result of Teapot Dome, Sinclair served seven and one-half months in a Washington jail on two concurrent sentences for contempt of the Senate and jury tampering. But Fall's bribery conviction was the federal prosecutors' only real victory in the naval oil criminal cases. When the Teapot Dome committee unearthed its sensational findings, the *New York Times* now observed, many had predicted that soon "the prisons would be bulging with politicians and millionaires." Those boastful predictions had fallen far short, because a decade later it was Albert Fall, "old and ill, broken in reputation and at the end of his financial resources, who alone pays the penalty."

Fall became eligible for parole at the end of four months. When applying to the federal parole board for early release, he gave as his reason, "My version of the matter is simply that I was not guilty." The penitentiary warden favored Fall's liberation because of age and poor health, commenting that the prisoner had been "confined to the hospital since his admission." The judge in the bribery trial, although complaining that he had been deceived earlier about the severity of the defendant's health problems, did not unreservedly oppose a parole. Of the nine jurors who expressed an opinion, seven said that they endorsed the former cabinet officer's release. The FBI, which investigated Fall's financial capability of paying his $100,000 fine, reported that he was all but broke.

Senator Bronson Cutting and some of Fall's former Senate colleagues lobbied for the parole in Washington. On Sunday afternoons when he was at home in Santa Fe, Cutting often visited Fall, and, with Fall's daughter, Jouett Elliott, joining them, talked for hours about politics and national affairs. On one of these visits Cutting found Fall in a "wretched physical state" and worried about White House opposition to his release. In response to Emma Fall's urgent pleas, Cutting and Democratic Senator J. Hamilton Lewis of Illinois conferred with President Hoover, but got an ice cold reception. It was difficult to "describe the degree of discourtesy with which the President received us," Cutting wrote Fall's wife, adding that he had not imagined Hoover would be "vindictive in so petty a way." In January 1932 the parole board denied Fall's application for early release because, given the nature of his crime, it was "unjustifiable and incompatible with the welfare of society."

Under time-off provisions for good behavior Fall could now hope for his freedom in the spring. After serving nine months and nineteen days of his sentence, he left the New Mexico penitentiary on May 9, 1932, riding in the same ambulance that had brought him to Sante Fe. His entire incarceration was spent in the prison hospital. Although the original commitment order seemed to require payment of his $100,000 fine before his release, Fall did not pay the fine, nor did he sign a pauper's oath. Justice Department officials, who issued amended commitment papers, declared that Fall's sentence had contained neither the "direction nor implication" of imprisonment until liquidation of the fine, or until he claimed insolvency. Technically, by serving an additional thirty days in jail and taking a pauper's oath, Fall could have wiped out the monetary penalty. He never paid the $100,000, nor did his financial situation ever tempt the government to force the issue, so his fine became a dead letter. His bribery conviction had also deprived him of his basic civil rights. Despite the unceasing efforts of his wife, who died in 1943, and various individuals and organizations to clear his name and restore his rights, the former United States senator and interior secretary went to his grave without ever regaining full citizenship privileges.

From the state prison Fall, with family members and friends in the procession, went straight to the Three Rivers ranch, the root of all his troubles. By this time a slow, tortuous process was underway by which he would lose this cherished property. Doheny stated in the Teapot Dome hearings that his $100,000 loan to Fall for the Harris ranch purchase was secured by a note, which he later produced in a mutilated form. In the Fall-Doheny conspiracy trial of 1925 it was revealed that Fall had also assigned one-third of the ranch corporation's capital stock to Doheny as collateral security. During the next four years the oil magnate, to protect their joint interests, acquired control of the Three Rivers property by lifting a foreclosed mortgage held by other creditors and through a special master's sale and a second lien turned over to him by Fall. Meanwhile, in an agreement with Doheny involving a nominal rent, Fall continued to live on the home place and use adjoining land, with the expectation of realizing a modest equity when the Three Rivers holdings were sold. Doheny returned a herd of purebred cattle, obtained in the mortgage sale, to his friend for the minimum amount required for legal purposes, one dollar. He also gave Fall half of the range cattle and soon bought back 770 head for $38,500. In effect, Fall had become a tenant on what had been his vast ranch domain—but under rather generous terms.

Fall and Doheny remained friends throughout these complex land and livestock transactions. The oilman's acquisition of control over the Three Rivers property obviously added substance to their contention in court that the $100,000 was a loan, not a bribe. And Doheny's increasing financial involvement in the ranch also saved it from falling into other hands and gave Fall hope of collecting an equity someday. Sinclair, on the other hand, simply declined to protect his one-third interest at Three Rivers, originally valued at $233,000, and took no part in the various mortgage and other legal proceedings. Fall's personal relationship with Doheny began to unravel before his bribery conviction when the oil magnate's only son and heir, Edward L. Doheny, Jr., died mysteriously in a hushed-up murder-suicide case involving young Doheny and his male secretary. As the key witness in Fall's trial a few months later, the grieving father wept and nearly collapsed when he spoke of his son on the stand. Doheny was "completely crushed" and never recovered from the shock of his son's bizarre death. Fall received no more warm philosophical letters from the oilman, nor did he see his friend again after the bribery conviction. While Fall was in prison, Doheny's wife declared that he had written no one since Fall's trial. "He has lost interest in everything," she said, "and I can almost say in everybody." In fact, he spoke no more than "ten words in the entire day."

Soon after he assumed control of the ranch, Doheny announced his intention to sell it if a suitable buyer could be found. In the naval oil cases the defense attorneys had steadfastly maintained that the Three Rivers property was worth approximately $700,000. After the stock market crash of 1929 Fall informed Doheny that $400,000 would be a good price, even though the spread still represented an investment of $700,000. By 1931, when Fall went to prison, the oilman had spent at least $460,000 in acquiring and operating the ranch. These calculations meant that Fall now had little or no hope of realizing anything from his equity.

Doheny assigned management of the Three Rivers property to one of his subsidiaries, the Petroleum Securities Company. By 1935, because of advancing senility, the oil magnate had lost his grip on the extensive corporate operations he had built up over the past forty years. In August, Petroleum Securities unexpectedly notified Fall that it was disposing of the ranch and asked him to vacate the premises within two weeks. Fall refused to budge, contending that the home-place ranch house and one hundred acres of surrounding farmlands had not been included in the mortgage foreclosures. In a public statement he said: "The order to move came from Mrs. Doheny, who is really running the company. Mr. Doheny has been in ill health and I don't know whether he knew about the letter sent me. He and

I are still friends." While legal steps were underway to evict Fall, news came from Los Angeles that Doheny, who reportedly had been bedridden for nearly three years, had died on September 8, 1935. As one more irony of his fabled career, Doheny had hired the famous Montana artist Charles M. Russell to paint two large friezes depicting the western heritage for display at 8 Chester Place. At Doheny's insistence Russell, who favored cowboys and Indians, reluctantly brushed in three small, nondescript oil derricks but hid them on the wall behind a staircase. Prone to romanticize his part in the frontier saga, Doheny considered the paintings a failure.

The Palomas Land and Cattle Company, which had bought the ranch, offered to let the Fall family stay on the home place "indefinitely as our guests" for an annual rental of one dollar. If the battle against eviction continued, however, the family would be "thrown off the property." Still a fighter, Fall refused this proposal and took his struggle to the courts. Several neighbors and friends sent word that they were armed and ready to resist the eviction by force, but he did not accept these offers of assistance. After a year-long controversy characteristic of Fall's tumultuous life, his appeal was dismissed by the state supreme court. Sadness as well as acrimony marked the family's forced departure from their Three Rivers home of thirty years. When Emma Fall attempted to take a flock of domesticated geese with her, a representative of the purchasers stopped a Hispanic hired hand from catching the fowls, saying that the Palomas company now owned everything on the ranch. Just before going to prison, Fall had written of such an eventuality: "To part with it [the ranch] forever would be almost more than I could bear. When it is gone the last vestige of security is gone." This was the final crushing blow.

In the heat of the eviction battle Fall had suddenly become critically ill, and an ambulance had rushed him to the army's William Beaumont Hospital near El Paso. For months it was touch-and-go. While suffering from severe bronchial pneumonia, the former interior secretary, whose grandfather had been a Campbellite patriarch, became a Catholic upon his baptism by

Father Albert Braun, pastor at the Mescalero reservation. From 1935 to 1942 Fall spent most of his time in Beaumont Hospital or in Veterans Administration facilities at Albuquerque and Fort Bayard, New Mexico. When not hospitalized, he lived in the El Paso home owned in his wife's name. Although Emma Fall received some meager returns from inherited Texas farmland and other sources, probably the only regular income the family had after losing the ranch was Fall's Spanish-American War veteran's pension of between $70 and $100 a month. Many always felt that Fall had not been punished enough. For this proud, headstrong man, broken in health and finances, humiliated as the first cabinet officer sent to prison, and held up to public scorn even today, his punishment was complete. Moreover, he faded into obscurity, cut off from the seats of power. It was the worst possible fate imaginable—a living hell.

In 1942 Fall's friends made arrangements, reportedly paid for by Doheny's widow, for his care in Hotel Dieu, an El Paso Catholic hospital. His old respiratory and heart ailments plagued him constantly, and arthritis made his life especially miserable, crippling him until he could not walk. Still he read omnivorously, preferring history, periodicals covering current events, and sometimes fiction, mostly stories of the Old West. He never lost interest in politics. To some newspaper reporters he seemed bitter, cynical, and "ice-eyed." He told one of them in 1938: "I'll never get out of bed—I haven't long to live. I've paid my debt to society. I owe it nothing." But old friends of southwestern frontier days and political battles found him cordial and eager to chat with them when he was well enough to do so. On several successive evenings a little boy, whose grandfather was recuperating from gallbladder surgery at Hotel Dieu, slipped into an old man's room across the hall for welcomed visits. The old man turned out to be Fall. On November 30, 1944, as he read a newspaper in Hotel Dieu, the world of events slipped out of sight, and Albert Fall, the principal figure of "the most sordid scandal in the history of the Federal government," slumped over on his pillow, dead. It was four days past his eighty-third birthday.

Epilogue

ALBERT Fall always had his share of enemies and critics, but even at the time of his death, when the national ignominy had been piling up for years, *Newsweek* assessed his career with impartiality by stating: "The ugly chapter in Fall's life could not have been foreseen by the public. His reputation for honesty, integrity, and fearlessness had been impeccable." One of Fall's former Senate colleagues recalled his amazement when the oil scandal broke, feeling that "a monument of manhood toppled when he fell." On the other hand, many of Fall's contemporaries, with the advantage of hindsight and the fear of splattering oil from the scandal, attempted to give the impression in both written and public statements that everyone always knew Fall was a villain even before Teapot Dome. In fact, some of his more prominent associates of earlier years tried to conceal their previous admiration and respect for him.

President Coolidge had placed great value on Fall's advice in Mexican affairs. When the Teapot Dome investigation first began raising questions about the naval oil leases, Coolidge told a group of reporters, "My judgment about it would be based on the confidence that I had in President Harding and Secretary Fall." Yet the most important files on Fall and Teapot Dome were apparently purged from Coolidge's presidential papers deposited in the Library of Congress. Oilman William F. Buckley was a staunch backer of Senator Fall's Mexican-affairs investigation of 1919–20. A memorial volume published by Buckley's family quotes most of his testimony before the subcommittee but omits an explanation of his close association with Fall. At the Interior Department, Fall's picture was slashed and relegated to a storeroom until finally restored and displayed among the portraits of the other interior secretaries—in 1967. And such slights were only the beginning.

About a year after Fall left the Senate to become interior secretary, Senator Henry Cabot Lodge stated frankly that Fall's departure to the cabinet had been a serious blow to him because they had become good friends. Later Lodge edited his correspondence with Theodore Roosevelt as his last published literary effort. The first manuscript of this work included some flattering references to Senator Fall. But before it went into print the naval oil scandal broke. Lodge did additional editing; he pored over the manuscript and eliminated every mention of Fall. On the other hand, Roosevelt, who died in 1919 before the scandal erupted, had described Fall as "the kind of public servant of whom all Americans should feel proud."

As already pointed out, Herbert Hoover was plagued by Teapot Dome because of his service as commerce secretary in the Harding cabinet. Later Hoover's detractors said that he must have known about the manipulations in the Interior Department and should have exposed them. This was enough to put Hoover under a cloud and link him, as the Republican presidential candidate in 1928, to Teapot Dome, the main corruption issue in that election. Nor was Hoover allowed to forget the warm farewell letter he had written to departing Secretary Fall in March 1923, saying that this department had "never had so constructive and legal a headship as you gave it" and expressing the hope that Fall would soon return to public office. Fall published the letter in the series of nationally syndicated newspaper articles he wrote just before going to prison, thus adding another coal of fire on the Great Depression president's head.

Hoover would not admit any friendship with Fall and disclaimed any knowledge of his cabinet colleague's wrongdoing. After Fall publicized the letter, Hoover turned on him with a vengeance, as Senator Cutting discovered during his White House visit in behalf of Fall's pardon. Yet Hoover's continued prominence in the Republican party was one of the main reasons the Democrats found Teapot Dome an effective campaign barb for so long. As late as 1952, when Hoover hurled charges of corruption at the Truman administration, the Democrats immediately confronted him with the letter he wrote Fall in 1923 and his association with the oil-splattered Harding administration.

Until the day he died, Fall would never admit that he was guilty of any graft or corruption in the naval oil negotiations, nor would his family. To him the money exchanges with Doheny and Sinclair were normal business transactions and the resulting Teapot Dome scandal was a partisan political vendetta. As with every public servant, however, he must stand responsible for his record in the Interior Department, and clearly he insisted on being master in his own realm. Yet he did not conceive and negotiate the complicated contracts and leases single-handedly without the knowledge and aid of his own subordinates as well as Navy Department staff members, several of whom testified to the worthiness of the arrangements. The failure to encourage competitive bidding and to announce the Teapot Dome and Elk Hills deals until Congress demanded information inevitably cast suspicion on these negotiations. But the Doheny and Sinclair agreements, if separated from Fall's personal financial transactions, were defensible, theoretically at least. In the long run, when Pearl Harbor became America's last major stronghold and the nerve center of the Pacific Theater in World War II, Fall was convinced that his thwarted efforts to build a great fuel depot there twenty years before, as a part of the contracts with Doheny, had been vindicated.

In terms of modern leasing practices for federal oil lands, Fall's handling of the naval reserves was, in some ways, visionary and enlightened. His policy is cited as the first major governmental implementation of unit operation, or large-tract leasing, intended to consolidate production, reduce waste, and promote efficiency. In short, this concept recognized an oil field as a geological structure, not a legal or political issue. The Buena Vista Hills Reserve, which had been parceled out in small tracts until it practically ceased to exist as a reserve, provided an example of the old program's evils. Instead of relying primarily on multiple individual leases, Fall negotiated contracts with Sinclair for all of Teapot Dome and with Doheny for large blocks of Elk Hills. Assuming that drainage was a serious threat, as Fall contended, his policy of leasing large units to major oil companies with advanced technology, proven track records, and abundant financial resources might have resulted in more efficient operations and utilitarian conservation on the reserves.

The revelation of Fall's money deals with the two oil millionaires obliterated any advantages his plan may have offered. The Supreme Court canceled the contracts in 1927, but Congress amended the General Leasing Act three years later to allow the unitization process of consolidating leases on federal lands. In 1938 the navy was authorized to apply this principle on the Elk Hills Reserve. By June 1944, during World War II, the government had drawn up and signed a full-fledged unit-plan contract that would make Standard Oil of California (now Chevron) the navy's operational agent on Elk Hills for the next fifty years. Responding to the Arab oil embargo of the early 1970s, Congress contracted all three California and Wyoming reserves for full commercial production at their "maximum efficient rates" to help offset American reliance on imported petroleum, and, in 1977, transferred their management from the navy to the newly created Department of Energy. Only then did the Teapot Dome Reserve confirm long-held suspicions that it was a lemon and would never fulfill Harry Sinclair's grandiose expectations for it.

Moreover, in 1996 Congress mandated the outright sale of Elk Hills to the highest private bidders and the study of specified options, including direct sale, to determine what would "maximize the value" of Buena Vista Hills and Teapot Dome as well as three naval oil-shale reserves in Colorado and Utah. The navy did not require such strategic reserves, the Department of Defense stated, because these needs could be satisfied by the world market. Some of the official announcements strangely echoed the Harding administration's departmental reorganization program, which had helped spawn the Teapot Dome scandal. Since a downsized, streamlined government was "not in the business of making money," an Energy Department spokeswoman declared, the production of petroleum in competition with the private sector constituted an undesirable "federal function."

Elk Hills is among the nation's richest producing oil fields. In late 1997, after receiving twenty-two competitive offers, the Energy Department announced that the successful bidder for the government's 78 percent share in the field was the Occidental Petroleum Corporation of Los Angeles. The sales price of $3.65 billion made the transaction, scheduled for conclusion in early 1998, the largest privatization of federal property in American history, exceeding the previous record divestiture of the eastern freight railroad Conrail for $1.6 billion in 1987 ($2.3 billion in late 1990s dollars). An Energy official justified the deal by saying: "We're getting maximum value for this asset, and we're turning one of the nation's premier oil and gas fields over to the private sector. . . . The Navy no longer needs Elk Hills, and this sale helps get the government out of the oil and gas business." Elk Hills no longer served a defense purpose, an Energy Department press release added, because the Strategic Petroleum Reserve now held the country's emergency oil supply. Historically, this concept of artificial oil storage for national security needs was curiously reminiscent of Interior Secretary Fall's program, on a smaller scale, that called for naval fuel facilities at Pearl Harbor and elsewhere.

Albert Fall must have started spinning in his grave with indignation. Even as an unflinching corporation man he had never seriously proposed the outright sale of the naval reserves. Textbooks might still roundly condemn him as a notorious villain, but his oil policy had been adopted as gospel, indeed, in spades, by the federal government.

In fact, it is difficult to fix the degree of Fall's guilt. Taking the money from Doheny and Sinclair while he held a public trust was clearly both foolish and wrong, but were the oil deals a sinister, well-conceived plot in which Fall brazenly bargained with the highest bidders to rob the nation of vital resources affecting the national security? Or, was he guilty of a gross indiscretion in his personal affairs at a time when he badly needed money? Because of his anticonservation philosophy as a corporation man, and for this reason alone, Fall undoubtedly would have turned over the naval reserves to Doheny and Sinclair anyway, or to some other representatives of private enterprise. Such a long-standing attitude made bribery unnecessary. If bribes were his main objective, he should have held out for $4,000,000 instead of $400,000. As for the $100,000 from Doheny, on which Fall's bribery conviction was based, the oil magnate probably would have made the loan regardless of the oil leases because of Fall's role in the Senate as the protector of American property rights in Mexico. An equally compelling reason was Doheny's desire to secure Fall's influence and expertise in Latin-American affairs after he retired from the cabinet.

It is possible to speculate, although the solid evidence is missing, that the two oil millionaires simply took care of a loyal comrade who, while serving their corporate cause in the Senate and the cabinet, had been deprived of making his own fortune and was now in need. Further speculation could lead to the conclusion that business leaders like Doheny and Sinclair had promised Fall, perhaps implicitly, that if he continued in the Senate, they would make it up to him, and then they sweetened the pledge when his cabinet offer arose. Certainly, after two of his children died of influenza just before his Senate reelection in 1918—a personal tragedy he tended to equate with his political sacrifices—Fall felt that he was owed extra compensation for remaining in public office. In this context the money from Doheny and Sinclair was a payoff or bonus but not a bribe. The trouble was that these private deals, whatever their form and circumstances, spawned a monstrous public spectacle called the Teapot Dome scandal in which an ailing former interior secretary went to jail and two millionaire oilmen went free.

One sunny spring day in 1934 a throng of 4,650 southwesterners, many of them "old pioneers," gathered for a big picnic and dedication of the "Great White Sands Monument" near Alamogordo. Large delegations came from El Paso, Las Cruces, and Roswell, and smaller groups from several distant communities. Eight hundred automobiles rumbled over a half-finished New Deal road to a natural amphitheater deep in the glistening White Sands, with the majestic San Andres Mountains, towering Sierra Blanca, and the Sacramento Mountains in full view around the horizon. The entertainment included a baseball game between two African American teams and "plenty of good music" by two school bands, followed that evening by dancing under the stars to fiddle and banjo renditions. A brush arbor provided shade for the handicapped and elderly.

The numerous prominent orators included two former governors, but Albert Fall, the main speaker, drew the crowd's "spell-bound attention." This warm response was less for what he said—which was mostly about past proposals and his own legislative attempts to capitalize on the White Sands—than for his conspicuous presence among them, as if he had suddenly returned from a long journey. The *Alamogordo News* reported:

> For those who knew Judge Fall in the days when his eloquence and personal magnetism held audiences at wrapt [*sic*] attention, and who knew of his great ability it was indeed a pathetic sight to see that he had to be assisted from his car and supported during his talk. After he had spoken for a few moments he sat down and talked while sitting. Unfortunately his voice was so weak that he could be heard only in a radius of a few feet.

The faint words made little difference to the hundreds of his friends present, who remembered his fearlessness and brash crusading ardor years ago as a lawyer, judge, and champion of the underdog ranchers. He was "visibly affected," shedding tears unashamedly as they paid their respects. On that day his life had come full circle.

Sources

Three major collections of Albert Bacon Fall papers are crucial to any understanding of his life and activities: Huntington Library, San Marino, California (54 linear ft., 1887–1941); University of New Mexico Library, Albuquerque (9 linear ft., 1916–27); and New Mexico State University Library, Las Cruces (2.5 linear ft., 1907–41). A fourth Fall collection in the Washington State University Library, Pullman (2 linear ft., 1912–41), consists of photocopies of papers now at New Mexico State University. For the Teapot Dome affair specifically, the UNM Library has extensive material on its various aspects, especially the naval oil court cases, while the NMSU Library possesses important original Fall correspondence exchanges with Warren G. Harding, Edward L. Doheny, Harry F. Sinclair, and other prominent public figures, as well as some general oil information. Separate indexes have been compiled by the various libraries for their own holdings. Although the composite Fall papers are apparently incomplete, all of them together present a fairly continuous representation of Fall's life. In particular, the voluminous files of his dictated correspondence, characterized by lengthy, often digressive letters, capture both his reasoning and a rapid-fire manner of speaking. Significantly, there is no indication of wholesale purging in this remarkable composite manuscript collection.

The manuscript collections of the following persons also made substantial contributions to this account: in the Library of Congress, Washington, DC, papers of Calvin Coolidge, Bronson M. Cutting, Charles Evans Hughes, William G. McAdoo, Evalyn Walsh McLean, Gifford Pinchot, Theodore Roosevelt, Theodore Roosevelt, Jr., William H. Taft, Thomas J. Walsh, William Allen White, and Woodrow Wilson; in the Huntington Library, San Marino, CA, papers of Eugene Manlove Rhodes; in the University of New Mexico Library, Albuquerque, papers of Thomas B. Catron and Carl C. Magee; in the Duke University Library, Durham, NC, papers of Harry A. Slattery; in the Ohio Historical Society, Columbus, papers of Cyril Clemens and Warren G. Harding; and in the Kentucky Historical Society, Frankfort, papers of Philip Slater Fall.

After more than seventy years the Teapot Dome affair is still often depicted as an enigma enshrouded by an impenetrable conspiratorial cloud. Yet numerous documentary and other revealing primary sources are readily available. The published hearings and reports of the Teapot Dome investigation panel (Senate Committee on Public Lands and Surveys), which provided information for all parts of this book, appeared under a common title, *Leases upon Naval Oil Reserves* (1924, 1924 and 1925, 1928), except for one report, *Investigation of Activities of Continental Trading Co.* (1928). Besides the testimony of those involved in the scandal and the findings of the committee, these proceedings include as exhibits pertinent documents and correspondence on Fall's leasing negotiations with Doheny and Sinclair, his personal financial arrangements with the two oilmen, and many aspects of his family, ranching, and other private activities. Other essential primary sources are the voluminous correspondence and records spawned by the Senate inquiry (largely in the ensuing litigation), held in the Naval Oil Reserve Investigations collection (Teapot Dome file) of the National Archives. This file contains letters and memoranda of the special federal prosecutors, Atlee Pomerene and Owen J. Roberts, as well as legal papers, transcripts of the trials and appeals, and other documents. A small part of this material has been reproduced on microfilm as *The Teapot Dome Documents* (University Publications of America, Arlington, VA). The National Archives also has the extensive records of the Office of Naval Petroleum and Oil Shale Reserves, which include an abundance of technical and bureaucratic information, and of the Interior, State, Justice, and Navy departments, which contain scattered pertinent material. Another published document with valuable information for several parts of this book, *Investigation of Mexican Affairs* (1920), resulted from Fall's Senate Foreign Relations subcommittee inquiry of 1919–20. For his Senate tenure (1912–21) the *Congressional Record* faithfully portrays Fall's broad knowledge as well as his bare-knuckled oratorical skills.

No thoroughgoing biography of Fall exists, although one is long overdue. The two best book-length studies available dwell on broader aspects of the scandal: Burl Noggle, *Teapot Dome: Oil and Politics in the 1920's* (Baton Rouge: Louisiana State University Press, 1962), and J. Leonard Bates, *The Origins of Teapot Dome: Progressives, Parties, and Petroleum, 1909–1921* (Urbana: University of Illinois Press, 1963). My doctoral dissertation, "Albert B. Fall and the Teapot Dome Affair" (University of Colorado, 1955), deals mostly with Fall's role in Teapot Dome, while my related periodical articles flesh out several aspects of his career: "President Wilson's Smelling Committee," *Colorado Quarterly* 5 (Autumn 1956); "New Mexican Machiavellian? The Story of Albert B. Fall," *Montana: The Magazine of Western History* 7 (Autumn 1957); "Behind Teapot Dome: Some Personal Insights," *Business History*

Review 31 (Winter 1957); "Splattered with Oil: William G. McAdoo and the 1924 Democratic Presidential Nomination," *Southwestern Social Science Quarterly* 44 (June 1963); and "Two Western Senators and Teapot Dome: Thomas J. Walsh and Albert B. Fall," *Pacific Northwest Quarterly* 65 (April 1974). Fall's own account of his early life to 1891, which he dictated in 1925, appears in *The Memoirs of Albert B. Fall*, edited and annotated by David H. Stratton (El Paso: Texas Western Press, 1966). A Fall granddaughter, Martha Fall Bethune, gives a touching, almost novelized view from inside the family in *Race with the Wind: The Personal Life of Albert Fall* (El Paso: Novio Book, 1989). Although Fall testified only in the early stages of the Teapot Dome investigation, and not at all in the court cases, he explained his role and motivations several times, most notably in his correspondence with Doheny, Sinclair, and the various defense lawyers and in his deposition for *United States vs. Sinclair* (1928), the Sinclair conspiracy trial (copy in Teapot Dome file of the National Archives). In addition, the autobiographical series of fifteen syndicated newspaper articles by Fall, in collaboration with *El Paso Times* editor Magner White, for the North American Newspaper Alliance (July–August 1931) covers the Teapot Dome affair and some aspects of his cabinet service.

The newspapers most often used here are the *New York Times*, *Santa Fe New Mexican*, *Albuquerque Morning Journal*, and, under varying titles, *El Paso Herald* and *El Paso Times*. Handy summaries of national press opinion in the 1920s were obtained from the *Literary Digest*.

CHAPTER 1 ("THE ORIGINS OF A FRIENDSHIP")

For information on the Lindbergh flight and America in the 1920s see John W. Ward, "The Meaning of Lindbergh's Flight," *American Quarterly* 10 (Spring 1958); Walter L. Hixson, *Charles A. Lindbergh, Lone Eagle* (New York: Harper Collins, 1996); and Frederick Lewis Allen, *Only Yesterday: An Informal History of the Nineteen-Twenties* (New York: Harper & Row, 1931).

The importance of Philip Slater Fall as a leader of the Christian Church in the South is shown in Prince E. Burroughs, *The Spiritual Conquest of the Second Frontier* (Nashville: Broadman Press, 1942), and two unpublished theses that rely heavily on archival material: Herman A. Norton, "The Life of Philip Slater Fall, 1798–1890" (Vanderbilt University, 1951), and James A. Cox, "Incidents in the Life of Philip Slater Fall" (College of the Bible, 1951).

Details related to Fall's early mining experiences in southwestern New Mexico were provided, for Apache-white conflicts, in three works: Ralph E. Twitchell, *The Leading Facts of New Mexican History*, 5 vols. (Cedar Rapids, IA: Torch Press, 1912–17); Dan L. Thrapp, *Victorio and the*

Mimbres Apaches (Norman: University of Oklahoma Press, 1974); and Robert M. Utley, *Frontier Regulars: The United States Army and the Indian, 1866–1891* (New York: Macmillan, 1973). For the Black Range district see, Fayette A. Jones, *New Mexico Mines and Minerals* (Santa Fe: New Mexican Printing Co., 1904), and Paige W. Christiansen, *The Story of New Mexico Mining* (Socorro: New Mexico Bureau of Mines and Minerals, 1974). Lively reminiscences, although not always reliable, are found in James A. McKenna, *Black Range Tales* (1936; Chicago: Rio Grande Press, 1965).

Secondary works that aided me in formulating the profile of Doheny included Caspar Whitney, *Charles Adelbert Canfield* (New York: privately printed, 1930); B. C. Forbes, *Men Who Are Making the West* (New York: B. C. Forbes Publishing Co., 1923); and Ruth Sheldon Knowles, *The Greatest Gamblers: The Epic of American Oil Exploration*, 2nd ed. (Norman: University of Oklahoma Press, 1978). For the best capsule version of his experiences in New Mexico see Martin Ansell, "Such Is Luck: The Mining Career of Edward L. Doheny in New Mexico, 1880–1891," *New Mexico Historical Review* 70 (January 1995).

Local newspapers helped fill several gaps in chapter 1, namely the *Clarksville (Texas) Standard*, for Fall's activities in that town and his first exposure to Mexican mining, and the *Hillsborough Sierra County Advocate* and the *Chloride Black Range*, for events in and around Kingston in the 1880s.

CHAPTER 2 ("FIGHTING THE DEVIL WITH FIRE")

Information characterizing Fall as a westerner included my interviews with family members and others who knew him. Especially helpful printed or written portrayals are found in the *Bulletin* of the National Parks Association in 1923; the letters of H. Foster Bain, after he served as Bureau of Mines director under Interior Secretary Fall (copies in Fall papers, New Mexico State University); Louis Siebold, *Current Opinion*, July 1921; and Mark Sullivan, *The Twenties*, vol. 6 of *Our Times: The United States, 1900–1925* (New York: Scribner's, 1935). For Eugene Manlove Rhodes's life and writings, including his use of Fall as a character, see W. H. Hutchinson, *A Bar Cross Man: The Life and Personal Writings of Eugene Manlove Rhodes* (Norman: University of Oklahoma Press, 1956).

General coverage of the Dona Ana County range war and politics, as well as the Fall-Fountain rivalry, may be found in C. L. Sonnichsen, *Tularosa: Last of the Frontier West* (New York: Devin-Adair, 1960); William A. Keleher, *The Fabulous Frontier: Twelve New Mexico Items*, rev. ed. (1945; Albuquerque: University of New Mexico Press, 1962); and Earl S. Pomeroy, *The Territories and the United States, 1861–1890* (Philadelphia: University of Pennsylvania Press, 1947). A recent book,

Gordon R. Owen, *The Two Alberts: Fountain and Fall* (Las Cruces, NM: Yucca Tree Press, 1996), contains a mass of biographical material on its two subjects. The two indispensable Las Cruces newspapers are the *Rio Grande Republican* and the *Independent Democrat*, both of which display the vicious political journalism of the day.

On Thomas B. Catron and the Santa Fe Ring these works were especially useful: Victor Westphall, *Thomas B. Catron and His Era* (Tucson: University of Arizona Press, 1973); Oscar D. Lambert, *Stephen Benton Elkins* (Pittsburgh: University of Pittsburgh Press, 1955); and Tobias Duran, "Francisco Chávez, Thomas B. Catron, and Organized Political Violence in Santa Fe in the 1890s," *New Mexico Historical Review* 59 (July 1984). Darlis A. Miller, *The California Column in New Mexico* (Albuquerque: University of New Mexico Press, 1982), contains details on Albert J. Fountain, William L. Rynerson, and 338 other members of General James H. Carleton's command who stayed in New Mexico after the Civil War.

For the death of Colonel Fountain a good place to start is A. M. Gibson, *The Life and Death of Colonel Albert Jennings Fountain* (Norman: University of Oklahoma Press, 1965), although the author, who calls Fall the "principal figure in the Fountain case," is often unduly favorable to Fountain. Material collected by Katherine D. Stoes, now housed in the New Mexico State University Library, include her historical notes and copies of the Pinkerton Detective reports on the Fountain murders. In November 1954 at Las Cruces, I interviewed Mrs. Stoes, who had lived in Dona Ana County since 1892 and knew Fall, Fountain, Pat Garrett, and others who figure prominently in this chapter. Among the myriad of accounts on the shootings of John Wesley Hardin and Pat Garrett, two books by Leon C. Metz were the most helpful to me: *John Selman, Texas Gunfighter* (1966; Norman: University of Oklahoma Press, 1980), and *Pat Garrett: The Story of a Western Lawman* (Norman: University of Oklahoma Press, 1974).

Fall's appointment and service as a Spanish-American War captain, including his rapprochement with Catron, receive attention in Miguel A. Otero, *My Nine Years as Governor of the New Mexico Territory, 1897–1906*, ed. Marion Dargan (Albuquerque: University of New Mexico Press, 1940). The role of assassination in New Mexico's territorial politics is explained in Richard Maxwell Brown, *Strain of Violence: Historical Studies of American Violence and Vigilantism* (New York: Oxford University Press, 1975).

CHAPTER 3 ("CORPORATION MAN")

The broader aspects of this chapter are treated in George Curry, *George Curry, 1861–1947: An Autobiography*, ed. H. B. Hening (Albuquerque:

University of New Mexico Press, 1958), and Frank D. Reeve, *History of New Mexico*, 3 vols. (New York: Lewis Historical Publishing Co., 1961). General information on Fall's law practice, his association with W. A. Hawkins, and his rise as a corporation man may be found in J. Morgan Broaddus, Jr., *The Legal Heritage of El Paso*, ed. Samuel D. Myres (El Paso: Texas Western College Press, 1963), and Ira G. Clark, *Water in New Mexico: A History of Its Management and Use* (Albuquerque: University of New Mexico Press, 1987). Personal interviews with one of Fall's former law partners, Harris Walthall, November 23, 1954, at El Paso, and with Gardiner Hawkins (son of W. A. Hawkins), August 24, 1956, at Boulder, Colorado, helped give me an understanding of Fall's law practice and economic philosophy, as well as his activities in Mexico.

By far the most useful book on Fall's involvement with William C. Greene in Mexico was C. L. Sonnichsen, *Colonel Greene and the Copper Skyrocket* (Tucson: University of Arizona Press, 1974). Ira B. Joralemon, *Romantic Copper: Its Lure and Lore* (New York: D. Appleton-Century, 1934), takes a more sensationalist view of Greene than does Sonnichsen. Other detailed secondary information came from David M. Pletcher, *Rails, Mines, and Progress: Seven American Promoters in Mexico, 1867–1911* (Ithaca, NY: Cornell University Press, 1958); Marvin D. Bernstein, *The Mexican Mining Industry, 1890–1950: A Study of the Interaction of Politics, Economics, and Technology* (Albany: State University of New York, 1964); and Ramón Eduardo Ruiz, *The People of Sonora and Yankee Capitalists* (Tucson: University of Arizona Press, 1988).

For Fall's party switch, his role in the New Mexico statehood movement, and his first two Senate elections, the most informative volume is Robert W. Larson, *New Mexico's Quest for Statehood, 1846–1912* (Albuquerque: University of New Mexico Press, 1968). Howard R. Lamar's *The Far Southwest, 1846–1912: A Territorial History* (New Haven: Yale University Press, 1966) outlines the interpretive aspects of both the New Mexico and Arizona statehood movements, while Herbert T. Hoover's "History of the Republican Party in New Mexico, 1867–1952" (Ph. D. diss., University of Oklahoma, 1966) gives insights into the partisan political struggles of this period. For the "Tall Timber Cases," Elmo R. Richardson, *The Politics of Conservation: Crusades and Controversies, 1897–1913* (Berkeley: University of California Press, 1962), clarifies the interaction between westerners and the federal government. The *Proceedings* (Albuquerque: Morning Journal Press, 1910) of the New Mexico constitutional convention, although limited in coverage, provide some essential facts about the delegates and the committees. Over the years the *New Mexico Historical Review* has run a series of articles by or about convention delegates, and *New Mexico Magazine*, March 1969, carried another reminiscence: Winfred E. Garrison, "The Constitutional Convention's Last Man."

For observations on events in Santa Fe involving statehood and the senatorial elections see Richard Lowitt, *Bronson M. Cutting: Progressive Politician* (Albuquerque: University of New Mexico Press, 1992), and Elting E. Morison et al., eds., *The Letters of Theodore Roosevelt*, 8 vols. (Cambridge: Harvard University Press, 1951–54). The Cutting papers contain lengthy Burns Detective Agency investigative reports on Fall's Senate elections.

CHAPTER 4 ("RIDING WITH ROOSEVELT")

A helpful framework for Fall's attitude toward progressive reforms came from Howard W. Allen, *Poindexter of Washington: A Study in Progressive Politics* (Carbondale: Southern Illinois University Press, 1981), which mistakenly classifies Fall as a progressive Republican but otherwise furnishes a good analysis of reform votes in the Senate. For the characterization of Fall as a senator, I am especially indebted to the late Senator Henry F. Ashurst of Arizona for access to his diary, later published as *A Many-Colored Toga: The Diary of Henry Fountain Ashurst*, ed. George F. Sparks (Tucson: University of Arizona Press, 1962), and for his letter to me, November 1, 1956. These two studies provided guidance on conservation topics: E. Louise Peffer, *The Closing of the Public Domain: Disposal and Reservation Policies, 1900–50* (Stanford: Stanford University Press, 1951), and a fine case study of another western Republican senator, Thomas G. Alexander's "Senator Reed Smoot and Western Land Policy, 1905–1920," *Arizona and the West* 13 (Autumn 1971). Lawrence C. Kelly's *The Assault on Assimilation: John Collier and the Origins of Indian Policy Reform* (Albuquerque: University of New Mexico Press, 1983) is extremely critical of Fall's relations with Indians and his national park proposals, both as a senator and later as interior secretary, while C. L. Sonnichsen, *The Mescalero Apaches* (Norman: University of Oklahoma Press, 1958), is less so.

The myriad of works on the Mexican Revolution and its effects on United States–Mexico relations, most of which at least mention Senator Fall, is almost overwhelming. Older studies that I used included Howard F. Cline, *The United States and Mexico*, rev. ed. (New York: Atheneum, 1965), and Merrill Rippy, *Oil and the Mexican Revolution* (Leiden: E. J. Brill, 1972). Of the newer books, the one I relied on most was Jonathan C. Brown, *Oil and Revolution in Mexico* (Berkeley: University of California Press, 1993), and, to a lesser extent, I used Robert F. Smith, *The United States and Revolutionary Nationalism in Mexico, 1916–1932* (Chicago: University of Chicago Press, 1972). By far the most pertinent scholarly work, however, is Clifford W. Trow, "Senator Albert B. Fall and Mexican Affairs, 1912–1921" (Ph. D. diss., University of Colorado, 1966). Fall himself presented his early views on the

Mexican situation and intervention in his article, "The Crisis in Mexico and Its Cause," *Leslie's Illustrated Weekly*, August 14, 1913.

Fall's differences over Mexican policy with President Taft may be readily understood by referring to Paolo E. Coletta, *The Presidency of William Howard Taft* (Lawrence: University Press of Kansas, 1973), and Henry F. Pringle, *The Life and Times of William Howard Taft*, 2 vols. (New York: Farrar & Rinehart, 1939). Similarly, for President Wilson, the authoritative work of Arthur S. Link helped clarify the conflicting viewpoints: *Woodrow Wilson and the Progressive Era, 1910–1917* (New York: Harper & Row, 1954), *Wilson*, 5 vols. (Princeton: Princeton University Press, 1947–64), and Link et al., eds., *The Papers of Woodrow Wilson*, 69 vols. (Princeton: Princeton University Press, 1966–94).

For the Roosevelt-Fall relationship, including the presidential election of 1916, I drew from George E. Mowry, *Theodore Roosevelt and the Progressive Movement* (Madison: University of Wisconsin Press, 1947), and, especially for the political context of their early association, from Gerald D. McKnight, "Republican Leadership and the Mexican Question, 1913–1916: A Failed Bid for Party Resurgency," *Mid-America* 62 (April–July 1980). Senator Lodge's influence is shown in Henry Cabot Lodge, ed., *Selections from the Correspondence of Theodore Roosevelt and Henry Cabot Lodge, 1884–1918*, 2 vols. (New York: Scribner's, 1925). In addition, these books furnished information on the election itself: Merlo J. Pusey, *Charles Evans Hughes*, 2 vols. (New York: Macmillan, 1951), and S. D. Lowell, *The Presidential Election of 1916* (Carbondale: Southern Illinois University Press, 1980).

CHAPTER 5 ("MEXICO STILL BECKONS")

The most useful monograph for my understanding of Wilsonian wartime policies was Seward W. Livermore, *Politics Is Adjourned: Woodrow Wilson and the War Congress, 1916–1918* (Middletown, CT: Wesleyan University Press, 1966), while Robert H. Ferrell, *Woodrow Wilson and World War I, 1917–1921* (New York: Harper & Row, 1985), helped explain the chain of events. Fall's article, "Where Are Our Statesmen?" *Forum*, July 1918, indicates his thinking on Wilson's early peace plans. For Fall's senatorial reelection in 1918, especially his dealing with the New Mexico governor, I drew insights from Ira C. Ihde, "Washington Ellsworth Lindsey," pt. 2, *New Mexico Historical Review* 26 (October 1951). The dramatic events surrounding the deaths of Fall's two children became clear to me through a typescript interview with Jack Fall's widow, Mrs. Anna Millar, May 6, 1969, conducted by C. L. Sonnichsen, who sent me a copy.

Fall's role as an irreconcilable in defeating the Versailles Treaty is shown in older standard works, including Henry Cabot Lodge, *The Senate and the League of Nations* (New York: Scribner's, 1925), and W. Stull Holt, *Treaties Defeated in the Senate . . .* (Baltimore: Johns Hopkins Press, 1933). Among later accounts the most helpful was Ralph Stone, *The Irreconcilables: The Fight against the League of Nations* (Lexington: University Press of Kentucky, 1970). Fall's hurried departure from the White House conference in August 1919 is described in an unpublished manuscript by Kathleen Lawler (a Fall admirer and Republican insider), "The Hardings I Knew," copy in Harding Papers.

Additional information for the context of my presentation of Mexican matters came from Lorenzo Meyer, *Mexico and the United States in the Oil Controversy, 1917–1942*, 2nd ed., trans. Muriel Vasconcellos (Austin: University of Texas Press, 1977), which gives the Mexican viewpoint on several issues, as does Gene Z. Hanrahan, *The Bad Yankee (El Peligro Yankee): American Entrepreneurs and Financiers in Mexico*, 2 vols. (Chapel Hill, NC: Documentary Publications, 1985). Doheny's career is treated in Dan La Botz's hostile biography, *Edward L. Doheny: Petroleum, Power, and Politics in the United States and Mexico* (New York: Praeger, 1991), and Fritz L. Hoffmann's more balanced account, "Edward L. Doheny and the Beginnings of Petroleum Development in Mexico," *Mid-America* 24 (April 1942). The best, most-detailed presentation, however, is Martin R. Ansell, "Hero or Villain: A Reinterpretation of the Life and Career of Edward L. Doheny" (Ph.D. diss., University of Texas at Austin, 1996).

The smelling committee episode is recounted in a popular book, sometimes inaccurate in its details, by Gene Smith, *When the Cheering Stopped: The Last Years of Woodrow Wilson* (New York: Bantam, 1965). For the diplomatic ramifications of the Jenkins kidnaping see Clifford W. Trow, "Woodrow Wilson and the Mexican Interventionist Movement of 1919," *Journal of American History* 58 (June 1971), and Charles C. Cumberland, "The Jenkins Case and Mexican-American Relations," *Hispanic American Historical Review* 32 (November 1951). Edith Bolling Wilson's hindsight observations on the smelling committee visit, as well as the Versailles Treaty amendments and reservations, came from her book, *My Memoir* (Indianapolis: Bobbs-Merrill, 1939), while her firsthand notes on the sickroom scene are in the Wilson Papers.

The idea of an oil conspiracy behind the Mexican-affairs investigation, with Fall at its center, appears in several accounts, including Mark T. Gilderhus, *Diplomacy and Revolution: U.S.-Mexican Relations under Wilson and Carranza* (Tucson: University of Arizona Press, 1977). For William F. Buckley's activities I drew on a favorable but not uncritical group biography, Charles L. Markmann, *The Buckleys: A Family Examined* (New York: Morrow, 1973).

CHAPTER 6 ("KICKER IN THE CABINET")

For the Harding administration, including its various scandals and Harding's presidential reputation, an invaluable secondary source is Robert K. Murray's sometimes overly favorable *The Harding Era: Warren G. Harding and His Administration* (Minneapolis: University of Minnesota Press, 1969). Two other books provided important insights: Francis Russell, *The Shadow of Blooming Grove: Warren G. Harding and His Times* (New York: McGraw-Hill, 1968), and, especially for bureaucratic details, Eugene P. Trani and David L. Wilson, *The Presidency of Warren G. Harding* (Lawrence: Regents Press of Kansas, 1977). Harry M. Daugherty was a seminal figure in Harding's presidency, but his memoirs, *The Inside Story of the Harding Tragedy* (New York: Churchill, 1932), are self-serving and must be augmented with a scholarly study by James N. Giglio, *H. M. Daugherty and the Politics of Expediency* (Kent, OH: Kent State University Press, 1978).

An overview for Fall's cabinet appointment is given in Wesley M. Bagby, *The Road to Normalcy: The Presidential Campaign and Election of 1920* (Baltimore: Johns Hopkins Press, 1962). The political differences between Fall and Holm O. Bursum are discussed in Donald R. Moorman, "A Political Biography of Holm O. Bursum, 1899–1924" (Ph. D. diss., University of New Mexico, 1962).

The early conflicts Fall experienced while interior secretary have been chronicled but often only incidentally. For his role in the Colombian treaty these studies were helpful to me: Richard L. Lael, *Arrogant Diplomacy: U.S. Policy toward Colombia, 1903–1922* (Wilmington, DE: Scholarly Resources, 1987), and J. Fred Rippy, *The Capitalists and Colombia* (New York: Vanguard, 1931). On recognition of Mexico, I obtained new perspectives from Donald C. Baldridge, *Mexican Petroleum and United States–Mexican Relations, 1919–1923* (New York: Garland, 1987), and Linda B. Hall, *Oil, Banks, and Politics: The United States and Postrevolutionary Mexico, 1917–1924* (Austin: University of Texas Press, 1995).

Secretary Fall's battles over conservation and resource development may be followed in these books, by topic as indicated: a general treatment, Donald C. Swain, *Federal Conservation Policy, 1921–1933* (Berkeley: University of California Press, 1963); on the national forests, Russell Lord, *The Wallaces of Iowa* (Boston: Houghton Mifflin, 1947), and Donald L. Winters, *Henry Cantwell Wallace as Secretary of Agriculture, 1921–1924* (Urbana: University of Illinois Press, 1970); on the Colorado River, Norris Hundley, Jr., *Water and the West: The Colorado River Compact and the Politics of Water in the American West* (Berkeley: University of California Press, 1975); on the national parks, Robert Shankland, *Steve Mather of the National Parks* (New York: Knopf,

1951), Donald C. Swain, *Wilderness Defender: Horace M. Albright and Conservation* (Chicago: University of Chicago Press, 1970), Horace M. Albright, *The Birth of the National Park Service: The Founding Years, 1913–1933* (Salt Lake City: Howe Brothers, 1985), and Dietmar Schneider-Hector, *White Sands: The History of a National Monument* (Albuquerque: University of New Mexico Press, 1993).

For Fall's attempts to change Indian policy, and his plans for the Mescalero reservation, I relied most heavily on Lawrence C. Kelly, *The Navajo Indians and Federal Indian Policy, 1900–1935* (Tucson: University of Arizona Press, 1968), as well as his *The Assault on Assimilation*, previously cited for chapter 4. Also helpful were Kenneth R. Philp, *John Collier's Crusade for Indian Reform, 1920–1954* (Tucson: University of Arizona Press, 1977); John Collier, *From Every Zenith: A Memoir* (Denver: Sage, 1963); and a series of articles by Collier and others in the early 1920s attacking Fall's Indian proposals in *Sunset*, *New Republic*, *Survey*, and other periodicals.

CHAPTER 7 ("LEASING THE NAVAL OIL RESERVES")

Among the best sources on the post–World War I oil crisis and its repercussions are Herbert Feis, *Petroleum and Foreign Policy*, Commodity Policy Studies, no. 3 (Stanford: Food Research Institute, Stanford University, 1944); Gerald D. Nash, *United States Oil Policy, 1890–1964: Business and Government in Twentieth Century America* (Pittsburgh: University of Pittsburgh Press, 1968); Stephen J. Randall, *United States Foreign Oil Policy, 1919–1948: For Profits and Security* (Montreal: McGill-Queen's University Press, 1985); and John A. DeNovo, "The Movement for an Aggressive American Oil Policy Abroad, 1918–1920," *American Historical Review* 61 (July 1956).

The General Leasing Act, the "Daniels bill," and the status of the naval oil reserves are explained in John Ise, *The United States Oil Policy* (New Haven: Yale University Press, 1926); Max W. Ball, *Petroleum Withdrawals and Restorations Affecting the Public Domain*, United States Geological Survey, Bulletin 623 (Washington, 1916); Reginald W. Ragland, *A History of the Naval Petroleum Reserves* . . . (n.p., [1944]); and J. Leonard Bates, "Josephus Daniels and the Naval Oil Reserves," *United States Naval Institute Proceedings* 79 (February 1953).

For the Colombian treaty, as discussed in chapter 7, and Secretary Fall's battle with the Royal Dutch Shell combine, see E. Taylor Parks, *Colombia and the United States, 1765–1934* (1935; New York: Greenwood, 1968); Stephen J. Randall, *The Diplomacy of Modernization: Colombian-American Relations, 1920–1940* (Toronto: University of Toronto Press, 1977); and Kendall Beaton, *Enterprise in Oil: A History of Shell in the United States* (New York: Appleton-Century-Crofts,

1957). Flanagan's undercover role for Standard Oil in Latin America, as well as other sharp insights on the petroleum industry, is recounted in George S. Gibb and Evelyn H. Knowlton, *History of Standard Oil Company (New Jersey): The Resurgent Years, 1911–1927* (New York: Harper, 1956), and Bennett H. Wall and George S. Gibb, *Teagle of Jersey Standard* (New Orleans: Tulane University, 1974). Frederick Wright's investigative article on the rumored payoff to Fall appeared in the *Chicago Sunday Tribune*, April 20, 1924.

President Harding's executive order transferring the naval oil reserves to the Interior Department and Fall's policy for them are scrutinized by Senator Thomas J. Walsh in Theodore M. Knappen, "What I Think of the Oil Scandal: An Exclusive Interview with Senator Walsh," *Magazine of Wall Street*, March 15, 1924. Besides giving background issues for the leasing legislation of 1920, Keith W. Olson, *Biography of a Progressive: Franklin K. Lane, 1864–1921* (Westport, CT: Greenwood, 1979), shows that Wilson's longtime interior secretary also favored generous treatment for oil companies on the reserves. Burl Noggle, *Into the Twenties: The United States from Armistice to Normalcy* (Urbana: University of Illinois Press, 1974), sets the stage for Harding's and Fall's actions.

The Sinclair and Doheny agreements are analyzed in Charles G. Hagland, "The Naval Reserve Leases," *Georgetown Law Journal* 20 (1931–32), and Marcus E. Ravage, *The Story of Teapot Dome* (New York: Republic Publishing Co., 1924). The reaction to them is interpreted in Robert A. Waller, "Business and the Initiation of the Teapot Dome Investigation," *Business History Review* 36 (Autumn 1962), and Belle C. and Fola La Follette, *Robert M. La Follette*, 2 vols. (New York: Macmillan, 1953). Gene Fowler, *Timber Line: A Story of Bonfils and Tammen* (New York: Covici-Friede, 1933), gives a colorful account of the *Denver Post* and Teapot Dome.

The odds against Fall's appointment to the Supreme Court (for one reason because Chief Justice William Howard Taft exercised a virtual veto power over such appointments) may be seen in Henry J. Abraham, *Justices and Presidents: A Political History of Appointments to the Supreme Court*, 3rd ed. (New York: Oxford University Press, 1992).

CHAPTER 8 ("THE TEAPOT DOME INVESTIGATION")

My description of the Fall ranch, its operations, and the necessity for the Harris-Brownfield purchase was influenced by Fall's own account in his deposition for *United States vs. Sinclair* (1928), copy in Teapot Dome file. Observations of a courtly Fall as the patriarch of his majestic ranch are presented in Dorothy Emerson, *Among the Mescalero Apaches: The Story of Father Albert Braun, O.F.M.* (Tucson: University of Arizona

Press, 1973). I am indebted to the Cleveland, Ohio, Public Library staff for sending me biographical material on Price McKinney, especially his front-page obituary in the *Cleveland Plain Dealer*, April 14, 1926. For firsthand insights into the Fall-McLean relationship see Evalyn Walsh McLean, *Father Struck It Rich* (Boston: Little, Brown, 1936). These accounts of Harry F. Sinclair and his oil companies were particularly helpful to me: Edwin Wildman, *Famous Leaders of Industry* (Boston: Page Co., 1921); *The National Cyclopaedia of American Biography*, vol. A—current (New York: James T. White & Co., 1926); P. C. Spencer, *Oil—And Independence! The Story of the Sinclair Oil Corporation* (New York: Newcomen Society, 1957); and *A Great Name in Oil: Sinclair through Fifty Years* (New York: F. W. Dodge Co./McGraw-Hill, 1966).

On Fall's trip to Russia with Sinclair I found helpful information in Louis Fischer, *Oil Imperialism: The International Struggle for Petroleum* (New York: International Publishers, 1926); Frank C. Hanighen, *The Secret War* (New York: John Day Co., 1934); W. L. Connelly, *The Oil Business as I Saw It: Half a Century with Sinclair* (Norman: University of Oklahoma Press, 1954); Floyd J. Fithian, "Dollars without the Flag: The Case of Sinclair and Sakhalin Oil," *Pacific Historical Review* 39 (May 1970); and Edward M. Bennett, *Recognition of Russia: An American Foreign Policy Dilemma* (Waltham, MA: Blaisdell, 1970).

For the Teapot Dome investigation and Senator Walsh's role in it I relied heavily on J. Leonard Bates, "Senator Walsh of Montana, 1918–1924: A Liberal under Pressure" (Ph. D. diss., University of North Carolina, 1952), and "Thomas J. Walsh: His 'Genius for Controversy,'" *Montana: The Magazine of Western History* 19 (October 1969); and by Walsh himself, "The True History of Teapot Dome," *Forum*, July 1924. Another essential account, about a Republican Teapot Dome committee member, is Herbert F. Margulies, *Senator Lenroot of Wisconsin: A Political Biography, 1900–1929* (Columbia: University of Missouri Press, 1977).

The importance of Carl C. Magee and the New Mexico witnesses is emphasized in William G. Shepherd, "How Carl Magee Broke Fall's New Mexico Ring," *World's Work*, May 1924. Magee's complex problems in court and politics are explained succinctly in Susan Ann Roberts, "The Political Trials of Carl C. Magee," *New Mexico Historical Review* 50 (October 1975). A copy of D. F. Stackelback's unpublished investigative report for the *Denver Post* is in the Walsh Papers. The motivations and sequence of events involved in the Roosevelt brothers' influential testimony are outlined in Eleanor B. A. Roosevelt, *Day before Yesterday: The Reminiscences of Mrs. Theodore Roosevelt, Jr.* (Garden City, NY: Doubleday, 1959).

CHAPTER 9 ("THE FINAL CRUSHING BLOW")

The political atmosphere and the stakes of the 1924 election are portrayed in J. Leonard Bates, "The Teapot Dome Scandal and the Election of 1924," *American Historical Review* 60 (January 1955), and Robert K. Murray, *The 103rd Ballot: Democrats and the Disaster in Madison Square Garden* (New York: Harper & Row, 1976); and, for the 1928 election, in Paul A. Carter, "The Other Catholic Candidate: The 1928 Presidential Bid of Thomas J. Walsh," *Pacific Northwest Quarterly* 55 (January 1964). An influential, but now outdated, journalistic account of the scandals inherited by President Coolidge is Samuel Hopkins Adams, *Incredible Era: The Life and Times of Warren Gamaliel Harding* (Boston: Houghton Mifflin, 1939).

President Coolidge's predicament and his crafty maneuvering to escape it may be seen in Howard H. Quint and Robert H. Ferrell, eds., *The Talkative President: The Off-the-Record Press Conferences of Calvin Coolidge* (Amherst: University of Massachusetts Press, 1964), and Donald R. McCoy, *Calvin Coolidge: The Quiet President* (New York: Macmillan, 1967). The liabilities of holdover Harding cabinet members, particularly Navy Secretary Denby and Attorney General Daugherty, are presented by two of their Senate nemeses: Thomas J. Walsh, "The Senate as Censor," *Forum*, October 1927, and Burton K. Wheeler, *Yankee from the West* (Garden City, NY: Doubleday, 1962). Although often superficial, William Allen White, *A Puritan in Babylon: The Story of Calvin Coolidge* (New York: Macmillan, 1939), was also helpful.

My understanding of the Fall-Doheny relationship and Doheny's attempted publicity projects during the naval oil litigation was enhanced by a letter to me from Hollywood producer Cecil B. DeMille, January 6, 1955, and *The Autobiography of Cecil B. DeMille*, ed. Donald Hayne (Englewood Cliffs, NJ: Prentice-Hall, 1959). Anecdotal details about Doheny's social and political activities and his Los Angeles home at 8 Chester Place are provided in Ward Ritchie, *The Dohenys of Los Angeles* (Los Angeles: Dawson's Book Shop, 1974); Stephen Birmingham, *California Rich* (New York: Simon and Schuster, 1980); and Kevin Starr, *Material Dreams: Southern California through the 1920s* (New York: Oxford University Press, 1990).

For the court cases resulting from the Teapot Dome affair, these two works were especially useful: Francis X. Busch, *Enemies of the State* (New York: Bobbs-Merrill, 1954), and M. R. Werner and John Starr, *Teapot Dome* (New York: Viking, 1959). Werner also wrote *Privileged Characters* (New York: Robert M. McBride, 1935), which portrays the various Harding scandals in a sensationalist light. The civil cases are given special attention in Dale R. Gardner, "Teapot Dome: Civil Legal Cases that Closed the Scandal," *Journal of the West* 28 (October 1989). On

Sinclair's jury-tampering conviction see William R. Hunt, *Front-Page Detective: William J. Burns and the Detective Profession, 1880–1930* (Bowling Green, OH: Bowling Green State University Popular Press, 1990).

President Hoover's speech at the Harding Memorial dedication and associated issues are discussed in Herbert Hoover, *The Memoirs of Herbert Hoover*, 3 vols. (New York: Macmillan, 1951–52); Calvin Coolidge, *The Autobiography of Calvin Coolidge* (New York: Cosmopolitan, 1929); and William Allen White, *Masks in a Pageant* (New York: Macmillan, 1929) and *The Autobiography of William Allen White* (New York: Macmillan, 1946). Mrs. Fall's version of her visit with President Harding in the Muelbach Hotel is given in a feature article, *Kansas City Star*, July 12, 1931.

Brief overviews of Fall's life, with emphasis on the naval oil affair, may be found in my two biographical sketches of him: *Dictionary of American Biography*, suppl. 3 (New York: Scribner's, 1973), and *American National Biography* (New York: Oxford University Press, forthcoming). The *DAB* also includes biographies of Doheny (suppl. 1) and Sinclair (suppl. 6). Doheny's final years and the continued philanthropic projects of his wife, Carrie Estelle (Betzold) Doheny, are outlined in Lucille V. Miller, "Edward and Estelle Doheny," *Ventura County Historical Society Quarterly* 6 (November 1960), which correctly states that Doheny disliked Charles M. Russell's artwork at 8 Chester Place. John Taliaferro, *Charles M. Russell: The Life and Legend of America's Cowboy Artist* (Boston: Little, Brown, 1996), contends that Doheny "happily paid" Russell $30,000 for the friezes.

EPILOGUE

The best place to start on any aspect of the Harding administration's historical standing, especially its myths, is Robert H. Ferrell, *The Strange Deaths of President Harding* (Columbia: University of Missouri Press, 1996). Priscilla L. Buckley and William F. Buckley, Jr., *W. F. B.—An Appreciation by His Family and Friends* (New York: privately printed, 1979), gives extensive information about William F. Buckley's involvement in Mexican affairs but mentions Fall only incidentally. Senator Lodge's excision of Fall's name from his manuscript is pointed out in John A. Garraty, *Henry Cabot Lodge: A Biography* (New York: Knopf, 1953).

On my comparison between Fall's proposals for the naval reserves and later federal oil policies, see two items by Gary D. Libecap: "The Political Allocation of Mineral Rights: A Re-Evaluation of Teapot Dome," *Journal of Economic History* 44 (January 1984), and "What Really Happened at Teapot Dome?" in *Second Thoughts: Myths and Morals of*

U.S. Economic History, ed. Donald N. McCloskey (New York: Oxford University Press, 1993); Jeffrey M. McKeage, "The Naval Petroleum Reserves: A Modern Perspective," *Journal of the West* 28 (October 1989); Department of Energy news releases, September 8, 1995, May 7, 21, October 6, 1997; *Wall Street Journal*, May 22, October 7, 1997; *New York Times*, October 7, 1997. For a broader historical framework see William K. Wyant, *Westward in Eden: The Public Lands and the Conservation Movement* (Berkeley: University of California Press, 1982).

The dedication ceremony at the White Sands National Monument was taken largely from the *Alamogordo News*, May 3, 1934.

Index